The Conservative Party
from Peel to Major

Robert Blake was a student and tutor in politics at Christ Church, Oxford, and Provost of The Queen's College, Oxford from 1968–87. Educated at King Edward VI School, Norwich, and Magdalen College, Oxford, where he took a First in Modern Greats, he served in the Royal Artillery during the war, became a prisoner of war in Italy from 1942–4, escaped and was mentioned in despatches. He was Senior Proctor, 1959–60, and a Conservative member of the Oxford City Council, 1957–65. In 1967 he was elected a Fellow of the British Academy. He was made a Life Peer in 1971. He was Chairman of the Historical MSS Commission, a Trustee of the British Museum, Editor of *The Dictionary of National Biography* and a Director of Channel Four Television. He edited *The Private Papers of Douglas Haig* (1952) and *The English World* (1982) and he has written *The Unknown Prime Minister: the life and times of Andrew Bonar Law 1858–23* (1955), *Disraeli* (1966), *The Office of the Prime Minister* (1975), *A History of Rhodesia* (1977), *Disraeli's Grand Tour* (1982) and, in the *Paladin History of England* series, *The Decline of Power 1915–64* (1985).

The
Conservative Party
from Peel to Major

ROBERT BLAKE

ARROW

Published in the United Kingdom in 1998 by
Arrow Books

1 3 5 7 9 10 8 6 4 2

This revised edition first published in the United Kingdom
in 1997 by William Heinemann

Arrow Books Limited
Random House UK Limited
20 Vauxhall Bridge Road, London SW1V 2SA

Random House Australia (Pty) Limited
20 Alfred Street, Milsons Point, Sydney,
New South Wales 2061, Australia

Random House New Zealand Limited
18 Poland Road, Glenfield, Auckland 10, New Zealand

Random House South Africa (Pty) Limited
Endulini, 5a Jubilee Road, Parktown 2193, South Africa

Random House UK Limited Reg. No. 954009

A CIP catalogue record for this book
is available from the British Library

Papers used by Random House UK Limited
are natural, recyclable products made from wood grown in
sustainable forests. The manufacturing processes conform to
the environmental regulations of the country of origin

Printed and bound in the United Kingdom by
Cox & Wyman Ltd, Reading, Berkshire

ISBN 0 7493 2297 7

Contents

Tables

Plates

Cartoons

The author and publishers wish to thank owners for permission to reproduce the cartoons. Acknowledgements are included in the captions beneath the pictures.

Foreword
to the 1970 edition

This book is an expanded and revised version of the Ford Lectures which I delivered in Oxford in 1968. I would like to thank the Ford Electors for the honour that they conferred on me and the opportunity that they gave me of concentrating my mind on a subject which had always intrigued me. On any plausible dating of its origin the Conservative or Tory party has had a longer continuous existence than any other British political party which can still be described as a major party capable of forming a government. This fact alone makes it a historical phenomenon worthy of study.

My book does not purport to be a connected history, like Sir Keith Feiling's two great works on the Tory party from 1640 to 1832[1]. It is, rather, a commentary upon the history of the party from 1830 to 1955 – a history which perhaps someone will one day write in detail on a suitable scale. I begin where I do because Wellington is so often regarded as the last 'Tory' Prime Minister. I end where I do because Sir Winston Churchill's resignation marks the end of an era. Perhaps Britain ceased to be a world power in 1945, but she believed herself to be one for another ten years. Whether or not it was cause and effect, the illusion vanished within two years of Churchill's departure. The consequences are still unfolding in every aspect of public life, not least in the Conservative party itself.

I would like to acknowledge with thanks kind permission from the following to quote from privately published or unpublished material in which they have the copyright: the Earl

[1] Sir Keith Feiling, *A history of the Tory party 1640–1714* (1924); *The second Tory party 1714–1832* (1938).

of Derby (Derby Papers); the National Trust (Disraeli Papers); Messr Hodder & Stoughton (Lady Gwendolen Cecil, *Biographical studies of the life and political character of Robert Marquis of Salisbury* (n.d.)).

I would like to thank Mr F. T. Dunn for his care in compiling the Index and Miss Marion Weir for her patient editing of my typescript.

The Queen's College, Oxford   ROBERT BLAKE
1970

Note on the 1997 edition

The new edition reprints the old one more or less as it stands, though with one or two corrections and with a slightly expanded version of Chapter VIII which ends in 1955. I have added five more chapters to bring the story as near as I can to the present day – perhaps a presumptuous enterprise for a historian. I have also revised the Bibliographical Notes and added a new Postscript to the Epilogue

Norfolk   ROBERT BLAKE
1997

The Conservative Party
from Peel to Major

INTRODUCTION

The ancestry of the party

The ancestry of the Conservative party has been variously traced. Some discern a continuous tradition from Strafford, Laud and Charles I, 'the holocaust of direct taxation', as Disraeli termed him, through the Tories of the time of William III and Anne to the younger Pitt and his successors. Others have been unwilling to go back so far. Suspecting that the old Tory party, which Walpole was able to ruin (thanks to the Hanoverian succession and the cowardice of Bolingbroke), had little connection with anything that came after, they have preferred to place its origin with Pitt and the great crisis of 1782-4. Yet others, uneasy at the fact that Pitt never called himself a Tory let alone a Conservative, have endeavoured to place the ancestry later with Perceval, Liverpool, or most commonly with Peel.

It is not easy to date the origin of a political party with any precision. As Sir Ivor Jennings observes:[1]

> We must remember that in Britain a party is not a legal entity except in the sense that any association having funds vested in trustees or a committee is a legal entity. . . . If a party were a legal entity created by charter or legislation, like a college or a public company, we could give it an age and celebrate its birthday.

This is exactly the trouble. Even if we were to take the matter of central party funds vested in some sort of trustees it is difficult to discover the facts. The researches of Professor Gash[2] show the obscurity of the subject. It is not clear that any such fund existed

[1] Sir Ivor Jennings, *Party politics*, II, *The growth of parties* (1961), 61.
[2] Norman Gash, *Politics in the Age of Peel* (1953), 434-7.

for the Conservative or Tory party before 1832, or even in
the election of 1832. There was, however, an election fund in the
elections of 1835, 1837, 1841 and 1847. Sir Robert Peel and the
Duke of Wellington were its trustees and it was administered by
the Earl of Rosslyn, the leading member of the party's election
committee. But one would hardly date the origins of the Conservative party in 1835, merely because of the fund.

Are there other institutional features which would enable us to
identify the continuity of a political party? One characteristic of a
modern political party is a centralised bureaucracy and a country-
wide mass organisation. As far as the Conservatives are concerned
one can be reasonably precise here. Both these features came into
being as a result of a challenge created by the first major step
towards mass democracy, the Reform Bill of 1867. In that very
year on November 12 at the Freemasons Tavern, London, was
founded the National Union of Conservative and Constitutional
Associations with the avowed purpose of organising working class
support for the government. True, a Mr Eadie of Newcastle who
said he was the son of a working man declared that the word
'Conservative' would be a fatal handicap in Radical areas, adding
that he personally 'was not a Conservative, he never pretended to
be one, and he never should be'. But his attempt to elaborate on
this interesting theme was drowned not surprisingly 'in hisses and
confusion'. In 1870 the Central Office was founded and it is thus
possible to say that a century ago the most characteristic institutions of the modern Conservative party had come into being.

The form and features of the National Union and the Central
Office today would be fully recognisable to a Conservative party
worker of the 1870s. Considering how much has changed in political life since then, one can only be surprised at this continuity – a
tribute to Disraeli's organisational power, or if not to his, to that of
the people whom he selected to do the work. Is there, then, a case
for stopping our search into the past at the early 1870s and dating
the Conservative party from then? This would accord with the
idea of Disraeli as the founder of modern Conservatism – a notion
widely held and by no means devoid of substance. For Disraeli not
only innovated in the field of organisation. He did so too in the
far more important field of ideas; or, if this is too big a claim, he

certainly expressed old ideas with a personal style and colour which made them seem new. It cannot be wholly accidental or erroneous that so many modern Conservatives look back on Disraeli as their prophet, high priest and philosopher rolled into one.

Yet however strong these arguments, it simply does not sound plausible to begin the story of the Conservative party then. To do so is to ignore a continuity of outlook, of parliamentary organisation and of succession to the leadership which undoubtedly goes back earlier, though just how far is the point we are trying to discover. The Conservatives of the late 1860s and early 1870s did not feel themselves to be in any sense a new party or to be making a fresh start; many of them distrusted Disraeli; a small minority positively detested him. No contemporary Conservative would have regarded him as the founder of the party – least of all Disraeli himself.

Perhaps at this stage it is worth glancing at Disraeli's own theory of the history of the party which he came in the end to lead. As so often in his career his view of history varied with the political circumstances in which he found himself. It depended upon whether he was a rebel or an Establishment man. In 1880 when he had just resigned as Prime Minister but had accepted an invitation from the party to continue as their leader, he wrote to Lord Lytton: 'They [the Tory party] have existed for more than a century and a half as an organised political connexion and having survived the loss of the American Colonies, the first Napoleon, and Lord Grey's Reform Act, they must not be snuffed out.' This suggests belief in continuity since the early eighteenth century. The same view in more detail is expressed forty-five years earlier in his *Vindication of the English constitution* where Bolingbroke is regarded as the founder of a Tory tradition which continues through William Pitt the younger, Burke and apparently Lord Liverpool (for although he is not named his measures are praised), the Duke of Wellington and Peel himself. Disraeli makes no attempt to contrast Tories and Conservatives, merely observing that 'in times of great political change and rapid political transition it will generally be observed that political parties find it convenient to re-baptise themselves'.

But in between the time when he was seeking Peel's favour in the 1830s and the time of his own ascendancy a generation later the story was quite different. He was a rebel in the 1840s. Needing a Tory philosophy of history as a counterweight to the Whig philosophy, and at the same time determined to put Peel in his proper place he advanced in his novels an ingenious version of 'true Toryism'. This begins with Charles I, and an inclusive list of members contains the Jacobite, Sir John Hynde Cotton, Sir William Wyndham who was Bolingbroke's lieutenant, Bolingbroke himself of course, Carteret, Shelburne and the younger Pitt. But at this juncture it becomes necessary to distinguish. If Pitt's successors in the leadership were to be included, then, as Disraeli saw it, there would be no means of avoiding a lineal descent through Addington, Portland, Perceval and Liverpool, which would end in Peel; and Peel, for a number of reasons, one of which was his refusal of office to Disraeli in 1841, was just the man on whom he least wished to confer this accolade.

Therefore it becomes necessary to argue that things somehow went wrong during Pitt's reign. Pitt himself was a great man but the Tory apostolic succession stopped with him. He is 'the best of the Tory statesmen but who [sic] in the unparalleled and confounding emergencies of his later years had been forced unfortunately for England to relinquish Toryism'. His successors were not in any sense standard-bearers of 'true Toryism' or, as Disraeli sometimes and significantly called it, 'the English system'. They were a 'factitious league' who 'had shuffled themselves into power by clinging to the skirts of a great minister'. They are the ancestors of 'Conservatism'.

Disraeli's denunciation in *Coningsby* of Conservatism as practised by Peel is famous.[1] Less well known is his apostrophe to Toryism in *Sybil*.

But we forget; Sir Robert Peel is not leader of the Tory party – the party that . . . [and a long list follows of its virtues and achievements]. In a Parliamentary sense, that great party has ceased to exist; but I will believe it still lives in the thought and sentiment and consecrated memory of the English nation.

[1] See below, p. 27.

It has its origin in great principles and in noble instincts; it sympathises with the lowly, it looks up to the Most High. It can count its heroes and its martyrs; they have met in its behalf plunder, prescription, and death. Nor when it finally yielded to the iron progress of oligarchical supremacy, was its catastrophe inglorious. Its genius was vindicated in golden sentences and with fervent arguments of impassioned logic by St John; and breathed in the intrepid eloquence and patriot soul of William Wyndham. Even now it is not dead but sleepeth; and in an age of political materialism, of confused purposes and perplexed intelligence, that aspires only to wealth because it has no other accomplishment, as men rifle cargoes on the verge of ship-wreck, Toryism will yet arise from the tomb over which Bolingbroke shed his last tear, to bring back strength to the Crown, liberty to the Subject, and to announce that power has only one duty – to secure the social welfare of the PEOPLE.[1]

In effect what Disraeli is saying here – and we must not forget the circumstances in which he was saying it – is that some sort of true blue stream has been flowing from the days of the Cavaliers, through the turbid whirlpools of the reigns of William III and Anne, becoming thinner but nevertheless remaining discernible in the marshes and thickets of the mid-eighteenth century, broadening out with the rise of the younger Pitt, and then flowing underground for half a century or so, but always there, ready to be brought to the surface again by the wand of some magical water-diviner. And it is not difficult to guess whom he had in mind.

With the fall of Peel, and his own elevation to the leadership of the party in the House of Commons only four years after *Sybil* had been published, Disraeli altered his attitude, or – perhaps one should say, since he never repudiated his past professions – became silent. But the distinction which he drew between Toryism and Conservatism has always had its supporters. In an essay on Coleridge in his *Sketches in nineteenth-century biography*, Sir Keith Feiling dwells on the distinction, and draws up pedigrees for the two concepts. Conservatism's ancestors are Clarendon,

[1] Benjamin Disraeli, *Sybil, or, The two nations*, 3 vols (1845), Bk IV, ch. XIV.

Blackstone, Eldon, Peel; Toryism's are Harley, Bolingbroke, Pitt, Canning, Disraeli. The great ideologists or thinkers are Burke for Conservatism, and Coleridge for Toryism. Conservatives, broadly, defended the existing order. Tories, while pruning the abuses of their era, 'looked behind the institutions of their own generation to the spirit of the nation which gave them life'. The distinction is of value in terms of ideology though it would be interesting to know how it ought to be continued after Peel and Disraeli. But it is not intended as a means of categorising the organisational development of the party.

There is much room for argument about the precise ancestry of the Conservative party. But it is at least clear when it got its name, although we do not know from whom. The word 'conservative' in its modern political sense was first used in an article in the *Quarterly Review* in January 1830 – 'We now are, as we always have been, decidedly and conscientiously attached to what is called the Tory, and which might with more propriety be called the Conservative Party'. Like 'Liberal', the word had a continental derivation, as is shown by the alternative use 'conservator'. Baron Vincent writing to the Duke of Wellington in 1819 rightly observed that *'les principes conservateurs ont en vous un fort et noble appui'*. As late as May 1832 we find a correspondent of the Duke observing that Birmingham was far from radical, 'the majority of respectable persons being decidedly conservators'. But this usage soon faded out. By December 1831 the *Standard* was referring to the 'Conservative party' as if the phrase was a well established expression, and, although for a year or two some people still tended to use it with a conscious feeling of novelty, in actual or metaphorical inverted commas, it soon became the normal word for the party of the Right. The article in the *Quarterly Review* has traditionally been attributed to John Wilson Croker, a minor politician, a journalist and a friend of Peel and Wellington. But one of those persons who would be stigmatised by Sir Winston Churchill as 'a tiresome researcher' has discovered that Croker was not writing for the *Quarterly* at that particular time. So the godfather of the Conservative party remains anonymous even if we know the date of the baptism.

This brief chronology shows that the expression was not, as it is sometimes claimed, invented in the aftermath of the great *débâcle* of 1832. It was in use before that. On the other hand there can be little doubt that its adoption by the leading figures of the party and by leading journals of the Right such as the *Standard* from 1832 onwards was a deliberate attempt to purge the party of its old associations and to symbolise, if not a break with the past, at least a change of course. Was this change so great as to constitute a real break with the past?

There was certainly continuity of a sort. In one sense the Duke of Wellington may perhaps be regarded as the last Tory Prime Minister and Peel as the first Conservative one. But Wellington remained leader of the party after 1832, and the Carlton Club which was to be the organisational headquarters of the party until the creation of the Central Office was founded before the carrying of the Reform Bill – though, admittedly, not long before. On the whole such machinery as there was for co-ordinating party activities seems to have survived the double defeats of 1831–2. It is true that the Chief Whip, William Holmes, the last Tory whip in the unreformed House, did not carry on with his duties with the new House, but this was merely because he lost his seat. It is also true that some important organisational changes took place in the years immediately after 1832. But these were the result of new circumstances, the response of a defeated party to new problems. There was no fundamental break with the past. Peel's emergence in 1834 as Prime Minister was the result not of any party rebellion but of the Duke's deliberate decision to withdraw.

If the party retained a basic continuity in terms of institutions and persons, it is equally true that no drastic change occurred in Conservative as compared with Tory political ideas and attitudes. One can easily overdo the contrast between the party of Lord Liverpool and the party of Peel. Almost the whole of Peel's political experience had been under Liverpool, and there is little to suggest that he was critical or even doubtful about his chief. Liverpool was not the figure of reaction depicted by Disraeli. He aimed at a middle of the road policy even as Peel was to do in the 1830s and 1840s. All in all it is hard to argue that the change of name from Tory to Conservative represented any more of a gap in continuity than the change from Conservative to

Unionist sixty years later. Both names remained in concurrent use. The name of Tory is far from extinct even today.

It will be argued in this book that the real gap in organisational continuity is provided by the corn law crisis of 1846 and that the Protectionist party founded by Lord George Bentinck and Lord Stanley constitutes a new departure in a sense to which there is no exact parallel in the period covered. If this interpretation is correct, the party of Peel is not a different party from that of his predecessors, Wellington, Canning, Lord Liverpool. It is basically the same. The question then arises as to when that party first came into being. No doubt it can be argued that there is some sort of continuity in ideas – a Tory attitude to political problems – which can be traced back through the eighteenth century to the political struggles in the reign of Charles II when the words 'Whig' and 'Tory' originated. Both were at first terms of abuse subsequently appropriated with defiant pride by those who were abused. 'Whig' originally meant a Scottish horse thief and was applied first to Presbyterian rebels and then to all those who in the crisis of 1679 supported Ashley's attempt to exclude from the succession James, Duke of York, the Roman Catholic heir to the throne. 'Tory' meant an Irish papist outlaw and was applied to those who supported the legitimate heir to the throne in spite of his adherence to Rome.

As long as the succession to the throne remained a political issue – and it did not finally cease to be so until after the failure of the rebellion of 1745 – the use of the terms Whig and Tory in the old sense had some meaning. But even by then the political structure of Britain had become virtually a one party system with the Whigs providing in effect both government and opposition. It is not easy to trace any organisational continuity between the Toryism of Bolingbroke and the Toryism of Lord Liverpool. The best way of looking at the Whig and Tory parties as they had become by 1830 is to take the second of the three alternatives suggested at the beginning and to regard them as descending from the two sides in the crisis of 1782-4, the Whigs from those who supported Charles James Fox, the Tories from those who supported the younger Pitt.

But it is important to remember that the term Tory was for a long while not used of themselves by the party later to be described as Tory. Pitt always called himself a Whig. Spencer Perceval, Prime Minister from 1809 to 1812, never spoke of himself as a Tory. Until 1806 the most common party names in the House of Commons were Pittite and Foxite. Canning appears to have been one of the first Cabinet ministers on the Pittite side who actually called himself a Tory. Peel himself only admitted to the appellation of Tory on one occasion, and that was with heavy irony when on May 1, 1827, he gave an account to parliament of his reasons for resignation. 'I may be a Tory, I may be an illiberal, but . . . Tory as I am, I have the further satisfaction of knowing that there is not a single law connected with my name which has not had as its object some mitigation of the severity of the criminal law. . . .'[1] Nevertheless by 1830 when this survey of the history of the party begins, the names Whig and Tory had a clear meaning and were in regular use. There is no need to go back beyond 1784 for the origin of the parties to which they refer, and there is little profit in pursuing a Disraelian search for continuity through the eighteenth century.

[1] Norman Gash, *Mr Secretary Peel* (1961), 437.

CHAPTER I

Peel's problem

In 1830 the Tory party fell from power. In 1832 it sustained the greatest defeat in its history, bar one – the landslide of 1906. In a house of 658 members it had only 185 – a drop of 70 from the figure in the last unreformed parliament, which itself, however, represented a great decline from the situation only two years earlier when the Duke of Wellington had been Prime Minister and Sir Robert Peel leader of the House of Commons. The reason for the collapse is clear enough. It was not, as the Whigs and Liberals were liable to argue, the just retribution for long years of reactionary government by the 'stupid party'. It was not, as Disraeli would later maintain, the consequence of the personal deficiencies of 'the Arch Mediocrity', his unflattering and unjustified soubriquet for Lord Liverpool who had been Prime Minister from the murder of Spencer Perceval in 1812 till his own incapacitation by a stroke in 1827 – the longest tenure of the office in the nineteenth century. Those were years of great turbulence and stress. Lord Liverpool was certainly not a mediocrity. Nor was either he or his party reactionary – at least after their early fears of post-war revolution had died away. From 1822 onwards under the influence of Peel at the Home Office, George Canning at the Foreign Office, and William Huskisson (the most famous railway casualty in history) at the Board of Trade the Tory government had charted a course that was in contemporary terms by no means illiberal, witness its policy in matters fiscal and penal. Even when the disappearance of Liverpool and Canning within a few months of each other had brought power to what might be considered the 'right wing' of the party, the repeal of the Test and Corporation Acts of 1828 and the passage of Catholic emancipation in 1829[1] showed that the Tories were capable of moving with the times, of opting to bend rather than to break.

The rock on which they foundered was parliamentary reform. There was nothing inevitable about the shipwreck. They could have steered differently, and the party's past did not preclude a compromise on this issue. Indeed it was not obviously more difficult than surrendering to the agitation for Catholic emancipation. On both questions traditionalists could find precedent for a liberal approach in the attitude at various times in his career of their hero, the younger Pitt. If anything the demands of the Irish Catholics raised even greater problems than those of the parliamentary reformers. Anglican exclusivism was even more closely bound up with the party's past than the preservation in every detail of an electoral system which had hardened into its present form in the seventeenth century and had been fossilised ever since. The point was emphasised by the decision of a section of the 'Ultras', as the men of the extreme right were termed, to support parliamentary reform after 1829 on the ground, probably well founded, that a more liberal franchise would have resulted in a less liberal treatment of the Catholics.

But precisely because Peel had given way on the Catholic question he was inhibited from repeating the performance in another field. Peel was highly sensitive to charges of 'betrayal' — more so than most politicians who sensibly come soon to recognise that it is the necessary price paid by those who conduct the government of the country with some regard to changing circumstances and new situations. It was Peel's merit as a statesman that he normally adapted his policies to the need for change. It was his defect as a politician that he did so in a manner which, combining as it did prickliness, egotism, self-exculpation and unctuousness, gave a formidable handle to his enemies. No doubt Peel was against the Reform Bill on its merits but he had been equally hostile to Catholic emancipation on its merits. The truth was that reform was not simply a matter of political philosophy. Professor

[1] The effect of these measures was to open legislature and executive to non-Anglican Christians. They already had the vote and Protestant dissenters could sit in parliament. Roman Catholics had been wholly excluded. Henceforth they could sit in parliament and hold any office except Lord Chancellor of England or Ireland, or Viceroy of Ireland.

Gash, the leading historian of the period, has put it admirably. 'It is clear that given the contemporary political assumptions accepted by both sides the Tories were in the right. . . . Sooner or later all the major prophecies of the opposition came true.'[1] But he goes on to point out that the thing which counted for the Whigs was not the verdict of posterity but the force of contemporary society, the need to conciliate popular demand. 'What the Tories said was true; but what the Whigs did was necessary.'[2]

Although Peel consistently opposed the Whig Reform Bill he did not declare himself hostile in principle to all parliamentary reform of any kind. His attitude seems, rather, to have been that circumstances while he was in office made it impossible for him to bring forward proposals of his own, and that he had every right to find fault with the particular measure submitted to parliament by the Whigs. This moderate attitude was not shared by the duke whose resignation in 1830 had been precipitated by his extraordinary declaration that the constitution had reached a state of perfection and that no reform could improve it. There can be little doubt that Wellington's attitude corresponded to the sentiments of the Tory hard core, a body diminishing in size but powerful nevertheless. Their view of the English constitution was amusingly satirised by Peacock in *The misfortunes of Elphin*. Elphin, it will be recalled, drew the attention of the Welsh Prince Seithenyn to the condition of an embankment on his property, which was supposed to keep out the sea.

'That is the beauty of it,' said Seithenyn. 'Some parts of it are rotten and some parts of it are sound.'

'It is well,' said Elphin, 'that some parts are sound: it were better that all were so.'

'So I have heard some people say before,' said Seithenyn, 'perverse people, blind to venerable antiquity; that very unamiable sort of people who are in the habit of indulging their reason. But I say that the parts that are rotten give elasticity to those that are sound: they give them elasticity, elasticity, elasticity.[3] If it were all sound it would break by its own

---

[1] N. Gash, *Politics in the age of Peel*, 3.   [2] ibid., 11.

[3] 'Elasticity' was a favourite virtue attributed by contemporary defenders of the old constitution.

obstinate stiffness. . . . There is nothing so dangerous as innovation. . . . This immortal work has stood for centuries and will stand for centuries more if we let it alone. It is well: it works well: let well alone. Cupbearer fill. It was half rotten when I was born, and that is a conclusive reason why it should be three parts rotten when I die.'

This was not an attitude which could be successfully sustained in the era of social transformation and economic struggle between 1815 and 1846.

England in the 1830s was, and had been since Waterloo, the battleground of competing class ideologies. Class was a relatively recent concept. In the old eighteenth-century society where the two great political parties had their origin the language of class did not exist. That society has been admirably described as 'an open aristocracy based on property and patronage.'[1] It was a hierarchical society with an immense number of gradations from a tiny minority of rich landowners through a multiplicity of 'middle ranks' to the propertyless poor who constituted the numerical majority of most pre-industrial societies. Its links were vertical, secured by patronage, dependence and influence, rather than horizontal, secured by a common feeling of class consciousness among persons with a common economic interest. But, although an aristocratic system, it was for a number of reasons never a caste system. Younger sons did not inherit the land and titles of their fathers; they were sent out into the world to fend for themselves and might or might not re-emerge from the middle ranks into which they were thrust. On the other hand people from those ranks who had vigour, enterprise, intelligence, or good fortune could rise to the very top. Commerce, law, lucky marriages, office under the crown could bring the wealth to purchase a landed estate; and for the landowner, as long as he owned enough, the various stages in the peerage followed almost automatically.

Professor Perkin argues that this social mobility, unique in contemporary Europe, was one of the preconditions of that other unique English phenomenon, the Industrial Revolution.[2] This is

[1] Harold Perkin, *The origins of modern English society 1780–1880* (1969), 17.
[2] Ibid., 63.

a difficult question. What is certain is that an industrial revolution occurring in England in the second half of the eighteenth century produced a class of confident, self-conscious, capitalist factory owners whose social and economic demands could not be accommodated by the old open aristocracy. Individuals, like the elder Sir Robert Peel, might go up the steps of the eighteenth-century hierarchy and never think in any other terms. But a host of less rich, less individually aspiring business men regarded the old order as wrong in itself, a clog on industry, a barrier to 'free trade in everything', an immoral corrupt encumbrance preventing the achievement of that beneficent economic growth which seemed to them of paramount importance. It was a strange trick of fate that the younger Sir Robert, in spite of his Toryism and his landed estate, in spite of Harrow and Christ Church, should have become the idol of this new class and should have broken his own political career in the pursuance of its interests.

The 'middle class', thus differentiated from the 'middling ranks' of the old order, did not find itself in acute conflict with the aristocracy till the end of the Napoleonic Wars. For the first fifty years of the Industrial Revolution the interests of the two classes were not markedly divergent. The aristocracy was more than ready to meet the new ideology of competition and *laissez-faire* half way. They were for example only too happy to jettison their already much diminished paternalist duties, the social *quid pro quo* of the paternalist authority which gave them their claim to govern the country. Nowhere was this clearer than in the case of the poor laws whose evils were denounced as vigorously by the gentry as by the manufacturers. The substitution of a cash nexus for the old social nexus which had its roots back in the days of feudalism did not immediately damage the position of the landowner. On the contrary the Industrial Revolution made his rent roll larger than ever and he continued to reign supreme in the countryside. In the long run, perhaps, the change was injurious to him. Just as today in 'White Africa' the European population has been digging its own eventual grave by the attempt, however natural, to substitute a cash economy for the subsistence economy of tribalism, so too the aristocracy of the eighteenth century was destroying its own *raison d'être* by accepting the arguments of the economists. But the long run can be very long indeed, as proved to be the case with the English aristocracy, and well may be in White Africa too.

The issue which brought conflict to a head was the corn law of 1815. Passed by a parliament of landowners it was one of the most naked pieces of class legislation in English history, and a clear sign that the capitalist ideal was not going to prevail without a struggle. The middle class became consciously militant and began to look for allies. The aristocracy and the employers were not the only groups which had emerged as classes from the old hierarchical pre-industrial order. The same period saw the conversion of a substantial element of what had been 'the lower orders' into 'the working class'. This development was no doubt an inevitable long term result of urbanisation and the factory system, but what immediately provoked it and made the working class hostile to the aristocracy was the campaign to abolish the poor laws. Coming on top of the refusal to regulate wages and the passing of the Combination Acts it seemed the last straw, the open and palpable abandonment of the paternalist tradition.[1]

It was a combination of the discontented middle class with the disillusioned working class which brought about the Reform Act of 1832. But the measure could never have been peacefully passed if a section of the aristocratic class which dominated parliament had not supported it also. The descendants of the Foxite Whigs led by Lord Grey had been the 'outs' of politics almost ever since the death of their leader and hero in 1806. For nearly a quarter of a century the descendants of the Pittite Whigs, now called Tories,[2] had possessed a monopoly of political power and patronage; and by 1830 it seemed to the 'outs' that the rules of the game were so adverse to them that only an accident could ever put them in. If that accident occurred, it was essential to seize the opportunity and change the rules.

The Whigs thought about reform in quite distinct terms from the middle and working classes. To both the new classes it was a vital prerequisite for the creation of the type of society, very different in each case, where they hoped to flourish and prosper economically – a stepping stone to further changes such as the repeal of the corn laws. The Whigs flourished economically as it

---

[1] Perkin, op. cit., 189 et sq.   [2] See Introduction, p. 9.

was. Most of them were immensely rich and were growing richer. To them reform was essentially a move in the party game like Fox's India Bill[1] in 1783. Their basic social attitudes were those common to the whole landed class and were not very different from those of the liberal Tories who controlled the government during the 1820s. In a broad sense this outlook accepted the middle class ideals of competition, non-interference and *laissez-faire*; even free trade, though not 'free trade in everything'. The Whigs like the Tories were in favour of the corn laws and, again like the Tories, were in favour of the Established Church, but in the latter case with a difference of emphasis. They were perhaps rather nearer than the Tories to 'free trade in religion', although it is fair to say that a Tory government repealed the Test Acts and emancipated the Catholics. As for 'free trade in land', both parties would have none of it, and the failure of land reform to make any headway throughout the nineteenth century, except to a limited degree in Ireland where special circumstances prevailed, is clear evidence of the continued strength of the aristocracy.

The Whigs' support of parliamentary reform should not be condemned because they thought of it largely in terms of party advantage. They were, after all, right as well as shrewd. The old system was fundamentally indefensible, and, if the landed class was to preserve any part of its old ascendancy, concessions had to be made to popular demand. It will never be possible to say how near to revolution England was in 1832, but it would be hard to argue that reform could have been postponed for much longer without an explosion. The party that successfully invested in the movement for reform was bound to secure great dividends. It was by no means self-evident in the 1820s which of the two parties this would be. The accident of personalities and events ensured that it would not be the Tories.

In terms of parliamentary representation the Reform Act was a far less conclusive victory for the middle classes than old fashioned historiography allows. As for their working class allies it was in a sense a defeat, largely depriving them of such representation as the

[1] This was a measure designed to vest the patronage of the East India Company in Foxite hands and thus indirectly consolidate Fox's control of the House of Commons. Under strong pressure from George III the House of Lords rejected the bill. The king dismissed the Fox-North coalition and the long rule of the younger Pitt began.

quirks and eccentricities of the old system had, as it were by accident, given them. The preponderance of the small boroughs, the continued under-representation of the north of England and of the big towns, left the middle class without a big enough base from which to launch a party of its own. There is nothing surprising in this. The measure was drafted and carried by a section of the aristocracy. Not unnaturally it was electorally advantageous to that section, but it did not substitute middle class for aristocratic ascendancy. At most it gave the middle class a junior partnership in power.

Representation, however, is not everything. The archetypal middle class business man in his counting house, constantly concerned with the active employment of his capital, ever alert to buy in the cheapest and sell in the dearest market, had no time for politics. The leisure needed for that occupation could only be possessed by the man who derived his income not from active employment of capital but from passive enjoyment of property, whether in the form of land or what Disraeli called 'the sweet simplicity of the three per cents'. The middle class had won or was in process of winning, a much more important struggle than the struggle for the House of Commons; this was the battle for the heart, for 'the control of the prevailing morality', as Harold Perkin describes it.[1] It was the successful subjection or conversion of the other classes to the ideals of hard work, competition, continence, thrift, non-intervention, freedom of commerce, labour, religion, which marked the real triumph of the middle class. In short they had behind them everything that is summed up by that vague but nonetheless useful phrase 'the spirit of the age'. With this on their side there was no need to push the aristocracy out of parliament. The aristocracy, except perhaps in a few matters not vital to middle class aims, would do the good work themselves, and the political party which adapted itself most readily to the new ethic was the one which would enjoy the ascendancy in the years to come.

In spite of the failure of the Tories to come to terms with 'the spirit of the age' in the matter of rotten boroughs, they stood a very reasonable chance of winning this battle. For they possessed a

[1] Perkin, op. cit., 273.

potential dynasty of leadership which came far closer to the middle class ideal than any Whig equivalent. Peel and his disciple, William Gladstone, were the statesmen who seemed the embodiment of the aspirations of the new order, and at the same time they were singularly well qualified to reconcile these aspirations with the old order to which by education, upbringing and background they themselves belonged. Yet in the event both were to be repudiated by their party, Peel to wander in political limbo till his death, Gladstone to go over to the other side and lead it.

Peel was one of the greatest statesmen of his age. He was a most able administrator. He possessed a remarkable capacity for hard work. He was humane. He cared intensely about the distress and poverty of the society in which he lived. He had, till Disraeli broke it, an ascendancy in the House of Commons unequalled by any rival. He was very rich; he was most happily married; he achieved his ambition of becoming Prime Minister. Yet there is something curiously uneasy about him. Perhaps he never entirely recovered from the strain of living up to the expectations of his father who looked at him rather as Joseph Kennedy looked at his sons, with intense pride, affection – and vicarious ambition. Although he had an aristocratic upbringing, he did not belong to the aristocracy. His manner was awkward and he spoke like Gladstone with a provincial accent. Disraeli in some reminiscent jottings wrote:

Peel always pût a question and to the last said 'woonderful' and 'woonderfully'. He guarded his aspirates with immense care. I have known him slip. The correctness was not spontaneous. He had managed his elocution like his temper: neither was originally good.'[1]

Peel, again like Gladstone, lacked the gift of managing people. He did not bother to conciliate his supporters, and he was 'peppery', finding it difficult to suffer fools gladly or to make the effort to win over the malcontents and rebels. He had an unfortunately egotistical manner and was even more addicted than most politicians to the first person singular. He had mannerisms and phrases which were unnoticed when he was in the ascendancy

[1] Hughenden Papers, Box 26 A/X/A, 45, 1862.

but gave a handle to mockery when things went wrong. He was, for example, too fond of claiming that he was being 'frank and explicit'.[1] Disraeli did not let this go without comment. The 'gentleman in Downing Street' instructs his Secretary, Mr Hoaxem how to deal with two delegations by telling them each precisely the opposite story. 'I have no doubt you will get through the business very well, Mr Hoaxem, particularly if you be "frank and explicit"; that is the right line to take when you wish to conceal your own mind and to confuse the minds of others.'[2]

These were superficial defects no doubt, but they may explain some of the suspicion with which he was regarded by his aristocratic followers and the venom with which they treated him over the repeal of the corn laws. But in the early 1830s this lay far ahead. Peel seemed indispensable, the one hope of a shattered party to recover from the plight in which it found itself.

In a broad sense there were three possible policies open to the Tory or Conservative party[3] after 1832. They could remain simply an aristocratic landed interest group obdurately opposing the wind of change which was blowing through English society in the early nineteenth century. The late Evelyn Waugh once expressed his regret that the Conservatives had never put the clock back for a single minute. There was a section of Peel's supporters who would gladly have done so, or at most would have settled for stopping the hands where they were. The chief representative of the 'Ultras' was Disraeli's patron, Lord Chandos, who later achieved celebrity when as Duke of Buckingham he went bankrupt to the tune of a million pounds, largely thanks to his propensity to buy land whose rental was far below the interest on the money that he borrowed in order to buy it. He was known as 'the Farmers' Friend'. His supporters came from the squirearchy, particularly those who had little aspiration to office. They formed the backbone of the 'agriculturist' malcontents of the 1830s and were largely the same people who opposed Catholic Emancipation.

---

[1] The phrase appears in the Tamworth Manifesto (so called from Peel's constituency in Staffordshire). The manifesto is given in full in Lord Mahon and E. Cardwell (eds), *Memoirs by the Right Honourable Sir Robert Peel* (1857), II, 58–67.

[2] *Sybil*, Bk VI, ch. 1.

[3] The question of nomenclature and continuity is discussed in the Introduction, pp. 5–8.

Their shibboleth was 'Protection, protestantism and no popery.' They fussed about the malt tax. The shadowy intrigues of the Duke of Cumberland and Lord Lyndhurst[1] to whom Disraeli acted for a time as private secretary were connected with the same section of the party. They stayed uneasily with Peel for the time being, but they voted against the Maynooth grant in 1845, and finally and fatally against the repeal of the corn laws in 1846.

The advantage of the Ultra policy was that it corresponded to the actual beliefs of a large section of the political nation. Probably a majority of the electorate or of those who influenced the electorate were basically conservative with a small 'c'. They believed in the preservation of the traditional institutions of England, the monarchy, parliament, the Church, primogeniture, the rights of property landed as well as commercial. Many of them would not have dissented at heart from the opinions of Prince Seithenyn, quoted earlier. The great majority of the effective political nation wished to keep things more or less as they were.

The disadvantage of the Ultra attitude, however, was that this same basically conservative electorate had to be convinced that the Conservative party with a big 'C' was the party best capable of achieving that objective. After the events of 1830–2 this seemed far from certain. Conscious of other classes knocking ever louder at the door those who controlled the constituencies had to consider whether to open it a little and let some of them in or to stand firm, in which case the door might be battered down and the house pillaged. Over parliamentary reform the Tory party cut itself adrift from moderate opinion which saw in blind adherence to the old constitution paradoxically a more dangerous and more revolutionary course, in the sense that it was likely to lead to revolution, than a policy of cautious concession.

The truth, as Peel and the abler members of the party saw, was that the landed interest by itself constituted too narrow a base on which to build a viable opposition. If the policy of the Ultras had won the day, the landed gentry would have become an isolated class of internal *émigrés* like the French aristocracy after 1870; the

---

[1] John Singleton Copley, Tory Lord Chancellor 1827–30, 1834–5, 1841–6. Renowned alike for his legal acumen, brilliance in debate, lack of scruple, and raffish mode of life.

Conservative party as their organ would have been as ineffective
as the Jacobites a century earlier. As Professor Gash puts it, 'For
the sake of the landed interest itself Conservatism as a national
party could not take its stand on landed Toryism alone.'[1] Thoughtful Conservatives therefore looked for more positive policies.

There were two alternatives. One which seemed in some ways
attractive was to fight the advancing middle class by an alliance
with the working class. Why should not the landed aristocracy
join hands with the socially dispossessed, the victims of the
Industrial Revolution, against the northern 'millocracy' which
threatened them both? The concordat between the middle and
working class, which had forced through the Reform Act was
short-lived. It soon became clear that the middle class had no
intention of using its victory for anything but its own purposes. The
new poor law enshrining the principle of 'less eligibility' was as
obvious a symbol of this purpose as one could find. True, it did not
satisfy the doctrinaires who would have liked the total abolition
of all provision for paupers, but *Oliver Twist* and a multiplicity of
less famous denunciations are enough to show that no one who
could help it was likely to enter the new Bastilles. The split
between the middle class and working class was confirmed and
widened by the growth of the Chartist movement. There seemed a
genuine opening for a Tory-Radical alliance.

The possibility appealed particularly to idealists, romantics,
escapists, all who harked back to a largely imaginary pre-
industrial golden age, all who disliked and feared the harsher
manifestations of the industrial revolution and the bleaker aspects
of the Utilitarian philosophy expounded by Jeremy Bentham.
The paternalistic side of the aristocratic ideal had never wholly
died. A sort of *noblesse oblige* spirit of responsibility for the lower
orders animated such figures as Thomas Sadler in the 1820s and
his disciples, Richard Oastler and John Wood, who fought against
the new poor law in the 1830s. To supply them with a philosophy,
not perhaps a very clear one, there was S. T. Coleridge whom J. S.
Mill ranks with Bentham as one of 'the two great seminal minds
in England of their age'. The intellectual organ of this group was
Blackwood's Edinburgh Magazine edited by John Wilson, under the

[1] N. Gash, *Reaction and reconstruction in English politics 1832–52* (1965), 139.

pseudonym of 'Christopher North'. He was also Professor of Moral Philosophy at Edinburgh University. Its most original contributor was David Robinson, a heterodox economist who challenged the dominant 'classical', *laissez-faire* doctrine of David Ricardo and advocated, though without the mathematical apparatus to prove his case, many of the measures associated with the name of John Maynard Keynes a century later: governmental intervention to ensure full employment, a reflationary money policy, increased public expenditure, and control of the economy by taxation and tariffs.[1]

High Tory paternalism of this sort was associated not only with protectionism but with a strong attachment to the Anglican Establishment. The whole trend of liberal Toryism both in terms of religious and economic policy during the 1820s inspired its deepest distrust. Canning and Huskisson came in for severe strictures from *Blackwood's*. As for Peel no words were too strong. In 1830 the journal observed: 'Mr Peel's public life has been one continuing course of despicable, grovelling, mercenary faithlessness to principles and party.'[2] It was not only the Ultras but high Tories of this paternalist school led by Sadler, who voted against Wellington and Peel in 1830, letting in the Whigs, and thus making the chances of their own success thinner than ever.

This strain in Toryism was to end, at least for the time being, with the Gothic absurdities of 'Young England' in the early 1840s, of which more later.[3] The numerous manifestations of popular Toryism between 1830 and 1845 show that the approach was not simply romantic nonsense: Tory Chartism; the attack on the new poor law; Ashley's campaign for Factory Acts; the parliamentary efforts of Sadler, Oastler and Wood; and the writings of Carlyle (not that the Sage of Ecclefechan could ever be described as a Tory, but he was at any rate no friend of the Liberals).

Yet the Tory-Radical approach had two grave defects. In the first place it ran clean contrary to 'the spirit of the age'. It was in almost every respect at loggerheads with the confident 'progressive' challenge of the active capitalist ideal which was rapidly

---

[1] See Perkin, op. cit., 244–52, for an illuminating discussion of the role of *Blackwood's* in general and Robinson in particular.

[2] Perkin, op. cit., quoting *Blackwood's*, XXVII (1830), 41.   [3] See pp. 55–6.

hardening into current orthodoxy. There is nothing discreditable in being against the spirit of the age. Indeed if one is against it long enough one may suddenly find oneself on its side; the spirit of the age does not last for ever. The progressives of any particular generation are often conceited, doctrinaire, blinkered and intolerant. Few of us today can read Macaulay's attack on Southey without feeling a great deal of sympathy for Southey. The asininities of those who are 'with it' frequently surpass the follies of those who are against 'it' (whatever 'it' means). But, in terms of political headway, opposition to the reigning intellectual orthodoxy is very difficult. After observing that 'the fallen, degraded, liberal Tory must servilely echo all the Whig advances, though public ruin be the consequence', Robinson went on to bewail the fate of those who challenged the liberal consensus.

You are treated as unworthy of argument, and are silenced by derision. Discussion and information are thus excluded from Parliament. The Holy Whig and Tory Fathers must preserve their political faith from the heresy of truth – they must canonize their saints, sell their relics, worship their images, exact credence to their legends and consign unbelievers to the moral rack and faggot, because in this is involved their public existence. They are destroyed, if argument and fact be suffered to kindle the blaze of reformation.

The press naturally follows its parties, surpasses them in guilt, and covers every point which they are incapable of defending...

Say that the Holy Fathers – the Wellingtons and Hollands – the Huskissons and Broughams – the Peels and Burdetts can err; and this press dooms you to the stake for uttering such an impious impossibility.

He ended with a series of rhetorical questions, two of which may serve to illustrate the rest.

Am I to applaud that which has sacrificed the foreign interests of my country and destroyed her influence amidst other nations merely because it is called liberal and enlightened policy? Am I to support laws which demonstrably have plunged half my countrymen into ruin and misery, because it is said that they are founded on liberal and enlightened principles?

Evidently the answer was no.

And he signed his piece which was an open letter to the heads of Oxford colleges (a body of men not in those days much given to enlightenment and liberalism) 'One of the Old School'.[1]

[1] One can sympathise. There is something deeply frustrating about those confident fashionable orthodoxies which at times seem indefeasibly established in the media of communication, supreme in academic circles, taken for granted by the intellectuals, an integral part of the mental equipment of civil servants, even of MPs. It is particularly frustrating when the majority of both sides in parliament either take the current fashion for granted or dare not argue against it for fear of ridicule, with the result that any criticism meets not rational argument but the automatic conditioned reflex of indifference and incredulity.

This became increasingly the position of the Tory-Radical paternalists as the decade wore on. The truth was that they were both too far ahead and too far behind their times; ahead, in that their shadowy prevision of the welfare state and a planned economy would not be generally accepted even a hundred years later; behind, in that their views on such subjects as the Church were as reactionary as those of the Ultras. To the ordinary commonsensical Tory M.P. who had already jettisoned the responsibilities of aristocratic paternalism, who was already half converted to the new middle class ethos except in so far as it directly damaged his own traditional interests, and who sought above all an accommodation with capitalism in order to retain as much as possible of the old order, the ideas of the Tory-Radicals seemed chimerical.

And even if they had not, there was a second major defect in that approach – a defect more practical, tangible and damaging. The class to which the Tories were to appeal had not got the vote. What is more no Tory or Whig M.P. had the slightest intention of giving it the vote. Tory-Radicalism made no sense as an effective policy unless a substantial element of the working class was enfranchised. Disraeli and the Young Englanders of the early 1840s were perhaps the most articulate exponents of the creed, but they never faced this issue squarely. There is no hint of a new Reform Bill in *Coningsby* or *Sybil*. Nor can it be claimed that the Conservative Act of 1867 represented a belated awareness of the possibility of such an alliance. Derby and Disraeli were primarily influenced then by short term tactical considerations, and did all in their power to counteract the consequences of household suffrage in the boroughs by trying to redraw the constituency boundaries on a massive scale. Reluctance to tamper with the franchise in the 1830s and 1840s is fully understandable and certainly not discreditable. To give the vote to the starving, illiterate, semi-revolutionary masses, victims of every sort of delusion from Chartism downwards, would have seemed lunacy to the possessing classes. Rightly or wrongly they had no intention of risking it, and that fact alone ruled Tory-Radicalism out of the realm of practical politics.

The other positive policy open to the post-reform Tory party was the one actually chosen, viz, to continue the liberal Toryism of the 1820s, the tradition of Liverpool, Canning, Huskisson, Peel himself. This, broadly, meant acceptance of the industrial revolution, compromise with the forces of change and adaptation of traditional institutions to the new social demands. Above all it meant a libertarian fiscal policy which would in the end bring increased affluence to every class in society and thus relax the tensions which in the hungry 1830s and 1840s threatened revolution in Britain. In this way the traditional constitution of Church and State and land could be preserved and strengthened, and the danger of its destruction at the hands of an alliance of the non-aristocratic classes much diminished or even averted altogether. The policy amounted to one of compromise with the middle class; a reversion in fact to the old course off which the party had been temporarily blown thanks to bad steersmanship in the eye of the wind of parliamentary reform.

Peel's acceptance of the new order of society should not be overstated. He considered that the existence of the territorial aristocracy as the governing class of England was essential for the welfare of the nation. On May 4, 1846 during the corn law debates he put his point of view clearly:

> I believe it to be of the utmost importance that a territorial aristocracy should be maintained. I believe that in no country is it more important than in this, with its ancient constitution, ancient habits and mixed form of government. I trust that a territorial aristocracy, with all its just influence and authority will be long maintained. I believe such an aristocracy to be essential to the purposes of good government. The question only is – what in a certain state of public opinion, and in a certain position of society, is the most effectual way of maintaining the legitimate influence and authority of a territorial aristocracy. . . . I said long ago that I thought agricultural prosperity was interwoven with manufacturing prosperity; and depended more on it than on the Corn Laws. . . . I believe the interests direct and indirect of manufacturing and agricultural classes to be the same.'[1]

By the time he spoke those words a large section of his supporters either believed, or had been pressed by their constituents into saying, that the interests of the two classes were not the same. Hence the split over the repeal of the corn laws with its ruinous effects on the party's fortunes for nearly thirty years. But in the immediate aftermath of the Reform Act the potential divergence was not so obvious. The corn laws were upheld by both parties. The Conservatives were in opposition, and in opposition fragmentation of opinion, as long as it does not lead to a group actually going over to the other side, is not so important. Throughout the 1830s Peel had trouble with Ultras, 'agriculturists' and other varieties of malcontents, but there was no haven for them among the Whigs; and no specific issue arose to cause a major secession.

The policy followed by Peel after 1832 had much to recommend it. More realistic than that of the Tory-Radicals, less rigid than that of the Ultras it offered the best opportunity of obtaining political power for his party and, what was more important in Peel's eyes, harmony and prosperity among the various classes in an era of poverty, violence, distress, and revolution. In fact it was

[1] *Speeches*, IV, 684, quoted, Gash, op. cit., 139.

the only line that he could have followed with any prospect of success, which does not in the least detract from his credit for doing so.

The main disadvantage which he had to face was the difficulty of distinguishing his policy from that of the Whigs. This is the problem which a Conservative opposition trying to swim with the general current of enlightened opinion so often has to face. If it speaks too much in the language of its opponents it incurs the charge of being an echo rather than a voice. If it speaks too much in its own language it incurs the charge of being a voice from the past. Peel did not escape the former charge, and Disraeli's famous satire in *Coningsby* which must be quoted in any survey of the history of the Conservative party had some truth in it.

> There was indeed considerable shouting about what they called Conservative principles; but the awkward question naturally arose, what will you conserve? The prerogatives of the Crown, provided they are not exercised; the independence of the House of Lords, provided it is not asserted; the Ecclesiastical estate provided it is regulated by a commission of laymen. Everything in short that is established, as long as it is a phrase and not a fact. . . . Conservatism discards Prescription, shrinks from Principle, disavows Progress; having rejected all respect for Antiquity, it offers no redress for the Present and makes no preparation for the Future. . . .[1]

Later in the same book he wrote:

> Whenever public opinion which this party never attempts to form, to educate or to lead, falls into some violent perplexity, passion or caprice, this party yields without a struggle to the impulse, and, when the storm has passed, attempts to obstruct and obviate the logical, and ultimately the inevitable, results of the very measures which they have themselves originated, or to which they have consented. . . .
>
> The man who enters public life at this epoch has to choose between Political Infidelity and a Destructive Creed.[2]

[1] Benjamin Disraeli, *Coningsby, or, The new generation*, 3 vols (1844), Bk II, ch. 5.
[2] ibid., Bk VII, ch. 2.

This was one aspect of the difficulty faced by Peel in pursuing his cautious middle course: the alienation of the section of his own party, which did not accept the 'consensus'. It is unlikely that it worried him unduly then, though it was to be fatal later. More awkward was the problem of inducing supporters of the Whigs to come over to his side. If he was an echo, if the policies for which he stood were virtually indistinguishable from those of the party in power, why should the floating vote – and even in those days of close constituencies there was such a thing – move away from the government and support the opposition? That was the real problem for Peel and his followers on the morrow of the great Reform Bill.

CHAPTER II

Peel's achievement
1832-46

I

The Tory party had no clearly recognised leader when the first reformed parliament met. This situation was not as abnormal as it would be today. Throughout the nineteenth century, indeed until some indeterminate date between 1911 and 1922, the leadership of a political party out of office went into 'commission' or 'abeyance', as between its two leaders in the two Houses of Parliament, unless one of them happened to be an ex-Prime Minister. In that case though not formally elected he was usually regarded as the leader of the whole party and, *ceteris paribus*, could expect to be invited to form an administration if the government of the day resigned on defeat at a general election or in the House of Commons.[1] If there was no active ex-Prime Minister the monarch was free to choose the leader in either the lower or the upper house.

An obvious example of the two situations can be taken from the history of the Conservative party between 1874 and 1885. After the Conservative electoral victory in 1874 Disraeli as ex-Prime Minister was regarded not only as leader of the party in the House of Commons but of the whole party and had the expectation which was not disappointed of being asked to form the next government. In 1876 he became Earl of Beaconsfield and exchanged the leadership of the lower for that of the upper house, Sir Stafford Northcote succeeding him in the former position. In 1880 he lost the election and died a year later. The peers elected

[1] The first person to be elected as 'Leader of the Conservative and Unionist Party' was Bonar Law on October 23, 1922.

Lord Salisbury as his successor. For the next four years there was no leader of the party as a whole, and when Gladstone resigned in 1885 it was open to the Queen to choose Northcote or Salisbury. In fact she chose the latter for reasons which are discussed below,[1] but she could have chosen either man without infringing constitutional propriety. In practice the situation always depended in some degree on personalities and circumstances. After 1846 there was no ex-Prime Minister in the ranks of the anti-Peelite Protectionists who constituted the new Conservative party, and so in theory the leadership should have been held jointly by Lord Stanley (Derby) in the Lords together with Lord George Bentinck in the Commons. But in practice no one doubted that Stanley was the party's only possible Prime Minister. His experience and prestige made any other choice absurd; he was regarded as the sole leader long before 1852 when he actually formed his first administration.

The situation in 1833 was unusual. There existed an ex-Tory Prime Minister in the person of the Duke of Wellington.[2] The duke had not retired from politics. He continued to lead the Tory peers whenever he cared to do so. On the other hand it was well known that, when his vain attempt in 1832 to form a government for the paradoxical purpose of carrying a Reform Bill collapsed amid general obloquy, he had expressed his intention of never accepting the premiership again. However, people can change their minds. The duke's attitude made Peel's position uncertain. Nor was it beyond all doubt that Peel would be Prime Minister even if the duke did step down. A move to elect him formally as leader of the opposition came to nothing because of the hostility of a group of discontented Ultras.[3] There was gossip that the Speaker, Charles Manners-Sutton, would be the king's choice if a Tory ministry was formed.[4] The Tory party was in the mood of fractious disarray which so often overcomes it after a defeat.

---

[1] See pp. 134–7.

[2] In fact there were three, for Lord Sidmouth (Addington) was still alive and so was Lord Ripon (Goderich) but the former had long ago retired, and the latter, after the most ignominious premiership in English history, had gone over to the other side.

[3] Gash, *Reaction and reconstruction*, 140–1.

[4] ibid., 141. Manners-Sutton, son of an Archbishop of Canterbury and later created 1st Viscount Canterbury, would not have been a very suitable selection in an age of rising moral standards. Greville writes of his wife, formerly Mrs Purves, 'She lived with the Speaker during Purvis's [*sic*] life, but they managed their affairs with great skill or

This book is not a political history of the times but no analysis of
the development of a political party can ignore what was happening on the other side. This applies with particular force to a party
of the right. Inevitably the main initiative comes from the left, and,
although one can be legitimately rebuked for talking about 'right'
and 'left' at all in discussing the politics of the early nineteenth
century, nevertheless it is true that the Whig–Liberal–Radical
coalition was the 'party of movement', and that a large part of
Conservatism then, and ever since, consisted in resisting or deflect-
ing or slowing down 'movement'. It is therefore necessary to see
what the government was doing. The aftermath of the Reform
Act saw a spate of legislation. Most of it was not in the least
revolutionary, or notably different from the sort of measures which
Peel might have promoted, but there was one issue on which the
two parties did emphatically differ and which was to split the
reigning coalition.

This had nothing to do with economics or social reform. The
differences about those subjects which loom so large in modern
politics did not on the whole divide the parties from one another;
they created a line of division within the Conservative party, but
not between that party and the Whigs. What really did divide the
parties was a constitutional question. The Tory party never tired
of proclaiming its determination to uphold the traditional
institutions of the United Kingdom, the monarchy, the House of
Lords, and the Protestant Establishment, both its property and its
privileges. Closely tied to this was the concept of law and order, a
strong executive government. This was a favourite theme of the
Duke of Wellington, and in a period of popular agitation, great
poverty in places, frequent riots, and the constant threat of violence, it had all the relevance that such a theme has today in
America and Ulster.

No doubt it is true that the Whigs also proclaimed their determination to enforce law and order, and to uphold the constitution.
Here are utterances from four prominent figures about their and
their party's purposes:

else good luck for she had no children by him till after they were married, and then
two who appeared as triumphant witnesses of her immaculate virtue.' Lytton Strachey
and Roger Fulford (eds), *The Greville memoirs*, 8 vols (1938), III, 178.

The maintenance of our settled institutions in Church and State, and also the preservation and defence of that combination of laws, of institutions, of habits and of manners which has contributed to mould and form the character of Englishmen.

To the Constitution of this country in all its branches I stand pledged by feeling, by opinion and by duty.

You are determined to uphold the Protestant religion, the Church of England in Ireland as well as in England; you are determined to maintain the independence of a House of Lords.

I wish to rally as large a portion of the British people as possible around the existing institutions of the country – the Throne – Lords – Commons and The Established Church.[1]

The first, second and fourth are respectively by Peel, Russell and the Whig Lord Durham, 'Radical Jack'.[2] The third is from a letter of Wellington to Peel.

But this unanimity was little more than one would find in an interdenominational agreement to be 'against sin'. What mattered, as with the general question of preserving the territorial aristocracy, was the interpretation of ways and means, of tactics; and here one can find some important differences. Perhaps the most significant of all was over the question, partly religious, partly constitutional, of the redistribution and 'appropriation' of the revenues of the Church of Ireland. Both parties were determined to preserve the union of England and Ireland. Both parties recognised that the revenues of the Church of Ireland – and the Church of England too for that matter – were indefensibly maldistributed, and that parliament had a right to reallocate them. As far as the Church of England was concerned there was no real battle between the parties on the question of lay appropriation. It was agreed to be the national church and its total resources were not regarded as too much for its potential legitimate expenditure. The Church of Ireland was another matter: it catered for only about

---

[1] I have lifted all these quotations from Gash, *Reaction and reconstruction*, the first and third are on p. 132, the second and fourth on p. 165.

[2] Also known as 'King Jog', from his immortal remark to Creevey that a man may jog along on £50,000 a year.

one-eighth of the Irish population, although its establishment was designed to deal with the whole nation. Its revenue was claimed in some quarters to be not only inequitably distributed within the Church but altogether excessive.

The majority of the Whigs, and of course the Radicals to a man, were in favour of appropriating to lay purposes the 'surplus' thrown up by redistribution of the revenues of the Church of Ireland. The Conservatives were strongly opposed. Behind the two attitudes lay the deeper question of the best way to preserve the Union. The Conservatives believed that any weakening of the Protestant Establishment in Ireland would weaken the Union. The Whigs believed that the Union would only survive if concessions were made to the Catholic majority. There were some who went further and considered that the Union would be safer if the Church of Ireland was jettisoned altogether, but this view was not to prevail for another thirty-five years when Gladstone passed the Act of Disestablishment in 1869 – against relatively lukewarm Conservative opposition, such was the changed temper of the times.

The question of appropriation of Church revenues for lay purposes produced the first overt split in the uneasy coalition which had carried the Reform Bill. The Duke of Richmond, Lord Ripon, Edward Stanley, and Sir James Graham resigned in May 1834 because of an indiscreet declaration by Russell in favour of the principle. The moving spirit in this secession was Stanley, heir to the earldom of Derby. Hence the name given to his group, 'the Derby dilly'.[1] He was one of the most brilliant orators of his day, but essentially an impetuous and disruptive force at this stage in his career. The departure of the 'dilly' was a damaging blow to the Whigs, although it was not immediately followed by a union between Stanley and the Tories. He refused to join Peel in his 'hundred days' ministry of 1834–5. It was not till the session of 1836 that he consulted Peel on tactics and sat next to him on the opposition front bench and not till 1840 that he joined the Carlton

---

[1] 'Dilly' is an abbreviation for a diligence or coach which carried six passengers and the allusion is to lines by J. H. Frere, in the *Loves of the triangles*:

'So down thy hill, romantic Ashbourn, glides
The Derby dilly, carrying *three* insides.'

Club.[1] Meanwhile 'appropriation' had brought down two
ministries: it was the real reason behind William IV's dismissal of
Melbourne in November 1834, for Russell, on whose appointment
as Chancellor of the Exchequer and Leader of the House Melbourne insisted, was unacceptable to the king largely because of his
opinions about the Irish Church. It also brought down Peel's
ministry in April 1835 when Russell managed to carry a resolution
in the House of Commons in support of appropriation.

To modern minds the whole subject may well seem a footling
one. In the end appropriation never got through; Russell dropped
it in 1838. What is more the whole debate turned on the disposal
of a surplus whose existence was quite uncertain. Nevertheless it is
worth attention for it reminds us of something easily forgotten
today when Ireland and religion no longer dominate the legislature,
viz, the immense amount of political time which both subjects
occupied throughout the nineteenth century. In modern times the
great issues have been economic and social. In those days they
were religious and constitutional. The first parliament in which
economic issues were dominant was that of 1900, thanks to Joseph
Chamberlain's crusade for tariff reform. Despite Peel's great
budgets, despite the struggle over the corn laws, even the parliament of 1841 was more concerned with religion than economics.
In these circumstances one would expect to find the dividing line
between the parties to lie largely in religious and constitutional
issues, and this is certainly borne out by contemporary evidence.
'In the main it is undoubted,' wrote Stanley to J. W. Croker in
1847, 'that the Whig Governments fell, and the Conservative
party was formed upon questions affecting the maintenance of the
Established Church, and the integrity of the institutions of the
Country, the House of Lords included.'

A brief survey of the changes of government between 1832 and
1847 confirms Stanley's statement. The changes in 1834 and 1835
from Whig to Conservative and back again turned on the Irish
Church. The Whigs resigned in 1839 on the question of suspending
the constitution of Jamaica, and came back within a day or so on

---

[1] He retired from Brookes's in 1836, but so did a number of Whigs in protest at
O'Connell who was a member and who declined to resign despite having publicly
denounced the House of Lords as 'a set of stupid, ignorant, half-mad fops and cox-
combs'.

another constitutional question, that of the Ladies of the Bedchamber.[1] In 1841 they fell on a straight vote of no confidence. In
1846 Peel was defeated on an Irish Coercion Bill, though admittedly the real reason was the repeal of the corn laws. In 1851
Russell resigned nominally on a franchise question but fundamentally because his anti-papal declaration had deprived him of
Irish support, and, although he came back again thanks to Derby's
failure to form a government, the same basic reason brought him
down a year later. The fall of the Derby government in December
1852 owing to the defeat of Disraeli's budget was the first occasion
since the Reform Act where a government was formally ousted on
a question which could be described as purely economic or fiscal.

The Conservatives differed from the Whigs principally on
religious and constitutional matters, and they had considerable
success in resisting what they regarded as the threat of the Whig-
Radical alliance to 'the existing institutions of the country'. Their
success is too often masked by the tendency, not extinct even now,
to look at the history of the years between the death of Pitt and the
repeal of the corn laws through Whig-tinted spectacles; a quarter
of a century of Tory misrule, of obdurate resistance to change, is
succeeded in 1830 by a decade of progressive reformist legislation;
true, the Whigs are ousted in 1841 but only because Melbourne
was not a real Whig, and because Peel, having imbibed the
principles of his opponents, has shown his ability, though in 'the
wrong party', to carry out a programme of enlightened progressive
reform; when he founders on the rock of the reactionary Tory
squirearchy the 'natural' condition of politics reasserts itself; the
Whig party gradually developing into Gladstonian liberalism
becomes the normal governing party of the country.

The picture is nearer to reality at the end of the period than at
the beginning. There it is palpably incorrect. However reactionary
the Tories may have been in the years between Waterloo and Peter-
loo, they undoubtedly changed their course in the early 1820s.
The policy of Liverpool, Huskisson, Canning, and Wellington,
was in effect an attempt to secure what it has become fashionable

---

[1] Peel asked that the Queen as a mark of confidence should replace some of the Whig
Ladies of the Bedchamber by wives of Tory noblemen. She refused, and Peel declined
to take office.

YOUNG GULLIVER AND THE BROBDINGNAG MINISTER

IT WAS AT THIS PERIOD THAT MR DISRAELI COMMENCED THE ATTACKS UPON SIR ROBERT PEEL
WHICH WERE CONTINUED DURING THE LIFETIME OF THE STATESMAN—1845

April 4, 1845. Reproduced by permission of Punch

to call a 'consensus', that is to say a policy which accorded with
the general views of intelligent but not very far-sighted men
of affairs and with the material advantage of the politically
effective spiritual and economic interests of the country. Of course
there were many mistakes, omissions, imperfections in what they
did, but to see their tenure of office as a period of frozen reaction is
to fall for a trick of political propaganda – no doubt a perfectly
legitimate move in the game, like the Labour claim in 1945 that
the Conservatives had thrived on stagnation and unemployment
between the wars, but not a statement that any historian should
take seriously.

Peel after 1832 followed very much the same line as he had
when he was in Liverpool's administration during the 1820s. He
supported cautious piecemeal changes, he accepted the new
parliamentary system and its logical corollaries, he endeavoured
to win back the moderate men and the great 'interests' in the
nation alienated by the Tory attitude to the Reform Bill, and he
encouraged the removal of abuses; but he resisted with much
determination any move to disturb the balance of that 'mixed
constitution' which the Tories regarded as sacrosanct, and which,
though the Whigs paid due tribute to it, their Radical followers
frankly derided.

The Tories were highly successful. Anyone who surveyed the
various parts of the constitution in the heady aftermath of the
Reform Act might have hoped or dreaded, depending on his
political creed, that within a few years the Crown would lose its
prerogatives, the House of Lords would have its wings clipped, the
churches of England and Ireland would be disestablished, the
secret ballot introduced and local government democratised in
town and country. In the event very little of this programme was
realised. The Crown did lose some of its power but by an almost
imperceptible process of silent adaptation rather than any overt
political stroke. The House of Lords kept its privileges for nearly
eighty years. The Church of Ireland survived till 1869, open
voting till 1872. The corporations were democratised in 1835 but
the rule of the country gentlemen in the counties remained
inviolate till 1888. As for the Church of England it has not been
disestablished yet, and at the time of writing its senior bishops still

sit in the House of Lords. Of course much legislation was passed
by the Whigs between 1832 and 1841 but little of it was such as to
be objectionable to a liberal Tory like Peel whose ideas had been
shaped by his experiences under Liverpool in the 1820s.

Peel would not have become such a dominant figure if there had
been an equivalent of himself on the other side. The difficulty of
pursuing a middle course when you are in opposition is to distinguish yourself from the government, for most governments find
themselves obliged by circumstances to adopt a middle course too,
a cautious and moderate policy, whatever their members may
have declared when they were unrestricted by the responsibilities
of office. In these conditions political differences do become those
of men rather than measures, and if the Whigs had had a Peel, it is
hard to see how the Conservatives could have made much headway. However, they had not. Their nearest candidate was Lord
Althorp but he hated office and his inheritance of the Spencer
earldom in 1834 gave him the welcome opportunity to retire from
active politics.

2

The events of 1834–5 were crucial in the development of the
Conservative party – and this constitutes a second reason for the
importance of the appropriation clause which was the underlying
cause of the crisis. Historians often refer to the accession of the
Conservatives to office as 'premature'. If 1841 is seen as the culmination of an inevitable process of Tory advance with the
elections of 1835, 1837 and 1841 as milestones on the road this
judgment may make sense, but is there any reason to regard the
process as being inevitable? Surely a more plausible verdict is that
the king's dismissal of Melbourne, however ill-considered in terms
of the interests of the Crown, was a gratuitous boon to the Conservative party and put it on the road to success in a manner as
unpredictable as it was advantageous.

There were three reasons why the political crisis of 1834
benefited the Conservatives. First, it put Peel's own position
beyond doubt. Wellington's refusal to accept the premiership and
his advice to the king to send for Peel settled the leadership of the

party for the next eleven years and settled it in favour of the party's greatest and most distinguished statesman. He no longer had to seek the position. He was *there*, and only a major revolt could pitch him out. Secondly, it caused a general election which compelled the Conservatives as the minority party to organise themselves on a scale hitherto unknown. The Conservative and Constitutional Associations, the forerunners of modern constituency organisations, nearly all came into being during 1834-5. Thirdly, although the election itself did not result in victory, the party gained a hundred seats. This was in itself highly encouraging to morale. It was, moreover, enough in the parliamentary conditions of that epoch to give Peel the opportunity to try out his new men, to show that he could govern, to demonstrate that he could practise what he preached – conservative reform.

The Tamworth Manifesto,[1] given the highly restricted opportunities for political publicity at that time, was another bonus conferred by the crisis of 1834-5. Peel did not say anything that he had not said before, but he said it at the outset of a general election and he said it as Prime Minister and leader of the Conservative party; the attention paid to the manifesto in contemporary memoirs and letters shows that he got his message across to the political nation with considerable success. The document is a trifle heavy, like Peel himself, and to modern taste dwells rather too much on the author's own honour, integrity and uprightness. But it is a clear exposition of Peel's doctrine. As he puts it to the 586 electors of Tamworth, he is

> addressing through you to that great and intelligent class of society of which you are a portion, and a fair and unexceptionable representative – to that class which is much less interested in the contentions of party, than in the maintenance of order and the cause of good government, that frank exposition of general principles and views which appears to be anxiously expected, and which it ought not to be the inclination, and cannot be the interest of a Minister of this country to withhold.

Peel went on to make a significant declaration about his own position:

[1] See Mahon and Cardwell, *Sir Robert Peel*, II, 58–67.

Now I say at once that I will not accept power on the condition of declaring myself an apostate from the principles on which I have heretofore acted. At the same time I will never admit that I have been, either before or after the Reform Bill, the defender of abuses or the enemy of judicious reforms. I appeal with confidence . . . to the active part I took in the great question of the Currency – in the consolidation and amendment of the Criminal Law – in the revisal of the whole system of Trial by Jury . . . as a proof that I have not been disposed to acquiesce in acknowledged evils, either from the mere superstitious reverence for ancient usages, or from the dread of labour or responsibility in the application of a remedy.

This is interesting not only for what he says but what he omits. Although in a later passage he disclaims an illiberal attitude to dissenters, he nowhere mentions the repeal of the Test and Corporation Acts, nor does he make any reference to Catholic emancipation. Like all good Prime Ministers Peel was a politician as well as a statesman. It was not prudent to draw the attention of Conservative electors, even liberal Conservative electors, to three of the most controversial liberal measures with which he had been associated.

Peel dealt with the challenge of his opponents that a minister must accept the Reform Bill and act in its spirit. He had, he rightly said, already made it clear that he accepted the Act as 'a final and irrevocable settlement of a great Constitutional question'. As for 'the spirit of the Reform Bill' it depended what was meant. If it meant living 'in a perpetual vortex of agitation' and 'abandoning altogether that great aid of government – more powerful than either law or reason – the respect for ancient rights and the deference to prescriptive authority', then he had no intention of acting in its spirit.

But if the spirit of the Reform Bill implies merely a careful review of institutions, civil and ecclesiastical, undertaken in a friendly temper, combining, with the firm maintenance of established rights the correction of proved abuses and the redress of real grievances – in that case I can for myself and my colleagues undertake to act in such a spirit and with such intentions.

As with 'the spirit of the Reform Bill', much depends on the actual meaning given to these unexceptionable sentiments. Suppose that some 'proved abuses', or at least some 'real grievances', could not be corrected or redressed without infringing some 'established rights', what was the good Conservative to do? It is a problem far transcending the issues of Peel's day. Indeed it is perennial, and the sceptical anti-Peelite is tempted to say that in practice Conservative governments too often judge the reality of grievances by the amount of fuss made by the grievers, and sell out established rights whenever there is enough agitation against them.

This was to be the gravamen of Disraeli's charge in *Coningsby*, quoted at the end of the previous chapter: 'The Tamworth Manifesto of 1834 was an attempt to construct a party without principles: its basis therefore was necessarily latitudinarianism; and its inevitable consequence has been Political Infidelity.'[1] But politics, as someone or other has observed, is the art of the possible. If Peel had adopted the principles of Lord Eldon, or if – even less probably – he had been converted to the ideas of Sadler or Young England, he would have conceded a perpetual monopoly of power to the Whigs. The truth is that the Marquis of Monmouth, however low his motives, was nearer to reality than Coningsby –

'I wish to be frank, sir,' said Coningsby . . . 'I have for a long time looked upon the Conservative party as a body who have betrayed their trust . . .'

'You mean giving up those Irish corporations?'[2] said Lord Monmouth. 'Well between ourselves I am quite of the same opinion. But we must mount higher: we must go back to '28 for the real mischief. But what is the use of lamenting the past. Peel is the man; suited to the times and all that; at least we must say so and try to believe so; we can't go back.'[3]

[1] *Coningsby*, Bk II, ch. 5.
[2] A reference to Conservative acquiescence in the Irish Municipal Corporation Act of 1840.
[3] ibid, Bk VIII, ch. 3.

It is amusing to note that Disraeli too once believed that 'we can't go back' – but in the days when he was an aspirant for Peel's favour, not a disappointed office-seeker anxious for revenge. Of the policy carried out by Peel in 1835 he wrote in a celebrated pamphlet which took the form of an open letter to Lord Lyndhurst:

> This great deed, therefore, instead of being an act of insincerity or apostasy, was conceived in good faith, and in perfect harmony with the previous policy of the party: it was at the same time indispensable and urged alike by the national voice and the national interests, and history will record it as the conduct of patriotic wisdom.[1]

Peel recognised that his declaration of principle needed to be made more specific, and the rest of the manifesto is devoted to the actual problems before parliament. He will not interrupt the inquiry instituted by the Whigs into municipal corporations. He will maintain a liberal attitude to Dissenters, and, though he will not admit them to the universities, he will see that they are not at a disadvantage in the professions of law and medicine. He will resist retrospective inquiry into the Pension List but confer future pensions only on grounds of public service or intellectual merit. He will not countenance the alienation of Church property from ecclesiastical uses but he is prepared to commute tithe and to 'remove every abuse that can impair the efficiency of the Establishment'. The only reference to fiscal policy is vague – 'the enforcement of strict economy – and the just and impartial consideration of what is due to all interests – agricultural, manufacturing, commercial'.

Peel only had three months in office. A series of defeats forced him to throw in his hand at the beginning of April. His most important measure was the setting up of the Ecclesiastical Commission of which Dr Kitson Clark has observed, 'it, more than any other one reform, made possible the renewed usefulness of the Church of England in the 19th century'.[2] It was indeed a quint-

---

[1] Benjamin Disraeli, *Vindication of the English Constitution in a letter to a noble and learned lord* (1835), 201.

[2] G. Kitson Clark, 'The Life and Work of Sir Robert Peel', a spoken address presented to the County Borough Council of Bury (1950), 4.

essential instance of cautious liberal Conservative renovation. Peel's resignation was much less of a defeat for him than it was for the king. The Conservative party emerged incomparably stronger than it had been in November 1834 on the eve of Melbourne's dismissal. There does indeed seem something inevitable about its progress over the next six years. The king's death in 1837 caused another election which gave the Conservatives further gains, some 35 seats. In fact they had a majority of nine in the English constituencies and of sixteen if Wales is counted as a part of England, which it usually was – however deplorable this may seem in some quarters today. For their precarious tenure of power the Whigs depended on their majorities in Scotland (13) and in Ireland (42). It was this situation which gave such plausibility as there was to Disraeli's frequently repeated charge that the Whigs were 'only maintained in power by the votes of the Irish and Scotch members. The reason for this is that the Whigs are an anti-national party.'[1] He first made the charge in 1835 when it was not true. The Whigs had a majority of 56 in the 500 English and Welsh seats, 61 if Wales is excluded. But it was true that Ireland and Scotland kept them in power from 1837 to 1841. However, neither Disraeli nor any other Conservative drew the logical conclusion that the party should either press for home rule in those two countries or else stop grumbling.[2]

In 1839 Melbourne resigned. Stanley and his followers were now prepared to join Peel. He could legitimately have expected a spell in office, for a dissolution of parliament would undoubtedly have given him an easy win. It was forestalled by the Bedchamber crisis.[3] The attitude of the monarch, which had been so helpful to Peel in 1834, frustrated him in 1839, and the Whiggery of Queen Victoria gave Melbourne another two years of office, if not power. In 1841 beaten in the House he dissolved. The ensuing election gave Peel a majority of 76.

[1] *Vindication*, 181.
[2] It is in general true that from 1832 to the present day, elections in the U.K. as a whole have produced the same verdict as they would have done if confined to England only. The exceptions are those of 1837, 1892, January and December 1910, 1950, 1964, and February 1974. At each of these the Conservatives had a majority in England. The Liberals and in latter days Labour have certainly been reinforced by their support in the 'Celtic fringe', but it has seldom made the difference between winning and losing.
[3] See above, p. 35, n.

3

The electoral figures of 1841 are worth looking at. The party won 283 out of the 471 English seats and 19 out of the 29 Welsh seats. They thus had a majority of over a hundred in England and Wales. In Ireland and Scotland they did less well, winning 43 out of 105 Irish seats and 22 out of 53 Scottish seats. Their success was particularly striking in the two largest constituencies in England, each with an electorate of over 18,000. It was the only occasion between the first two Reform Acts when they won two of the four seats for the City of London, normally a Whig–Liberal stronghold, and both the seats in the West Riding of Yorkshire – perhaps the most important industrial constituency in the country.

As one would expect the Conservative triumph was most complete in the English counties where they won 124 out of the 144 seats. In 1832 the figure had been 42; in 1835, 73; in 1837, 99. Of the 323 borough seats they won 155. They also won all four university seats. These figures are the more striking when one remembers the disproportionately high representation of the borough electorate, 275,000 compared with 345,000 for the counties. If there had been anything like justice between borough and county representation, the Conservative would have won 330 of the 471 English seats, instead of 283.[1] On the other hand it has to be remembered also that the borough representation was itself very uneven. There were only 58 seats for boroughs with an electorate of over 2,000, although they accounted for 155,000 out of the 275,000 borough electors. The Conservatives only won 15 of these seats, and the Whigs 43. Had these big boroughs carried their proper weight, the Whig proportion of a reduced borough representation would have gone up, to something like 130 out of 210, and the Conservatives would have been down to 80.[2] They would have gone down even more if London had been accorded the proportion that its electorate numerically warranted. The 18 London seats represented 61,627 electors, nearly 10 per cent of the

[1] Numerical equality would have given 267 county seats and 210 borough seats, of which the Conservatives would have won 228 and 100 respectively, together with 4 university seats.

[2] There should have been about 118 seats for big boroughs and 92 for the rest.

whole English electorate. The Whigs even in this peak Conservative year won as many as 15. On a proportionate basis there should have been 46 or 47 London seats of which the Whigs would have won 39. The whole system was probably rather nearer to some sort of very rough numerical justice than one might suppose at first glance, but the point was not of any contemporary importance, for people simply did not think in those terms.

It is perhaps convenient at this stage to look at the elections between the Reform Acts of 1832 and 1867 as a series. Table A on page 46 shows the Conservative strength broken down in England between counties and the various types of borough, together with totals for Wales, Scotland and Ireland.

At a glance one can see the nature of Tory support. It was overwhelming in the counties. The party had a majority there in every election except 1832, and usually a heavy one. But Peel broke all records in 1841. Never again even in that favoured category was the party to win both seats in Bedfordshire, three out of the four Surrey seats, all four seats in Wiltshire, Worcestershire and Lancashire, three out of four Cornish county seats, five out of the six Yorkshire seats. The Conservatives also did well, though only relatively, in the boroughs with an electorate of over 1,000, winning 44 out of 121 seats (in 1837, 43). Their score was not to exceed 31 in subsequent elections. Performances in this sphere which were not destined to be repeated after 1841 were the success in the City of London already mentioned, the winning of one seat in Westminster City, one in Newcastle, one in Bristol, both the seats in Hull, Bedford, Reading, Southampton, Lancaster, Lincoln and Shrewsbury.

The counties and the big boroughs not only accounted for the vast majority of the electors but also constituted the area where public opinion was most capable, or least incapable, of expressing itself at elections in spite of the numerous barriers and checks imposed by bribery, corruption, intimidation, etc. The total number of English seats in these two groups came to 265. The Conservatives had an overwhelming majority of 71 in 1841, a modest majority (19) in 1837, a majority of only five in 1852. In all other elections they were in a minority.

The fluctuations in public opinion can be best measured by

Table A

Conservative members of parliament 1832–65[1]

	Total	1832 C	1835 C	1837 C	1841 C	(*) Total	1847† C	1847† P	(*) Total	1852† C	1852† P	1857† C	1857† P	1859 (*) C	1859 (*) Total	1865 C
English counties	(144)	42	73	99	124	—	99	10	—	108	8	89	3	99	(147)	95
English boroughs over 2,000	(58)	8	16	17	15	—	7	4	—	5	1	7	1	8	(59)	10
English boroughs 1,000–2,000	(63)	12	26	26	29	—	18	8	—	22	2	18	2	23	—	20
English boroughs below 1,000	(202)	63	90	98	111	(200)	64	38	(198)	90	15	72	6	86	—	94
English universities	(4)	4	4	4	4	—	2	2	—	2	2	3	1	3	—	4
English Total	(471)	129	209	244	283	(469)	190	62	(467)	227	28	189	13	219	(471)	223
Cons. majority England		-213	-53	13	95		-89			-13		-89		-29		-25
Wales	(29)	13	17	18	19	—	12	7	—	12	6	12	3	15	—	11
Scotland	(53)	10	15	20	22	—	8	11	—	12	8	8	7	15	—	12
Ireland	(105)	33	38	32	43	—	33	9	—	39	3	47	3	57	—	50
Total	(658)	185	279	314	367	(656)	243	89	(654)	290	45	256	26	306	(658)	300
Majority in U.K.		-288	-100	-30	76		-170			-74		-142		-42		-58

[1] Based on F. H. McCalmont, Poll book (1906).

the Conservative score out of 265 in these seats: 1832 (62); 1835 (115); 1837 (142); 1841 (168); 1847 (124); 1852 (135); 1857 (114); 1859 (130); 1865 (125). The smaller boroughs taken as a whole were the least representative of public opinion – which is not to say that public opinion had no effect there, any more than it had a completely unimpeded expression in the larger constituencies. The Whigs won a majority of these at every election in the series, except in 1841 when the Conservatives with 111 wins scored seventeen more than they ever did before or after. The general trend of opinion was, however, to some extent reflected in the smaller boroughs, and with the exception of the change between 1859 and 1865, they mirrored, albeit imperfectly, the direction of movement in the more popular constituencies, that is to say, when the Conservatives improved their fortunes in the latter group they normally did so in the former too and vice versa.

The table does not reveal geographical distribution. There are any number of ways of looking at this but the same broad conclusion emerges. As far as England is concerned, in Peel's time and even more markedly thereafter, the Conservative strength is to be

---

Notes for Table A

(*) In 1844 Sudbury with 2 seats was disfranchised, and in 1852 before the election St Albans also lost its two seats. In 1861 these were redistributed by giving one to Birkenhead (hitherto unrepresented), a third seat to South Lancashire, and two more to Yorkshire by dividing the West Riding.

(†) P = Peelite. Conservative majorities in England and the U.K. at the elections of 1847, 1852 and 1857 are calculated by regarding the Peelites as being for practical purposes on the Liberal side. This is an assumption which can reasonably be made for the first two elections. Its validity in 1857 is more questionable, and the usual figure given for the Liberal majority as *c.*90 assumes that the Peelites had reverted to their old party. It is often difficult to judge exactly who were or were not Peelites at any one time and particularly at that stage. I have taken as Peelite McCalmont's label of LC (Liberal Conservative) with amendments where it is obviously wrong. From 1859 onwards I have disregarded it, treating well known Peelites, such as Gladstone, Graham, Cardwell and Herbert as Liberals, and adding the relatively small residue to the Conservatives.

found in the centre, south and east (except for London), and the Whig–Liberal strength lies in the north and to some extent in the south-west. If we divide the English constituencies as evenly as possible by drawing a line from the Humber estuary to the Bristol Channel following the northern and western county boundaries of Lincoln, Notts, Leicester, Warwick, Worcester and Gloucester, if we then turn the line south-east along the south-west boundaries of Gloucester, Wilts, Hants to the sea, and if we omit London and Middlesex, we have enclosed what can be called the Conservative 'heartland', consisting of 236 seats. Apart from the election of 1832 when they fared disastrously everywhere, and that of 1857 when their score was only 103, the Conservatives had a majority in this area at every general election in the period. In the remaining 231 seats they never had one at all, their nearest approach being in 1841 when they won 113. Excluding that election and the disaster of 1832 they averaged about 36 per cent of the seats in this area. The poorness of their performance is emphasised by the accident of geography which on this line of division puts Shropshire and Westmorland, two of the most consistently Tory countries, on the wrong side of the fence.

The growing weakness of the Tories as one moves further away from the 'home counties' is emphasised when we look at the election returns in the non-English parts of the United Kingdom. Wales, it is true, had a Tory majority in all Peel's elections, apart from 1832, and it remained fairly evenly divided after that. A semi-colonial economy, dominated by an anglicised squirearchy, it was far more closely integrated politically to England than was either Scotland or Ireland. The high-water mark of Conservative success was in 1841. The 'natives' did not begin to revolt till the very end of the period covered by this series of elections. The loss of four Conservative seats in 1865 was the portent of troubles to come, and the election of 1859 remains the last occasion on which the party has won a majority of Welsh seats. Conservatives became like white expatriates in a black world. In 1906 they failed to win a single seat.

Scotland until 1832 had been a vast Tory pocket borough, or rather, a governmental pocket borough which the Tories had controlled for a political generation. The Reform Act produced a revolution. The 53 Scottish seats[1] were dominated by the Whigs and Liberals for the rest of the century and beyond. Indeed Conservatives and their allies only once had a majority – in the election of 1900, and this proved to be merely a flash in the pan. However, as in our other categories – English counties, English boroughs, large and small, and Wales – Peel in 1841 touched the high point of Conservative success between the first two Reform Acts, winning 22 seats.

The one exception to this pattern was Ireland which followed a course of her own. In every other category of seat there is a steady rise in the Conservative score at each of Peel's elections. In Ireland, however, he actually lost 6 seats at the election of 1837 – probably a consequence of the Lichfield House compact.[2] It is true that 1841 saw Peel's best achievement in Ireland as it did everywhere else, but it was not the top level of Conservative success between the Reform Acts. For reasons to be discussed later there was a remarkable revival in the party's fortunes in Ireland during the late 1850s; in 1859 the Conservatives actually won a majority of the Irish seats, and although this was never to be repeated, they won as many as 50 seats in 1865.

4

The election of 1841 was a striking vindication of Peel's policy. Before 1828 the Tories had on their side the weight of the most important interests in the country: the solid support of the Crown, the Church of England and the universities; a majority of the aristocracy; the vast majority of the squires; important commercial interests of the older sort. Against them led by a section of the aristocracy were the dissenters, the Catholics, the more aggressive middle class business men, and – though this is not easy to measure at all accurately – the preponderance of the intellectual world. The Tories lost much of their support, including that of the Crown, between 1828 and 1832. By 1841 they had recovered nearly all of it. The Crown admittedly was still hostile; but Peel aided by the Prince Consort soon managed to overcome the prejudices of

[1] 60 after 1867; 72 after 1885.
[2] A bargain made at Lord Lichfield's house between O'Connell and the Whigs.

Queen Victoria. The Church was solidly behind him. The 'old' commercial interests – shipping, sugar, timber, etc. – were still on his side. The new industrial interests, the 'field of coal' and the 'field of cotton' may not have been exactly with him but they were nothing like so much against him as they had been ten years earlier.

In office he consolidated his middle class support. His great budgets of 1842 and 1845 scraped away the fiscal barnacles of many generations, and enabled the ship of English trade to sail more freely than ever before. He did this by the substitution of a single direct tax for a multiplicity of vexatious duties which clogged, choked and distorted the channels of commerce. Peel's courage in reintroducing income tax in time of peace should not be underestimated. Hitherto it had been regarded as a desperate war-time expedient, and it had been promptly abolished in 1815. He is not to be blamed for the monster which personal taxation has become today; he would have been horrified at the spectacle. The Tory ministry of 1841–6 was one of the ablest of the whole century. It contained five past or future Prime Ministers, and the adhesion of the 'dilly' gave a notable boost to its talent.

Peel was responsible for many other important measures both at home and abroad. If any are to be singled out, perhaps his Bank Act should have pride of place in domestic affairs, and in foreign policy the settlement of the Maine and Oregon boundaries with Canada; but for that, the harmonious relations which on the whole prevailed between Britain and the USA for the rest of the century would not have been possible.

Perhaps Peel's greatest claim to fame is that, alone of the Conservative leaders in our period, he made a serious effort to deal with the Irish question. He did not of course succeed, but nor did anyone else either then or later. At least Peel tried to tackle it rather than sit back and draw political profits from the prejudice that it engendered in England. Ireland was regarded by Derby with well-reciprocated detestation, by Disraeli with perceptive cynicism,[1] by Salisbury with pessimistic despair, by Balfour with

[1] His summary of the Irish question in a speech in the House of Commons is lapidary: 'Thus you have a starving population, an absentee aristocracy and an alien Church, and in addition the weakest executive in the world. That is the Irish question.' But he did nothing whatever about it when he came to power thirty years later, merely observing correctly that it would ruin Gladstone.

tenacious obduracy, by Bonar Law with ancestral prejudice. Only
to Peel was it a problem to be solved like others, though more
difficult, complicated and intractable. It broke him, as it was to
break his pupil, Gladstone, a generation later. Of all statesmen in
their day those two great men came closest to embodying the
moral and political spirit of the new Britain emerging from the
stresses of the Industrial Revolution. There is something both
appropriate and symbolic in the fact that what Disraeli luridly
called the 'sinister catastrophe' of Peel's career should have been
connected, as Gladstone's was to be, with Ireland – the one area of
the United Kingdom where the Industrial Revolution had never
penetrated and where the social and political presuppositions of
the new Britain simply did not apply.

The real problem of Ireland was to satisfy nationalist sentiment
affronted by the Act of Union of 1801 which withdrew the limited
autonomy conceded in 1782. The triple problems of the Church
of Ireland, education and land tenure under which the Irish
question was normally divided, were ultimately subordinate to
that of self-government. It was a measure of the greatness of
Gladstone that late in life he came to see this truth and devoted
the rest of his political career to the cause of Irish Home Rule. In
fact self-government itself posed intractable problems, for there
were two nations in Ireland; and it was one of Gladstone's
limitations that he never perceived the force of Orange sentiment
in Ulster – something which the Conservatives were later to
exploit with much success.

All this, however, lay far ahead. Neither of the great parties
thought at this time in terms of repeal of the Union. The most that
the Whigs were prepared to do, as a result of the Lichfield House
compact with O'Connell, was to provide limited remedies for
specific grievances in return for the general support of O'Connell
and his followers in the House. Peel as leader of the Tory party
could not contemplate any disturbance of the special position of
the Irish Church, nor was this a matter of acting à contre cœur. He
strongly and genuinely supported the Establishment. Education
and land were different. Peel was ready to do something in both
fields. He set up the Devon Commission to enquire into Irish land
tenure, but even a modified version of its reasonable, though far

from drastic, recommendations foundered in the House of Lords. With education Peel did manage to achieve some progress, but the process was highly damaging to the unity of his party and can in retrospect be seen as the prelude to the revolt which was to bring him down.

Of Peel's two measures to deal with Irish education, one proved relatively uncontroversial in England. This was a Bill to set up and endow three colleges providing education for middle class Irishmen irrespective of religious creed. The trouble was that the Catholics in Ireland immediately took offence at the foundation of 'godless colleges', and Peel's measure though sensible enough in itself did little to placate the Irish. His other measure raised a storm, although it is hard for us nowadays to understand why. In 1795 the Irish parliament had initiated an annual grant to the Catholic seminary at Maynooth, and this contribution to the education of Irish priests had been continued by the U.K. parliament after the Act of Union without causing any special attention. In 1845 it was £9,000 p.a. Peel proposed to increase it to £26,000. At once a storm blew up which threatened to capsize his Cabinet. Since the principle of state subvention had already been conceded and no one proposed to abolish the existing grant, it is difficult to see the logic behind this extraordinary commotion. But politics is not always a matter of logic. It was a defect in Peel that he could not make sufficient allowance for the strength of irrational sentiments which he was far too sensible to share himself. After his experiences in 1829 he should perhaps have known better the strength of the 'No popery' cry. However, it must have been difficult to take seriously arguments of which the following is a good specimen, from a letter to *The Times* by Canon MacNeile on April 29, 1845.

As the Word of God forbids the bowing down to images as expressly as it forbids theft or adultery – consequently as we could not without wilful rebellion against God's authority, approve or co-operate in the endowment of a college for instruction in theft or adultery, so neither can we approve of or co-operate in the endowment of a college for instruction in bowing down to images.

Peel was able to carry the increased Maynooth Grant with large majorities in both Houses of Parliament, but the Conservative opposition to it was formidable, and the third reading in the lower House would have been defeated without Whig support. The Conservatives divided 159–147 for the second reading, 149—148 *against* the third reading. It is interesting to note that of the 159 Conservatives who voted for Maynooth on the second reading, 82 voted for the repeal of the corn laws on the third reading in 1846, and 59 against; whereas of the 147 opponents of Maynooth, 111 voted against repealing the corn laws and only 19 voted for.[1] In 1845 Peel had affronted one of the deepest prejudices of his supporters – protestantism. He survived narrowly, but neither he nor his colleagues were in any doubt about the damage done to the party. A year later he affronted another of those prejudices – protection. This time he did not survive.

5

The story of the corn law crisis is too well known for detailed repetition here. Peel was convinced that the famine looming ahead as a result of the failure of the Irish potato crop compelled him to remove the duties on imported grain. There are several difficulties in accepting his own arguments on this point, and it is clear now that for many reasons the repeal of the corn laws did not make – and could not have made – much difference to the famine. It has also long been known that Peel was already converted to free trade for quite other and indeed much better reasons which he found it politically impossible at first to avow in public. Peel was evidently feeling the strain of office and was acutely impatient of the dullards in his party. Nevertheless, with all allowance made, his conduct is puzzling. Why did he not persist in his original decision to resign instead of accepting the 'poisoned chalice' back from the hands of Lord John Russell? Why did he do so with such alacrity and 'glee' as Gladstone described it? It was quite unnecessary and he would have been far less likely to break up his party by giving support to Russell from the opposition benches than by repealing

---

[1] Gash, *Reaction and reconstruction*, 152, n. 2, quoting figures supplied by Professor Aydelotte.

the corn laws himself. It is true that he carried nearly all the Cabinet with him, the only resignation of significance being that of Stanley; but why did he make no attempt to conciliate his back-benchers? Why, if he considered the matter to be one of urgency, did he not as a temporary measure suspend the corn laws at once by order in council, which could be done under the Act, and leave it to the sense of Parliament to decide whether the suspension should be permanent, instead of introducing a bill which gradually tapered off the import duties over a period of three years? Peel answers some of these questions in his memoirs but not very convincingly.

At times one feels that he is almost courting defeat, or if not going quite so far, that he is deliberately overriding party prejudices, flouting their beliefs in an almost arrogant spirit of 'take it or leave it'. Peel was a proud man and a highly sensitive man. That he should have resented the language of Bentinck and Disraeli is natural enough; and, by the end of the long battle, having ensured the passage of repeal he may well have deliberately ridden for a fall over the Irish Coercion Bill. But his earlier conduct before the great debate began cannot be thus explained, unless we suppose that his troubles with his party over successive revolts on the Ten Hours Bill, the sugar duties and Maynooth had bitten deeper than appeared at the time. Whatever the reason, Peel seems to have cared less than most leaders about preserving the unity of the party, and the ensuing split is one whose significance in terms of party continuity, both institutional and ideological, has been sometimes underestimated. For in 1846 there was a real break away from the Conservative party of Peel. Moreover, it cannot be equated with a revival of any sort of romantic pre-Peel, pre-Liverpool, back-to-Pitt Toryism, let alone anything going even further into the past. The nature of the division created in Peel's party by his decision to repeal the corn laws is not always understood. The rebellion against him headed by Lord George Bentinck under the suzerainty of Stanley[1] and with Disraeli as adjutant led in a very real sense to the creation of a new party.

First, it is necessary to decide what the rebellion was all about.

---

[1] Stanley had been called up to the House of Lords at his own request in 1844, during his father's lifetime. He succeeded as 14th Earl of Derby in 1851.

One can easily be confused over this. The part which Disraeli's actions – his oratory and political intrigues – played in it has made posterity assume that the rebellion also must have had something to do with the ideas which he had been throwing off like an erratic catherine wheel during the last three or four years. Disraeli's ideas were extremely critical of Peel and of 'Conservatism'. Disraeli's actions during the crisis were extremely damaging to Peel and to the Conservative party. It would therefore seem *prima facie* reasonable to suppose that there was a connection, and that the conflict was one of ideas – a collision between the principles of 'Young England' and those of the Conservative Establishment in the 1840s.

In a previous work I described Young England as 'the Oxford movement translated by Cambridge from religion into politics'.[1] This may be an over-simplification of a complicated matter to which someone ought to devote a monograph if not a book, but there is undoubtedly a sense in which the two movements had a common origin – a romantic revolt against Erastianism in Church affairs and against liberal utilitarianism in the secular field. The name was given to a small coterie of youthful aristocratic Tories elected to the 1841 parliament, fresh from Eton and Cambridge: George Smythe, later 7th Viscount Strangford; Lord John Manners, later 6th Duke of Rutland; Alexander Baillie-Cochrane, ennobled by Disraeli in 1880 as Lord Lamington. The origin of the name is obscure. It may have been a carry over from Cambridge days, or it may have been (like 'Whig' and 'Tory') a term of derision subsequently adopted by the group itself. Disraeli was at an early stage regarded as their leader, though some of them had reservations about him. Fifteen years older than the rest, he taught them – but he also learned from them.

Their philosophy was a curious high Tory hotch-potch based on Clarendon's *History of the great rebellion*, Bolingbroke's *Patriot king*, Scott's novels, the *Tracts for the times*, and a forgotten book, *The broadstone of honour* which appeared in 1822 from the pen of a young Catholic convert and miscellaneous writer, Kenelm Digby; the book's sub-title was *Rules for the gentlemen of England*. The best and

---

[1] Robert Blake, *Disraeli* (1966), 171. See ibid., the whole of ch. VIII, for a discussion of this subject.

most entertaining expression of their outlook is Disraeli's *Coningsby*, in which the principal Young Englanders and their friends appear under thin disguise. Like Tractarianism and the Gothic revival, Young England was essentially nostalgic and escapist – the reaction of an aristocratic class that was on its way out, half conscious of defeat, yet determined to make a final protest against Benthamism, Whiggery, Peelism and consensus politics.

There was a great deal of nonsense mixed up with it. For example Smythe recommended the revival of 'touching for the King's Evil' as a means of resuscitating the monarchy. But it had a serious side. Viewed in terms of Conservative party thought it was the latest expression of that Tory paternalism discussed in the first chapter. The Young Englanders were indeed swimming against the tide, but it was not an ignoble effort, and, though they achieved little, it would be in the long run an asset to the party that some generous young men of high birth had urged the landed classes first to put their own house in order and then to attack the abuses of the millocracy, that they had declared property to have its duties as well as its privileges, that they had denounced the harshness of the poor law, and that they had shown some consciousness of the gulf between the Two Nations.

Disraeli probably took these ideas at least half seriously, though one cannot be sure, but the battle which he waged against Peel had nothing to do with them at all. The conflict was, indeed, one of clashing principles or attitudes, but it did not involve Young England nor did Disraeli claim that it did. In fact Young England was dead by the beginning of 1846, killed by the Maynooth debate, in which its members voted on different sides. They were not united on the corn law question either. George Smythe – 'Coningsby' himself – actually joined Peel's government in the consequential reshuffle. The great majority of the inarticulate squires who voted against the repeal of the corn laws neither understood nor cared about the romantic, Gothic, high Church, quasi-Jacobite notions of Lord John Manners and his friends. What Bagehot called 'the finest brute vote in creation' had little in common with Young England. It was Lord George Bentinck, the King of the Turf and owner of one of the best studs in England, whom they were following; not Disraeli, the alien adventurer and mountebank. The conflict was not between Peelism and any other brand of romantic or popular Toryism. It was between Peelism and the Ultras.

It is not surprising that responsible, prudent and orthodox Conservative 'men of business' had opted for Peelism. The steady rise in Conservative seats at three successive general elections seemed to confirm their wisdom. But a policy of consensus, involving, as it must, much distress to the faithful adherents of party doctrine or party prejudice, is easier to carry out in an era of rigid party obedience than one of independence and frequent cross voting. Perhaps, too, it depends for success on leaders who possess a certain indefinable genius for blurring differences, softening conflicts, cajoling recalcitrants, talking in one style, acting in another, giving an impression of orthodoxy while ever adapting it to the needs of common sense and political reality; leaders like Palmerston, Disraeli, Lloyd George, Baldwin – it is better not to venture upon more recent parallels. Peel clearly did not possess this gift, in spite of his many other political virtues. Whether he could have prevented the great schism of 1846, had he been differently constituted, must remain one of the 'ifs' of history. It may be that no one could have preserved party unity on such an issue, but Peel set about the task in the worst possible way. Indeed one could argue that he never set about it at all.

No one should underestimate the importance of personality in politics. There is another 'if' to be considered. Would Peel have had to face any real revolt from the Ultras, however disgruntled, if that strange figure, Lord George Bentinck, had not suddenly decided that his leader was no better than the horse-copers, sharpers, crooks, fraudulent trainers and corrupt jockeys of whom he had for years past been trying to rid the turf? And would Bentinck have got as far as he did, if he had not been aided by an embittered man of genius, the greatest master of invective in the House of Commons? And would Disraeli have played that role at all, if Peel had made him, say, a Junior Lord of the Treasury in 1841?

These are speculations. What is certain is that by repealing the corn laws Peel split his party irrevocably. It was not a straight division of landed gentry against the rest. It was a division between those who considered that the retention of the corn laws was an essential bulwark of the order of society in which they believed and those who considered that the Irish famine and the Anti-Corn Law League had made retention even more dangerous to that order than abandonment. This was to be a perennial dichotomy in the Conservative party and we shall find it recurring again and again in its history.

Peel carried with him all the institutional elements of the party. He was followed by every member of the government in and out of the Cabinet except three. In the crucial first vote on the corn laws 80 per cent of the Conservatives who supported Peel were office holders, or in one way or another dispensers of governmental patronage. Moreover, the Chief Whip, Sir John Young, went with him, and so did the manager of the party's electoral affairs, R. F. Bonham. In the election of 1847 the party fund was used to support only Peelite candidates; and after that the whole system constructed by Bonham collapsed with his departure.

The rebels, if that is the right word, had therefore to begin *de novo*. It was not like the Labour split in 1931, for Ramsay Mac-Donald carried few members with him; nor was it like the Conservative divide in 1922, when the party organisation repudiated Austen Chamberlain and the coalitionists – hence F. E. Smith's famous gibe at Sir G. Younger, its chairman, as 'the Cabin Boy who has taken charge of the political ship'. In 1846 the new party had to elect new leaders (Bentinck in the Commons, Stanley in the Lords), had to create their own organisation, appoint their own Whips, raise their own funds. It does not seem that Peel ever formally resigned his position as leader, nor for that matter was he ever formally deposed. However, almost all the pro-Peel Conservatives who carried any weight moved in the end, after an uneasy period of floating in the centre, over to the Liberal camp. For a while the anti-Peelites were averse to using even the name of Conservative, and played with the idea of calling themselves 'Protectionists'. In the end for reasons of tactics the name survived.[1] Yet, in spite of the ultimate continuity of nomenclature, there seems a better case for dating the modern Conservative party from 1846 than from 1832. The most that can be

<hr>

[1] See below, pp. 79–80.

said for 1832 is that at about that time the party rebaptised itself. Otherwise there is no distinct breach with the past, no distinct point of take-off. From every aspect of institutional continuity whether as a party within parliament or outside, 1846 is a better year of birth than 1832 or 1833; the genealogy of the party can be indisputably traced from that year on.

To say this is not to cast an adverse verdict upon Peel. His decision to repeal the corn laws, however evasive some of the arguments he used, however maladroit his management of men, was surely as right as any major political decision has ever been. But virtuous men may die childless. Rakes and roués may found dynasties. The party of Pitt, Perceval, Liverpool, Canning, Wellington and Peel vanished in the smoke and confusion of the corn law conflict. The party led by Stanley and Bentinck was in a real sense a new party, and it lived to fight another day.

CHAPTER III

The years of frustration
1846–65

I

In the early months of 1846 what was in effect a new party came into being. Those who organised it were fully conscious of the implications of their action, and, anyway in the House of Commons, knew that they were doing something more than organise a back-bench rebellion on a single issue. According to Disraeli's *Lord George Bentinck*,[1] the movement originated with an invitation from the Council of the Protection Society to all sympathetic MPs to attend a joint meeting. The Protection Society was a body presided over by the Duke of Richmond and founded as a counterblast to the Anti-Corn Law League. The meeting must have taken place early in February – at all events after January 27, the day when Peel's proposals were first put in detail to the House, and the inadequacy of the so-called 'compensations' to the landed interest became clear.

Even before that day there was a move, as Disraeli puts it, 'to test the possibility, to use the language of that day, of forming a third party, an achievement hitherto deemed by those learned in parliamentary life as essentially impossible'.[2] But the move was postponed till after Peel's statement. Now it was decided to proceed, and the Protection Society's invitation, to quote Disraeli again:

. . . occasioned the first public appearance of Lord George

[1] Benjamin Disraeli, *Lord George Bentinck, a political biography*, 4th edn, revised (1852), 78.
[2] ibid., 58.

Bentinck as one of the organizers of a political party; for he aspired to no more. The question was, whether a third political party could be created and sustained; a result at all times and under any circumstances difficult to achieve, and which [sic] had failed even under the auspices of accomplished and experienced statesmen.[1]

Bentinck had convinced himself from the very start that Peel was premeditating an unparalleled act of treachery. It was natural that he should make early contact with the only minister of any weight who had resigned from the Cabinet in December. He already knew Stanley quite well through the turf where both were conspicuous figures. Hitherto their correspondence had not dwelt much on politics. Horses, jockeys, trainers, or the cost of grouse moors were the main themes. On the last subject Bentinck passed on in characteristic style a warning from his brother 'that the Highland proprietors are one and all the greatest Robbers, Liars and Swindlers that can possibly be & you are never safe with them unless you have them tied down by their leases even in the most minute detail.'[2] Sir Robert Peel and his colleagues at the beginning of 1846 were regarded by him in the same light as these predatory highland lairds. On January 9 he wrote to Stanley and, after declaring that his father was 'going to stake his purse against that of the Corn Law League' and that he himself had written to the Duke of Richmond 'deprecating *any compromise*', he went on:

I met Captain Alexander Gordon at Goodwood three days ago – he told me you were going to act a second Edition of '*Gladstone on Maynooth*'[3] – is that so? I told him I thought Sir Robert Peel and his colleagues were not better than common cheats and ought to be dealt with as such – I believe the punishment in the good old times for offences of this kind used to be cropping the ears and putting the vagabonds in the pillory.[4]

[1] ibid., 78.
[2] Derby Papers, Box 132/13, January 9, 1841.
[3] Gladstone, though agreeing with the Maynooth Bill, resigned because its principle was inconsistent with the doctrine of a book which he had written some years earlier but in which he now no longer believed. His behaviour was widely regarded as incomprehensible. He re-entered Peel's Cabinet after the crisis of 1845, replacing Stanley.
[4] ibid., 132/13 January 9, 1846.

This was the sort of language habitual to Bentinck in private and he came close to it in public. There has probably seldom been a political figure, certainly not a party leader, who regularly spoke in such virulent terms of his antagonists and who so consistently ascribed to them the worst possible motives.

Stanley's attitude was quite different. He was a natural government man, a man of business in the eighteenth-century sense of the word. True, he had resigned, but he had not shed his sense of responsibility, nor was he prepared to view his late colleagues as a pack of power-loving scoundrels clinging on at all costs to office. In his reply to Bentinck we can discern the essence of a difference which no longer applies to the same degree – the difference between the official man who went into politics with the idea of holding office and carrying on the Queen's government, and the man who never expected or even thought of office, the natural back-bencher who knew himself as such. Of course there are plenty of natural back-benchers today, but not many who know they are.

After pointing out the obvious differences between his own position over the corn laws and Gladstone's over Maynooth, Stanley went on to say that Peel had not yet made his statement about the new measure.

> I think . . . that the Landed interest ought not to allow them-selves to be influenced by the personal feelings which they may entertain towards those by whom it is introduced; that they ought to consider it as a whole, and as a system of Government, not merely as an isolated measure in which the interests of different classes of the community are to be pitted against each other.[1]

He urged Bentinck to think hard before trying to eject the present government. Was there any practical chance of forming one on any other system with a likelihood of lasting 'and composed of any other materials'? Although he was not saying it in so many words to Bentinck he clearly did not regard the sort of people who were likely to rebel against Peel on the corn law question as capable of putting up any kind of show as ministers. He did not know then

[1] ibid., 176/2, January 14, 1846 (copy).

that Disraeli was to be one of them, but it would not have affected his judgment; and on the general point he was quite right. As he was himself to experience, when events had put him half-unwillingly at the head of the rebels, and after six years of opposition he had to form the famous 'Who? Who?' ministry of 1852,[1] want of official experience was a grave defect. It was to handicap the new party for twenty years.

The truth was that, although Stanley felt in honour bound to resign over the corn law question, he did not at this time see any real alternative.

> I own [he continued] that I would rather accept from the present Administration a measure of which I did not wholly approve, though I might think it would come with better grace from others, than the risk of all the evils which must result from a long interregnum in the formation of an Administration or from a long continued struggle on such a subject as Corn Laws, to be finally decided by an appeal to the excited passions of a general Election. Such are my views at the present time – I am afraid they will not be very satisfactory to you, and I have no great reason to hope that they will be adopted by the bulk of the Agricultural party either in or out of Parlt.[2]

Bentinck confirmed his dissent.

> I think you are wrong, but I do not presume to expect I can persuade you you are . . . I think the most damming fact of the whole of this bad business will be the shock that will be given to the mind of the Middle Classes of the English People by such wholesale examples of lying and pledge breaking on the part of the more educated and more exalted Rank of Men who constitute their Representatives and the Peers of Parliament.[3]

Stanley remained unconvinced. His attitude was summed up in a letter which was read out by Lord Norreys to the Oxfordshire Protection Society on January 14. Lord Stanley, said Lord Norreys, saw a lack among the Protectionists of 'public men of

---

[1] So called because of the Duke of Wellington's repeated questions in the stentorian tones of the deaf when Stanley tried to tell him their unknown names during a debate in the House of Lords.

[2] Derby Papers, loc. cit.   [3] ibid., 132/13, January 20, 1846.

public character and official habits in the House of Commons to carry on a government'.

This was true enough, but the rebels, especially Bentinck, were not concerned with acting 'responsibly' or helping to 'carry on the Queen's Government'. They were determined to stop the repeal of the corn laws, and, if one may use a phrase later current in a not dissimilar situation, to 'damn the consequences'. The Protectionist MPs seem from the first to have regarded Bentinck as one of their natural leaders, but he did not become *the* leader till April. During the interval they were guided by a committee of three consisting of George Bankes, William Miles and Stafford O'Brien.[1] O'Brien relied much on Disraeli for advice, as did Bentinck. The latter's exact relationship with the committee is not clear, but in late April Bentinck was unanimously elected as leader. The committee continued in being like a sort of shadow Cabinet. The election was presided over by Bankes who occupied a position faintly analogous to that of chairman of the 1922 Committee today: it was into the hands of Bankes that Bentinck placed his resignation twenty months later.

Bentinck is surely one of the most curious characters ever to have led a political party. He had scarcely spoken in the House before, and, now that he was really interested, he actually thought of hiring a lawyer to put his case for him. His quiescence in parliament did not correspond to any peacefulness in character. On the turf he pursued a career of incessant disputation involving duels, litigation and rows of every sort. His influence however was for the good and his exposure of one of the most famous of all racing frauds – the *Running Rein* affair in the Derby of 1844 – resulted in a presentation to him of 2,000 guineas which he generously made over as basis of that once well-known charity the 'Bentinck Benevolent and Provident Fund for Jockeys and Trainers'. It is no derogation to his generosity to add that, unlike most other younger sons of millionaire dukes, he was rich in his own right, anyway in terms of income. This was what enabled him later to set up Disraeli, a better bet than any lawyer, as a country gentleman and thus qualify him as spokesman for the 'Country Party'.

Bentinck was personally in no sense an Ultra. He had been

[1] Members for Dorset, Somerset (East) and Northants (North) respectively.

private secretary to Canning, who was his uncle-in-law. He had voted for Catholic relief and had supported Grey in 1830, though he refused office. He had followed Stanley, his great political exemplar, into Peel's camp after 1835. He was offered a post by Peel in 1841 but he again refused. He had been a faithful adherent of Peel thereafter and supported him over Maynooth. But the proposal to repeal the corn laws had upon him an effect which can only be described as seismic. It changed his entire life. What really lay behind this extraordinary convulsion no one knows – some strange psychological upheaval which there is now no means of understanding. In the absence of evidence one must assume his motive to be what he said it to be.

'I keep horses in 3 counties, and they tell me I shall save £1,500 a year by free trade. I don't care for that. What I cannot bear is being sold.'

As a parliamentarian, Bentinck was clumsy and ponderous. He was no orator and so nervous that he could never eat a meal before his speech with the result that he often had no dinner or supper till the small hours of the morning. He had, however, an excellent head for figures acquired by the habit on the turf of quick calculation of the odds, and this stood him in good stead in debates on prices and tariffs. He was no respecter of persons and on one occasion in what must be the longest sentence in *Hansard* rebuked the Prince Consort for appearing in parliament to give moral support to free trade. His relations with Disraeli were most friendly to the end, and they were a formidable combination 'the Jockey and the Jew' as their enemies called them.

Bentinck was in no sense a puppet of Disraeli, although he leaned much on him for advice. Disraeli could never have led the Protectionists at this time, but his speeches, unmatched for their wit and invective, kept up the party's morale and Peel simply could not answer them. Even Gladstone admitted that his hero was 'altogether helpless in reply' to Disraeli's sallies. 'Dealt with them with a kind of righteous dullness.' But it is a moot point whether invective pays in the end. Cobden might have persuaded the House to repeal the corn laws earlier, if he had been less bitter. Disraeli's attacks on Peel were resented long and deeply; they were a real stumbling block for many years to a Peelite-Conservative reunion, perhaps the main reason why it was never achieved.

By the time Bentinck became leader in the Commons there was already a leader in the Upper House. A meeting at the Duke of Richmond's London mansion on March 8 had elected Stanley in his absence. Given his resignation from Peel's Cabinet, it was a post which he could not very well refuse at this stage, without opting out of politics entirely. But he does not seem to have regarded himself as anything more than leader of the Protectionists in the House of Lords. A letter from the Duke of Newcastle on May 5 shows that he continued to take this attitude for quite a time. The duke admitted that Stanley and he had not always been in accord on political matters.

> On all questions of Reform I have always been a most decided opponent and mainly because I am a stupid matter of fact man and adhere to practice attaching little or no value to theory.

The duke, however, believing – and correctly – that Stanley was much more to the Right than hitherto (the duke did not put it like that) appealed to him to take the lead.

> Pardon the freedom of such expressions – but permit me to remark that I believe your Lordship to be actuated by the highest motives which should guide a Christian and a Patriot and that your nobility of nature, as well as of descent, places you above all mean considerations and prompts you to worthy deeds. . . . *Political virtue* [the duke somewhat platitudinously continued] should in all instances be substituted for and opposed to political laxness . . . the name of Stanley will [?rise] to eclipse the illustrious name of Chatham.
>
> I trust therefore your Lordship will now stand forward and allow us to rally to you as our 'great Captain' and the upholder of our preeminent interests in Church and State.[1]

Since Stanley was already the leader of the Protectionist peers this appeal must have been for him to take on some wider role. Stanley's reply is therefore significant. After the usual compliments he wrote:

[1] Derby Papers, 147/14.

... highly as I value the expression of your confidence and similar assurances which I have received from others, I cannot say that I have ever been ambitious of becoming the Leader of a Party; and certainly the aspect of affairs at present is anything but calculated to stimulate such an ambition. . . . I think that the attempt to form any party except so far as relates to an united effort to reject or greatly modify the measures now contemplated would be premature. I shall most willingly consult and co-operate with those who concur with me in opinion as to the best mode of giving effect to our views . . . but I do not think it would be for the public advantage, and I am sure it would not be for my own comfort and happiness, that I should at this moment take upon myself the onerous and responsible duty of the avowed Leader of the great section of the Conservative party who still adhere to their principles.[1]

But at some time between then and early July Stanley changed his attitude. During the corn law controversy he confined his activity to the House of Lords, and made little attempt to interfere with Bentinck and his parliamentary committee. It is by no means clear that he was privy to, or approved of, the 'blackguard combination', as Wellington called it, of Whigs and Ultra Protectionists which overthrew Peel on the Irish Coercion Bill at the end of June. But after Peel had resigned, Bentinck at a dinner on July 18 consisting of Protectionists from both Houses publicly announced that he looked upon Stanley as leader of the whole party,[2] and in the absence of any machinery of electing to such an office, this must be regarded as the nearest thing to a definite date for the start of Stanley's leadership. It was also the occasion to confirm the continued intention of the Protectionists to operate as a 'third party'.

2

After the fall of Peel the parliamentary situation was highly confusing. Peel himself never abdicated, and he retained the old

---

[1] ibid., 176/2 (copy).
[2] cf., ibid. 132/13, Bentinck to Stanley, July 10, 1846, referring to an overture from Lyndhurst: 'I have shunned the interview and have referred him to you as my superior.'

party organisation. Its funds were used in the 1847 election to support Peelite candidates, and the election was managed, in so far as there was any central management at all, by F. R. Bonham and Sir John Young, respectively Peel's party manager and Chief Whip. In the House of Commons Peel took his seat opposite Russell on the opposition front bench.

The Protectionists in the lower House were far more bitter against the Peelites than those in the House of Lords. There, Peelite and Protectionist peers as far as seating was concerned merged in a general mass on the opposition benches. But among the MPs a great debate at once arose on seating. Should they, as Lord Redesdale advised, anticipate Peel and occupy by *force majeure* the opposition front bench? Stanley was strongly against this course which, he thought, would scandalise public opinion; and even Bentinck considered it excessive. Should they occupy the benches on the opposition side but below the gangway, as Stanley recommended? Or should they show their detestation of Peel by remaining where they were – on the government side of the House, leaving the Peelites in a state of lonely obloquy on the opposition benches?

This was in fact the course adopted for the rest of the 1846 session, but the insanely lopsided appearance of the House, together with the inconveniences of seating when it was full, brought about a change in 1847. The Protectionists henceforth sat with the opposition, and their leaders occupied the front bench from the gangway up to the red box, while Peel and his friends took the places from there to the Speaker's chair. Great care was taken to prevent the possibility of Peel being next to either Bentinck or Disraeli; 'the buffers of the two parties', as Lord Lincoln put it in a letter to Peel who was absent at the start of the session, being 'the not very thickly wadded forms of Mr Goulburn[1] and Mr Bankes'. Significantly Russell discussed these arrangements not with Peel or any deputy of Peel but with Bentinck who now occupied the traditional seat of the leader of the Opposition.[2]

The old Conservative party which had won the election of 1841 was thus divided in its allegiance among three chieftains. A minority of MPs looked to Peel, a majority to Bentinck whose

[1] Peel's Chancellor of the Exchequer.   [2] Disraeli, *Bentinck*, 372.

avowed policy was to reverse as soon as possible Peel's principal achievement. In the upper House Stanley was undisputed leader of the opposition. No Peelite peer stood out comparably to Peel himself. Stanley also had a general suzerainty over the whole Protectionist party – MPs as well as peers. He was quite ready to use this authority. He frequently spoke his mind to Bentinck about the latter's violent language, personal attacks and general vituperation. As time went on the whips looked to him for orders rather than to the leader of their own House.

Let us briefly survey the intentions, attitudes and characters of the three men. Peel occupied an ambivalent position. He had no intention of retiring. He bitterly resented the tactics of the Protectionists especially the hard core of seventy or so who actually voted against the Irish Coercion Bill. On the other hand he never seems to have contemplated any serious attempt to reunite the party. When his whip, Sir John Young, sent a circular to 240 possible supporters at the beginning of the 1847 session, Peel refused to endorse his action. Gladstone disapproved.

> It might have been in his power [he wrote] to make some provision for the holding together and the reconstruction of that great party which he had reared. . . . But although that party was the great work of so many years of his matured life his thoughts seemed simply to be 'it has fallen; there let it be'. A greater idea still had overshadowed it; the idea of his country now became the Stewardess of his fame.[1]

It was an impossible and unsatisfactory situation. Peel would neither lead a party nor allow others to lead it. His attitude was an anachronism in an age of increasing party domination. 'The position of Sir Robert Peel in the last four years of his life was a thoroughly false position,' wrote Gladstone.

Peel had performed a great service for his party by regaining the centre ground once held by Liverpool and Canning, and later lost by the Duke of Wellington. He had taught it a lesson which in the long run was to be learned – that the old order could not survive if it relied on the narrow foundations of the past. But the lesson was

---

[1] From a memorandum dated 1855, B.M. Add. MS. 44745, quoted, J. B. Conacher, 'Peel and the Peelites 1846-50', *English Historical Review*, LXXIII (1958), 431-52.

not learned quickly. Tory landed gentlemen could accept Peelism
during the 1830s, for they were in opposition and internal party
differences were masked. Power proved fatal. Maynooth offended
their spiritual creed – Anglican protestantism. The corn law crisis
outraged their economic creed – protectionism. They had failed
to see their own interest in terms of political success and had
refused to make the compromises which were necessary for the
retention of political power. Peel could not bring himself to
attempt to reconstruct for a second time the party which he had
done so much to rehabilitate after 1832. Perhaps he could not have
succeeded with the best will in the world. The fact remains that he
never made – or wished to make – the attempt.

Stanley's attitude was quite different. He was anxious to
reconstruct the party and was determined to do all he could to
soften the acerbities caused by the language and demeanour of
Bentinck and Disraeli. It is easy to forget his importance as a
political figure if only because Disraeli has in retrospect come to
overshadow him, although Disraeli himself never underestimated
the stature of his chief, nor did his contemporaries.

Stanley was heir to vast estates and an ancient title. These assets
alone could bring a man who bothered about politics at all very
near to the top. If as late as 1876 an amiable mediocrity like the
Duke of Richmond could be considered in some circles as a
possible contender for the premiership – admittedly *faute de mieux*
and as a compromise – then how much stronger was the position
of Stanley in the still more deferential climate of the 1840s.
Described as 'the cleverest eldest son for a hundred years', Stanley
was a brilliant orator and an able administrator with experience
in two important posts, the Irish Secretaryship and the Colonial
Office. He towered above the other Protectionists.

His defect was a certain casualness and a perhaps excessive
spread of interests – racing, shooting, translation of Homer and,
incongruously, religious instruction; his book, *The use of parables for
young children*, was a great success and was translated into several
European languages. Despite his authorship of this pious best-
seller he was liable to display a certain levity which accorded ill
with the serious tone of the times, and for some reason, he never
quite carried it off in the way that his great rival, Palmerston,

succeeded in doing. At times he undoubtedly treated his own party in an off-hand manner, as the private criticisms of Disraeli and others show. But they seldom dared to protest direct to him. His control when he chose to exert it was absolute, and for twenty-two years with three spells as Prime Minister he led his party unchallenged to the end – the longest leadership in its history.

Stanley as a practical politician with a sense of the realities of power was anxious to try to reunite the opposing wings of his party. In the House of Lords this was not so difficult. It was quite another matter in the House of Commons. Lord George Bentinck never thought of such an attempt. His brief career was highly unusual in parliamentary history; he was one of those rare political figures who placed prejudices or principles – it depends on the point of view – before everything else and yet headed his party in the House of Commons. George Lansbury was about as unlike Bentinck as one could conceive but he is the only party leader whose career and attitude suggests a parallel. Compromise, middle-of-the-roadism, were utterly alien to Bentinck's nature – like Lansbury's. Perhaps it is wrong to call Bentinck a doctrinaire. At any rate he was not a Tory doctrinaire. He regarded the intolerant protestantism of the new party which his revolt had called into being with contempt. His vote in favour of the admission of the Jews to the House, which inspired protests from his whips, Beresford and Newdegate, and led to his resignation of his short-lived leadership, was not simply the result of personal loyalty to Disraeli, still less of sympathy with Disraeli's views on Jewry. Bentinck really did in his Whiggish way believe in religious toleration, and was unwilling, in his own words, to 'give in to the prejudices of the multitude'.

Where Bentinck was unusual was in his complete indifference to the practical problems of obtaining political power. Politics to him was a matter of fulfilling certain principles, of satisfying his own conscience and of punishing those who offended it. His decision to sell his stud with the result that he missed the chance of winning the Derby shows how genuine his feelings were. It was a real sacrifice. Such figures as Bentinck cannot long survive as political leaders if their followers see the possibility of office. It was no accident that like Lansbury he became leader at a moment of party disintegration and disaster when political success seemed far away. The grand gesture, the striking of attitudes, can be afforded and applauded by a party whose prospects are hopeless and whose main sentiment is anger at betrayal, but they are not luxuries in which a party of government can indulge. On the morrow of the corn law crisis the Protectionists were not a party of government.

3

The election of 1847 was fought – if that word can be fairly applied to an election in which 236 out of 401 constituencies were not contested – in an atmosphere of confusion, disorder and recrimination, although Stanley endeavoured to exercise a moderating influence and to discourage as far as possible conflicts between Peelites and Protectionists. He was successful on the whole and was helped by the desire to avoid expense. Often, therefore, two candidates from the rival sections would fight the Whigs as a pair or enjoy a walk-over.[1] There are only ten clear cases of Peelites fighting Protectionists, seven won by the former, three by the latter. It is hard to estimate the result of the election accurately, though it is clear that the Protectionists were decisively beaten. The number of Peelites has been put as high as 120, as low as 80. The problem of accuracy is increased because Peel himself refused to behave as a party leader and, despite the adherence of the whole of the old party 'machine', declined to authorise any systematic organisation of his group. So it is not easy to say who was or was not a Peelite. If one accepts McCalmont's figures with one or two corrections, the Peelites won 89 seats[2] – an estimate which is perhaps on the low side, but complete accuracy is impossible. If this is correct the strength of the Protectionists was 243 (England 190, Wales 12, Scotland 8, Ireland 33).

---

[1] A striking example was King's Lynn where Bentinck, Peel's arch foe, was returned unopposed together with Lord Jocelyn, a Peelite.

[2] See note to ch. III, below, p. 96, for details about the Peelites in the elections of 1847, 1852 and 1857. McCalmont divides the party into C, P and LC; Conservative, Protectionist and Liberal-Conservative (i.e. Peelite). He lists both Disraeli and Peel as C. It is true that Peel was in one sense not a Peelite, and that Disraeli soon tried to drop protection, but one suspects that the classification is the result of error, not design.

The Conservative party – and the name must be given now not to Peel's but Stanley's followers, for the future lay with them – was forced back on to the counties further than at any time before or since. More than half their English members sat for county seats. Regionally they were concentrated largely in the centre and East Anglia with outlying garrisons in Shropshire, Worcestershire, Westmorland (a fief of the Lowther family) and Sussex. They had a majority of seats (county and borough combined) in only fourteen of forty-one English counties,[1] 83 seats out of a possible 126. These were Berks, Bucks, Cambridge, Hunts, Leicester, Lincoln, Norfolk, Notts, Rutland, Shropshire, Suffolk, Sussex, Westmorland, Worcestershire. In three more counties they tied with their opponents, and won 11 out of a possible 22. These were Bedford, Essex and Northants. Everywhere else they were in a minority. The remaining twenty-four counties included most of the big ones in terms of seats amounting altogether to 317, of which the Conservatives only won 94. The four university seats, hitherto a Tory monopoly, were divided equally. Gladstone (Oxford) and Goulburn (Cambridge) were strong Peelites. Goulburn only scraped in, and Gladstone, though defeating the runner up by a rather larger margin than this, came far behind that slightly comical figure, the High Tory, Sir Robert Inglis.

A comparison can be made with 1841, which as regards party division of English seats as a whole was more or less the mirror image politically of 1847. The Whigs had majorities in only eight counties (Cumberland, Derby, Devon, Durham, Gloucester, Hereford, London, Staffs) and a tie in seven more (Cheshire, Lancashire, Middlesex, Northants, Northumberland, Rutland, Sussex), leaving Peel with a majority in the remaining twenty-six. The Whig strongholds provided them with 54 out of 87 seats, and the counties where there was a tie with another 38 seats. In the remaining twenty-six counties with a total of 304 seats, they won 95.

The geographical distribution of party strength is clear enough from this comparison. It is perhaps worth anticipating events for a moment and looking at the next election, that of 1852. (See

[1] For this purpose the eighteen London constituencies are regarded as constituting a county.

Tables B and C, p. 75). This was the one where during the whole of what might be called the Derby–Disraeli period the Conservatives came nearest to winning a majority of the English seats, 227 out of 467. They had majorities in nineteen counties. The counties 'gained' in this sense since 1847 were Cornwall and Kent (the only occasion between the Reform Acts, apart from 1841), Essex (all 10 seats), Hereford, Herts, Monmouth and Somerset. There was only one loss, Worcestershire where the spread of industry from the Midlands was steadily weakening their control. In the counties where they had a majority they won 125 out of a possible 180. They tied in seven counties, winning 34 out of 68 seats. These were Bedford, Derby, Devon, Dorset, Northants, Rutland and Warwick. In the remaining fifteen counties which accounted for the remaining 215 seats they won only 66.

These figures, and those of the next three general elections confirm, with minor variations, the general pattern of early Victorian post-Peel electoral geography. It would be an oversimplification to say that it was simply a matter of the field of corn against the field of coal, but the fact remains that Conservative strength was very largely based on the areas where traditional rural influences prevailed, and that the party was weakest in those where the new industrialism was dominant. For example, even in 1841 they only won 59 of the 126 seats in Staffordshire, Cheshire, Derby, Yorkshire and the counties to the north. In 1847 they sank to 35. In 1852 their score was 38.

If we take the historian's advantage of hindsight and again look back at the election figures in table A on p. 46 we can see that the Conservatives needed somehow to win some 40 to 50 more seats in England during the post-Peel period. Admittedly there were two elections, 1847 and 1857, where they needed a much larger addition, if they were to have a hope of power. But these can be written off as being fought in particularly adverse conditions, one in the confused aftermath of the corn law crisis when the party had virtually no organisation at all, the other against the full force of Palmerston's 'patriotic cry'. In the election of 1852, 50 extra seats could have given them a majority of 26, and in those of 1859 and 1865 when they did better in the Celtic fringe, majorities of 58 and 42 respectively.

Table B

Table to show changes in England compared with 1852. Conservative members only are given, Peelites being omitted (total numbers of seats is given in brackets)

	1841	1852	1865	1874
Counties where Conservatives had a majority in 1852	(184)*132	(180)125	102	(167)122
Counties where Liberals had a majority in 1852	(215)†111	66	(219) 86	(225)125
Counties divided equally in 1852	(68)‡ 36	34	31	(62) 37
University seats	(4) 4	2	4	(5) 4
Total	(471) 283	(467)227	(471)223	(459)288

* Berks, Bucks, Cambridge, Cornwall, Essex, Hereford, Herts, Hunts, Kent, Leicester, Lincoln, Monmouth, Norfolk, Notts, Shropshire, Somerset, Suffolk, Sussex, Westmorland.

† Cheshire, Cumberland, Durham, Gloucester, Hants, Lancashire, London, Middlesex, Northumberland, Oxford, Staffs, Surrey, Wilts, Worcester, Yorkshire.

‡ Bedford, Derby, Devon, Dorset, Northants, Rutland, Warwick.

Table C

Table to show the only two Conservative victories between 1832 and 1885 in terms of electoral geography in England. Conservative members only are given, Peelites being omitted (total numbers of seats is given in brackets)

	1841	1852	1865	1874
South, Centre and East (omitting London, Middlesex, Surrey)*	(165)118	(161)108	94	(155)115
North†	(126) 59	38	(130) 51	(143) 73
London, Middlesex, Surrey	(27) 9	5	2	(31) 19
West and South-west‡	(149) 93	74	72	(125) 77
University seats	(4) 4	2	4	(5) 4
Total	(471)283	(467)227	(471)223	(459)288

* Beds, Berks, Bucks, Cambridge, Essex, Herts, Hunts, Kent, Leicester, Lincoln, Norfolk, Northants, Notts, Oxford, Rutland, Suffolk, Sussex, Warwick.

† Cheshire, Cumberland, Derby, Durham, Lancashire, Northumberland, Staffs, Westmorland, Yorkshire.

‡ Cornwall, Devon, Dorset, Hants, Hereford, Gloucester, Monmouth, Shropshire, Somerset, Wilts, Worcester.

The politics of the Celtic fringe were incalculable. The bonus of an Irish majority in 1859 was not likely to be – and was not –

repeated. Scotland was inveterately hostile. Wales was slipping away. The hope was in England. In counties where they had a majority or a tie in 1852 they won in that year 159 out of 248 seats.[1] In the same area Peel in 1841 had won 168 out of 252 (132 out of 180 in counties with a Conservative majority in 1852, and 36 where there was a tie). Therefore Derby in 1852 managed almost as well as Peel had in those areas. The picture is very different if we look at the counties where the Conservatives were in a minority in 1852. They won only 66 out of 215 seats, whereas Peel in the same counties eleven years earlier had won 111.

Clearly this was the field in which the post-Peel party had to make up lost ground. In the 'good' counties Derby was unlikely to do any better than Peel himself had done in 1841, and even if he equalled Peel's performance there, he would gain only 9 seats. In fact he was to find it impossible even to hold the position of 1852. Whether it was because the protection issue had been removed or because of Palmerston who led the Liberals after 1855, the Conservative strength declined even in the areas where they had seemed best placed. In 1857, 1859 and 1865 they won 89, 104 and 103 seats out of 180 in counties which had Tory majorities in 1852 when they had won 125 seats. They certainly could not afford a drop of 20 to 30 seats in this area. They declined also in the seven counties where there had been a tie in 1852, winning only 22 seats out of 68 in 1857 and only 27 seats at each of the next two elections.[2]

The Conservatives, therefore, had a double problem; to hold their ground in the south and centre – 'the field of corn'; and to make gains in the north – 'the field of coal'; and also in the big cities, particularly London and its suburbs which, just as much as the north constituted the new expanding England. In fact they did make some progress in the counties where they had been outnumbered in 1852. In 1859 their score went up from 66 to 72 and in 1865 it was 79. But this was nothing like enough to offset the losses in their traditional areas, let alone to give them a majority in England.[3]

What they needed in fact was just what Disraeli achieved in

[1] See Table B, above, p. 75.
[2] If Peelites are added the figures would be 29 in 1859 and 31 in 1865.
[3] See Table C, above, p. 75.

1874. The franchise by then had been extended, and the electoral weight given to the various counties altered, but the figures are interesting even though there is no proper comparability. The Tory minority areas of 1852 now accounted for 225 seats instead of 215 in Peel's day. Disraeli won 125, a slightly better performance than Peel's 111. The Tory majority areas of 1852 now covered 167 seats of which Disraeli won 122, much the same proportion as Peel's 132 out of 189. The counties where there had been a tie in 1852 provided 62 seats in 1874. Disraeli won 37, which was superior both proportionately and absolutely to Peel's score of 36 out of 68. The detailed distribution was not the same as Peel's, but a comparison of the 1852 election with either Peel's or Disraeli's victory shows clearly enough the weakness of the mid-century Conservative party.

But this is to anticipate events. The election of 1847 left the party in a state scarcely less feeble than its condition after 1832. True, it was numerically stronger, by 56 seats, and if the Peelites could be recovered the party would, depending on one's estimate of Peelite numbers, have either a small majority or be so near to the government's strength as to render Russell's position impossible. But the bitterness caused by the split over the corn laws made such a reunion impossible for the moment. There had been no comparable division after 1832. Moreover, the Conservatives after 1846 not only possessed no one with the stature of Peel, they had scarcely any one with any experience at all of office. This was a grave handicap to a party whose tradition was essentially that of a party of government, indeed *the* party of government. Between 1806 and 1846 the Tories in one guise or another had ruled the country for twenty-nine out of forty years, and the period during which the Whigs held office had been too chaotic and faction-ridden to make them an acceptable substitute. During their last four years they had scarcely governed at all. Hence Peel's victory in 1841 for the traditional party of government.

The situation was very different after 1846. The Whigs might not have gained greatly in public esteem, but with the Peelites out of office, and the Protectionists regarded as unfit to rule, they were the only possibility. The period that followed was one of party weakness, great confusion, much cross-voting, and – inevitable concomitant – weakness in government too. The 1830s seem in contrast a period of almost modern party discipline.

There was also great weakness in organisation. The Peelites wholly lacked it. As we saw, it was the swan song of Young and Bonham, respectively Peel's Chief Whip and Principal Agent. Peel himself refused to act as a leader even of his own supporters. They voted without orders or guidance. But the confusion among the Protectionists was equally bad. They had no agent equivalent to Peel's Bonham, and the whips had to do everything. They seem to have captured the political committee of the Carlton and to have raised an election fund, but otherwise all was chaos. The correspondence of Beresford with Stanley shows this well enough. 'I am in despair about the Elections . . . I can get no Candidates. Every second man falls away when it comes to the point The luke-warmness and shiftiness of those I have to deal with is most disheartening.'[1] Beresford was on bad terms with both Bentinck and Disraeli. He believed that Bentinck's lack of Protestant zeal was a grave defect, and in Disraeli he had no confidence whatever. After the election was over he wrote to Stanley about them both:

> I fully acknowledge his [Bentinck's] good qualities but I feel that he is what is called impracticable to that degree that I look at his future career with fear and apprehension. I know that with all that obstinacy of character which is inherent in his nature that [sic] he is greatly in the hands of D'Israeli, and whatever my opinion of that person's talents, I cannot think him a safe Mentor for G.B. Entre nous I would not trust D'Israeli any more than I would a committed felon.[2]

This was not a happy relationship between the Chief Whip and the two leading figures in the lower House. Matters became even worse when Bentinck accused Beresford of making an improper use of the election fund. After the debate on the 'Jew Bill' Bentinck on December 21 replied to Beresford who had reproached himself for having written a strong letter of protest without sufficient previous warning:

¹ Derby Papers, 149/1, n.d., but evidently May–June 1847.
² ibid., 149/1, Beresford to Stanley, postmarked September 23, 1847

You have no reason to reproach yourself on the score you have written down. Whether or not you might with more reason have reproached yourself as a Trustee of the Funds and the Interest of a Party divided in opinion upon particular questions bearing upon religious feeling for having used a common purse and a common trust to fan into flame the flickering embers of prejudices entertained only by one division of the Party and openly and *from all time* disavowed and repudiated by the other must remain a question to be settled between you and your conscience.[1]

Beresford replied in a rage:

I will not be tempted by a very unjust accusation to say more than that you are entirely misinformed with regard to the corrupt misapplication of a common fund which you have laid to my charge.

There was a subscription contributed by several Peers & Members whose opinions on religious questions coincide with mine, for the express purpose of upholding those opinions. That money was kept quite distinct from any Election Fund. . . . I could not allow you to remain under this false impression which could have been only insinuated into your mind by some designing person from the worst of motives.[2]

Although there is no means of sorting out the truth it seems highly probable that this was yet another of the reckless charges flung about by Bentinck when in a temper, and that though Beresford was, as he himself admitted, a 'bigoted Protestant'[3] he had not done anything dishonourable. But the interest of the correspondence lies, rather, in the light it throws on the general working of the party machine at this time.

Apart from electoral weakness and disputes about funds a delicate problem of nomenclature arose. The word 'Conservative' by its association with Peel personally had become repugnant to a large section of the party. Should they rebaptise themselves? The name 'Country Party' nostalgic of the eighteenth century was

[1] ibid., 149/1, copies sent by Beresford to Stanley.
[2] ibid., Beresford to Stanley, n.d.   [3] loc. cit., 149/1.

canvassed. Peel's Chief Whip used it of them – and not in any sarcastic or ironic sense. 'Protectionist' was a more general usage. If McCalmont is reliable, over 150 MPs were returned under that description in 1847 – or at any rate could be plausibly given that name. Evidently, however, it was applied only to a section, albeit the largest in the party. But Beresford showed good sense in opting for the established name. On November 2, 1847, in a postscript to a letter to Stanley about the circular letter to supporters he wrote, 'I considered it best to put in the "Conservative Party" as it left the door open to any man who liked to join us and who might shy [sc. at] the "Protectionist or Country Party".'[1] It was neither the first nor the last occasion when the name has inspired misgivings. In 1867 when the National Union was founded there were objections to the title and the word 'constitutional' was added to meet the criticism – 'National Union of Conservative and Constitutional Associations'. As late as 1945 Lord Woolton had to quash a quite serious move to abolish it. But to give it up would have been a sign of weakness. In 1847 it would also have meant abandoning all hope of bringing the Peelites back into the fold. They did not in fact come back as events turned out, but they would have been even less likely to do so if there had been a change of name.

The chaos in the ranks of the Stanleyites was enhanced by a major crisis in the autumn session of 1847. Bentinck resigned at the end of December on the Jewish question. He acted impetuously after receiving a letter from Beresford expressing the party's dissatisfaction at his vote for the admission of Jews to parliament. Bentinck was feeling ill at the time and did not try to find out the real strength of the dissentients. He probably could have secured a vote of confidence had he wished. Nevertheless the episode has a significance which is usually overlooked: it was the first occasion on which rebellion from below – or the rumour of such rebellion can be said to have brought about the resignation of a party leader. It was over sixty years before this was to recur, but the episode can be seen as an early pointer to the situation which obliged Balfour in 1911, Austen Chamberlain in 1922 and Sir Alec Douglas-Home in 1965 to retire from the leadership.

[1] Derby Papers, 149/1.

Part of the trouble in Bentinck's case was the ambiguous chain of command. Were the whips responsible to Stanley as the acknowledged, though never formally elected, leader of the whole party, or to the leader in the House of Commons? 'I cannot help giving you this friendly advice [wrote Bentinck to his successor Lord Granby] . . . to appoint your own Whippers-in; and let them take orders from you and no one else.' Granby, eldest son of the Duke of Rutland, was, alas, in no position to take this advice. Disraeli some years earlier had referred to his 'high Castilian emptiness', and his leadership was surely the shortest of any party in either House during our history. He was elected on February 10, 1848, a week after the session began. He resigned at the beginning of March, acutely conscious of his total inadequacy. Disraeli had been the successor for whom Bentinck hoped. But he was impossible, given the circumstances of Bentinck's own resignation, and if he was impossible in February he had not become less so in March. The dearth of talent on the Protectionist benches was such that no one could be discovered to lead for the rest of the session. Stanley had to manage his party's affairs in the Lower House as best he could through the whips. The result was confusion.

Bentinck's death in September 1848 raised the whole question again, for, as long as he lived, there was always the chance of persuading him to reconsider his resignation. This time Stanley and the Whips could not evade Disraeli. They distrusted him profoundly, as did a large section of the party. They endeavoured to restrict him by putting the leadership into commission under a committee of three, reviving the arrangement which prevailed after the original Protectionist revolt in the early months of 1846. The other two were Granby and J. C. Herries, an elderly 'official man' who would probably have been in Peel's administration had he not lost his seat in 1841. Disraeli neither accepted nor rejected this face-saving but absurd arrangement. He disregarded it, and behaved as sole leader. Nevertheless, his position was anomalous, and for some years he was regarded by Stanley and many others in the top echelons of the party as a stop-gap leader, pending the hoped-for reunion with the Peelites.

But this reunion, although for a long time it seemed to be just round the corner, never occurred. That uncertainty together with the ultimate perpetuation, indeed widening, of the gulf between the two sections of the old Conservative party is the key to the confused and shifting politics of the 1850s. The importance of the Peelites was not simply numerical. The rank and file fell, through conversion, retirement, and a few defeats, from 89 to only 45 after the election of 1852, and to 26 after 1857. Their importance lay in their talents. They were what Gladstone called 'the Official Corps' – and this was just what the 'Who? Who?' ministry lacked. Why did the obvious not occur? Why did the Peelites remain a separate group – a head without a tail? While Peel was alive there could of course be no question of reunion, nor could there be any chance of it as long as the Protectionists refused to drop protection. Peel died in 1850 and thus one barrier was removed. Disraeli did his best to drop protection as soon as he succeeded to his ambiguous leadership early in 1849. But for a number of reasons, most of them quite comprehensible at the time, the party would not follow, and Derby, as we must call Stanley after the summer of 1851, was unwilling to press the matter. The question was still open when events forced Derby to take office early in 1852. It was not until after the general election in the summer that the party finally gave up any serious idea of reimposing the corn laws; and then not out of conviction but necessity. Even so there remained a hard core of 53 MPs who remained obdurate. Their attitude had much support among the squirearchy. In Anthony Trollope's *Barchester Towers* (1857) we have an affectionate picture of the type.

In politics Mr Thorne was an unflinching Conservative. He looked on those 53 Trojans who, so Mr Dod tells us, censured Free Trade in November 1852 as the only patriots left among the public men of England. When that terrible crisis of Free Trade had arrived, when the Repeal of the Corn Laws was carried by those very men whom Mr Thorne had hitherto regarded as the saviours of his country he was for a time paralysed. . . . Now all trust in human faith must be for ever at an end. . . .

He had within him something of the feeling of Cato who

gloried that he could kill himself because Romans were no longer worthy of their name. Mr Thorne had no thought of killing himself, being a Christian and still possessing his £4,000 a year; but the feeling was not on that account the less comfortable.

Why did the feud continue after 1852? Partly it was the familiar phenomenon of the hardening of attitudes. When once there has been a great split in a party on a vital issue all experience suggests that it is extremely difficult for the combatants to shake hands and make it up with any degree of sincerity. It was seven years before Cranborne and his friends rejoined Disraeli after their resignation on the second Reform Bill. The Liberal Unionists never went back to the Liberals. There was no real reconciliation between the friends of Asquith and those of Lloyd George. The rift in the Labour party created by Ramsay MacDonald in 1931 was never mended. The scars from the wounds caused by the great battle over 'appeasement' had not vanished from the Conservative party as late as 1957.

There was another reason. Although the Protectionists had dropped protection they had not yet dropped the principle which underlay protection, viz, that in return for the special duties and burdens alleged to fall upon the landed interest it was entitled to special reliefs in taxation. From this point of view Disraeli's autumn budget of 1852 deserves a closer scrutiny than has usually been given to it. His attempt to halve the malt tax while raising the house tax was palpably designed to compensate the agricultural industry as a whole, including the landowners, for the potential damage done to it by free trade. As Macaulay commented, this was 'nothing but taking the money out of the pockets of people in towns and putting it into the pockets of growers of malt'. But this preferential treatment was just what 'progressive opinion' could not stomach, and, tagging along behind Cobden, Bright and the standard bearers of the new Radical free trade orthodoxy were the Peelites and the heterogeneous Whig-Liberal majority thrown out of office ten months earlier thanks to the ineptitude of their leaders. It was on opposition to Disraeli's budget that they sought to return; and the most formidable of all the attacks launched upon it was that of Gladstone. There could be no early chance of reunion after that. Moreover, the gap at once widened. The narrow balance of power in the House together with the discredit into which the Whig leaders had fallen alike in the eyes of the court and parliamentary opinion gave an opening to the Peelites. A coalition Cabinet was formed in which they captured the premiership and half the offices. They had not yet committed themselves decisively to the other side. That did not occur till 1859. But they had taken up a position which rendered a return to the Conservative party far harder.

What was more, the Derbyites, though not Derby, became less and less ready to receive them back even if they had wished to be received. The truth was that the electoral system was exactly wrong from the point of view of the long term interests of the new post-1846 Conservative party. Had it been more favourable to the counties, as it well might have been if the numerical distribution of the electorate had been more accurately reflected, the party would have had a reasonable chance of sometimes winning a general election on its own and forming a government based on a working majority in the House of Commons.

On the other hand if the landed base of the party – the English counties and small boroughs of the southern half of England – had been palpably too narrow and inadequate, then perhaps the party would have seen, and acted on, the need to widen it by looking elsewhere. As it was, the Conservatives did well enough in the four successive elections, 1852, 1857, 1859, 1865, to be the biggest homogeneous party, for the Whig-Liberal-Radical-Peelite-Irish coalition was a loose assemblage of groups rather than a coherent party. The Conservatives therefore perpetually saw dangling before them the carrot of a clear majority, but they never did well enough actually to put tooth to vegetable. The mass of the party was reluctant to co-operate with the smaller groups which held the balance of power in the Commons, and this reluctance was shown even towards the Peelites – the group with which they had most affinity. Derby and Disraeli did indeed see the need to do something, but Disraeli was too ready to snatch at adventitious alliances of opportunity – e.g. with Bright and the Manchester Radicals or with the Irish – manœuvres which only aroused suspicion among his own supporters and could not in any case have led to lasting results. As for Derby, he was prepared to do what he could with the Peelites, but when once that failed – and a Peelite alliance was really a dead duck after 1852 – he was unwilling to do anything except, as his son put it, 'obstruct "progress"', and take office on those occasions when the parties behind the normal governing coalition fell out among themselves and let in a minority administration.

He was not always ready to do so even then. One of the most controversial passages in his career is his failure to take office in 1855 when the scandals of the Crimea brought Lord Aberdeen's coalition to an end. Both Gladstone and Disraeli privately censured him for this refusal, and since they scarcely ever agreed about anything, it is natural to think that, when they did, they must have been right. But it does not follow, and the theory that Derby could have put the Conservative party on the map by giving them the kudos of being the party that won the Crimean War does not stand close examination. It seems likely that a government formed by him in 1855 would have had no less precarious and short-lived a career than that of 1852 or of 1858. Moreover, there was a deeper reason for doubting its longevity. As Derby himself told Queen Victoria, 'the whole country cried out for Lord Palmerston as the only man fit for carrying on the war with success'. The political philosopher may view such an expression with scepticism, but common sense gives it a meaning. The country cried out for Lloyd George in 1916 and Churchill in 1940. Surely Bonar Law on the former occasion and Lord Halifax on the latter, were right to stand down and refrain from pressing their claims?

Disraeli's well publicised complaints should not lead one to suppose that Derby's refusal was universally condemned. Sir William Joliffe,[1] the Chief Whip, wrote to Derby on October 23:

I am unable to participate in the regret which Disraeli no doubt feels that he has missed a chance of taking office, when of course it was the object of his life. I believe that these regrets of his are very much fermented by the secluded life he leads associating

[1] He succeeded Beresford who had been made Secretary at War in 1852. He retired in 1859 and was created Baron Hylton in 1866.

only, as it appears to me, with his most intimate friends or with his followers and political supporters in Buckinghamshire who of course are all of the same mind. I therefore greatly regret that he is not more frequently brought in contact with those who being more his equals, would have greater weight upon his judgement and ideas. I write these smaller reflections because they may lead to greater results, and if I see them my Chief for whom [I] wish to labour should not be ignorant of such influences.[1]

Joliffe's letter is interesting, apart from the question of taking office in 1855. He put his finger on one of Disraeli's weaknesses. Disraeli never seems to have enjoyed the society of his equals. He had patrons as a young man, disciples as he grew older. With both categories he could be on terms of great intimacy, as with Lyndhurst on the one hand, George Smythe or Lord Henry Lennox on the other. But partly because he had missed the normal education of public school and university, partly because he was to a singular extent 'unclubable', preferring the society of women and disliking men's dinners or even the monosexual circulation of the post-prandial port at a mixed dinner, Disraeli in middle age saw little of those whom Joliffe would have liked him to meet. To a far greater degree than most politicians he lived in a world of his own.

Disraeli's position in the Conservative party was by no means assured. Had Derby retired or died in the 1850s or the early 1860s, he might well have been passed over for the succession. His talents in the House of Commons made him an indispensable second-in-command, and he was the only man on his side who could put on a real display of fireworks, the only man who could give as good as he got to the formidable orators on the other side – Gladstone, Palmerston, Russell, Herbert, Bright, Cobden. But a great many people continued to distrust him, and the venom with which he had attacked Peel made his presence on the Conservative front bench in itself alone a grave impediment to reunion with the Peelites. This was what Gladstone meant when on one occasion he described him as 'at once the necessity of Lord Derby and his curse'.

[1] Derby Papers, 158/10.

Derby did not look at his second-in-command quite in that light. He recognised his talents and he was not prepared to throw him over, but he was at times irritated by Disraeli's love of implausible alliances and fantastic reshuffles of the political pack. A propensity of Disraeli which he particularly disliked was a tendency to woo the Irish vote by flirtation with popery. Disraeli with some logic believed that Roman Catholics were naturally conservative. This was indeed the case on the continent where the Catholic Church was a bulwark against liberalism and 'progress'. Could not this innate conservatism be harnessed somehow into support of the Conservative party in the United Kingdom? It was certainly true that the Catholics in Ireland and England disliked the Liberal party's anti-papal foreign policy. The Tories gained eleven seats in Ireland in 1857 when they were losing ground almost everywhere else and another seven in 1859, giving them a clear majority there – the only occasion in the whole period between the Reform Act of 1832 and the dissolution of the Union in 1922.

Derby saw no future in this kind of thing. He did not believe it could last: the Conservatives as the party of the Church of Ireland as well as England could not make any real concessions to Irish popery, and the mere show of doing so would only alienate their own Protestant support. After all in 1852 the Tories had exploited the repercussions of the 'papal aggression' every bit as vigorously as Russell and his friends. Nor was it just a matter of political calculation or pandering to the Orange vote. Derby was thoroughly hostile to papal pretensions, and, as an old Whig, rejoiced in the triumph of Italian nationalism and the decline of the temporal power of the Pope. To Disraeli's consternation he called on Garibaldi when the Italian hero visited England in April 1864 and, in the run up to the election of 1865, by accident or design he greatly offended the Roman Catholics by comparing them with dangerous dogs which needed muzzling. Canine metaphors should be avoided by politicians, as a more recent example shows.[1] Whether or not it was cause and effect, the Conservatives in 1865 lost 7 seats in Ireland, and one of the seats which in 1859

[1] I leave this sentence as delivered if only as a reminder of the ephemeral nature of political allusions. It is doubtful whether many people now remember Harold Wilson's reference to dog licences not being renewed when there was a Labour back-bench revolt in 1967.

they had gained in South Lancashire where there was an unusual concentration of English Roman Catholics.[1]

4

The choices open to the Conservatives after 1846 were not fundamentally different from those open to Peel in the 1830s. These, as we saw, were either to 'obstruct "progress"' – the policy of the old 'Ultras'; or to take some quite new unorthodox line – the policy of Sadler, Oastler, Young England; or to dispute the middle ground with the party in power. And each was subject to just the same difficulties. Obstruction might work up to a point, for the Conservatives still predominated in the House of Lords, and the possibilities of at least delaying legislation were considerable. The most intelligent proponent of this view and a bitter critic of Disraeli was Lord Robert Cecil[2] for whom few people in the 1850s would have prophesied his later role as leader of the party. Opposing the abolition of church rates, which he regarded as the prelude to disestablishment, he said that even if the Conservatives were beaten

> ... at any rate they had obtained delay and delay was life. They had kept church rates alive for thirty years and with their present numbers they could keep them alive for ten years longer. At that rate they might keep tithes twenty years after that and endowments twenty years longer still. That brought them to fifty years and that period was something in the life of a nation.

The snag in this policy was the same snag as existed in the 1830s: it offered no hope of political power.

The same applied to the possibility of some new ideology challenging the conventional wisdom of the day. This could only

[1] In 1859 the Conservatives contested South Lancashire for the first time since the repeal of the corn laws and won both seats. In 1861 a third seat was allocated to the division and at the ensuing by-election they won this too: but at the general election of 1865 Gladstone displaced one of the sitting Tory members, although the other two were ahead of him by slight margins.
[2] Younger son of the 2nd Marquess of Salisbury. On his elder brother's death he became Viscount Cranborne, served under that name in Derby's third Cabinet till he resigned in 1867 over the second Reform Bill. Succeeded father, 1868; Prime Minister, 1885-6, 1886-92, 1895-1902.

be some variant of the social paternalism which had never made much headway in the party even at a time when bitter working class discontent seemed to render at least plausible an alliance with the landed interest against the millocracy. But the working class was itself becoming permeated by bourgeois middle class ideas, and, as the tide of mid-Victorian prosperity flowed higher, social conflict became much less acute than it had been in Peel's day. It is difficult to say quite how seriously Disraeli had ever taken the ideas of Young England. He had voted against the new poor law and for the Ten Hours Bill, but he also voted against the Public Health Act of 1848 and the Mines Act of 1850. These votes might be discounted as belonging to a later period of his life but it is hard to see him even in the early 1840s as an ardent social reformer even remotely comparable to Lord Shaftesbury. The Conservatives were not wholly neglectful of the condition of the people, but there was not a conscious party policy in the matter. As Dr Paul Smith puts it, 'Conservative support for social reform was very much a matter between 1846 and 1866 of the sporadic efforts of individuals'.[1] It was one thing to seek to ameliorate the lot of the poor, quite another to found upon this a strategy for winning political power. That came up against the same old difficulty. The lower classes had not got the vote and no Conservative leader could afford to offer it to them in the 1840s and 1850s without splitting the party just as disastrously as Peel had over the corn laws.

The only viable policy, therefore, was to imitate Peel and to woo the middle class. This was in fact just what Derby and Disraeli tried to do after Bentinck's death, though of course they did not put it like that even in the secrecy of private correspondence. There were differences of emphasis between the two men. Disraeli wanted to drop protection at once. Derby believed that an abrupt *volte face* would be even more damaging than clinging to a defeated cause, but basically his attitude was not different, as is shown by his own genuine efforts to bring back the Peelites after Peel's death. The policy which Peel had pursued with ultimate success after 1832 was the only real hope for Derby and Disraeli, but it involved two major difficulties. First, it was extremely difficult to 'sell' to a party – in many respects a new party – which had come

[1] Paul Smith, *Disraelian Conservatism and social reform* (1967), 20.

into being precisely because of Peel's alleged 'treachery'. There
had been no comparable problem after 1832. Secondly, there was
a major obstacle in terms of personalities. Derby and Disraeli were
not in the least like Peel, however much they might in practice
try to copy his policy. 'What a curious thing it is,' wrote the historical painter, Benjamin Haydon, a keen Liberal, in December
1845. 'I never feel comfortable with Sir Robert and the Duke
out.'[1] This was about the last thing that any Liberal was likely to
feel about Derby and Disraeli. And from 1855 there was a further
obstacle. The Liberals had Palmerston as their leader and he was
a far greater asset than Grey, Melbourne or Russell.

It seems to have been Palmerston's ascendancy which decided
Derby that there was little point in pursuing an active policy any
more. There is a revealing exchange of letters between him and
Lord Malmesbury, one of his closest friends and Foreign Secretary
in his first two administrations. It admirably epitomises the mid-
century Conservative dilemma. Malmesbury wrote on December
7, 1856:

> . . . for the first time in my life I own that I feel discouragement
> with regard to our political position. If Palmerston knew our
> unprepared & I may say *destitute* condition he ought to dissolve
> immediately. It is moreover useless to conceal that the animus of
> our Party is very unsatisfactory. . . .
>
> The best men [he went on] confirm this fact and say that you
> are supposed to be tired of politics & no longer ambitious of
> office & that this fact and the unpopularity of Disraeli are
> distracting our Party. My answer has always been that the
> Conservative body can never be an active one except in office,
> or in opposition to . . . a Minister who attacks our institutions,
> & that we are without either of these stimulants & therefore
> dormant.

Malmesbury ended on an unwonted note of implied criticism of
his chief and old friend:

> It is nevertheless clear that both the present & the future require

---

[1] *Diary of B. R. Haydon*, ed. W. B. Pope (1963), V, 501; quoted, Gash, *Reaction and
reconstruction*, 130, n. 3.

all your energy and abilities if during *our lifetime* the Conservatives are to remain an organised class in the political comity of England.[1]

Derby replied on December 15 in a letter printed in Malmesbury's *Memoirs*.[2] He did not deny, he said, or wonder at, 'a certain state of disorganisation' in the Conservative party.

> . . . indeed I am disposed to be rather surprised to find how mere fidelity to party ties, and some personal feeling, has for so long a time kept together so large a body of men, under most adverse circumstances, and in the absence of any cry or leading question, to serve as a broad line of demarcation between the two sides of the House. The breach which was made in the Conservative body by Peel in 1845-6, and which might have been healed to a great degree if his followers had only given us a fair support or even stood neutral in the session of 1852-3, was widened by the formation of the Coalition Government, on the avowed principle (or no principle) of discarding all previous party ties.

Public attention since then, he went on, had been mainly concentrated on the war, and Palmerston had played his cards so skilfully as to avoid attacks on our institutions or ground for Conservative censure.

> In short he has been a Conservative Minister working with Radical tools and keeping up a show of Liberalism in his foreign policy which nine in ten of the House of Commons care nothing about. That a Conservative party should have held together at all in such circumstances is rather to be wondered at, than that there should be apathy and indifference when there is nothing to be fought for by the bulk of the party.

Derby had put his finger on the crucial point. The decade from 1855 to 1865 was dominated by Palmerston. His role in foreign policy has had plenty of attention from historians. His part in home affairs deserves more study than it has been given. For he

[1] Derby Papers, 144/1.
[2] Earl of Malmesbury, *Memoirs of an ex-minister*, 2 vols (1884) II, 54.

supplied in a singular degree the political needs of the age. A parliament to which for whatever reason successive general elections invariably failed to return a party with an absolute majority required as Prime Minister an adept at the politics of consensus. This was just what Palmerston was. English to the core, an ex-Tory, in fact a Canningite turned Whig, on the popular side over the Reform Act and the corn laws, the darling of the Jingos including the Radical Jingos, exponent of a shrewd foreign policy decked out in Liberal language, cautious over institutional changes, an able party manager and one of the first politicians to humour and keep in with the press, he had all the attributes required by the age; except, perhaps, one – high moral tone.

It was appropriate that this solitary lack of rapport with the new era helped to give him his only toss in the whole decade. His appointment in 1857 of Lord Clanricarde to the Cabinet, a man of notoriously disreputable private life, contributed just as much as the Orsini affair to the defeat of the government in 1858, which gave Derby another brief lease of office, if not of power. But high moral tone was not exactly the *forte* of Derby either – witness the Prince Consort's horrified comment on his list of appointments submitted for the Household in 1852: 'all the roués and dandies of the Turf'. Nor did Disraeli help much in this respect.

The intellectual world was largely liberal or neutral. Although in Derby and Disraeli the Conservatives had two of the cleverest men in politics, it was hard for the party as a whole to escape the charge of being 'the stupid party'. Nor did their traditional assets help. They were the party of the Church of England but no one could say that Palmerston was putting the Church in danger. They were the party of the Crown but the Crown (i.e. the Prince Consort) regarded them with dislike and distrust. They could not claim superior efficiency. Disraeli's 1852 budget which not only offended financial orthodoxy but muddled up all the income tax schedules settled that. Moreover, they were damaged by a notable row early in 1853 about political jobbery in their dockyard appointments. Like the Whigs in the 1830s the Conservatives in the 1850s were disinclined to adopt that austerity in matters of patronage which a party with a long lease of power can more easily afford. Nor did their brief spells of office give them any chance to strike out on some new and contrasting policy of their own. Disraeli's budgets, after the failure of 1852, were mere imitations of Gladstone's. Indeed he carried Treasury economy on military and naval estimates to the point where Derby had to overrule him in the interests of national security. The government neither in 1852 nor in 1858-9 (apart from a Reform Bill palpably designed to favour themselves) put forward any distinctly Conservative measures. 'Everyone knows,' wrote Disraeli to Derby in 1859, 'that all we did, would really have been done by our predecessors.' It is difficult to see what the Conservatives could have put forward as a contrasting policy or programme – if indeed one can use such language at all about mid-nineteenth century politics.

Confronted with Palmerston they could play neither the 'constitutional' nor the 'patriotic' card; and it was hard for Derby or even Disraeli to avoid the charge of being 'not a voice but an echo'. It is not surprising that Derby gave up the attempt and resolved to throw his party not against Palmerston but rather in support of Palmerston against his own potentially rebellious Liberal followers. From 1859 to 1865 the inter-party parliamentary battle became a tacit truce only enlivened by occasional raids and sporadic gunfire.

In his recent study of nineteenth century Britain,[1] Dr Kitson Clark makes the point that for a large part of the time 'there were ... in Britain two nations struggling in the bosom of one land – an old nation based upon the old nobility, upon the squires and upon the Established Church, and a new nation based upon commerce and industry, and in religion largely Dissenting'. This conflict was far more important than that between the two nations of *Sybil* and in many ways more bitter, but the significant fact about it in terms of parliamentary history is that the new nation was for long after the first Reform Act under-represented in what may be termed 'the political nation', i.e. the electorate, parliament, and particularly the government. The political nation was dominated by the old nation. It remained, as we saw earlier, largely conservative with a small 'c', attached to what Malmesbury

[1] G. Kitson Clark, *An expanding society* (1967), 11.

called 'our institutions' – or in a phrase often used at the time 'the just influence of land'.

Yet, as we also saw earlier, conservatism with a small 'c' did not necessarily involve adherence to the Conservative party. The real bone of contention within the political nation was how much the old nation should concede to the new, for the more thoughtful members of the old nation believed that some concessions had to be made, unless there was to be a revolution. The judgment involved in deciding just where to dig one's toes in was tricky, but it seemed to moderate men that the old Tory party had got it wrong once – over the Reform Act; and then, despite their new name of Conservative, had got it wrong a second time – over the corn laws. Twice was too much, and after the second occasion their plight was enhanced by the mediocrity of all their leading men in the House of Commons – except Disraeli, whose character inspired more distrust than his genius commanded respect.

Whether for this reason or from sheer apathy the electorate continued to return an anti-Conservative majority. In 1852 it was, in round numbers, about 70; in 1857 it was 140; in 1859 it fell to 40; but in 1865 the Liberal majority rose to nearly 60. It was a gloomy prospect.

There were slight gains in Lancashire where a sort of primeval, Protestant, working class, anti-Irish conservatism was making its way, fed by such edifying literature as *Geralda, the demon nun* and *The secrets of the confessional*. Lancashire lacked the ecumenical spirit. But these gains were more than cancelled by losses in the 'Celtic fringe'; 4 in Wales, 3 in Scotland, 7 in Ireland. Derby wrote despondently to Disraeli:

. . . I come to the same conclusion with yourself, that looking especially to the utter rout of our party in Scotland, and to the amount of democratic spirit which prevails there, a purely Conservative Government is all but hopeless, until upon Palmerston's death . . . Gladstone tries his hand with a Radical Government, and alarms the middle classes. Then there *may* come a reaction; but it will probably be too late for my time; and I see no prospect of any state of affairs which shall again place me at the head of a government – which is equivalent to saying, in office at all. . . .[1]

In other words if the new nation pressed its claims too far, if it acquired a positive sympathiser at the head of affairs the situation might change. As it was the new nation had not been pushing very hard during the last decade, thanks partly to affluence, partly to Palmerston's genius at obscuring and muffling dissension.

But Palmerston, though at times he seemed immortal, could not last for ever. By early October he was seriously ill. On October 18 he died, the last Prime Minister to expire while still in office, the only one since 1832, apart from Harold Wilson and Margaret Thatcher, to have increased his majority at two successive general elections. The opening which Derby anticipated had come at last.

[1] Hughenden Papers B/XX/Derby/335, Derby to Disraeli, Knowsley, August 4, 1865.

Note

Fate of the Peelites

McCalmont's *Poll book* suitably amended gives 89 Liberal Conservatives i.e. Peelites returned at the election of 1847; 62 in England, 7 in Wales, 11 in Scotland, 9 in Ireland. 16 of them had been office holders in Peel's government. Geographically their strength in England lay in the west and 35 of them were returned for counties or boroughs west of a line drawn along the eastern boundaries of Lancashire, Cheshire, Staffordshire, Warwick, Gloucester, Wiltshire and Dorset. At the election of 1852 there were 45 Peelites; 28 in England, 6 in Wales, 8 in Scotland, 3 in Ireland. In both parliaments, therefore, they held the balance of power, and used it to such effect at the end of 1852 that they secured the premiership and half the Cabinet in a coalition government.

In the election of 1852, 31 of the original Peelites stood again and won as Peelites for the same seats as in 1847, 2 for different seats; 10 were beaten for the same seats, 1 for a different seat. 9 stood and won as straight Conservatives for the same seats, 2 stood and won as Liberals for the same seats, 3 stood and lost as Conservatives for the same seats. 15 did not stand (no reason given), 4 applied for the Chiltern Hundreds between 1847 and 1852, 8 died, 2 succeeded to peerages, 2 accepted offices of profit under the Crown. There were 11 new Peelites who got in at the 1852 election, 6 of them for seats won by Peelites in 1847, 5 for different seats.

In the election of 1857 26 Peelites were returned, 20 of them for the same seats as in 1852. The distribution was England 13, Wales 3, Scotland 7, Ireland 3.

The Peelites won 10 English county seats in 1847, 8 in 1852, 3 in 1857. In English boroughs with an electorate over 1,000 they won 12 seats in 1847, 3 in 1852 and 3 in 1857. In English boroughs below 1,000 the figures were 38, 15 and 6.

CHAPTER IV

Disraelian revival
1866–81

I

We now enter on to one of the most fascinating periods of modern British political history. The fifteen years in question cover a major extension of the franchise, the creation of the institutional framework of the modern state, and the great duel between Disraeli and Gladstone which has coloured political attitudes ever since. Moreover, it saw the beginning of an important change in the balance of political power. During the thirty-five years from 1830 to the end of 1865, the Conservatives had a parliamentary majority for less than five (Peel 1841–6). They were in office but without effective power for short intervals totalling another two and a half (Peel 1834–5, Derby 1852 and 1858–9). But over the next thirty-five years ending in 1900 they had an effective majority for seventeen (Disraeli 1874–80, Salisbury 1886–92, and 1895–1900). They were in office though in a minority for a further three years (Derby–Disraeli 1866–8, and Salisbury 1885–6).

But it is fair to say that this change was by no means obvious at the time of Disraeli's death or just after it. To a detached observer in 1881, the improvement in the Conservative party's fortunes was far from self-evident. True, there had been the Reform Act of 1867, but it had been followed by a resounding electoral rebuff in 1868, the first election on the new franchise. Admittedly Disraeli had staged a notable recovery in 1874, and the Conservatives, for the first time since Peel, were in power as well as office. But what Gladstone called 'Beaconsfieldism' apparently dissolved in ruins in 1880, and five years later a further extension of the franchise was carried, which was expected by most people to give further strength to the Liberals. The first election on the new suffrage did not entirely confirm that judgment, for the Liberal majority was slightly down, but it seemed quite enough for practical purposes. Although the political convulsion caused by Gladstone's espousal of Irish Home Rule brought the Conservatives back in August 1886, few people even as late as that would have predicted the prolonged ascendancy which followed.

This is a period which has attracted much more attention from historians than the previous twenty years and there is lively controversy about some of its problems.

The first great question is the Reform Act of 1867. The issue came to the fore because of the death of Palmerston. Russell who was his successor had long wished to carry a second Reform Act, and Gladstone who became leader of the House of Commons was also by now a convinced reformer. As Derby had predicted, the change involved a distinct shift in the Radical direction. Parliamentary reform had been debated off and on ever since 1851. It was the symbol, the patent mark as it were, of progressivism. It was the flag and shibboleth of the new nation against the old. It is true that since 1859 the Liberals had ceased to have a monopoly in this field. Derby and Disraeli in their unsuccessful Reform Bill of that year had staked the Conservative claim to legislate too. But everything depended on what was meant by reform. The Conservative measure was so palpably designed, despite Disraeli's euphemistic phrase, 'lateral extension of the franchise', to improve the party's electoral fortunes that it was bound to be rejected by a House in which the Conservatives were a minority. Seven years later it was clear that proposals for reform, however advantageous they might in practice be for a particular political party, had to bear the appearance of having some impartial non-partisan principle behind them. Palpable gerrymandering would not do.

The events of the next two years are seemingly paradoxical. The Liberals bring in a moderate Reform Bill in 1866. There is a right wing revolt against it within the party. The Conservatives in alliance with the rebels defeat the Bill. The government resigns. So far all is going according to form. But the new government, which is not as one might have expected a coalition of the anti-

THE HONEST POTBOY.

DERBY (*aside*). "DON'T FROTH IT UP THIS TIME, BEN. GOOD MEASURE—THE INSPECTORS HAVE THEIR EYE ON US."

March 16, 1867. Reproduced by permission of Punch

reform groups but a straightforward Conservative minority government, like those of 1852 and 1858-9, does not act according to form. It brings in and carries a Reform Act which by giving household suffrage in the towns extends the franchise much more widely than the Liberal Bill that the Conservatives have helped to reject only twelve months earlier.

To explain this paradox there have been three main theories. The first theory is the Liberal one that the Bill in its final form was forced on Disraeli by Gladstone; that acceptance of Gladstone's amendments widening the Bill was the price paid by an unscrupulous Tory minority ministry for staying in office. The true facts were recognised by the newly enfranchised urban householders who expressed their gratitude to Gladstone by returning the Liberals with an increased majority (up from 60 to 100) in the first election under the new Act. In a broad sense this is the theory favoured by Morley, Justin McCarthy, and G. M. Trevelyan.

The second theory which is a direct counter-blast to the first is that of 'Tory democracy'. According to this the Reform Act far from being forced on a reluctant Disraeli represented the fulfilment of his early aspirations. Had he not on frequent occasions in the 1830s maintained that the Conservatives were the truly democratic party? And in his Young England days, though contemptuous of the party that called itself Conservative, had he not seemed to advocate some kind of alliance between the aristocracy and the urban working class? It was of a somewhat hazy nature no doubt, but the Reform Act of 1867 at least on the surface seemed to be connected with it, and if the new franchise did not lead to a Conservative break through in 1868, the party indisputably triumphed in 1874. By then no doubt the urban householder had had time to see who was his true friend. The social reforms of 1875 and 1876 on one interpretation lend further colour to the view that the Conservative party was in some way appealing over the heads of the Liberal middle classes to that rather nebulous figure 'the Conservative working man'. Far from yielding to pressure in 1867, Disraeli was educating his party, and preparing it for the inevitable future.[1]

[1] The latest and ablest exponent of this general theory is Miss Gertrude Himmelfarb, an American historian. See *Journal of British Studies* (November 1966).

The third theory is that of the historians of the Labour movement – perhaps most conveniently accessible in Dr Royden Harrison's book, *Before the socialists*.[1] This lays emphasis on the degree
to which the leaders of the traditional parties were subject to
the pressure of mass working class agitation expressed through
the activities of the Reform League. According to this version the
really crucial event was the demonstration by the League in
Hyde Park on May 1867 in defiance of the government's pro-
hibition. This, it is alleged, is the direct cause of Disraeli's surrender over Hodgkinson's amendment eleven days later, i.e. the
amendment which abolished compounding and added another
400,000 potential voters to the borough electorate.

It is the achievement of Mr Maurice Cowling[2] and Dr F. B.
Smith[3] to have substituted a more convincing explanation. For, although there are points of truth and significance in all three theories,
none of them can stand by itself. Dr Smith effectively demolishes
the Gladstonian theory by showing that the amendments accepted
by Disraeli were not Gladstonian amendments. He also destroys
the Tory democracy theory which was always the least convincing of the three by demonstrating that Disraeli had no clear plan,
that he thought in terms of the old stereotypes (county = Conservative; borough = Liberal), that he was only 'educating his
party' in retrospect, that the final version of the Act though it
owed little to Gladstone was in no sense what Derby or Disraeli
intended. On the whole, Dr Smith's own explanation of events
seems to be nearer to the Labour theory than either of the
others.

Maurice Cowling's book gives the most convincing account of
what happened. He is the first person to see the full partisan
significance of the two Bills, when taken in conjunction with the
proposals for redistribution which accompanied them. The
Liberal measure of 1866 would have been extremely damaging to
the Conservatives, in spite of its relatively mild franchise provisions
– a reduction from £10 to £7 in the borough occupier franchise
and from £50 to £14 in the county. Derby described it in a letter

[1] Royden Harrison, *Before the socialists 1861-1881* (1965).
[2] Maurice Cowling, *1867, Disraeli, Gladstone and revolution* (1967).
[3] F. B. Smith, *The making of the second Reform Bill* (1966).

to a colleague as 'the extinction of the Conservative party . . .
and of the real Whigs'.[1]

This observation from a man who had spent a lifetime in
politics and who had been a member of the Whig government
which brought in the Reform Act of 1832 is not to be ignored. The
details are too complicated for discussion here. It is enough to say
that the reduction in the borough franchise, together with the
clause which added the borough leaseholders to the electorate in
the surrounding county, was bound in itself to involve some
Conservative losses, even if redistribution is entirely ignored. This
was also true of the final version of the 1867 Bill. But the redistribution provisions of the 1866 Bill, unlike those of the 1867 Act,
made matters much worse from the viewpoint of Conservatives
and 'real Whigs'.

The great hope of the Conservatives lay in their belief that
almost any redistribution was bound to increase the number of
seats in the counties which in terms of electors per M.P. were badly
under-represented. This, it was expected, would compensate for
the lowering of the franchise and certain other likely features of
redistribution such as the creation of extra seats for Scotland, for
new boroughs and for the big cities. The 1866 Bill did indeed add
seventeen seats to the counties, but not, as the Conservatives
wanted, by creating extra county divisions. Instead it turned
seventeen two-member counties into three-member constituencies
and, given the counties chosen for this addition, it is reckoned by
Mr Cowling that there would have been an actual bonus to the
Liberals of two or three seats.[2] The net effect of these and other
redistribution provisions, quite apart from the change in the
franchise, would have been enough to give the Liberals from eight
to fifteen extra seats.

These considerations illustrate the great importance which, in
that largely vanished[3] dimension of politics, attached to control
over redistribution. They also render the alleged paradox of
Derby's and Disraeli's attitude to reform a good deal less paradoxical than it seems at first sight. It made perfectly good sense for

[1] Cowling, op. cit., 70, quoting Derby Papers, 190/2, May 10, 1866.
[2] ibid.
[3] Not wholly, witness the 1969 dispute about the recommendations of the Boundary
Commission.

the Conservatives to ally with the right wing Liberals, the so-called Adullamites, in order to reject a Bill which was highly injurious to the party and then a year later to pass one which was far less so. Public opinion – not merely that of the Reform League but informed, intelligent, middle class opinion – was strongly in favour of reform, and the Conservatives could not simply sit back and do nothing. In 1867 they at least had the initiative over redistribution even if they did not have complete control. They were still in a minority and they had on occasion to defer to the House. But the Liberals were in a state of chaos thanks to Derby's and Disraeli's brilliant tactics. For a brief period the Conservatives were able to get their own way to a much greater extent than their numbers warranted.

The franchise provisions of the 1867 Act seem to have operated against the Conservatives – anyway in the next election – although it does not follow that the effect of Household suffrage was any more adverse than that of the more limited provisions of Gladstone's Bill or the abortive Ten Minute Bill. But the Conservative say in redistribution undoubtedly helped them. This is shown by the contrast between their ill fortune in constituencies where no change took place in boundaries or number of MPs and their relative prosperity in those areas of England where major changes were made. In the former the Liberals gained 25 seats (they won 57 and lost 32) – a net increase of 50 in their majority. In the fourteen counties where a large scale redistribution occurred there were in the old parliament 52 county MPs and 14 sitting for boroughs which were redistributed. Of these 66 MPs, 34 were Conservative, 32 Liberal. Under the new order the total representation rose from 66 to 87, of which 57 were Conservative. This meant a reduction of 25 in the Liberal majority, and it was a valuable offset to Liberal advantages such as the inescapable increase in Scottish representation.[1]

2

Why did the Conservatives tamper with reform at all? To understand this we must revert to the situation after the defeat of Gladstone's Bill in 1866. Indeed we must go back further. The

[1] Cowling, op. cit., 71–2.

Conservatives' great problem was to prove themselves as a viable party of government. Throughout the 1850s their position had been curiously analogous to that of the Labour party in the 1920s. Like MacDonald, Derby had to show that the new party created in 1846 – for there is a sense in which the Derby-Disraeli party was as new and untried as Labour after the First World War – was fit to rule. In 1852, the year of the 'Who? Who?' ministry, almost as many people entered the Cabinet for the first time and took their privy councillor's oath as in Ramsay MacDonald's Cabinet of 1924; and Derby's minority government lasted just about as long as MacDonald's. Their second chance in 1858 came at a similar interval of time to MacDonald's in 1929; in both cases it was again a minority administration; in both cases it ended in early defeat, although Derby's government did not break up in total disorder like MacDonald's in 1931. Perhaps because of the long shadow cast by Peel, the Right has been instinctively more cohesive than the Left, whether Liberal or Labour.

The reasons for Labour being out in the cold during the two decades after 1918 were basically the same as those which kept the Conservatives out during the two decades following the repeal of the corn laws – a deep distrust by middle of the road moderate opinion of their competence and capacity to govern. In the case of Labour, this was because the revolutionary language used by some of its supporters gave an impression of reckless irresponsibility; in the case of the Conservatives seventy years earlier, because the reactionary language of a section gave the whole party the reputation of being the 'stupid' party, likely to provoke revolution by pursuing a narrow agrarian class interest. Of course, anyone who examined the speeches and attitudes of Derby and Disraeli could see that they no more echoed the opinions of the red-faced country squires who thronged the back benches, than MacDonald and Henderson echoed those of the Clydesiders. But it was the general impression which had to be changed in each case, if the minority party was to be regarded as 'fit to govern'.

The difficulty is that the charge of being unfit to govern can only be disproved by governing; and the more the charge is believed the less chance there is of showing it to be false. Moreover, neither

Derby in the 1850s nor MacDonald in the 1920s had been particularly successful during their brief ministries. Derby's second
government was rather better than his first, but he had done
nothing to make public opinion positively prefer him to the
dominant Palmerstonian coalition. It was vital, therefore, that his
third chance should not be muffed. Palmerston was dead. Russell
and Gladstone had made a hash of their Reform Bill. The Liberal
party was split wide open. On the other hand the Conservatives
were outnumbered in the House and neither Derby nor Disraeli
believed that a general election would improve their position.[1]

In these circumstances the great need was for the Conservatives
to stay in office on their own for long enough to show at least that
they were *a* party of government, and ideally that they were *the*
party of government. These were the aims of the leaders and,
though they did not succeed in the second, for Derby never
acquired the mantle of Palmerston – nor did Disraeli, hard
though he tried – they did succeed in the first. In spite of the
election of 1868, in spite of the increased Liberal majority, the
events of the previous thirty months had permanently altered the
position of the Conservatives. They had ceased to be the 'stupid'
party. They had become a viable alternative to the still dominant,
but no longer unchallengeable Liberals.

This objective of establishing their party as a party of government explains most of the actions of Derby and Disraeli throughout
the crisis. It explains why they sabotaged in June 1866 the project
to form a fusion with the right wing of the Liberals: the Conservatives had to govern on their own; incidentally, fusion would
have been fatal to the personal position of both men, but this need
not alter one's judgment that they acted in the best interests of the
party as well as themselves. The same purpose explains why they
brought in a Reform Bill at all: it was vital to keep the Liberals
divided, and nothing was surer to do so than reform. Of course
'the climate of opinion' was relevant too, though not public
agitation which had little effect on Derby or Disraeli. But a viable
Conservative government had to show that it could move with the
times.

[1] Curiously enough Russell, and Brand, the Liberal whip, thought that the Conservatives would win if there was a dissolution. Cowling, op. cit., 131.

This aim to be a party of government also explains the form of
the Bill. It had to be based on a principle and the principle had to
appear different from Gladstone's. In reality all sides of an
intensely conservative House of Commons wanted a moderate
measure which would exclude the 'residuum' – i.e. the poorest,
most feckless and easily corruptible element in the urban working
class. The Conservative Bill based on personal payment of rates
would, with its original safeguards and restrictions, have produced
a very similar electorate to Gladstone's £7 rental limit. But it
seemed to embody a different and more democratic principle.
What was more, it seemed to provide a final resting place for the
question, whereas any named figure based on rental could always
be cut away till it was reduced to nothing at all, and turned into
straight manhood suffrage.[1] This argument had some substance.
True, Disraeli's safeguards all vanished, but household suffrage
(extended in 1885 to the counties) did remain the basis of the
electoral system for half a century. Adult male suffrage did not
come in till 1918, and female till 1928.

The same determination to keep the Liberals off balance – and
hence themselves in power – explains why Derby and Disraeli were
ready, after the first shock had worn off, to accept the resignations
of a powerful group in the Cabinet rather than put forward a Bill
which had no chance of achieving these objects. The group
consisted of Lord Cranborne, who later became 3rd Marquess of
Salisbury and leader of the party, Lord Carnarvon, a priggish
Puseyite much addicted to resignation, and Sir Robert Peel's son,
General Peel of whom Disraeli wrote to Derby, 'You will find him
very placable, except on the phrase "household suffrage", when
his eye lights up with insanity.' On February 25 as a result of
Cranborne's statistical calculations the group declared that they
must resign unless the Bill was withdrawn. Taken off balance the
Cabinet agreed to substitute a Bill based on a £6 rating franchise,
and did so only ten minutes before the party meeting at which
Derby was due to announce the proposals to a party meeting.
'The Ten Minute Bill', as it became called thanks to the indiscretion of another member of the Cabinet, Sir John Pakington,
pleased no one in the Conservative party. Worse still, it seemed to

[1] Cowling, op. cit., 172.

be a surrender not only to Cranborne's group but to Gladstone, indeed unlikely to be carried without his support. This explains why Derby and Disraeli changed their minds. It explains why Disraeli whipped up agitation among the back benches against concessions to the anti-party group in the Cabinet, thus setting a precedent for Harold Wilson's alleged intra-party activities over arms for South Africa, which so many journalists confidently said were unprecedented. It explains why Derby on March 2 accepted the resignations of ministers whom he had seemed ready to appease at great cost only five days earlier.

The leaders were perhaps lucky in that the resigning ministers were not ready to try to organise the sort of revolt that Disraeli himself, along with Bentinck, had organised against Peel twenty-one years earlier. Derby was by no means confident of the consequences of his decision. 'This is the end of the Conservative Party,' he is recorded by Lord John Manners as saying when Cranborne and his friends rose to leave the Cabinet room. But it was nothing of the sort, and, although the attacks made in the House were very bitter, especially against Disraeli personally, he survived and so did the party. Seven years later Cranborne (now Salisbury) and Carnarvon accepted Disraeli's invitation to join his Cabinet. This would not have seemed at all likely in 1867.

Desire to keep the Liberals divided probably also explains Disraeli's acceptance of Hodgkinson's amendment which in effect enfranchised all ratepayers and seemed the most sensational example of what his foes termed 'betrayal'. A cardinal feature of the Bill on its first introduction had been the restriction of the rating suffrage to those who paid their rates direct to the local authority. Disraeli had dwelt at length upon the special virtues of those who were personally responsible for their rates, contrasted with those who, in the jargon of the day, 'compounded', i.e. paid through the rent collected by their landlords. In fact Disraeli's argument was a dodge to combine a seemingly radical cry with a cautiously restrictive result – the exclusion of the 'residuum'. But it is unlikely that Disraeli himself cared greatly about the matter or feared that the enfranchisement of the compounder would necessarily damage the Conservatives, provided that he could deal with redistribution in a suitably pro-Conservative way while the

Liberals were still in a state of confusion. This meant getting on with things as quickly as possible. The Radicals had the power to filibuster, and they could have held up the Bill till an autumn session which Disraeli particularly wished to avoid for its own sake, even apart from the danger that delay would consolidate the opposition.

There may have been another reason. We are perhaps too ready to underestimate the extent to which even men as clever as Disraeli may find themselves the prisoners of their own arguments. After all Hodgkinson did not propose to enfranchise compounders. He merely proposed to abolish compounding and make every occupier personally responsible for his rates. Disraeli had never tied his colours to the retention of compounding, which was indeed open to much criticism in the form in which it was adopted. He had simply said that only those who paid direct should have the vote. Under Hodgkinson's amendment this was just what would still happen. The only difference was that there would be a great many more of them.

Perhaps it is permissible to draw a parallel with a more recent episode. When Sir Anthony Eden and M. Guy Mollet declared that their purpose in the Suez intervention was 'to separate the combatants', everyone except the inordinately naïve suspected that this was a form of words designed to cover another – and to many people entirely creditable – objective, viz, to seize control of the Suez Canal and bring down Nasser. But when after six days the combatants obviously had been separated, it was difficult to think of a plausible excuse to go on, even though the Canal zone had not been occupied and Nasser had not been brought down. No doubt there were other factors – world opinion, U.S. pressure on sterling, etc. But we should not forget the major difficulty raised by the particular *casus belli* chosen. At any rate, whatever the truth about Suez, one can see Disraeli's genuine dilemma over the compound householder.

The manœuvres of Derby and Disraeli over reform make good sense if their aim was to show that their party was fit to govern, and if they were hoping to inherit Palmerston's mantle in the changed circumstances caused by Palmerston's death.[1] The Bill

---

[1] See Cowling, op. cit., ch. IX, 'Palmerston's mantle'.

they carried was probably as conservative a measure as could have been carried by a minority Conservative government in 1867. Moreover, because of their say in redistribution, it was far less adverse to their party than any measure which the Liberals would have passed, in spite of Liberal support of a restrictive franchise.

The bid for the mantle of Palmerston was not immediately successful. The events of 1867 did, however, make the Conservatives a genuine alternative government. They also gave Disraeli personally a notable boost. When Derby retired early in 1868, Disraeli was bound to be his successor. This might not have been true two years earlier, nor one year later when the loss of the first election on the new franchise had dealt a heavy blow to his prestige. Fortunately he had by then the immense advantage of being an ex-Prime Minister – and there are only three examples in the whole of our period of a Conservative ex-Prime Minister being toppled when in opposition – Balfour in 1911, Home in 1965 and Heath in 1975. But the twice repeated efforts in 1869 and 1870 of the patrician section of the party to make Salisbury leader of the House of Lords show how shaky Disraeli's position was.[1] Had they come off, he would have been bound to resign, as no doubt Salisbury's supporters intended. The two men were not even on speaking terms, and Salisbury had recently described Disraeli in the *Quarterly Review* as 'a mere political gamester'.

But, although the Conservatives had become a plausible party of government, they did not yet look like becoming the majority party in the way that they had seemed to be under Peel in 1841 and that the Liberals really had been under Palmerston. Gladstone saw to that early in 1868 by taking up the cause of disestablishment of the Irish Church. He brilliantly turned the tables on Disraeli, and exploited one of his opponents' major weaknesses. The Conservatives had often been jeered at as the party of protestantism and protection. Maynooth and the corn laws showed the political danger of both these causes. Protectionism had been dropped, but not protestantism, i.e. defence of the Anglican Establishment interpreted in its evangelical sense which still commanded by far the greatest support in the Church.

---

[1] See E. J. Feuchtwanger, *Disraeli, democracy and the Conservative party* (1968), 4–7, for a full account of the intrigues over the leadership of the House of Lords.

Protestantism had often been a political incubus. It had caused
Bentinck's resignation in 1848. It had made a coalition with
Peelites and Irish impossible in 1852. It had wrecked Disraeli's
bid for Irish support in 1859. Derby, for all his grandeur and
insouciance, was the spirit incarnate of this attitude; his inveterate
hostility to popery in general and to Irish popery in particular
may well have enhanced his authority among the country squires,
but it positively repelled outside support.

Yet it is doubtful whether Derby's retirement early in 1868
made the situation any better. Disraeli from miscalculation made
the same error that Derby would have made from conviction; he
based his programme on identification of the cause of no-popery
with that of the Irish Church and hoped that popular uproar
would check disestablishment. Perhaps he had no choice. To
compromise over the Irish Church would have fatally split his
rank and file. When Gladstone chose the Anglican Establishment
in Ireland for attack he was no doubt acting from deep felt conviction, but he was also shrewdly moving the political battle on to
the Conservatives' weakest ground. The Church of Ireland was
predominantly evangelical, and the party was officially bound to
defend it in the last ditch. Yet its numbers and endowments were
not easily defensible in a Church ministering to only one-eighth of
the nation for which it was designed. A great many Conservatives
were uneasy about it. The Fenian troubles had made all parties in
England anxious to do something about Ireland. Disraeli's plan
had been the old one of Pitt and Castlereagh. It might be described
as levelling up instead of levelling down, for it involved concurrent
endowment of the Roman Catholic and Presbyterian Churches,
leaving the Anglican Establishment undisturbed. The difficulty
was that it also involved the tax-payer's money, and the English
tax-payer was not likely to look on expenditure for such a purpose
with any friendly eye. However, Disraeli believed that he might
succeed and at least that Cardinal Manning and the Catholic
hierarchy would be with him. But Manning, to Disraeli's anger,
ceased negotiation the moment that Gladstone announced his
plan. All hope of a Conservative alliance with the Irish vanished
overnight.

Gladstone could not have selected a better issue on which to unify his own party and divide his opponents. Whether this was the reason for his electoral victory must remain non-proven, for we know so little about the psephology of a century ago. But it seems certain that in England Disraeli's appeal fell flat, except in Lancashire, and at least probable that the big jump in the Liberal majority in Ireland (from 5 in 1865 to 25 in 1868) was a direct result of Gladstone's espousal of Irish disestablishment. It probably helped him in Scotland too where in any case the extra seats created by the Reform Act were bound to be advantageous (in 1865 the Liberal share was 41 out of 53 seats, in 1868 it was 52 out of 60 – a rise in their Scottish majority of 15). In fact the Liberal gain was mainly in the Celtic fringe, for their numbers also went up from 18 out of 29 in Wales to 22 out of 30.

Yet, although their English majority remained virtually the same, 17 instead of 25, there were some important changes within it. The Liberals made substantial gains in the big cities, but these were offset by two significant movements in favour of the Conservatives which are shown on Table D on page 112. The first was in Lancashire and Cheshire, where, as we already saw, the existence of a large Irish immigrant population had caused a Protestant anti-Irish reaction even in 1865 against the party which seemed more closely identified with the Irish. The extension of the franchise to working class householders, together with Gladstone's policy of disestablishment, greatly strengthened this trend. In 1859 the Conservatives won 15 out of the 36 seats in the two counties. In 1865 the figures had risen to 18, and in 1868 the Conservatives won no less than 31 out of the 46 seats allocated to the two counties by the new Reform Act. The second movement, which was even more significant for the future, was that of middle class opinion in the south. It was shown in Westminster where W. H. Smith, himself a symbol of the change, for he had been a Palmerstonian in 1865, defeated J. S. Mill, and in Middlesex where Lord George Hamilton ousted Henry Labouchere, although only the year before the seat had seemed so hopeless that no Conservative candidate could be found to fight it. It was the beginning of a slow move of both the world of business and that of suburban villadom away from the Liberal party – a move which was to contribute much to the Conservative ascendancy at the end of the century.

Table D

Table to show Conservative break-through 1859-1900 in (1) London, and (2) Lancashire and Cheshire, contrasted with (3) Yorkshire. Conservative members only are given (total seats for each area in brackets)

	Total 1859	1865	1868	1874	1880	1885	1886	1892	1895	1900
(1) London	(18) 0	0	(22) 3	10	8	(59) 35	47	36	51	51
(2) Lancashire and Cheshire	(36) 15	(38) 18	(46) 31	34	19	(69) 46	58	45	60	56
(3) Yorkshire	(37) 14	(39) 14	(40) 13	(38) 17	8	(52) 16	20	16	21	26

3

But however significant these developments may seem in retrospect, at the time they seemed a very thin lining to a very large black cloud. Gladstone was at the head of a triumphant majority. For the moment there was nothing much to do and Disraeli very sensibly decided to do nothing much. He played it cool and settled down to write a satirical novel, *Lothair*, in which he could at least get his own back on Manning. Of course there were the usual complaints from those who wanted 'instant' opposition. Disraeli's stock sank low during the next three years. Although the attempt to make Salisbury leader in the House of Lords as a lever to dislodge him failed and the Duke of Richmond, an amiable nonentity, was elected instead, it was a serious matter that the attempt should have been made at all.

In 1871 there was a strong move to persuade Disraeli to resign in favour of Derby's son, who succeeded his father as 15th Earl in 1869. The new earl, an addict of the Blue Book and Mechanics' Institutes rather than the Stud Book and the turf, was a totally different character from the old earl. He was at heart a Liberal, but he was paralysed by his frightening father who seems to have viewed his son with a curious mixture of affection and contempt, and who disliked his close relationship with Disraeli. The son once paid an unexpected visit to Knowsley where he found Lord Derby in the middle of a game of billiards. 'What brings you here, Edward?' was the earl's genial greeting, 'Are you going to get married, or has Disraeli slit his throat?' It is more than likely that Stanley would have joined Palmerston if he had been a free agent. He was offered office by Russell in 1865 but refused. More than anyone else he seemed the possible leader of a government of fusion in 1866. He had a much greater appeal to the floating vote than Disraeli, and his status in society made him more acceptable to the Tory faithful than an adventurer like Disraeli could hope to be until he justified himself by that success which in politics guarantees the forgiveness of all other sins. Gerard Noel, the Chief Whip, told some of the shadow Cabinet in February 1872 that Derby's name alone would be worth forty or fifty seats. But no one dared tell Disraeli this, and neither he nor Derby made any move.

Then quite suddenly Disraeli decided to assert himself. He had been by no means as inactive as he had seemed, even before this. The party organisation, on his initiative, was to some extent over-hauled by J. E. Gorst. To what extent is open to argument. But the Central Office with Gorst as Principal Agent and a forgotten but very able figure, the Hon. C. K. Keith-Falconer as secretary, was undoubtedly a more efficient instrument than Disraeli's personal firm of solicitors which had been originally chosen to deal with its client's finances rather than with the electoral management of a great political party.[1] Gorst and Keith-Falconer succeeded in fielding far more candidates in the 1874 election than ever before. In 1868 and 1874 about half the 650 or so seats in parliament were virtually uncontested in the sense that one of the two major parties was not in the battle at all. But, whereas in 1868 the Liberals had nearly twice as many walkovers as the Conservatives (213 compared with 116), in 1874 the pro-portions had sharply changed. Uncontested Conservative seats rose from 116 to 178; uncontested Liberal seats declined from 213 to 150. Altogether the Conservatives seem to have put between 40 and 50 more candidates in the field in 1874, whereas the Liberals had some 70 fewer.

The other important organisational change was the creation of the National Union of Conservative and Constitutional Asso-ciations in 1867. This was designed originally as a means of organ-ising the newly enfranchised working class men in the boroughs. At the time its significance did not seem very great. It was only one of a number of similar movements and organisations, and it got off to a poor start. The first annual conference was fixed with remarkable fatuity to take place four days after Christmas 1868. Not surprisingly only six members, apart from the chairman, Lord Dartmouth, turned up. It was Disraeli who put the National Union on the map. He made it his audience on two important occasions in 1872. The first of these was his speech on May 3 to a gathering of the Lancashire associations at the Free Trade Hall, Manchester. The desirability of Disraeli making some major pro-nouncement in this electorally promising area had long been can-

[1] For a fuller discussion of party organisation, see below, pp. 137–49.

vassed. It is a measure of his unpopularity that the invitation had not been issued much earlier, as Disraeli had hoped. In the event the delay may well have been beneficial. It resulted in Disraeli striking at just the right psychological moment when Gladstone was running out of steam and into trouble. He followed up his first blow with a second only seven weeks later, on June 24, when he addressed the London Conference of the National Union at the Crystal Palace.

The nature and effect of these two pronouncements have been to some extent distorted in retrospect. They do not constitute some kind of political charter like the Labour party's in 1918, nor even a positive programme, like the Liberals' Newcastle programme of 1891. Disraeli devoted most of his time to an essentially destructive theme; the ineptitude of the government, the harrassing and unsettling nature of its legislation, the dangerous attitude of its left wing. For Gladstone since 1868 had been engaged in a major programme of what would nowadays be called 'modernisation'. It was the overdue process of removing from the nation's institutions some of the ancient dust and cobwebs which had lain undisturbed for generations past. The army, the universities, the civil service, the judiciary, the Irish Church, the Irish land law, the conduct of elections, had all been reformed. Disraeli had been careful not to associate himself with the defence of really flagrant abuses, but he was fully prepared to take advantage of the mood of discontent, injured interests, and vague uneasiness about the future, which Liberal reforming zeal had created. And the extreme Left, then as always, provided an excellent target. In particular, the republicanism of some Radicals was a constant embarrassment to Gladstone. Here was a chance such as Palmerston never afforded for the Conservatives to be a voice and not an echo.

If this was true in home affairs it was even truer in external policy. To a great many people Gladstone here was an unwelcome contrast with Palmerston. He accepted the award of the arbitrators in the case of the *Alabama*, a southern warship which had escaped from Liverpool in the American Civil War and inflicted great damage on northern shipping. To many people the damages paid to the American government seemed grossly

THE CONSERVATIVE PROGRAMME.

"DEPUTATION BELOW, SIR.—WANT TO KNOW THE CONSERVATIVE PROGRAMME."

RT. HON. BEN. DIZ. "EH?—OH!—AH!—YES!—QUITE SO! TELL THEM, MY GOOD ABERCORN, WITH MY COMPLIMENTS, THAT WE PROPOSE TO RELY ON THE SUBLIME INSTINCTS OF AN ANCIENT PEOPLE!!"

[*See Speech at Crystal Palace.*

July 6, 1872. Reproduced by permission of Punch

excessive. There was also Russia's decision in 1870 to abrogate the clauses of the Treaty of Paris of 1856 which after the Crimean War forbade a Russian navy in the Black Sea. Britain could and did do nothing, but Gladstone's popularity was not enhanced. Finally there was Britain's palpable impotence during the Franco-Prussian War. All these episodes seemed signs of either feebleness or of the postponement of British interests to some sort of higher moral and international law. Many Liberals, moreover, appeared to display a certain shamefacedness, if not positive guilt, towards the overseas Empire. In all these fields Disraeli was an instinctive Palmerstonian. He had the intense alien patriotism not infrequently found among people whose country is in a sense adopted and not really their own; and with it went an acute dislike of those genuinely British figures who seemed to be letting down the side and who ought to have known better. This was largely what prompted Disraeli's emphasis on empire in both his speeches, and his attacks on Gladstone's foreign policy right up to the general election.

Disraeli did not say very much about empire to the National Union and what he said was vague. He said little more about social reform – the other question in which he is usually supposed to have made a major initiative; and here too he was equally unspecific. Not that vagueness should be regarded as a reproach. Disraeli had heeded the warning of his old chief against what Derby considered Bentinck's besetting sin 'of starting detailed projects when in opposition'.[1] But Disraeli did sound a new note when he declared that the English people would be idiots if they had not 'long perceived that the time had arrived when social and not political improvement is the object which they ought to pursue'.

This was a perfectly sensible bid for working class support. But it would be untrue to suppose that Gladstone had wholly neglected social reform, or to imagine that the Conservative measures in that field, largely enacted in 1875 and 1876, represented any departure of principle from what was regarded as acceptable by orthodox reasonably enlightened opinion on both sides. This is not to decry

[1] Derby to Disraeli, September 22, 1849, quoted, W. F. Monypenny and G. E. Buckle, *The life of Benjamin Disraeli Earl of Beaconsfield*, 6 vols (1910–20), III, 215–16.

their value, merely to put them into perspective. Electorally Disraeli's move can be seen as designed to conciliate the newly enfranchised borough voter. Moreover, some of Gladstone's reforms, being characteristically actuated by what he considered good for the lower classes rather than what they wanted, were far from popular. His Education Act had stirred up a sectarian hornets' nest. His Trades Union legislation dissatisfied the leaders of organised labour. His Licensing Act, though it did not, as Professor Hanham shows, have the cataclysmic electoral effect attributed to it by Sir Robert Ensor, was anything but a vote winner.[1]

To sum up, in 1872 and 1873 Disraeli was able to do something that no Conservative leader had done since Peel: to present his party as having not only a distinctive colour and style, but also a broad-based appeal on the one hand to the working class, on the other – and this was much more important – to the forces of property everywhere, not simply the landed interest, as a bulwark against the harassing, disturbing, restless legislation of the Liberals. At the same time – and perhaps this was even more significant – he boldly staked the claim of the Conservatives to be 'the patriotic party', something that could never be established while Palmerston lived.

It would be rash to say that this was why he won the election of 1874. Improved Conservative organisation and poor Liberal organisation must have played their part together with Gladstone's singularly inept timing of the dissolution. Divisions and dissatisfaction within the Liberal fold also contributed to the disaster, though it is fair to say that Disraeli exploited them to the full. Whatever the cause, the result was a complete reversal of 1868. The Conservatives swept the English counties where the Liberals only held 27 seats out of 180. They made striking gains in the bigger boroughs all over the U.K. If we define these as having a population of over 50,000 in 1871, there were 114. The Conservative share rose from 25 to 44. The party had a majority in

---

[1] H. J. Hanham, *Elections and party management: politics in the time of Disraeli and Gladstone* (1959), 222–5, demolishes the theory of R. C. K. Ensor, *England 1870–1914* (1936), 21–2, that a great movement by the publicans swung the results of the 1874 election and that henceforth the liquor interest was the principal source of Conservative funds. Long after 1874 the landed aristocracy continued to be the main suppliers of the Conservative sinews of war. See below, p. 143.

England of 110; in Scotland the Conservatives rose from 7 to 19 and they profited from the success of the new Home Rule party in Ireland, whose 51 seats were mostly won from the Liberals. In the whole U.K. the Conservatives had a majority of 50 over Liberals and Home Rulers added together. There were 352 Conservatives, 243 Liberals and 57 Home Rulers. The previous election had returned 279 Conservatives and 379 Liberals.[1]

This is not the place to describe the details of Disraeli's ministry. From the point of view of party history it is enough to say that, though he established no Palmerstonian or Baldwinian ascendancy, he confirmed the verdict of 1866-8 that the Conservatives were an alternative party of government. His Cabinet, man for man, was quite as able as Gladstone's. If he did not possess Gladstone's genius for legislation or his volcanic energy, these qualities were less necessary in a party brought to power largely by a reaction against exuberant activity. In the field of social reform valuable work was done, though, owing to Disraeli's unreadiness for victory and his propensity to leave initiative to his ministers, scarcely anything happened during the first session. It was in foreign policy that he achieved most, but it was here too that he provoked the bitterest hostility.

Disraeli had no sympathy with the notion that political questions are basically ones of morality. Gladstone took the opposite view, and the conflict has coloured the struggle between Left and Right from that day to this. Unluckily for Disraeli, he lived at a time when great moral explosions were liable to convulse the country. Gladstone could seem on occasions the very embodiment of moral fervour. It is hard to overestimate the formidable, indeed terrifying effect as of some Old Testament prophet that he had on those who met him. The Bulgarian atrocity campaign of 1876, prompted by Turkish massacres of their Christian subjects in what is now Bulgaria, was the greatest of all expressions of the 'Nonconformist Conscience', and it created a confrontation as bitter as anything in recent history; Gladstone standing for what he believed to be the higher moral law, Disraeli for what he considered to be the 'permanent and abiding interests of England', which he

---

[1] The difference in the total number of seats is explained by the disfranchisement of Beverley (2), Bridgwater (2), Sligo (1) and Cashel (1) in 1869.

equated with the preservation of Turkey as a bulwark against Russian expansion.

Being tough and in office with a majority ('the best repartee' as he once described it) Disraeli got his way and brought back 'peace with honour' from Berlin. But it is the way of the world that those who defend the cause of *realpolitik* against moral arguments may, if they are careless or if their opponents are skilful, appear to be positively condoning immorality. Gladstone managed to equate in many people's minds the cause of empire with the cause of evil, and when two expensive and initially disastrous campaigns (the Afghan and Zulu wars of 1879) had to be fought on the confines of empire largely because of the 'prancing proconsuls' on the spot disobeying orders, he had the further charges of waste and incompetence to add to that of wickedness. Hence the apparent success of the two Midlothian campaigns at the end of 1879 and at the election of 1880, when Gladstone successfully challenged the sitting member for Midlothian, the Earl of Dalkeith, son of the greatest Conservative landowner in Scotland, the Duke of Buccleugh, and used the occasion for a whirlwind denunciation of Disraeli's foreign and imperial policy.

Yet, although Gladstone may well have projected a picture of Disraeli's extravagance, gaudiness and lack of principle, he would not have been so successful in 1880 but for the industrial and agricultural depression which had been growing deeper during the last two years of the ministry. 'Hard times' Disraeli believed to be the cause of his downfall. He may have been right. The agricultural depression raised the whole question of re-enacting protection. Disraeli wisely rejected it. The urban working class suffering from unemployment and finding its only consolation in cheaper food would never have tolerated measures which made it dearer. Roughly 70 per cent of working class budgets went on food and drink, and these items accounted for as much as 45 per cent even of middle class budgets. By enfranchising the urban working class householder in 1867 Disraeli, the defender of protection in 1846, had made its revival electorally impossible. But by refusing he weakened the party's position in its traditional stronghold – the English counties where the Conservatives lost no less than 27 seats. The party's organisation was badly run down too for reasons which will be discussed in the next chapter. Nor was Disraeli's election address very inspiring. It contained nothing about social reform on which he could legitimately have congratulated himself, and was principally concerned with cryptic warnings about the danger of Irish separatism. Although the warning was to come true remarkably soon, it seemed a mere chimera to most people in 1880 and only served to alienate even further the Irish vote in England. These factors, along with the setbacks in India and Africa, are quite enough to explain the disaster that followed. Even Lancashire let down the Tory cause, and things went well only in south-east England. The Liberals made a net gain of 103 seats which gave them 353 to the Conservatives' 238, while the Home Rulers rose from 51 to 61.

Un-English though he was, Disraeli had one quality on which Englishmen pride themselves. He was a good loser. He did not repine or recriminate, or throw up the leadership in a huff, as Gladstone seemed to the public to have done in 1875. Old and ill, he accepted the unanimous request of a party conclave to continue.

The situation [he wrote to Lord Lytton] requires youth and energy. When they are found – and they will be found – I shall make my bow. In the meantime I must act as if I were still young and vigorous and take all steps in my power to sustain the spirit and restore the discipline of the Tory party. They have existed for more than a century and a half as an organized political connexion & having survived the loss of the American colonies, the first Napoleon & Lord Grey's Reform Act, they must not be snuffed out.

I prophesy [he ended] as becomes one in the sunset of life – or rather I should say the twilight of existence.[1]

But he did not behave like this at all. He completed a new novel, *Endymion*, for which he received the largest publisher's advance hitherto recorded, and he began another – a lampoon on Gladstone, very funny but, alas, never completed. He gave confident and totally misleading advice to the Queen on her constitutional position (luckily she did not act on it). He led his party in the

[1] Blake, *Disraeli*, 721-2, quoting Knebworth Papers.

House of Lords with vigour and aplomb. He attended a series of fashionable routs in London. It could not last. The winter and spring were among the coldest in the century. Returning from a dinner party he caught a chill, and died of bronchitis a month later on April 21, 1881. The true significance of his career has been and will be endlessly debated. At least there must be agreement that he remains the most extraordinary, incongruous, fascinating, fresh and timeless figure ever to have led the Conservative party.

What had Disraeli achieved for his party? It is a measure of the enigma of his career that there is no agreed answer to this question. One can certainly say that, if he wrecked the party in 1846, he had gone a long way towards rebuilding it by the end of his life. The Conservatives were a party of government between the second and third Reform Acts, whereas they had not been one in the twenty years after the repeal of the corn laws. The change cannot be attributed to the ability of a single individual. There was an element of chance in personalities; the replacement of Palmerston by Gladstone gave an opening which might not otherwise have come. There were, moreover, deep social currents moving favourably for the Conservatives, and these were largely outside the control of any single person.

Disraeli had a measure of luck, but the test of a political leader is his ability to exploit his luck, and on this test Disraeli comes out well. He carried the Reform Act of 1867 without splitting his party. Could Peel have done it? If Disraeli lost the ensuing general election the reason was that the cards were so heavily stacked against him that he could have done nothing else. He had at any rate the good sense to keep calm after defeat, wait on events and hit back at the right moment. He also showed that he had learned not to snatch. His refusal to take office in 1873 was an act of notable sagacity, the more remarkable because it was by no means in keeping with his previous character. The victory of 1874 owed as much to his prudence and patience as to his capacity to dazzle with new ideas and fresh proposals.

His achievement in office has been exaggerated by some writers. Dr Paul Smith,[1] however, has analysed his social legislation more

[1] *Disraelian Conservatism and social reform.*

clearly and convincingly than any previous historian. Without belittling the Conservative performance in this field, which was undoubtedly very considerable, he shows that it had little connection with Disraeli's early Tory philosophy, and that it was neither a rebellion against conventional wisdom, nor a revival of Tory paternalism, nor a precursor of redistributive state intervention in the interest of the have-nots. In fact one has only to word the suggestion like this to see its essential improbability. Apart from anything else, collectivism of that sort would have clashed with a far deeper conviction of Disraeli – his detestation of centralisation, bureaucracy and the whole of that side of Benthamism which is associated with the name of Sir Edwin Chadwick, the great civil servant and health reformer. Disraeli believed strongly and quite consistently throughout his life in a Burkean concept of diversity, multiplicity of centres of power, the importance of independent institutions like the Church, the universities, the county Bench, etc. Indeed those who seek a lesson from Disraeli to the modern Conservative party in the sphere of domestic policy are better advised to look at that side of his philosophy than at his social legislation.

The principal Conservative measures – the Sale of Food and Drugs Act, the Public Health Act, the Artisans' Dwellings Act, the Rivers' Pollution Act, the Factory Acts of 1874 and 1875, the labour legislation of 1875 – did not differ very greatly from the type of legislation which a Liberal government might have carried. They added up to a substantial instalment of social reform, but not to a major new departure. Disraeli took up the social cry in opposition largely because there was a general movement in that direction and partly because it was likely to divide the Liberals. In office he was bound to do something about it. The electoral situation made complete negativism a recipe for disaster. But there was no question of a Tory–working class alliance of the mode advocated by Sadler nearly half a century earlier. The working class was kept at arms length. In the election of 1880 the National Union was a feeble affair compared with the Liberal Caucus, which under Joseph Chamberlain's rule was a tail that wagged the dog.

The truth was that a really vigorous policy of paternalistic

collectivism on behalf of the working class ran into direct conflict
with another great electoral force which was moving, almost
without the need for any special Conservative effort, into the
Conservative party. The middle classes began to be frightened
by Gladstonian liberalism, as Gladstone's ministry approached
its end. This may seem surprising in view of the number of
measures which he carried in their interest – reforms of the
judicature, the universities, the civil service and the army, for
example. But gratitude is not a characteristic of voters. Having
got much of what they wanted from the Liberals, the middle class
began to be alarmed at working class militancy, Joseph Chamberlain's radicalism, Sir Charles Dilke's republicanism, and other
manifestations which a Conservative government under Disraeli
seemed more likely to check than Gladstone, however much he
personally disapproved. Disraeli knew what he was doing when he
revived all the traditional Conservative slogans about the monarchy, Church and constitution. It was vital to avoid doing anything which would frighten away these new allies. A quiet, low
temperature election is nearly always better for the Conservatives
than their opponents. Gladstone was able to raise the temperature
high in 1868 and to fever pitch in 1880, but he could not do it in 1874.

The middle class was susceptible to one appeal which also
affected the working class. The patriotic card which Palmerston
had played with such effect was played no less effectively by
Disraeli. It had the great advantage over social questions that it
involved no conflict of interest, and fitted into the whole concept
of 'one nation', that repudiation of class warfare which was one of
Disraeli's great themes. No one can prove it for certain, but, apart
from straight conservatism – and we should never underestimate
its strength in all classes – this was probably the most effective
vote-winner for Disraeli and perhaps his most notable long term
contribution to the future success of the Conservative party. It did
not always work. Gladstone persuaded the electorate in 1880 that
it was immoral. Campbell-Bannerman and his colleagues managed to do much the same in 1906, although in both cases there
were other reasons also for the Conservative defeat. But those
elections were abnormal. 'Patriotism' since the late 1860s has
usually been a valuable weapon in the Conservative armoury.

This had not always been the case. At times in opposition to Palmerston, the Conservative leaders had taken almost a 'Little-Englander' line. Disraeli was in favour of a pacific policy towards the end of the Crimean War, though he was overruled by Derby. Derby himself attacked Palmerston's high-handed attitude towards China in 1857. It is true that Disraeli on that occasion was more wary. He remembered how Palmerston had extricated himself when he was attacked for throwing Britain's weight behind the dubious cause of Don Pacifico seven years before. Nevertheless, he put his doubts aside and joined with Gladstone and all the leading statesmen of the day in attacking and defeating the government in the House of Commons. It was a Pyrrhic victory, for Palmerston at once dissolved on the patriotic cry and easily won the ensuing election. A few months later the boot was on the other foot and Palmerston was ousted for being insufficiently John Bullish over the Orsini affair. But he did not make that mistake again and for the six years of his last ministry the Conservatives once again found themselves out-trumped by 'the most English minister', as Palmerston was once described.

If the Conservatives could lay no special claim to be the patriotic party while Palmerston lived, still less could they be described as 'the party of Empire'. No doubt there was a sense in which no party could claim that description in the first half of Queen Victoria's reign. Apart from India, which was considered to be a necessary if troublesome buttress of British strength and therefore had to be kept at all costs, the colonies were in general regarded in the light of the 'ripe fruit' theory. It was assumed that they would drop off the tree in due course. This was the logical corollary of the triumph of the Manchester school, and the main object of the Colonial Office was to ensure that, when the white dependencies achieved inevitable self-government, their departure should occur in an atmosphere of friendliness and goodwill, not bitterness and revolt, as with the American Colonies.[1]

The Conservatives evinced no sign of deviating from this orthodoxy. Disraeli called the colonies 'millstones round our neck' on one occasion, and on another asked, 'What is the use of these colonial deadweights which we do not govern?' And he went

[1] A. P. Thornton, *The imperial idea and its enemies* (1959), 9.

on in the same letter to Derby, 'Leave the Canadians to defend themselves; recall the African squadron; give up the settlements on the west coast of Africa; and we shall make a saving which will at the same time enable us to build ships and have a good budget.'[1] These highly Gladstonian sentiments expressed as late as 1866 read oddly in the light of subsequent attitudes. Even India did not seem such a bright jewel as she was to become later. In 1858 it fell to a Conservative government to legislate for the future governance of India after the mutiny, but the party leaders showed no particular relish in bringing that most strange and exotic of all British possessions under the direct rule of the Crown. It was a very different matter eighteen years later when Disraeli made the Queen empress of India.

The emergence of the Conservatives as the party of England and empire can be dated, in so far as one can ever date these things precisely, from Disraeli's famous speeches in 1872. At the Manchester Free Trade Hall on April 3 he condemned Gladstone for his dealings with Russia over the Black Sea clauses of the Treaty of Paris and with America over the *Alabama* arbitration. He repudiated any propensity on his own part to 'a turbulent and aggressive diplomacy'. England's policy towards Europe, he said,

. . . should be a policy of reserve but proud reserve; and in answer to those statesmen, those mistaken statesmen, who have intimated the decay of England and the decline of her resources I express here my conviction that there never was a moment in our history when the power of England was so great and her resources so vast and inexhaustible. And yet, gentlemen, it is not merely our fleets and armies, our powerful artillery, our accumulated capital, and our unlimited credit on which I so much depend, as upon the unbroken spirit of her people, which I believe was never prouder of the Imperial country to which they belong.

He took up the imperial theme much more strongly at the Crystal Palace on June 24.

If you look at the history of this country since the advent of

---
[1] Monypenny and Buckle, *Disraeli*, IV, 478.

Liberalism – forty years ago – you will find that there has been no effort so continuous, so subtle, supported by so much energy, and carried on with so much ability and acumen, as the attempts of Liberalism to effect the disintegration of the Empire of England. And, gentlemen, of all its efforts this is the one which has been the nearest to success. . . . When those subtle views were adopted of granting self-government to the Colonies I confess that I myself thought that the tie was broken. Not that I for one object to self-government: I cannot conceive how our distant Colonies can have their affairs administered except by self-government.

But self-government, in my opinion, when it was conceded ought to have been conceded as part of a great policy of Imperial consolidation.

And Disraeli went on to adumbrate in a famous passage ideas to which Joseph Chamberlain was to give a more precise – indeed in electoral terms disastrously precise – articulation thirty years later: an imperial tariff, 'a representative council in the metropolis' and a military code of mutual defence, under which not only could the colonies call on the mother country for aid but vice versa.

All this, however, was omitted because those who advised that policy – and I believe their convictions were sincere – looked upon the Colonies of England, looked even upon our connection with India as a burden upon this country; viewing everything in a financial aspect and totally passing by those moral and political considerations which make nations great, and by the influence of which alone men are distinguished from animals.

Well what has been the result of this attempt during the reign of Liberalism for the disintegration of the Empire? It has entirely failed. But how has it failed? Through the sympathy of the Colonies for the Mother Country. They have decided that the Empire shall not be destroyed; and in my opinion no Minister in this country will do his duty who neglects any opportunity of reconstructing as much as possible our Colonial Empire, and of responding to those distant sympathies which may become the source of incalculable strength and happiness to this land.

Disraeli was sounding quite a new note – one that no English statesman of the top rank had ever struck before. True, he did little to implement these shadowy proposals after he had achieved power. But here, for whatever reason, he may have been right. When a concrete programme of imperial unity with its attendant drawbacks and sacrifices was put to the British public, it fell flat. Although Joseph Chamberlain's campaign for tariff reform may not have been the only cause of the landslide of 1906, it was certainly *a* cause. But Disraeli by being less specific was more successful. He managed, with remarkable prescience and no small degree of adaptability, to acquire for the Conservatives a monopoly in the partisan expression of a new *Zeitgeist* – the inchoate, half-romantic, half-predatory emotions and ideas inspired by the idea of empire during the last quarter of the nineteenth century. While these ideas remained vague and almost mystical they had an appeal to the imagination, which constituted one of the party's great assets. For a whole political generation the 'spirit of the time' had been puffing in the wake of the Liberal party. Now for the first time it was giving a fair wind to the Tories.

It was a very easy step from the claim that the Conservative party was the guardian of patriotism and of national and imperial unity to the claim that the Liberals were consciously pursuing the opposite policy, and that they were, as Professor McKenzie puts it in his fascinating study of working class Toryism 'in some sense a deliberately divisive force in the national community, the champions of sectional rather than national interests, and utterly to be distrusted where the fate of the nation's institutions and its imperial interests are concerned'.[1] Professor McKenzie's analysis of the popular polemical literature put out by the National Union shows how quickly the Conservatives made this argument one of the principal points in their propaganda.[2] The controversy aroused by the eastern crisis of 1876-8 gave an excellent oppor-

[1] Robert McKenzie and Allan Silver, *Angels in marble, working class Conservatives in urban England* (1968), 48.
[2] ibid., 51-73.

tunity to charge Gladstone and that element of the Liberal party, which supported him, with pro-Russianism, cowardice and lack of patriotism. When the same issue under another guise came up ten years later in the form of Irish Home Rule, the word 'traitor' was freely bandied about and applied even to Gladstone himself.

It goes without saying that these charges in their crude popular propagandist form had no substance. This is of course equally true of the counter-allegations made by the Liberals against Disraeli. Gladstone did not aim at the disintegration of the British Empire any more than Disraeli opposed the 'Atrocitarians' because of his Judaic detestation of Christian liberty. In fact the cause of imperialism was powerfully supported by some Liberals. Sir Charles Dilke's *Greater Britain*, published in 1868, was one of the first expositions of the imperial creed and he stood well to the left of the Liberal party. Lord Milner and Joseph Chamberlain, the two greatest imperialists of their day, began their careers as Radical-Liberals.

Nevertheless, the Liberal party under Gladstone was vulnerable to a less crude accusation by the supporters of empire. Granted that he did not wish to abandon it, in fact for a host of practical reasons could not do so even if he had wished, there remained the danger that he would pursue the imperial cause in a lukewarm, grudging spirit. Liberal imperialists were exceptions to a general rule of unenthusiastic, half-guilty acquiescence in the burden of empire. Nor should it be forgotten that a vociferous section of the Liberal party, though not the leaders, had long regarded with the profoundest suspicion almost any actions overseas by any government. Cobden and Bright, in the words of N. McCord, all too often 'seemed to start from the prejudice that anything done by their fellow countrymen abroad was likely to be evil, while conversely they were ever ready to accord to headhunters in Borneo or to a Burmese King the attributes of the noble savage'.[1] Their attitude during the Crimean War brought them to the nadir of popularity. With Palmerston at its head the Liberal party was in no serious danger of being tarred by the brush of anti-nationalism. Twenty years later when Gladstone was thundering denunciations

[1] N. McCord, 'Cobden and Bright, 1846–1857', in Robert Robson (ed.), *Ideas and institutions of Victorian Britain, essays in honour of George Kitson Clark* (1967).

of a Tory policy which seemed on the verge of producing a second
Crimean War, the picture was rather different.

That, then, is Disraeli's most lasting contribution to the success
of his party. He made it the 'national party'. It cannot be said that
this was an inevitable development. The most plausible alternative
leader to Disraeli in the 1870s had been the 15th Earl of Derby.
He certainly would not have led the party in that direction, even
if Disraeli was a trifle unfair when, after Derby's departure to the
Liberals, he rounded on his old friend and declared, 'I do not
know that there is anything that would excite enthusiasm in him
except when he contemplates the surrender of some national
possession.'[1] But Disraeli set a tradition from which the party has
never deviated. Again and again in the years to come the Conservatives were to try to pin the label of spiritual treason upon first
their Liberal then their Labour opponents, and if they did not
always succeed, they managed to do it often enough to make this
one of their most profitable moves in the party game. The Home
Rulers, the pro-Boers, the pro-Russians exposed by the Zinoviev
Letter, the Labour 'weaklings' denounced by Winston Churchill
in 1951 for surrendering to Iran and Egypt – one can multiply
examples. Nor was it simply a trick or a gimmick. If the 'Left' has
so often found itself pilloried as the anti-national party, this is because it has so often contained members who behaved as if they
were the friends of every country except their own. It is only a
superficial paradox that Disraeli, the least English of Englishmen,
should have been the person to ram the lesson home.

[1] In a speech in the House of Lords, March 1, 1881. Quoted, Monypenny and Buckle,
Disraeli, VI, 604.

CHAPTER V

Tory democracy and the rule of Lord Salisbury 1881–1902

I

The dominant figure of the next twenty-one years was Lord Salisbury.[1] He was the most successful of all the Conservative leaders in the period covered by this book, if we regard success as measured by the electoral performance of the party he led. He fought five general elections and won three of them easily. Of his two defeats, one – that of 1892 – was only marginal and profited his opponents little, while the other – that of 1885 – was reversed within seven months. Lord Salisbury led the Conservative peers for twenty-one years, the party as a whole for seventeen. He was Prime Minister for thirteen and a half years, and for just over eleven of these held the Foreign Office as well. It was a remarkable record. Only Baldwin, who also won three out of five elections, approaches it. But he had nothing like so long a tenure of the premiership.

Yet, although a major break-through occurred under his lead, Salisbury never seems to have had quite the place in the Conservative pantheon which one would have expected. Perhaps this is because he is so difficult to fit into any kind of stereotype. Peel is the middle-of-the-road reformer, Derby the dashing patrician, Disraeli the romantic adventurer, Balfour the intellectual in

[1] One of the great gaps in nineteenth century political biography is the lack of a satisfactory life of him. This is not to disparage his daughter's work – Lady Gwendolen Cecil, *The life of Robert Marquis of Salisbury*, vols I, II (1921), III, IV (1931) – which does indeed give a wonderful personal portrait such as we rarely have of any major statesman. But her four volumes end in 1892, and neither in their account of foreign policy nor in their account of Salisbury's relations with his party can they be regarded as wholly satisfactory.

politics, Bonar Law the new man representing in Tory terms a
new political class, Baldwin the liberal conciliator, Churchill the
war leader and the Chatham of his age. No doubt these stereotypes
are far from fitting satisfactorily and need many modifications if
they are to correspond with reality. The problem with Salisbury is
to think of any stereotype at all. Perhaps the nearest we can reach
is that of the aloof, sceptical inheritor of a great name and a
famous house, standing rock-like in the advancing tide of democracy, emblem of a vanishing world and, though a great Foreign
Minister, essentially negative, indeed reactionary in home affairs.

Certainly Salisbury took a sombre, almost fatalistic, view of the
secular world. He was deeply religious in his outlook and it was
this which gave him much of his strength. There is a memorable
passage in his daughter's biography which describes how he told
his family one day that he simply did not understand what his
recent guests meant when they condoled with him on 'the burden
of responsibility' that he had to bear.

> There were exclamations of protest from members of the family
> and he proceeded to explain further. He was about to start upon
> a walk and was standing at the moment at the open door, look-
> ing out upon the threatening clouds of an autumn afternoon. 'I
> don't understand,' he repeated, 'what people mean when they
> talk of the burden of responsibility. I should understand if they
> spoke of the burden of decision – I feel it now, trying to make
> up my mind whether or no to take a great coat with me. I feel
> it in exactly the same way, but no more, when I am writing a
> despatch upon which war or peace may depend. Its degree
> depends upon the materials for decision that are available and
> not in the least upon the magnitude of the results which may
> follow.' Then, after a moment's pause and in a lower tone, he
> added, 'With the results I have nothing to do.'[1]

It was a very different attitude from his predecessor's although
one could perhaps imagine Gladstone sharing it, but one cannot
see even Gladstone writing the following passage – in 1872
apropos of the Irish question.

---

[1] Lady G. Cecil, *Salisbury*, I, 118–19.

The optimist view of politics assumes that there must be some remedy for every political ill, and rather than not find it, will make two hardships to cure one. If all equitable remedies have failed its votaries take it as proved without argument that the one-sided remedies, which alone are left, must needs succeed. But is not the other view barely possible? Is it not just conceivable that there is no remedy that we can apply to the Irish hatred of ourselves? that other loves or hates may possibly some day elbow it out of the Irish peasant's mind, that nothing we can do by any contrivance will hasten the advent of that period? May it not, on the contrary, be our incessant doctoring and meddling, awaking the passions now of this party, now of that, raising at every step a fresh crop of resentments by the side of the old growth, that puts off the day when these feelings will decay quietly away and be forgotten? One thing we know we can do in Ireland, for we have done it in India and elsewhere with populations more unmanageable and more bitter. We can keep the peace and we can root out organised crime. But there is no precedent in our history or any other, to teach us that political measures can conjure away hereditary antipathies which are fed by constant agitation. The free institutions which sustain the life of a free and united people, sustain also the hatreds of a divided people.[1]

It is doubtful whether Salisbury can be categorised at all. To analyse his character would require a lengthy digression. It is enough for the purposes of this study to observe that a man can be personally sceptical about the trends of his time, pessimistic about the prospect ahead, dubious about the stock panaceas of intellectual fashion – and yet by no means ready to opt out, by no means convinced that the effort to delay what others call 'progress' is not worth making. Such a man may be far from neglectful of the practical problems of political technique, and quite ready to make limited tactical concessions to 'the spirit of the age' without feeling obliged to bow down to it, still less to believe in it. What Lord Salisbury's governments did is too often judged by what Lord Salisbury said.

[1] ibid., II, 38-9.

Salisbury did not at once succeed to the full inheritance from Disraeli. The latter's death vacated the leadership in the House of Lords, but, as we saw earlier, when a party was in opposition and possessed no ex-Prime Minister still active in politics, it did not normally have a single leader for the party as a whole. The leader in the House of Commons was Sir Stafford Northcote, Chancellor of the Exchequer throughout Disraeli's administration. He had been elected at Disraeli's behest in 1876 when the Prime Minister took his earldom. The alternative candidate had been Gathorne Hardy, the Secretary of State for War. He was a tough debater and in many ways a stronger character, but Disraeli disapproved of his tendency to neglect the House in order to dine at home with his wife. Subsequently Disraeli regretted his decision to pass over him and on at least one occasion declared that he would not have selected Northcote if he had anticipated Gladstone's return to politics later that very year. He perceived Northcote's defects – a lack of vigour and an excessive respect for Gladstone whose private secretary he had in distant days once been. He would have liked to hand on both his own posts, i.e. the leadership of the whole party as well as the Lords, to Salisbury. Had he lived, he might have managed it.

His death, however, came too soon. There was no doubt about Salisbury succeeding him in the Lords, but Salisbury's friends who were anxious to canvass his claims to the greater post were frustrated. Salisbury himself believed it unwise, and the leading figures in the House of Commons were not disposed to accept subordination to a member of the upper House without a struggle. Indeed, if it had come to a showdown, Northcote would probably have been the victor. The Queen wrote privately to him in May that

. . . *she* will look on Sir Stafford Northcote as the Leader of the Great Conservative Party, though it may not be necessary to *announce* this *now*, and she wished that Sir Stafford, who is so old and kind a friend, should *know* this . . .[1]

Northcote, therefore, knew at that time that if Gladstone's govern-

[1] G. E. Buckle (ed.), *The letters of Queen Victoria*, Second Series 1862–86, 3 vols (1926), III, 219, May 15, 1881.

ment was defeated he would be Prime Minister. It is impossible to say for how long afterwards he believed this, nor exactly when the Queen changed her mind. She seems to have had no hesitation in preferring Salisbury when Gladstone resigned in June 1885, but by then the combination of Lord Randolph Churchill's attacks and Northcote's own failings had altered the whole picture.

Northcote was an ineffective leader, too 'responsible', too courteous, too prosy – and it must be added too ill, for he had a grave affliction of the heart – to satisfy the more ardent Tories. The story of the way Lord Randolph Churchill undermined him is famous. He and the rest of the 'Fourth Party' made a point of treating their leader with public mockery – Lord Randolph had a particularly irritating high pitched laugh which he used with much effect when Northcote spoke – and with private contempt which soon buzzed round the clubs. To his friends he described Northcote as 'the Grand Old Woman', or alternatively as 'the Goat'. This was not for the reason which inspired people to give that soubriquet to Lloyd George – Sir Stafford's private life was impeccable – but because of the shape of his beard.

A word should be said about the Fourth party.[1] It consisted of four clever *frondeurs*, Lord Randolph Churchill, Arthur Balfour, Sir Henry Drummond Wolff and J. E. Gorst (of whom more below). The first two need no introduction. Drummond Wolff, who was descended from Sir Robert Walpole on his mother's side, had been a diplomat and financier before entering parliament. He was more easy-going and older than the rest, being just on fifty. Not that any of them was as young as one tends to imagine. Lord Randolph, a younger son of the Duke of Marlborough and father of Winston Churchill, was thirty-one. Much of life was behind him when he first appeared as the very type of political *jeunesse dorée*. Arthur Balfour was a year older. Urbane, inscrutable, ironical, he remains a puzzle to posterity. He was Salisbury's nephew and he never quite entered into the spirit of the others. Churchill, an addict of nicknames, gaily dubbing him 'Postlethwaite', could not have guessed the strength of those tenuous spider threads which

[1] The reason for the name emerges from an exchange in parliament, quoted, Winston S. Churchill, *Lord Randolph Churchill*, new edn. (1951), 122: 'There are two great parties in the State,' said a member one night. MR PARNELL: 'Three.' LORD RANDOLPH CHURCHILL, 'Four.' (Laughter.)

bound Balfour to his uncle, or the effect of the sub-acid com-
mentaries with which as time went on he enlivened the private
correspondence of the future Prime Minister.

It is hard to avoid the impression that the Fourth party began
in fun rather than earnestness. Not that this is any reason for
condemnation. Public life would be a dull affair if fun were to be
banished from it altogether. But it would be wrong to take them
too seriously. In many ways the Fourth party resembled Young
England. There was the same half-conspiratorial approach, the
same witty irreverence, the same desire to score off the seemingly
stuffy and pompous figures on the front bench. A similar ideology
can be discerned. Just as Disraeli, Smythe and Manners advocated some sort of vague Tory-radicalism, so too Lord Randolph
and Gorst tried to outflank Gladstonian measures by amending
them not in a more conservative but a more 'democratic' direction.
Both groups had the same common aversion – consensus politics,
embodied by Peel in the 1840s and, forty years later, by Northcote
whose policy was very much cast in the Peelite mould.

Of course there were differences. For one thing the Conservatives were in opposition under Northcote whereas they were in
power under Peel. Moreover, Peel was a far more formidable
opponent, and even in those days it was much harder to shake the
party leader when he was Prime Minister than when he was
merely leader of the opposition; in the case of Northcote not even
the sole leader but partner in a condominium. This may partly
explain the differing degree of success. Young England caused
quite a sensation but it never got near to overthrowing Peel. He
fell for quite different reasons, on a question which had nothing
to do with Young England, and on which they were not even
united among themselves. But Northcote was genuinely driven
out by the Fourth party. Their campaign was indirect. Their
effectiveness depended on their effectiveness in attacking Gladstone. Lord Randolph would not have endangered Northcote's
position as he did, if he had not appeared to a demoralised party
as a far more formidable opponent of the government than their
own front bench could ever hope to be. Had it not been for the
Fourth party's hard, brilliant, unrelenting campaign of ridicule
and obstruction from the Bradlaugh case onwards, the issue

between Northcote and Salisbury would have been far more doubtful. As it was the Queen when she chose Salisbury in 1885 only ratified an opinion already well established in the Conservative ranks. It was a wonderful example of what sheer parliamentary skill could do in circumstances which, though favourable, by no means guaranteed success.

2

Much of the struggle between the rebels and the Establishment centred round points of party organisation. To explain the situation it is necessary to take a brief glance at past developments.

The years between 1832 and 1867 had seen the heyday of 'club government'. The Conservative party's effective headquarters had been the Carlton Club. After an abortive effort in 1831, it came formally into existence in March 1832,[1] and, partly because it was the first specifically Tory club, its birth was not attended by the same internecine controversy which afflicted that of its rival, the Reform Club, four years later. The Reform had to compete with the great Whig citadel of Brookes's, whereas White's the nearest equivalent of Brooks's on the other side, had long ceased to display any obvious political colour. The Carlton's first premises were at No. 2 Carlton House Terrace – hence no doubt the name. In 1835 it moved to a specially designed building by Sir Robert Smirke in Pall Mall. This was replaced in 1854 by a new building on the same site, which survived till the bombs of 1940.[2]

The minutes of the club's political committee, if they ever existed, have not survived. But there is ample evidence to show that for a whole generation the club was the centre of such political organisation as the party possessed. It was there that F. R. Bonham, Peel's faithful henchman, had his desk, arranged for candidates, sought subscriptions, organised elections, and reported the

---

[1] See Gash, *Politics in the Age of Peel*, 393–401, and A. Aspinall, *Politics and the press* (1949), 336–40, for the house or 'office' in Charles Street from which the Carlton sprang. Sir Charles Petrie, *The Carlton Club* (1955), 39–41, is rather too cavalier in dismissing this part of the story as a myth.

[2] The Carlton Club is now housed in 69 St James's Street, the former abode of Arthur's.

gossip of the day to his master. To join it was for neophytes the first step in the rung, for eminent converts the outward and visible sign of grace.[1] Whips, election committees, provincial grandees, Tadpoles and Tapers – all the principals, stage hands, prompters, designers of the great party political drama congregated in its precincts.

The Carlton was very much more than merely a social focal point for those whose political opinions were broadly Conservative. It was a centre of power. When therefore a new club, the Conservative, was founded in 1840 with the ostensible purpose of catering for those who were excluded from the Carlton owing to the long waiting list, the party leaders and managers looked at it with a frosty eye. They did not wish to see a rival body interfering with the Carlton's monopoly of electoral arrangements. But in practice the Conservative Club, whatever the purpose of its founders, does not seem to have constituted any such threat.

Twenty years later the party leadership took quite a different line with the third Conservative London club to be founded, the Junior Carlton. On August 14, 1863 Disraeli wrote to Derby:

The Carlton & Cons[e] Clubs are filled to overflowing and hundreds of candidates are waiting their turn for a ballot, wh. will not in most cases come on for years.

They are also necessarily so exclusive that the working corpus of our party never can be admitted. The Carlton will rarely admit a professional candidate & the Conservative a small percentage only.

Our strength is great in country attorneys and agents who want a political and social focus in London. As Henry Drummond used to say, 'of all powers in the 19th century the power of attorney is the greatest'.

They want to form a new political club to be called the Junior Conservative or something of the sort, but to effect the purpose aimed at, it must be started under powerful and unmistakeable auspices. Taylor[2] says it will organise, strengthen & encourage

---

[1] Cf. Disraeli's successful, though feverish, intrigues to get elected in 1836, and Graham's and Stanley's decorous adherence in 1841.

[2] Colonel T. E. Taylor, Junior Whip, 1855–9, Chief Whip, 1859–68.

the party greatly & has written to me very strongly on the matter, with an unreasonable desire that I should communicate with you anent. What he wishes is that the five trustees of the new Club shd be yr Lordship, Ld Malmesbury, Ld Colville, Colonel Taylor and myself.

I believe the affair has been long maturing, is needed & will be useful – but of course I await your wishes & opinion, on wh: all must depend.[1]

No doubt the position of the Carlton as a party headquarters was beginning to decline by then, and so the danger of divided counsels in management was less. The Junior Carlton was founded the following year and its relations with the older club appear to have been entirely cordial from the start.

In the 1830s and early 1840s the Conservative party organisation consisted of a loosely bound triple alliance: there was the Chief Whip; there was Bonham who would have been called the Principal Agent if such a title had existed; and there was the Election Committee set up *ad hoc* for the election of 1835, but apparently continuing thereafter with a responsibility for co-ordinating arrangements for registration. In effect Bonham was the key figure in the extra-parliamentary organisation. He was a barrister of private means educated at Corpus Christi College, Oxford, and he was socially a cut above his opposite numbers on the Whig side, who were two middle class attorneys thrust into their positions by radical pressure.[2] He was through his mother a relation of Sidney Herbert. He held strong Tory views and once declared that from infancy he entertained a 'dread of any proposed reforms'.[3] He sat in parliament 1830–1 and 1835–7. He was an Assistant Whip in the parliament of 1835. He was Storekeeper to the Ordnance in both Peel's administrations.

The disruption of the party over the corn laws destroyed the whole organisation so carefully constructed after 1832. Bonham faded from the scene along with his master, Peel. The Carlton Club was itself bitterly divided. An unknown individual scratched

[1] Derby Papers, 146/1.
[2] See Gash, *Politics in the Age of Peel*, 412–27, and appendix K, for an excellent account of Bonham, and also of Parkes and Coppock, the Whig agents,
[3] ibid., 413.

Peel's name off the printed list of members and wrote against it
'withdrawn' after Peel brought forward his fiscal proposals in
February 1846. The committee, anxious to avoid heresy hunting,
recorded gravely that 'such a proceeding is unwarrantable and
should it occur again will require public notice'.[1] In the event Sir
James Graham appears to have been the only figure of importance
who resigned from the club during the crisis. Passions rose even
higher when the Peelites joined the Whigs in turning out Derby
and Disraeli over the budget of 1852. Lord Downshire, com-
plaining that the committee had failed to prevent the club
becoming 'a mixed society of Peelites, Radicals, Whigs and
Tories', asked to have his name taken off the books. Gladstone
while reading a newspaper after dinner was insulted by some
angry (and one may suspect tipsy) Tory MPs who, so we are told,
informed him that 'he ought to be pitched out of the window in the
direction of the Reform Club. Mr Gladstone addressed the parties
in the most courteous terms but they repeated their insulting
language, ordered candles in another room, and then left Mr
Gladstone alone.'[2] In fact Gladstone did not resign from the
Carlton till 1860.

The elections of 1847 and 1852 were managed by the Chief
Whip, Beresford, and the Assistant Whip, Newdegate. The
situation was chaotic and unsatisfactory. But after the fall of the
Derby administration at the end of 1852 Disraeli took up the question of the party's extra-parliamentary organisation. The new
Chief Whip, Sir William Joliffe, was a much better manager than
his predecessor and also much better disposed to Disraeli. At the
same time the position of Agent, left in abeyance since the days of
Bonham, was revived. Disraeli's solicitor and Buckinghamshire
neighbour, Philip Rose, who was a partner in the London firm of
Baxter, Rose, Norton & Co., took on the post. Thus in the 1850s
and 1860s the pattern has but slightly changed. The whips remain as always key figures, the Carlton Club is still very important. It is there that the county magnates meet and arrange
candidatures with little regard to the embryonic central organs
of the party. Their writ was largely confined to the counties

---

[1] Petrie, *Carlton Club*, 79.
[2] ibid., 82, quoting *Sunday Times*, December 26, 1852.

and the smaller boroughs which reflected agrarian interests but these of course accounted for the great majority of Tory seats.

On the other hand in the less rural boroughs the rudiments of a newer form of organisation were beginning to appear. Up and down the country in the boroughs there were a number of solicitors acting as what were called 'parliamentary agents' whose income was largely made out of the legal expenses of parliamentary elections and the trial of election petitions. Hence Disraeli's jest about 'the power of attorney'. This was a highly lucrative form of business and it was worth while doing the purely agency work for the party in return for the fees to be gained from electoral litigation Baxter, Rose, Norton & Co. had a big practice in this field at the London end and employed at one time as many as two hundred clerks. When in 1853 Disraeli looked for someone to be in charge of extra-parliamentary party organisation it was natural to choose a solicitor in this line of business especially if he happened to be a friend. It was natural too that Rose should have been widely though informally described as 'Principal Agent', to distinguish him from the ordinary run of Conservative parliamentary agents with whom he dealt and coresponded.

Rose personally acted in this capacity for only six years. In 1859 he was rewarded with a County Court treasurership and Markham Spofforth, a partner in the same firm, who had been acting as his assistant, became Principal Agent. He in his turn was assisted by Dudley Baxter, a statistician of some distinction.[1] Later he had another assistant to act as secretary to the Conservative Registration Association which was set up in 1863. Apart from their position as members of a firm of solicitors, the functions of Rose and Spofforth did not differ much if at all from those of Bonham. All three acted in a co-ordinate rather than subordinate role vis-à-vis the whips. Bonham dealt directly with Peel. Rose and Spofforth had direct access to Disraeli, though not apparently to Derby, for there are no letters from Spofforth and only three from Rose in the whole of Derby's political correspondence. This presumably was because Derby as a peer left electoral management to the Leader of the House of Commons, though subsequently Salisbury did not

[1] Hanham, *Elections and party management*, 357 and n.

take this line; on the contrary he kept a close liaison with 'Captain' Middleton, the Principal Agent from 1885 onwards.

In the 1860s therefore party organisation was much as it had been in Peel's time. There were the whips who decided on the expenditure of the party fund and dealt with the selection of candidates. They were assisted by Spofforth who appears to have been an enthusiastic and loyal worker but not always tactful or discreet. Getting him at long last a reward for his labours – as Taxing Master in Chancery at £1,500 p.a. – Disraeli wrote to the Lord Chancellor, Cairns, on January 13, 1875, 'Mr Spofforth served us for years, and years of adversity – if not always with perfect judgement, with great talent, honor and devotion. He was not well used by us but has never murmured.'[1] At general elections there would be an *ad hoc* committee formed consisting of the whips and suitable people interested in party management. In the election of 1868 Corry, Disraeli's private secretary, was a member. So was Lord Nevill, later Marquess of Abergavenny and destined to be one of the most powerful figures behind the scenes in Tory politics. He was a trustee of the party fund and, along with the whips played an important part in collecting and disbursing it. Lady Dorothy Nevill described him as 'the Tory Blood-hound'.[2]

A word should be said about the party fund. The existence of a central fund can be traced back to the general election of 1835.[3] Its trustees appear to have been Peel and the Duke of Wellington while Lord Rosslyn acted on their behalf in the matter of expenditure. Disraeli, though nominally an independent radical, was one of the beneficiaries, receiving £500 towards his expenses in his unsuccessful struggle for High Wycombe that year. This fund naturally remained in Peel's control after 1846, and some of it was used by the Peelite whip, Sir John Young, to help Lord Lincoln for his election in 1847. The Protectionists also had a fund of their own by then. It appears to have been under the control of the whips, for in December 1847 Bentinck had accused Beresford the

[1] Cairns Papers, quoted, Feuchtwanger, *Disraeli, democracy and the Conservative party*, 106–7.
[2] Ralph Nevill (ed.), *The reminiscences of Lady Dorothy Nevill* (1906), 70.
[3] See Gash, *Politics in the Age of Peel*, appendix C, for detailed discussion of the problem.

Chief Whip of diverting it to an irregular use.[1] Little is known about the central fund during the next twenty years. It seems to have represented in Peel's day only a tiny proportion of the total amount spent at elections, and one can reasonably surmise that the same was true in the period of Derby's leadership. Most candidates paid their own expenses or had them paid on their behalf by personal and private arrangements.[2]

The principal contributors to the central fund were peers. They had no election expenses, and, at least till the agricultural depression of the late 1870s, they were by far the richest class in society. But as they were also expected to give help directly to candidates in their own counties, they were often reluctant to support the central fund. The Chief Whip in the House of Lords who normally had the job of raising the money often found it hard work. For the election of 1868 Disraeli set a target of £100,000 and cajoled the Cabinet into producing £10,000. Despite this good example there is nothing to suggest that the target was reached.[3] The other source of supply only available when the party held office was the Secret Service money – £10,000 a year which was at the disposal of the Patronage Secretary, an office always held by the Chief Whip. The abolition of the Secret Service money in 1886 by Lord Randolph Churchill and the increasing tendency towards the end of the century to fight even the most unpromising seats made it still more important to raise money for the central fund. But the incomes of the peerage, unless they stemmed from non-agricultural sources, were on the decline. By the 1890s the Conservative party had been obliged to broaden the whole basis of its contributions. It was greatly helped by the move of the business and industrial classes into its ranks, and these became more and more the principal sources of supply. From 1886 onwards the Conservatives were in general far better placed to raise funds than the Liberals. It is not accidental that the Liberals should have been the first party to engage in the sale of honours as

---

[1] See above, pp. 78–9.

[2] In the election of 1880, the returned expenses of Conservative candidates was c. £900,000 – almost certainly a lower figure than the true expenses. The 'Carlton Fund' at the disposal of the Central Office was said to be only £24,000. See for these figures Trevor Lloyd, *The general election of 1880* (1968), 74–6.

[3] Hanham, *Elections and party management*, 371.

a source of their funds, though the Conservatives soon followed suit.

Meanwhile circumstances had brought about a major change in the organisational pattern of the 1860s. An alteration of electoral law in 1868 resulted in petitions being tried locally by a specially appointed judge instead of by a parliamentary committee in London. Baxter, Rose, Norton & Co. no longer had this valuable source of income and did not have the same interest in retaining the party agency. The Liberals had already changed or been obliged to change their arrangements. Their Principal Agent from 1857 to 1867 had been William Drake, a prominent city solicitor, but when he retired after the election of that year, no replacement was made. The work fell on the shoulders of successive Chief Whips who soon found themselves hopelessly overburdened. Yet it was not till 1886 that the party again appointed a Principal Agent.

The history of the Conservatives was different. Spofforth ran the election of 1868, but this was his last. Increasing friction between him and some of the principal figures in the party, a row over the election of the secretary to the Junior Carlton, and possibly his past associations with corrupt practices resulted in his either resigning or being asked to resign early in 1870.[1] But unlike the Liberals the Conservative whips did not intend to take on the job themselves, and in April 1870 Gerard Noel, the Chief Whip offered the post to J. E. Gorst, a barrister aged thirty-five who sat in parliament for Cambridge City from 1866 to 1868 but had lost his seat in the general election. Gorst's social and political standing was clearly above that of Spofforth, or even Rose. In fact it was more like Bonham's, though with the difference that Bonham seems to have regarded the position of agent as an end in itself whereas Gorst, a pushing, ambitious and prickly character, regarded it as a means of political advancement.

The leadership does not seem to have envisaged any startling change in the task of agent. Gorst was chosen because he was recognised as able and competent, above all perhaps because he had already shown a keen interest in the problems of urban Conservatism. It was against the solid strength of the Liberals in

[1] Feuchtwanger, op. cit., 111-12.

the big boroughs that the Conservatives had to make some inroads, if they were ever to escape from being a permanent minority party. Gorst, who had been chairman in the first meeting of the National Union of Conservative and Constitution Associations in November 1867, seemed well qualified to deal with the problem and indeed his performance justified these expectations. He was a genuine believer in working class Conservatism which, not perhaps entirely correctly, he understood to be the essence of Disraeli's creed. He was methodical, clear-headed, hard working and efficient.

His new office in 53 Parliament Street was not at first known as the Central Office but by the end of 1871 the name was in general use. The mass organisation of the party was constituted by the National Union which had not at first counted for much (see page 114). No members of the government attended its inaugural meeting on November 12, 1867 at the Freemasons' Tavern. It was overshadowed by the Metropolitan Conservative Alliance and the Central Conservative Registration Association. The idea of forming a federation of the numerous Conservative Working Men's Associations which had come into being just before the passing of the second Reform Bill was by no means universally welcomed even by the Associations themselves. The Manchester Association for example disliked it as a possible threat to its own independence. Although the Union took credit for a big part in the electoral successes of the party in Lancashire in 1868, the claim was bogus. The National Union as such did little or nothing.

When in 1870 Gorst became secretary of the Metropolitan Conservative Alliance as well as party agent the position of the National Union seemed even more shaky. But in the following year the whole situation changed. Leonard Sedgwick, the secretary of the National Union, retired, and Gorst, together with Major Charles Keith-Falconer, replaced him as joint secretaries. The headquarters of the Union was moved to 53 Parliament Street. Henceforth, apart from the split so nearly engineered by Lord Randolph Churchill in 1884, the Central Office and National Union acted in complete harmony, and from that day to this have operated under one roof. The National Union became the body to which constituency organisations were affiliated, though such

organisations were by no means universal then, being largely
confined to boroughs and not even covering all of them. However,
as we saw earlier, the seal of respectability was set on it by
Disraeli's decision to make it the sounding board for his great
oration at the Crystal Palace in June 1872. From then onwards it
was, in Feuchtwanger's words, 'an integral part of the Central
Office organisation and was used by the party leaders as a mouth-
piece and as an organisational front for popular demonstrations'.[1]

The party organisation in the 1870s was thus a threefold one
even as it had been in the days of Derby and of Peel. But there was
a difference. The Carlton Club had faded out as a political
headquarters. The party agency was no longer in its precincts as
it had been under Bonham, nor in the offices of a solicitors' firm
as it had been under Rose and Spofforth. It was in the Central
Office at 53 Parliament Street. The second vital organ of the
party, as has been the case all down its history, was of course the
position of Chief Whip. The exact relations of the whips with
Gorst were not clearly defined. They probably controlled the
funds but Gorst certainly had a big say in the choice of candidates,
and as the principal source of electoral information his advice
was crucial. The third organ, quite new, was the National Union
which can be regarded as in many ways the propaganda aspect
of the Central Office. The Central Office was at this stage chiefly
important for the big boroughs. The smaller ones were largely
controlled by local influences. As for the counties, Disraeli in 1873
set up a special committee of persons with suitable social status to
deal with elections.

Gorst's problem was to satisfy and harness urban conservatism
to a party which still remained predominantly landed and whose
funds still derived almost wholly from the purses of the great
territorial magnates. This did not mean a programme specifically
designed to appeal to the working class. The most profitable area
for Conservative exploitation was in fact the professional and
business classes frightened by Gladstonism. They were not only
shaken by his policies, they were beginning to lose their old
dissenting roots. They tended more and more in the 1870s and
1880s to send their sons to Anglican public schools. They were

[1] Feuchtwanger, 130.

moving out of city centres away from the world of counting house and chapel to that of prosperous suburbia. The era of the commuter had begun. The middle class provincial Tory leaders who controlled the associations of the National Union saw the party dominated by a 'magic circle' of landed proprietors whose methods were the traditional ones of 'influence', bribery and corruption. Those who exploited these techniques, described by Gorst as 'the Old Identity', could still claim success for them in the counties and pocket boroughs. But the traditional methods were increasingly irrelevant in the urban areas, and this was true whether the appeal was to the anti-Irish, anti-employer working class in Lancashire or to the suburban commuters of Middlesex, Surrey and Kent. And as time went on 'the Old Identity' became even more irrelevant. The Ballot Act of 1872, the Corrupt Practices Act of 1883 and finally the Reform Act of 1884 which extended the urban suffrage to that last stronghold of landed Toryism, the counties, all contributed to the change.

One has to remember the social exclusiveness of the day. A country squire with one or two thousand acres could move on terms far nearer to social equality with, say, Lord Derby or Lord Salisbury than a rich self-made manufacturer could move with the same country squire, even though he could buy him out several times over. It was another matter if a prosperous merchant or financier actually purchased an estate and set up as a country gentleman. The 'County' was remarkably unsnobbish and unprejudiced in that respect. Few people refused an invitation to a Rothschild ball. But the provincial business man who remained as such – and this applied *a fortiori* to the less wealthy – found himself separated by a great gulf from the traditional governing class. This gap was reflected in the Conservative party's internal politics. The urban Tory leaders were excluded from the world of the great country houses, and the grand London parties, in which Disraeli moved, alike incongruously and effortlessly, and where party affairs were settled over the port. What they sought was recognition and a just share of influence in the councils of the party, and they sought it through the National Union which was the only organisation capable of expressing their aspirations. 'Tory democracy' therefore had a dual meaning. It could signify a more democratic control over the party machine, which in practice meant a greater say for the urban middle class; or it could mean a policy designed to appeal to the working class. The two notions did not necessarily conflict, but they were not the same. Tory democracy was about party organisation just as much as sanitary legislation for the lower orders.

If we look at the matter in this light we can see that the career of Gorst has a significance comparable with that of Lord Randolph Churchill, for he was involved in the question from the very outset. He saw his task as one of building up Conservative organisation in the towns. It was clearly a very different job from that of Spofforth, Rose and the old fashioned parliamentary agents. Propaganda and persuasion were beginning to replace 'influence'. The question of suiting the constituency to the candidate became far more important than hitherto. Gorst kept closely in touch with this aspect of his trade. The 1874 election with its notable advance in the fortunes of borough Conservatism seemed a vindication of the new arrangements.

Precisely what went wrong thereafter is not wholly clear, for our only source is Gorst himself, and he undoubtedly had a personal grievance about his own lack of reward. His formal engagement as Principal Agent ended with the election. He took up his legal practice, and in 1875 got into parliament at a by-election. He seems, however, to have kept some sort of watching brief on the Central Office which was now much weakened, for Keith-Falconer had also left. In 1876 a new Principal Agent, W. B. Skene, a barrister and Scottish landowner, was appointed. He was not a success but, even before there was any means of knowing this, Gorst in 1877 severed his own relations with the Central Office and wrote a well known letter of protest to Disraeli.[1]

His own personal feelings may have coloured his views but they sound plausible. His main complaint was that the Chief Whip had interfered too much in matters which should have been the province of the Principal Agent, often by-passing him altogether. There was a new Chief Whip, Sir William Hart-Dyke, and the fact that the Conservatives were in office may have made a difference.

[1] See Feuchtwanger, op. cit., 137–8, for the full text, quoted from Hughenden Papers.

The Chief Whip was customarily the Patronage Secretary to the Treasury and the mere occupation of the post probably led him to do what Gorst regarded as 'the chief cause of all the mischief . . . the system . . . of managing elections at the Treasury'. The Liberal whip had done the same thing, and this, so Gorst alleged, was a factor in the previous government's defeat. He ended by adjuring Disraeli 'to separate entirely and for ever the electoral management of the Party from the Government Department of the Treasury'. But nothing seems to have been done.

Gorst may have exaggerated the contribution of organisational defects to defeat. It is the endemic malady of politicians to do this for they find it hard to believe that the electorate could have rejected them on their merits. But organisation undoubtedly makes some difference, and Gorst was right in prophesying disaster at the next election. As leader Disraeli must bear his share of the blame. After 1874 he showed little interest in the party machine, and his attitude was inevitably coloured by the preconceptions of his long past experience. After all he had been a county member since 1847, and had rarely been opposed. There was a sense in which he was himself a part of 'the Old Identity'. He had only sporadic appreciation of the importance of urban conservatism. True, he used the fact that W. H. Smith was M.P. for Westminster as an argument to Queen Victoria for giving him high Cabinet office in 1877, pointing out that the monopoly of House of Commons ministers which the county members had hitherto enjoyed was resented by the Conservative borough members. But he was probably using this as a justification for a promotion which he favoured on other grounds. He knew that the Queen would need some persuasion to accept a middle class man as First Lord of the Admiralty. In matters of honours and awards to the Tory bourgeoisie Disraeli was anything but generous. Nor did he make any effort to act on Gorst's warnings. The new Principal Agent, W. B. Skene, was of little use and hastily retired in 1880. After mismanaging the affairs of the Conservative party he departed to manage the estates of Christ Church whose dean, Liddell, was his father-in-law. The Chief Whip fell ill at the end of 1879 through overwork. The election of 1880 was conducted amidst the maximum of incoherence and confusion.

3

There was widespread discontent at the débâcle which ensued, especially among the associations of the National Union. Disraeli appointed a central committee under W. H. Smith to examine the whole party machine and it soon became permanent. Its principal members were W. H. Smith as chairman, Edward Stanhope as vice-chairman and Earl Percy who was chairman of the National Union. This was a sop to check a revolt on the part of that body. Gorst was brought back again to act as the committee's executive officer. He was as prickly and 'crotchety' as ever, and in no time found himself at daggers drawn with Smith. What was more he became almost at once involved with the Fourth party. It was obvious that in the long run Gorst could not join Lord Randolph and the *frondeurs* against Northcote within the House of Commons while at the same time loyally serving a committee which was responsible to the official leadership for party affairs outside the House. The situation was just tolerable while Disraeli was un-disputed leader. It could not continue when the leadership became a duumvirate in which Northcote was, to start with, the senior partner.

Disraeli, indeed, treated the Fourth party with consummate tact entering sympathetically into their feelings about Northcote but strongly advising against any open breach. 'Lord B. was in his talk anything but goaty,'[1] wrote Gorst to Lord Randolph in November 1880, and in the same autumn Disraeli told Wolff how much he regretted having passed the leadership of the lower House to Northcote, in the light of Gladstone's return to politics. But to both of them he firmly counselled public deference to their leader, '. . . you must stick to Northcote,' he told Drummond Wolff, 'he represents the respectability of the party. I wholly sympathize with you all because I was never respectable my-self. . . . Don't on any account break with Northcote.'[2]

Nor did they while Disraeli lived. But the situation became impossible after his death. Gorst resigned in 1882. The Fourth party was not his only reason. He had also quarrelled with the

[1] Churchill, *Lord Randolph Churchill*, new edn., op. cit., 129.   [2] ibid., 131.

whips over their alleged encouragement of corrupt practices –
the struggle again with the 'Old Identity'. His successor, G. C. T.
Bartley, fared no better, but he seems to have been as prickly as
Gorst. He complained that he was never consulted about policy,
although no other agent, not even Gorst, aspired to this status.[1]
He resigned in November 1884, publishing his reasons in the press,
and denouncing the leadership in the *Fortnightly Review* – a
Radical organ. He sat as a Conservative MP from 1885 to 1906
but – not surprisingly – was excluded from office, and, to quote
Professor Hanham, 'eventually brought his political career to a
suitable climax by declaiming against the number of Lord
Salisbury's relations in the government'.[2]

From 1882 'Tory Democracy', the affairs of the Fourth party,
the story of the National Union, and Lord Randolph's bid for
leadership are so closely connected that they have often been
blurred by historians. In fact they are separate, and it is necessary
to disentangle them.

The National Union had been founded as a propagandist body,
with a suitable gaggle of peers as vice-presidents, designed to
attract working class support. The initiative had come from
London, not the provinces, and the founders, Henry Raikes and a
group of young Conservatives, were supported and encouraged by
such central organisation as the party had in 1867. To encourage
local leaders in the boroughs it was decided to hold annual meetings to which the constituencies could send delegates. As the
1870s wore on, the character of the associations composing the
union changed. They became more middle class in composition
and less pliable. But the governing body of the Union known as the
council was largely co-optative and unrepresentative, being in
practice dominated by the Central Office. Moreover, as we saw
earlier, Conservative associations were far from universal even in
the borough constituencies, and not all of them were affiliated to
the National Union though the proportion was much higher than
in the counties. What the more militant spirits aimed at in the late
1870s were associations in every constituency to provide a permanent organisation for registering voters, making propaganda,
choosing candidates and conducting elections; these associations

[1] Hanham, op. cit., 364. [2] ibid.

to be linked in provincial unions, and the provincial unions to be properly represented on the council where they could make effective representations to the leadership about organisational matters.

Professor J. Cornford, in an article in *Victorian Studies*,[1] makes two important points: first, that though this movement had a lot to do with Gorst, it originally had nothing to do with Lord Randolph Churchill. It began before he was ever even heard of. Secondly, it was at no time a bid to control policy or to interfere with the political functions of the leadership. It was essentially a move on the part of the provincial Tory leaders to have their voice heard in matters of organisation which they regarded as essential in the new circumstances. They felt this more strongly than ever after the election of 1880.

There was, as was seen at the time, good reason for urban Conservatism to feel itself to be on the upgrade in spite of the losses in the boroughs compared with 1874. In the twenty-nine largest boroughs – those with an electorate of over 17,500 – the Conservative share of the poll since 1868 had gone up from 37·5 per cent to 44·3 – a rise of nearly 7 per cent in twelve years. Whatever the reason for this change, it was an encouraging sign, especially if one remembers that the electorate of these same towns had gone up from 460,000 to 655,000 – which was bound to mean a big increase in representation whenever ′redistribution took place. It also goes far to explain the determination with which, to Gladstone's surprise, Salisbury pressed for the seemingly radical proposal for single member constituencies in 1884. The Liberals had in these big cities a share of MPs altogether disproportionate to their poll – 45 against 17 in 1868, 43 against 19 in 1880. This was largely because in these two or three member constituencies villa Toryism was outvoted by the Radical masses. After 1885 the situation was transformed. As Cornford puts it, 'Where Conservative supporters had formerly been swamped in huge constituencies, they were now high and dry on islands of their own.'

In 1885 for the first time since 1832 Conservatives had a majority in the English boroughs; also for the first time a minority in the

[1] J. Cornford, 'The Transformation of Conservatism in the late 19th century', *Victorian Studies* (September 1963).

English counties though they recovered soon enough. Urban Toryism had come strikingly into its own. Indeed the Conservatives were to win the English boroughs with numbers varying from 132 to 177 at the next four elections.[1] It is not surprising that the remaining demands of the National Union were met in 1886. They had largely been met already in 1884 partly as a by-product of Lord Randolph's campaign.

If the satisfaction of those demands can be regarded as a by-product of that campaign a question remains to be answered: What was the main object of Lord Randolph's campaign? In spite of two outstanding biographies,[2] this is still not at all an easy question to answer. The more one examines what he said and did in parliament, on the platform, in the council of the National Union or as a minister, the less easy it is to discern any consistent thread.

It is clear that from 1880 onwards he was trying to sabotage Northcote's leadership in the House of Commons. It is clear that in 1883–4 he was endeavouring to capture the council of the National Union and destroy the central committee. It is clear that in 1886 he was seeking to force Salisbury's hand over the estimates and that he never expected a half-proffered resignation to be gladly accepted. But what were the forces he was enlisting, the cause he was supporting, the changes he wished to achieve? Or was it all a restless, feverish zigzag towards supreme power? Did he merely aim to be Prime Minister? What did he really mean by Tory democracy?

By far the most convincing answer to this last question was his own given in a cynical moment – 'mostly opportunism, I think'. And the answer to the previous two is simply, yes. It is easy to see the psychological reason that drove him on. He had an intense resentment of what would now be called the Establishment because he had been socially ostracised, indeed driven for a

[1] Conservative MPs in England:

	Boroughs (226)	Counties (239)
1885	114	105
1886	165	174
1892	132	136
1895	175	184
1900	177	162

[2] Winston S. Churchill, *The life of Lord Randolph Churchill* (orig. edn), 2 vols (1905); Robert Rhodes James, *Lord Randolph Churchill* (1959).

time into exile, as a result of the mortal offence that he had given to the Prince of Wales over the Aylesford affair in 1876 – an episode in which it is hard to decide who comes out worst, Lord Randolph or the prince.[1] If this explains what Bentham called 'the springs of action' in his case, it is also not difficult to find an explanation of his impetuous, erratic, at times outrageous behaviour. One can surmise that his excitability, his violent language and his growing lack of judgment, indeed of mental balance, stemmed, insofar as they were not inborn defects of temperament, from the premonitory symptoms of the disease of the brain which eventually killed him. In May 1884 Salisbury wrote to Lady John Manners:

> Randolph and the Mahdi have occupied my thoughts about equally. The Mahdi pretends to be half mad, but is very sane in reality. Randolph occupies exactly the converse position.[2]

The truth is that Churchill had no real policy. He talked about Tory democracy and the importance of the working class Tories, but he showed no sign of having any programme for them. The demands of the provincial notables of the National Union which Churchill used as a vehicle for his own bid for power in the organisation had little to do with Tory democracy in that sense, though they could be regarded as a sort of Tory democracy in another sense. In fact their need for local autonomy, co-ordinated activity and more efficient organisation was better understood by Salisbury whose early hostility to Disraeli and whose intransigence in 1867 to parliamentary reform has caused him to be regarded as a much more hide-bound figure than he really was. He saw the changing pattern of Conservative support more clearly than most. 'I believe there is a great deal in Villa Toryism which requires organisation,' he wrote to Northcote in 1882.[3] Under Richard Middleton, an ex-naval officer, always known (erroneously) as 'Captain' Middleton, 'the skipper', and under Aretas Akers-Douglas, the Chief Whip,[4] both appointed in 1885, the party organisation was in far better hands than ever before. When all is

---

[1] Philip Magnus, *King Edward the seventh* (1964), 140–50, gives the fullest account of this scandal which rocked London society.
[2] Lady G. Cecil, *Salisbury*, III, 88.
[3] Quoted, Cornford, op. cit., 52.
[4] One of the ablest holders of the office. Created Viscount Chilston, 1911.

said and done the party organisation had only been modernised
to a very limited degree under Disraeli. It is one of the oddities of
party history that an alien middle class adventurer should have
headed a party which to the end of his time was more like an
eighteenth-century aristocratic 'connection' than anything else,
whereas the owner of Hatfield, no doubt under pressure from
below, found himself adopting the techniques, if embryonic, of
modern mass electoral organisation. And we can compare what
he said two years earlier to the Duke of Richmond, 'Before this
Parliament is over the country gentlemen will have as much to do
with the government of the country as the rich people in America
have'[1] – an exaggerated prophecy of their decline but a not
unreasonable estimate of the trend.

The settlement which he made with Lord Randolph and the
National Union is too often represented as a surrender. In fact
Salisbury gave away nothing that mattered. Gorst himself regarded Churchill as the man who had surrendered. In so far as
Lord Randolph and Gorst were hoping to ape the Liberal Caucus
they lost all along the line. It is true that Salisbury wound up the
central committee, but the real charge against that body, the
charge which the majority of the union levelled, was not, as Lord
Randolph alleged, that it was undemocratic but that it was in-
efficient. All that the leadership had done constitutionally was to
delegate some of their own powers to it. Powers that they could
delegate they could resume, and this was just what Salisbury, now
palpably in command, proceeded to do. What he did not do was to
abandon a single jot or tittle of the powers that the leadership
inherently possessed.

Nor did most members of the National Union wish him to do
so. Churchill may have talked sometimes in terms of imitating
the Caucus, though it is an exaggeration to regard him as trying
to turn the union into a nominating convention on the American
model – which would have been a big step on, even from the
Caucus. But the great distinguishing feature of the Caucus did
not exist in the National Union. The Caucus was a grass roots
affair which grew up in the provinces without any fostering or

---

[1] Quoted, Feuchtwanger, op. cit., from Richmond Papers. America has changed
since then.

encouragement from the Liberal leadership at the centre, and its object was not only to reform the Liberal organisation but to impose a particular policy. The National Liberal Federation constituted a strong Radical pressure group in favour of the policies of Chamberlain and Dilke. The National Union began the other way round; it grew under the aegis of the Central Office, and it was the leadership which encouraged the associations to send delegates to an annual conference.

Whatever Gorst and Churchill wanted, the great majority of the associations were content with what they got in 1884, recognition and a voice in organisational matters, to which was added the creation of provincial unions in 1886. Thereafter the National Union went quietly to sleep till 1903. In fact Gorst wanted something more than this and felt himself let down by the compromise to which Churchill agreed. Exactly what Churchill did get out of Salisbury in return for dropping out of the National Union controversy and handing the chairmanship to Hicks Beach is none too clear. Indeed the whole dispute is highly obscure if we simply look at the proposals and counter-proposals – though less so if we look at the personalities. It was in the end Lenin's famous question – Who whom? And in this particular battle the cards were stacked more favourably for Salisbury than is always appreciated.

Lord Randolph's position really depended less on any policy or programme than on brilliant opposition demagoguery. His role is often compared with that of Joseph Chamberlain in the Liberal party. Did not Chamberlain too fight against his equivalent of what Lord Randolph called 'the old men crooning round the fires of the Carlton Club'? Did not Chamberlain battle with 'the goats' of his party? Did not he stand for democracy against oligarchy, for the new electorate against the old order? The parallel seemed to be emphasised by the genuine respect and friendship which grew up between the two men.

But in reality their situations were quite different, and, although both were to be frustrated in their purposes within their respective parties, it was for different reasons. Joseph Chamberlain really could afford to attack the aristocratic element in the Liberal party. He genuinely believed that the Liberals would be stronger without the Whigs, and he rightly saw that men like Lord Hartington, Lord Granville and Lord Spencer were only tied to the party by family tradition, not by any real common bond of interest. The Liberal party was more likely to make a broad appeal to the 'outs', to the dissenters, to the rural proletariat and the urban working class, if the Whigs no longer constituted two-thirds of the Cabinet and possessed an influence on policy wholly disproportionate to their numbers. Joseph Chamberlain rightly saw that democracy was on the march in England and he was ready to put himself at its head with a programme that was radical in content as well as being highly demagogic in its form of presentation. What wrecked him in the end was the fact that democracy was also on the march in Ireland, and Gladstone put himself at its head – not with a programme but a crusade.

Lord Randolph could not play the same part in the Tory party if only because the aristocracy was inextricably tied up with it at almost every level. To have pushed out the landed classes would have meant the total disruption and collapse of the party. Lord Randolph knew this well enough. He was a member of that class himself, a younger scion of one of its grandest families. What is more, the provincial middle class leaders in the associations of the National Union knew it too. They merely wished to be consulted. They did not wish to lead, although they did wish that those who led should be efficient like Lord Salisbury, not incompetent like Sir Stafford Northcote.

Randolph Churchill appealed to them not because he had a popular democratic programme. If he had, he would not have appealed at all. Indeed, as it was, some of his patrician gibes at the middle class Conservatives must have been received with mixed feelings. Smith and Cross, those pillars of the Tory bourgeoisie whom Disraeli treated (apart from an occasional secret sally for the benefit of Lady Bradford) with unfailing respect, were to Lord Randolph 'Marshall and Snelgrove'. And few people forgot his famous reference to Smith as one of 'the Lords of surburban villas, the owners of pineries and vineries'. His appeal was because he had style, colour, panache, a great gift for platform oratory in the heyday of that art, and a wonderful capacity for making Gladstone appear ridiculous. One example out of many must suffice. Here is Lord Randolph addressing a mass meeting at Blackpool in 1883.

The Prime Minister is the greatest living master of the art of personal political advertisement. Every act of his, whether it be for the purposes of health, or of recreation, or of religious devotion, is spread before the eyes of every man, woman and child in the U.K. on large and glaring placards. For the purpose of an autumn holiday a large transatlantic steamer is specially engaged. The Poet Laureate adorns the suite and receives a peerage as his reward, and the incidents of the voyage are luncheon with the Emperor of Russia and tea with the Queen of Denmark. For the purpose of recreation he has selected the felling of trees; and we may usefully remark that his amusements like his politics are essentially destructive. Every afternoon the whole world is invited to assist at the crashing fall of some beech, elm or oak. The forest laments in order that Mr Gladstone may perspire. . . . For the purpose of religious devotion the advertisements grow larger. The parish church at Hawarden is insufficient to contain the thronging multitudes who flock to hear Mr Gladstone read the lessons of the day, and the humble parishioners are banished to hospitable Nonconformist Tabernacles in order that mankind may be present at the Prime Minister's rendering of Isaiah, Jeremiah or the Book of Job.

In many ways he was like Disraeli on whom of course he modelled himself. He had the same wit, brilliance, invective, sheer humour. But he was less professional, less serious; above all he was less indispensable, and he was an intolerable colleague. The Tory party could not do without Disraeli, but Disraeli would never have dreamed of addressing Derby in the terms in which Randolph Churchill addressed Salisbury. And the very success of Disraeli in removing the once justified description of the Conservative as the 'Stupid party', meant that even as clever a figure as Lord Randolph could be jettisoned. When he forced a direct clash with the Prime Minister on an issue of old fashioned Treasury economy his defeat was total, humiliating and abject. Not only Salisbury but the whole Cabinet breathed a sigh of relief. Lord Randolph's parliamentary struggle had only resulted in substituting a far more

formidable barrier than Northcote to his own rise. His organisational campaign had merely consolidated the strength of the
Marshalls and Snelgroves of the provinces. His campaign in the
Cabinet merely resulted in his own ejection. He was in the end,
as Lord Lyttelton said of George Smythe, 'a splendid failure'.

4

The Conservative ascendancy was ushered in by the election of
July 1886. It is increasingly fashionable to minimise the importance of the Irish question in the reversal of fortunes which occurred at this time. But it is hard to explain what happened without
some reference to it. In December 1885 the Liberals had a majority
of 84 seats over the Conservatives (334 to 250), and the Conservatives secured only 47·3 per cent of the poll in Britain excluding
Ireland. Irish Home Rule was not on the political programme
of either of the major parties. Seven months later, after Gladstone
had taken up the cause, had seen his party break up, had been
defeated on the second reading of his Home Rule Bill, and had
appealed to the country on it, he sustained a shattering defeat –
'a drubbing', as he termed it to his son, Herbert. The Conservatives and Liberal Unionists combined had 53·7 per cent
of the vote winning 394 seats[1] to the Liberals' 191, and although
one can add the 86 Irish Nationalist seats to that figure, the
Liberals remained heavily outnumbered.

This remarkable swing can scarcely have any other explanation, and it is surely not unreasonable to suppose that the Liberal
party must have been greatly weakened by the secession of the
Whigs under Hartington on the one hand, and a number of the
Radicals led by Joseph Chamberlain on the other. No doubt there
was also a slower tide moving against the Liberals, viz, the trend
ever since 1868 for the non-landed propertied classes to go over to
the Conservative side. It is clear that the division between
Liberals and Conservatives ran increasingly on lines of class and
wealth towards the close of the century, but it is difficult to say
whether this was more important than that created by the Irish
question.

[1] Of these, 78 were Liberal Unionists.

Apart from anything else the Irish question was itself to some extent a class question. It was a class question for two reasons. The behaviour of the Irish extremists alarmed, by its implications, those concerned with the rights of property in England as well as Ireland. Moreover, those very remedial measures which the Liberals took in Gladstone's first and second administrations, involved in themselves interference with the rights of property in Ireland, which seemed a dangerous precedent for similar interventions elsewhere for different reasons. These were powerful causes for middle class hostility to Home Rule. Added to a growing sense of English nationalistic pride, a desire for imperial unity, and deep seated antipathy to Rome, they were quite enough to explain the increasing alienation of villadom from a Liberal party committed to the Irish cause.

Of course no one could argue that then any more than today the sole dividing line between Left and Right was that of wealth. If it had been, the Conservatives would never have won at all. In addition to the lords of suburban villas, a substantial but more volatile body of working class opinion must have voted for them too. It is certain that a considerable section of the working class was liable to be as much affected by the Irish question as the middle class – especially in areas where there was a substantial body of Irish immigrants. But working class opinion was concerned with other things as well. Bread and butter politics were even more important. Considerations of welfare and living standards were bound to affect working class votes in a big way at the very first moment that the policy of one of the major parties seemed more likely than that of the other either to improve or to lower those standards.

But, during the late 1880s and for the whole of the 1890s – indeed beyond – it would be hard to argue that either of the major parties had the edge on the other in this respect. The Liberals lacked the ideas and energy in this field which might have been supplied by Joseph Chamberlain, and so made no very special appeal to the working class. Although they probably remained the party which attracted most votes from that section of the community, they had lost the predominance which Gladstone possessed at the time of the election of 1880. As for the Conservatives the particular circumstances of the 1886 election made it impossible for them to pursue a totally static policy even if they had wanted to.

The impression is sometimes given that Salisbury could afford – and did get away with – a long period of cautious negativism in domestic affairs because the Irish question divided the opposition and rendered a reformist policy unnecessary. The opposite is true of both parts of the proposition. Salisbury could not afford to ignore reform, because the new electorate would soon start voting for Gladstone if he did – Home Rule or no Home Rule. Nor could he afford to dispense with the support of the Liberal Unionists who were certainly not going to acquiesce in a purely static policy.[1] What is more the record shows that his government was far from being static from 1886 to 1892.

The truth has been obscured by the fall of Lord Randolph and his own comments on his fall. He naturally tended to drama-tise the episode and see in his personal defeat the defeat of the 'progressive cause' in the Conservative party. But if Lord Randolph's ideas are epitomised in the Dartford programme of September 1886, then it is clear that his 'cause' survived him, for most of the measures which he favoured were enacted after his departure. No doubt something depends on what one regards as the 'progressive cause'. The Conservative government did not pass either then or later the sort of measures which would have satis-fied Keir Hardie, the trade unions new and old, the Social Democratic Federation or the Labour churches. But the Liberals during their brief innings of 1892–5 showed no sign of doing so either – witness Rosebery's reluctance to deal with one of the main Labour demands, payment of members, even though it was an item in the Liberal Newcastle programme of 1891. Hence no doubt the later emergence of a Labour party organised on the model of the Irish party as a parliamentary pressure group determined to extract in parliament benefits which pressure from outside had failed to secure from either of the traditional parties.

But in the late 1880s the kind of domestic reform which the 'progressive' elements in both those parties were bothering about

[1] See Michael Hurst, *Joseph Chamberlain and Liberal reunion* (1967), for a discussion of this point.

concerned not the urban but the rural working class. This was so for two excellent reasons. First, the country labourer was the man who had got the vote under the Act of 1884, and the Conservatives as well as the Liberals were just as anxious to placate him as they had been ten years earlier to placate the newly enfranchised urban householder. Secondly, there was far more economic distress in the country than in the towns. 'The Great Depression' which lasted from 1873 to 1896 did not hit the industrial working class very badly. Indeed the fall in prices especially of food caused a rise in real wages. But the agricultural slump really did hit the land and all who earned or 'unearned' their incomes from it. Not even a Conservative Prime Minister could reimpose straight agricultural protection, although it was possible to deal with other grievances. Hence the prominence in the Dartford programme, and in Salisbury's subsequent legislative record, of measures to assist smallholders, alter the incidence of tithe, facilitate cheap land transfer, change the agricultural rating system, reform the local government of the counties.

The neutrality of the urban working class, the unpopularity of Home Rule, concessions to the rural proletariat, an image of cautious progressivism, alliance with the Liberal Unionists under Chamberlain and Hartington, all these factors combined 'to make Salisbury's government, like Palmerston's a quarter of a century earlier, a broad-based coalition seemingly in safe occupation of the middle ground of politics which Peel had held for a few years but which had always evaded first Derby then Disraeli. Home Rule enabled Salisbury to play both the 'constitutional' and the 'national' cards. In the four elections which followed the great Home Rule split he won overwhelming majorities in England and clear majorities in Britain excluding Ireland. In only one, that of 1892, did the Irish Nationalists give the Liberals a narrow lead in the U.K. as a whole; and the disarray which followed Gladstone's second attempt to carry Home Rule, in particular the damaging struggle for the succession between Lord Rosebery and Sir William Harcourt in 1894, only seemed to confirm the Conservatives as the natural party of government, strengthened by the formal adherence of Chamberlain and Hartington in 1895.

Yet it is one of the fascinating features of historical study that appearances often, when closely examined, belie realities, and sometimes do so even when they are not so very closely examined. If we look at the actual course of events Lord Salisbury's regime does not seem quite so securely based as it has come to appear when with hindsight we telescope sixteen years into a period of 'Conservative ascendancy'. The election of 1886 was certainly a clear cut victory as long as the Liberal Unionist members voted straight, which on the whole they did though much management was needed. But, if by-elections are any test, the party's stock in the country went rapidly down in the late 1880s and although there was something of that rally to the government which one would expect in a general election, the Conservatives could not hold their ground in 1892.[1]

They certainly made a fine recovery in 1895, and, if there is a case for the view that Liberal feuds and incompetence put them in on an essentially negative vote, the answer is that this is just what one would expect in a two party system when the electorate is very often voting as much 'against' as 'for'. But once again the popularity of the party seems to have slumped rapidly, and its by-election fortunes were uniformly unfavourable until the outbreak of the Boer War when a national emergency rallied support to the government of the day; the more so since the Liberals appeared to be no less divided between pro-Boers and Liberal Leaguers than they had been five years earlier on the merits of Rosebery and Harcourt.

It is not obvious why the Conservatives lost ground in this way. Various explanations have been given: the waning importance of the Irish question; the lack of achievement in the field of social reform, in particular failure to do anything about old age pensions. It is impossible to give a single conclusive answer. What does seem clear, however, is that the rising tide of imperialist enthusiasm which is usually said to have reached high-water mark in the late 1890s did not bring any noticeable electoral

[1] It is sometimes said that the Parnell divorce scandal which burst in November 1890 damaged the Liberals and caused the result to be much closer than it otherwise would have been. If so one would have expected by-elections in 1891 and 1892 to have shown a more favourable – or less unfavourable – trend for the Conservatives. In fact this does not appear to have been the case, and no obvious change emerges from the statistics.

dividends to the political party associated with the cause of empire. Of course it may be the case that the Conservatives would have lost even more by-elections and suffered even heavier defeats but for their connection with imperialist movement. Alternatively, it may be that public enthusiasm for the empire was always much more limited than its supporters claimed; that it was largely an affair of the City, the middle classes and the metropolitan press; and that it never cut very much ice outside. Whatever its significance there seems no reason to regard it as anything more than a minor asset to the Conservatives, many of whom regarded it with a good deal of suspicion anyway.

A possible hypothesis about electoral behaviour between 1885 and 1900 can be advanced, though tentatively and with a strong awareness that it is an over-simplification. It is based on the assumption that the most persistent factor in the choice made by the enlarged electorate was the desire for collectivism, for social reform in the interests of the newly enfranchised urban and rural householders, but that this at moments of crisis, particularly when some 'national' issue came to the fore, could be elbowed out. After the Congress of Berlin and the Conservative failure to carry any further instalment of the reforms passed in 1875-6, it would be natural, in spite of Gladstone, to look to the Liberal party, with Chamberlain and Dilke as its men of the future, for this sort of legislation. Hence the Liberal victories of 1880 and 1885. But the Irish crisis, arousing strong national emotions and breaking up the Liberals, pushes Gladstone out and gives Salisbury six years of power. As the immediate crisis over Ireland recedes, however, the electorate again thinks in terms of social reform, and, although the Conservatives are by no means supine or apathetic in this field, they do not do enough. The grass is always greener on the other side of the fence. By-elections show the electorate's discontent, but Ireland is still an important question and the general election is bound to turn to some extent on Home Rule, still the major plank in Gladstone's platform. These two conflicting trends explain the ambiguous and indecisive result of 1892.

From 1892 to 1895 the Liberals make the worst of every world. They do nothing about social reform. The fact that this is

DIFFICULT STEERING.

Lord S-l-sb-ry (to Arth-r B-lf-r). "HANG THESE 'IMPROVEMENTS' ARTHUR! DO YOU THINK WE SHALL GET THROUGH?"

February 20, 1901. Reproduced by permission of Punch

by no means their own fault is irrelevant. 'Ploughing the sands' as a way of exposing the obstructionism of the House of Lords merely inspires contempt. They are defeated over Home Rule. They are divided over personalities. When they break up in disorder in 1895, a Conservative victory is assured. But the Conservatives in their turn disappoint. There is the great failure to do anything about old age pensions. The pendulum begins to swing towards the Liberals, but more as a protest than anything else. Increasingly, the leaders of the working class, in so far as they can be defined, think in terms of an independent party. The Boer War rallies opinion to the government. Lord Salisbury, apparently the symbol of a vanished age, still conducting foreign policy by private correspondence from Hatfield, yet, as so often in his life, curiously modern in his approach to the democratic politics which he regarded *en principe* with contempt, dissolves parliament at the most favourable moment, and the Conservatives emerge triumphant if slightly surprised from the election of 1900 – the first example in modern times of the electoral opportunism which is now taken for granted.

But the war that seemed to have been won lingers on for two more years. Disillusionment sets in. Moral doubts about the methods used begin to increase. The Boer War becomes almost as divisive an element in Britain as the Vietnam War in modern America. The old Queen dies in 1901, her death emphasising the end of an era and the beginning of a new century. Salisbury's powers are failing but he stays in office for another year till the coronation of the new monarch. As he hands over to his chilly, brilliant, nonchalant, enigmatic nephew, Arthur Balfour, the prospect for the Conservative party begins to darken.

CHAPTER VI

Defeat and recovery
1902–22

I

Balfour's succession to the premiership was generally expected, in spite of the presence of a more conspicuous figure in the Cabinet, Joseph Chamberlain. At the time that Salisbury resigned Chamberlain was in bed after a bad cab accident; he probably never quite recovered from its effects. Tempting though it is to suppose that Salisbury chose this moment to ease his nephew into power, there is no evidence to confirm the theory which is anyway implausible. Joseph Chamberlain laid no claim to the supreme office. He was not a Conservative even in name, for the Liberal Unionists were still a separate party with their own funds, whips and organisation. It would have been asking a great deal of the Conservatives to accept as Prime Minister the non-Anglican leader of a far smaller party, an ex-Radical whose earlier career had been devoted to scathing attacks upon everything that they stood for. This was the last period in Conservative party history when Anglicanism was still important, and when politics turned to any serious extent on the conflict between the Church of England and the Nonconformists. Chamberlain, nothing if not a realist, was fully conscious of his handicaps. Moreover, throughout his career he wanted to *do* things rather than *be* someone. He was ready to serve under Balfour, as long as he was given a reasonably free hand; but he had no intention of being a doormat.

The new Prime Minister was a person of immense charm, great intellectual power, and much political sagacity. Like his uncle, he took it for granted that parliamentary democracy would only work – if it could work at all – as long as 'the masses' continued to elect their leaders from 'the classes'. Not that he was himself, any more than Salisbury, a typical member of the order to which he belonged. He was too clever, too cool, too detached to be thus categorised. The tragic death of the girl he hoped to marry seems to have left a lasting scar upon his feelings. He remained a bachelor – Britain's first, though not her last, unmarried Prime Minister since the younger Pitt – and he was happy to move to the end of his days courteous, charming and self-contained in an adoring circle of female friends and relations. As a young man he belonged to 'the Souls', that fascinating, aristocratic, intellectual coterie whose history, like the history of all such groups, can never now be written, for so much of it has vanished with the echoes of their own brilliant talk. It was there that he met Curzon and perhaps acquired the seeds of that lasting doubt about his character, which was to deflect marginally yet decisively, the course of party history in the early 1920s.

There is no reason why a Prime Minister should be typical of his fellow-countrymen. In fact few if any can be so described. Yet there are probably limits beyond which remoteness from the man in the street becomes a liability. Balfour was not only a wealthy man and a member of the aristocracy, he was also an intellectual. No doubt this could be said of his uncle, Salisbury, and of his rival, Rosebery. But Salisbury, who was a younger son brought up with no expectation of succeeding to a grand title and a splendid estate, had at one time been relatively hard up and had actually worked for his living; and Rosebery was a devotee of the turf which was not only the sport of kings but of the masses too. Both men had at least some contact with the world of ordinary people.

Balfour's hobby was philosophy – a study in itself calculated to inspire mistrust in the 'plain man'. Nor was he helped by the title of his first and best known book on that subject, *A defence of philosophic doubt*. To most people – and of course most people never read it – this suggested scepticism about religious creeds, or even agnosticism. In fact Balfour was applying 'doubt' not to religion but to that very process of scientific reasoning which constituted the greatest challenge to religion. In effect he was saying that, looked at from one point of view, everything is doubtful – religion not more so than the rest; therefore why not believe in religion? Whatever the merits of this argument it was unlikely to get across to any but a tiny minority of his contemporaries. It was the title that stuck in men's minds and shaped Balfour's 'image', as a sceptical sitter on the fence incapable of giving a clear lead or making a definite decision – 'shivering in philosophic doubt on the steps of a metaphysical bathing machine', as the Tory *Pall Mall Gazette* unkindly put it.

Balfour had a very clear mind. More than most statesmen of his day he saw the new situation in which Britain found herself. He was aware of the changing balance of world power, acutely conscious of the long term threat implicit in the rise of German military strength and the growing economic preponderance of the United States. It was a time when Britain's 'role in the world' was the subject of much heart searching on the part of her leading politicians, publicists and thinkers. In retrospect this period of anxiety can be seen as beginning with the German victory of 1870. Disraeli's shadowy, high flown, but none the less genuine appeal to the cause of empire, made soon afterwards, was one of the first manifestations of anxiety about the indefinite continuance of the Victorian high noon, an early recognition that the shadows were growing longer and that something would have to be done if the nation was to protect itself against the evening chill which might not be so very far away.

But it took time and further changes for the situation to become at all clear. Thirty years after Disraeli's Crystal Palace speech when Balfour became Prime Minister in 1902 there was a far greater awareness of the altered position of Britain vis-à-vis her rivals. Kipling's poems written at the turn of the century are often taken as symbols of imperial complacency; they are in fact nothing of the sort as anyone who takes the trouble to read *Recessional* (1897), *The white man's burden* (1899), or *The dykes* (1902) will quickly see. Britain's security, her survival even, were no longer taken for granted.

The Boer War had enhanced all these misgivings. True, Britain had won it, but only after a prolonged campaign which reflected little credit either on the army's readiness for war or the competence of its commanders. If Britain was to retain her place as a great power, three important requirements had to be met: the country needed a new foreign policy to avoid isolation in a hostile world; it needed a new defence policy in order to cope with a war which seemed more and more probable; it needed a new educational policy to prevent its industry falling behind the technological standards of Germany and America. Salisbury, Balfour and Chamberlain, the triumvirate which dominated the Tory government from 1895 to 1902, were well aware of these needs. Balfour's clear brain, his personal interest in scientific and technological matters, his knowledge of defence problems made him in many ways the statesman personally best suited to deal with the situation. What is more, to the best of his ability and with the limited means at his disposal he really did do something about it.

A new course in foreign policy began with the formation of the Japanese Alliance (actually signed before Balfour became Prime Minister) and the creation of the *Entente* with France. The Committee of Imperial Defence was set up and a major reorganisation of both the army and navy was put in hand. There is evidence that Balfour's much criticised decision to hang on to office long after by-elections had shown a massive swing to the other side was caused less by hope that it would swing back than by his anxiety to place some of those changes beyond the power of the Liberals to reverse. Nor did he neglect education. The Act of 1902 which he personally piloted through the House while his uncle was still Prime Minister remained the basis of secondary education till the Butler Act of 1944.

Yet the Education Act also showed Balfour's great limitation: his range of vision excluded what might be called the middle distance in politics. He could discern what was happening far away and he had an eye for the signs of new trends and developments. He was, for example, quick to see that the real significance of the landslide election of 1906 was not the huge number of Liberal gains but the election of 29 members of an Independent Labour Party. At the other end of politics no one threaded his way more skilfully than he through those complicated personal and political mazes of Cabinet or shadow Cabinet, which so often bewilder lesser men. He always behaved with formal correctitude, though not always with generosity. The charges levelled against him over his treatment of the Free Trade ministers in the crisis of 1903, or of jettisoning his Irish Secretary, George Wyndham, in 1905, have been shown as baseless. He had every reason to dismiss a group which was caballing against him; and far from throwing Wyndham to the wolves he did all he could to dissuade him from resigning. But he could also behave with much ruthlessness. The preservation of the unity of the Conservative party was in his eyes a trust for which as leader he was personally responsible. He had no intention of letting others manœuvre him out of it until the moment came, as it eventually did come in 1911, when he concluded that his continuation as leader was a greater danger to that trust than his resignation. Meanwhile, as Winston Churchill puts it, who knew his formidable powers only too well, 'Had his life been cast amid the labyrinthine intrigues of the Italian Renaissance, he would not have required to study the works of Machiavelli.'[1]

Where Balfour went astray was neither in his dealings with cabinet colleagues, nor in his perception of the altered balance of power in the world, nor in his awareness of social changes in Britain. It was when he surveyed the middle distance bounded by the limits of the British electorate that his vision became hazy, his touch unsure. The truth was that he was too rational and that he made insufficient allowance for the unreason of the masses. He could understand what he regarded as a reasonable cause for complaint. For example, he rightly saw that Joseph Chamberlain's campaign for imperial preference would never be accepted if it involved food taxes. 'The prejudice against a small tax on food is not the fad of a few imperfectly informed theorists,' he wrote to Chamberlain on February 18, 1905, 'it is a deep rooted prejudice affecting a large mass of voters, especially the poorest class, which it will be a matter of extreme difficulty to overcome.'[2] Balfour was right, and the association of Chamberlain's proposals with dearer food was almost certainly a major element in the defeat of 1906.

But it was not the only one, and on at least two other matters

[1] Winston S. Churchill, *Great contemporaries* (1937), 242.
[2] Quoted, Kenneth Young, *Arthur James Balfour* (1963), 220.

Balfour's blind spots were responsible for trouble. One of these was the Education Act which greatly irritated Nonconformist opinion by putting Anglican Church schools 'on the rates'. Exactly how much support this cost the Conservatives is a moot point but it cannot have done them any good. In a sense the outcry was illogical. For years past the Treasury had subsidized Church schools, and it is hard to see any difference of principle between provision from central funds and provision from local taxation. But the fact was that people felt differently about the two methods, however illogically. This was something that Balfour with his cool, dispassionate mind failed to foresee – unlike Joseph Chamberlain who might be unsound on food taxes but knew all about nonconformity, and predicted clearly the unpopularity which would accrue to the government.

The second reproach which took Balfour by surprise, and most of his colleagues too, was 'Chinese slavery', the decision to allow the mine-owners of the Rand to import indentured Chinese coolies in order to fill the labour shortage which followed the end of the South African War. To the High Commissioner, Lord Milner, who recommended it, the policy seemed a sensible way of speeding up post-war reconstruction. Alfred Milner, a former Liberal partly German in ancestry, was at this time one of the heroes of the imperialist movement. He had great prestige and he regarded parliamentary democracy with contempt. It was not for him to consider the repercussions of his policy in Britain. The Prime Minister ought to have seen its implications, but Balfour was singularly insensitive to any save the most predictable reactions of the working class. This had already been shown by his unwillingness to press parliament to reverse the new and far more restrictive interpretation put by the judges in *Quinn* v. *Leathem* and the Taff Vale case on the trade union legislation of 1871–6 – legislation for which the Conservatives themselves could claim much of the original credit. *Quinn* v. *Leathem* greatly extended the liability of a strike organiser to civil actions by employers, and the Taff Vale case removed the protection which the law had hitherto been believed to give to trade union funds. Few things contributed more than Conservative inaction in this field to the rise of the Labour party and the alienation of the working class which had such disastrous effects on the Conservative party in the 1906 election. It is hard to believe that Disraeli would have made a similar error.

Nor is it likely that he would have agreed to 'Chinese slavery'. The policy asked for trouble from the working class for two reasons; it excluded a field of potential emigration, and it implied a commodity view of labour which was likely to be anathema to articulate trade unionists; if capitalists in South Africa were to be allowed to deal with shortage of labour by importing foreigners, the precedent might be extended to Britain and be invoked to undermine the unions whenever they found themselves in a favourable bargaining position. The policy also invited trouble from the 'Nonconformist Conscience' of a section of the middle class already affronted by the Education Act. The Nonconformist Conscience was not only highly sensitive about slavery, but also highly sensitive about sexual irregularities. What would happen, it was asked, if great numbers of young men for reasons of security were horded in 'compounds' for long periods of time without their wives or women? The answer was all too clear – in the jargon of the day 'nameless practices'; and although today we are readier to give them a name, even then everyone knew what was meant.

The Cabinet did indeed have some misgivings about Milner's proposal. Joseph Chamberlain when he made his prolonged visit to South Africa in the winter of 1902-3 vetoed it for the time being, declaring that he would only consent if there was incontrovertible evidence that the Europeans in South Africa wanted it. But he was out of office by the time the real crisis of labour shortage on the Rand came to a head late in 1903. His successor, Alfred Lyttelton, did not have the political stature to cope with Milner who appears to have been determined to get his way on this point at almost any cost. Milner visited London in the autumn. He believed that he had persuaded Asquith and the leading Liberal imperialists to remain at least neutral, and he convinced the Cabinet with cogent economic arguments. Early in 1904 the Legislative Council of the Transvaal by 22 votes to 4 asked for an ordinance sanctioning the importation of indentured Chinese coolies. The ordinance was promptly made and immediately a storm burst upon the heads of the Cabinet in London.

This is not the place to discuss the rights and wrongs of the measure except to observe that, although 'slavery' was a gross exaggeration which the Liberal leader, Campbell-Bannerman,[1] himself virtually withdrew later, and although the Chinese labourers earned wages some fifteen times as high as they could ever get in their native land, and although Milner's economic objective was undoubtedly achieved, nonetheless there were features about the conditions of work which could legitimately arouse humanitarian indignation. Even more to the point, the ordinance did alienate organised labour in Britain. The humanitarian 'do-gooders' tended to be Liberals anyway, but in 1895 and 1900 a substantial measure of working class support must have gone to the Conservatives. It was this which Taff Vale and Chinese slavery were to whittle away. As Balfour put it in a letter on June 15, 1904, to the Governor-General of Australia, Lord Northcote, a son of Sir Stafford Northcote, '. . . . our chief difficulty is the misrepresentation over Chinese labour . . . which is opposed on the preposterous ground that it is slavery but is really unpopular because it is erroneously supposed to substitute yellow for white labour.'[2] Balfour was not allowing for justifiable objections which seemed fully confirmed later when it became known that Milner with incredible folly had actually sanctioned illegal flogging of the coolies; but he had a genuine point when he said that the outcry was not wholly altruistic. However, this did not make it any less damaging to the Conservatives. Rather the contrary.

2

Balfour had many good qualities and his government achieved much success in the fields of foreign policy, defence and education. To these should be added the Licensing Act of 1904, a notable effort to bring sense and order into the jungle-like obscurity of the British laws on drink, and the Irish Land Purchase Act of 1903

[1] Sir Henry Campbell-Bannerman had been elected leader in succession to Harcourt, who gave up in a huff in 1898. Harcourt himself had led the party for only two years having succeeded Rosebery who resigned out of pique in 1896. The Liberal party suffered much at that time from *prima donna* leadership. Campbell-Bannerman, a cautious Scot, was a welcome contrast.

[2] Balfour Papers, quoted, Dennis Judd, *Balfour and the British Empire* (1968), 201.

which produced a lasting settlement of the Irish land problem. It was also the culmination of the policy of 'killing Home Rule by kindness'. Here it failed but that merely illustrates the truth which escaped the Conservatives though not Gladstone, viz, that nations, rightly or wrongly struggling to be free, are not going to be stopped by economic palliatives. To solve the Irish land problem was worth doing for its own sake; it was not an answer to Irish nationalism.

Balfour, however, had his blind spots, and their effects on the electoral fortunes of his party were considerable. It is fair to say that this myopia was shared by nearly all his colleagues, although Joseph Chamberlain, heir to another political tradition, was more percipient. The religious clauses of the Education Act with their effect on the Nonconformists, and the Chinese labour ordinance with its effect upon the conscience of the middle class and the fears of the working class were measures which Chamberlain regarded with much misgiving. But Joseph Chamberlain was as blind as anyone else in failing to see the need to do something about the judicial decisions reversing the interpretation of legislation believed for a quarter of a century to safeguard the position of the trade unions.

This neglect of working class interests gave a notable impetus to the newly founded Labour Representation Committee. Along with hostility to the Boer War and objection to the Education Act, it was an important factor in bringing about a secret agreement concluded early in 1903 between Herbert Gladstone, the Liberal Chief Whip, and Ramsay MacDonald, the secretary of the LRC. The gist of it was that, in return for a free run for LRC. candidates in some thirty-five seats, the LRC would not attempt to split the anti-Conservative vote elsewhere in England and Wales (the deal did not apply to Scotland). Despite the difficulties involved in encroaching upon local constituency autonomy the arrangement worked with remarkable smoothness. It was to be a vital feature of the political scene for the next fifteen years. No doubt the Conservatives would have lost in 1906, whatever the electoral arrangements of their opponents; but they would not have lost by so many seats, and they might have won the next election in January 1910 if there had been no coordination between Liberals and

Labour. It is hard to believe that the termination of the Liberal–Labour pact in 1918 and the simultaneous revival of Conservative fortunes were entirely coincidental. The election of 1922 where the Conservatives, with 5·5 million votes against the combined Liberal and Labour total of nearly 8·5 million, nevertheless won 344 seats out of 615 shows how well they could do when their opponents were cutting each others' throats.[1]

The desirability of reaching an agreement was enhanced by an important new development in May 1903. To explain it we must go back a year to the budget of 1902 when Hicks Beach, Chancellor of the Exchequer, with some hesitation reimposed after a lapse of thirty-three years the registration duty on imported corn. Hicks Beach was a rigorous free trader, and he had consented to this measure purely for revenue purposes. But at the Colonial Conference in the summer of 1902 the suggestion was made by Sir Wilfrid Laurier, the Prime Minister of Canada, that a reciprocal arrangement could be achieved if in return for a rebate on the tariff on British manufactured goods entering Canada, the British government were to remit the duty on colonial wheat entering Britain.

The notion of imperial preference had been in the air at least since the last Colonial Conference in 1897, and Joseph Chamberlain had long been intrigued by its possibilities; but the snag hitherto had been the non-existence of any British duties whose remission could be expected to make the slightest difference. Salisbury resigned in July, and Hicks Beach took the opportunity of retiring along with his old chief. The Cabinet discussed the matter during the autumn, and an interim decision was taken in favour of a rebate at the next budget. The new Chancellor, C. T. Ritchie, however, made it clear that he objected and that he reserved the right to argue the matter again nearer the day.

Chamberlain departed to South Africa, aware that Ritchie was hostile, but legitimately confident that the Prime Minister and the great majority of the Cabinet were on the other side. There is something about the veld, its thin air, its glittering sky by night,

[1] It is fair to point out that in this election there was also a division within the Liberal party itself between the Asquithians and the National Liberals who supported Lloyd George, but I can only find five seats which can be said to have been won by the Conservatives because of this split.

its vast horizons by day, which goes to the head and makes the problems of damp misty Britain appear small, remote and easily soluble. In South Africa Chamberlain became even more convinced that imperial preference was the only way in which the empire could be welded into a closer unity and thus constitute a counter-balancing force to the great new continental powers, the USA and Germany, which threatened the economic and military security of the British seaborne empire. Moreover he saw in the revenue to be obtained from the new duties a valuable source of finance for social reform.

Political unity in the form of imperial federation, economic unity in the form of a customs union, military unity in the form of the integration of the colonial forces – *Staatsverein*, *Zollverein*, *Kriegsverein*, to borrow the terms much in use at the time and symbolic of the prestige of post-Bismarckian Germany – these were the goals to be aimed at. Chamberlain was under no delusions about the difficulties which would confront anyone who attempted to reach them in a single stride, but he believed that a system of reciprocal preferences would · be an important step in the right direction, and that a rebate on the corn duty would provide an opportunity to start such a system. What is more he believed that the Cabinet had agreed to this step; that it would create a precedent when similar requests came, as they surely would, from other colonies; and that in this way without there being at any single moment a clear confrontation between free trade and protection, reciprocal colonial preferences would silently come into existence. The system once established would be for practical purposes impossible to repeal, and the Liberals when they came back into office would have to accept it.

A series of intrigues, misunderstandings and accidents frustrated this plan. The absence of any Cabinet minutes or written record of its decisions compounded the confusion. Stiffened by the Treasury officials, Ritchie, who had ironically in earlier days been a sympathiser with the 'fair trade' movement,[1] became an implacable opponent. Joseph Chamberlain's absence from England was disastrous. His son Austen, who represented him,

---

[1] This was a movement in the 1880s for the introduction of retaliatory tariffs. It soon faded out.

was a member of the Cabinet but felt himself too junior to make trouble. Ritchie threatened to resign if the Cabinet persisted in remitting the duty on Canadian wheat. Balfour hesitated. Free trade opposition in the Cabinet hardened. By the time Joseph Chamberlain returned, budget day was less than six weeks away. To press the issue now meant a show-down. It would be for either him or Ritchie to resign. He thought the issue of the corn duty by itself insufficient to resign on, and he was exhausted after his visit to South Africa. His biographer, Julian Amery, quotes a letter from Balfour to the Duke of Devonshire, describing Chamberlain as 'rather ill, rather irritable and very tired'. Amery goes on, 'He lacked the energy to mobilize his friends in the Cabinet. Accordingly he declined Ritchie's challenge. It may have been a fatal mistake.'[1]

One can but echo Amery's words. Confronted with a choice between Ritchie and Chamberlain Balfour must have opted for the latter. Chamberlain could have forced Ritchie's resignation on what might well have seemed to the public a narrow question. He might thus have rallied the Cabinet behind him and committed them to a policy of imperial preference. As it was, events went less favourably. Ritchie presented his budget in a highly anti-protectionist tone of voice. On May 15 Chamberlain made a memorable speech at Birmingham, in which he challenged the whole of the prevailing fiscal orthodoxy and posed the question of preference as a means of consolidating a great empire. He ended by urging his audience 'to consolidate an Empire which can only be maintained by relations of interest as well as by relations of sentiment'. He went on:

And, for my own part, I believe in a British Empire, in an Empire which, although it should be one of its first duties to cultivate friendship with all the nations of the world, should yet, even if alone, be self-sustaining and self-sufficient, able to maintain itself against the competition of all its rivals. And I do not believe in a Little England which shall be separated from all those to whom it should in the natural course look for support and affection – a Little England which shall thus be dependent

[1] Julian Amery, *Life of Joseph Chamberlain* (1969), V, 161.

absolutely on the mercy of those who envy its present prosperity, and who have shown they are ready to do all in their power to prevent its future union with the British race throughout the world [loud and continued cheers].[1]

The speech produced a great sensation. At once it gained the support of two elements in the Unionist party: the antediluvian figures who saw it as an attempt to reverse the repeal of the corn laws – men like Henry Chaplin, 'the Squire', and the aged Lord Halsbury; and, more welcome to Chamberlain, the younger generation sceptical about free trade and imbued with imperial enthusiasm. L. S. Amery, later to be a prominent Conservative minister in the inter-war years, describes how the morning after the speech he was as usual working in the offices of *The Times* on his history of the South African War when Leo Maxse, the combative owner and editor of the right wing *National Review*, burst in. 'Seizing both my hands in his he waltzed me round the room as he poured forth a paean of jubilation at the thought that, at last, there was a cause to work for in politics.'[2] People took these things more seriously than they do now. It is hard to imagine anything which would provoke similar excitement today. 'The Birmingham speech,' wrote L. S. Amery, 'was a challenge to free trade as direct and provocative as the theses which Luther nailed to the church door at Wittenberg.'[3]

This was true, but it was also the key to the difficulties that followed. There was no longer any hope now of sliding preference in by the back door as a minor gloss on free trade orthodoxy. Instead there was a confrontation. If the Birmingham speech rallied some sections of the Unionist party, it also infuriated others, and it led straight to a complicated Cabinet crisis in September, the cause of much subsequent controversy which needs no analysis here.[4] The upshot was that Chamberlain retired to campaign, with Balfour's blessing, for tariff reform from outside the Cabinet, while Ritchie and the free traders[5] whom Balfour regarded as having

[1] ibid., V, 29.   [2] L. S. Amery, *My political life* (1953), I, 238.   [3] ibid, 236.
[4] The most authoritative account which supersedes all previous ones is in Julian Amery, op. cit., V, 383–448.
[5] The others were Lord Balfour of Burleigh (no relation of the Prime Minister), Lord George Hamilton and Arthur Elliot.

intrigued against him were in effect dismissed. Balfour hoped to retain the Duke of Devonshire in spite of his free trade predilections. He thought he had succeeded, and when Devonshire resigned two weeks later on a hair-splitting interpretation of one of Balfour's speeches but really under pressure from the other free traders, he was not only very angry but, unusually for him, displayed his anger[1] in a withering letter to the unfortunate duke.

Balfour had wanted to get rid of Ritchie and his group. He would ideally have retained both Chamberlain and the duke. But he saw that he could not keep both, and he had agreed to let Chamberlain go on the assumption that the duke would stay. He had now lost the duke too and his reconstructed Cabinet seemed light in weight compared with the ministry he had inherited the year before. What was more the fiscal debate had become a wider one. Tariffs could be used for other purposes than preference. There was the possibility of retaliatory tariffs which Balfour himself favoured and which raised no question of dear food. Joseph Chamberlain himself conceded publicly that food taxes were not a practicable proposition for the moment. His object in resigning was to have a free hand for a great campaign to convert the electorate to the need for them. Thus the Unionist party spoke discordantly and with many voices.

All this was grist to the Liberal mill. The party began to close its ranks, and Labour, alarmed at the prospect of the 'little loaf', was determined to implement their bargain with the Liberal managers. All the evidence suggests that nothing was more disastrous to his party than Joseph Chamberlain's campaign for tariff reform. The attack on free trade alienated Whitehall, for the whole weight of Treasury orthodoxy was against protection in any form. It alienated the economists—only four of any standing were in favour of it. Far more important it frightened a great section of the working class to whom cheap food had been a much cherished boon for the last quarter of a century and it annoyed the middle class *rentiers* who saw the prospect of a reduction in the purchasing power of their fixed incomes. It split the Conservative party from

---

[1] The only other occasion that I can find was during the Parliament Act crisis of 1911 when he considered that he had been seriously misled by Lord Knollys, one of the king's private secretaries. See Kenneth Young, *Arthur James Balfour*, 301–8.

top to bottom, creating a disastrous appearance of vacillation and dissension. Finally, it united the Liberals who had been hitherto hopelessly divided on all the main political issues. This is quite an achievement for any campaign.

Moreover, it did not stop at the election of 1906. At the beginning of the controversy in June–July 1903, the Chamberlainites numbered about 130 MPs, and their all-out opponents, the Unionist Free Traders, were about 60. But the Tariff Reform League was in every way a more effective body than the Free Food League which tried to combat it. The latter was little more than a parliamentary group. The former operated on the grass roots of politics – and with great ruthlessness; by the time of the 1906 election it had some 300 Unionist constituency organisations under its control. The tariff reformers lost the election but triumphed in the party. Of the 157 Conservatives returned 109 were out and out tariff reformers and only 16 were Free Traders. The remainder adhered to a subtle Balfourian compromise which however, leaned far nearer to protection than free trade. Balfour in the new parliament moved rapidly closer to tariff reform. By 1910 the tariff reformers had completely captured the party, and Lord Hugh Cecil, appropriately elected for 'the home of lost causes', Oxford University, was almost the only Unionist Free Trader in the House.

The historian should frankly admit when he is baffled. The success of tariff reform within the party is something of a puzzle, given its total failure outside. One can see the reasoning behind it – ultimately uneasiness at Britain's world role; fear of the rise of the great land-based continental powers, America and Germany; belief that an imperial economic union would lead to an imperial federal union like the German *Zollverein*; a conviction that Britain as a small island (or, rather, two islands) must fall behind in 'the race' – a race whose goal then as today was never exactly specified – whereas Britain at the head of a great politically united empire could hold her own. It was certainly not an ignoble ideal, though its proponents gravely underestimated the obstacles they would have had to face even if they had managed to convert the British electorate. For example tariff reform ignored India and, even in the White Commonwealth for which it was essentially designed, cut far less ice than Joseph Chamberlain supposed. Indeed the trend in the empire was centrifugal not centripetal: first, its white European settlers, later its brown Asians, finally its black Africans sought nothing so much as the creation of nation states virtually independent of Britain though perhaps not unfriendly to her. That was the lesson they learned from Europe, not imperial federation.

One can also see the force which a new and clear policy had in a party which from 1902 was tired and running out of ideas – especially if that policy was championed by the most dynamic figure on the political scene. Joseph Chamberlain more than most politicians loved power rather than status. Hence his taking the Colonial Office in 1895. Hence his ready acceptance of the impossibility of his succeeding Salisbury as Prime Minister. Hence too too his ruthless determination, his harsh methods, the whiff of sulphur which hangs about so many of his actions. It is easier to be unscrupulous for a cause than for oneself.

But what baffles one is the persistence of the party in a cause that was politically so calamitous. True, it began well. The first by-elections in which ardent tariff reformers put the matter to the test were held at the end of 1903. At Dulwich Rutherfoord Harris, one of the shadiest of Rhodes's coadjutors over the Jameson Raid and a man who had been censured for electoral malpractices in 1900, came head of the poll. If tariff reform could get someone like that into the House it looked at any rate electorally promising. But in 1904 the tariff reformers fared disastrously at by-elections. Moreover, the question was dividing the party far more seriously than the feuds over the pro-Boers and the Liberal League had ever divided the Liberal party.

The old guard, the traditional landed classes, were split. Some detested protectionism, seeing in it not only economic disaster but an unsavoury attitude to life. Lord Robert Cecil told Balfour that he objected to the tariff reformers' 'whole way of looking at things. It appears to me utterly sordid and materialistic, not yet corrupt but on the high road to corruption.'[1] Others, with a certain nostalgia for the old high protectionism before 1846, supported tariff reform. If the driving force came from the representatives

[1] Brit. Mus. Add. MS. 49737 (Balfour Papers), Cecil to Balfour, January 25, 1906.

of heavy industry the fact remains that Chamberlain did not lack patrician allies. But his movement alienated some of the oldest and most respectable Unionists, Hicks Beach, Lord George Hamilton and the Duke of Devonshire. It also drove out some of the bright young men, 'the Hughligans' as they were called after Lord Hugh Cecil, a sort of Fourth party. The most famous of them was Winston Churchill who crossed the floor of the House in 1904. The Cecils remained – but were frustrated and discontented.

In spite of these palpable snags the persistence of the tariff reformers is perhaps explicable till 1906. After all, no one could really tell what would happen at the election. After 1906 it becomes harder and harder to understand. The cause had surely been an obvious vote-loser and yet it gained ground steadily even after its high priest had been paralysed by a stroke. Tariff reform was a major factor in pushing the party into rejecting the 1909 budget in the House of Lords. Thus, just at the moment when the record of the Liberals was producing a strong pro-Conservative swing, the party played into the enemy's hands. The elections of 1910 did, it is true, improve the Conservative position and were a disappointment to the Liberals. But this owed nothing to tariff reform, as Balfour seems to have seen, for he undertook, if returned at the December election, to submit tariffs to a referendum before bringing in legislation. And, although after the loss of the election the undertaking could be argued to have lapsed, his successor, Bonar Law, a far keener tariff reformer, felt obliged to renew the promise in 1913 (though in the form of a second election rather than a referendum).

Yet tariff reform remained an article of faith in the party. Like Clause 4 in the Labour Constitution it seemed irremovable, in spite of its obvious unpopularity with the public. When in 1922 Bonar Law renewed his pledge of 1913 the Conservatives won their first election since 1900. When in 1923 Baldwin asked for a mandate for tariffs he lost. In 1924 the party abandoned tariffs and won. In 1930 a row about tariffs nearly drove Baldwin out of the leadership. When at last in 1932 their huge majority enabled them to carry a moderate tariff which Neville Chamberlain professed to regard as the fulfilment of his father's ideals, it was in reality not tariff reform in the old sense at all. Imperial federation had long been as dead as the proverbial dodo. Seldom has a party persisted so long in such an unpromising cause. It almost gives credibility to the notion that there can be such a thing as a political death wish, improbable though that must seem amidst the normal wholesome pragmatism of British politicians.

3

The general election of 1906 was the most disastrous defeat that the Conservative party sustained in the whole of our period – worse even than 1832 when they only held 185 seats. In 1906 the Unionists sank to 157.[1] In Britain excluding Ireland they only secured 44 per cent of the popular vote.[2] If we look at Henry Pelling's 'regions' which, counting Wales and Scotland but not Ireland, amount to fifteen, the extent of the defeat is no less striking. In 1885 when the Conservatives did badly they had a majority of the popular vote in four out of the fifteen, in 1895 eleven, and in 1900 ten including Scotland. But in 1906 they were in a minority in all but one, the West Midlands. They were even out-voted in such normally impregnable fortresses as South-East England (114 seats), London (57) and Lancastria (76), in all of which they had a majority of the popular vote in 1885.

Until more work is done – and it is being done – on psephological history, one cannot be at all sure about the causes of this collapse. Indeed, even when it has been done, we may still be uncertain, for one cannot conduct political market research into the opinions of the dead. One can analyse the programmes of the parties, investigate their lines of attack and defence, read the newspapers – the Harmsworths and the 'heavies' – ascertain what the whips, the party managers and even the local constituency agents believed to be the causes of success or failure, but one cannot be sure just what swayed the voters. It is hard enough to understand contemporary elections – with all the devices of opinion polling at our disposal. How much harder to discover the truth about elections long vanished into the dusty archives of the past.

[1] Conservatives 132, Liberal Unionists 25; or on another mode of analysis, Chamberlainite tariff reformers 109, Balfourians 32, Unionist Free Traders 16.

[2] As calculated in Henry Pelling, *Social geography of English elections 1885–1910* (1967), 415. The book is a mine of information.

Statistically the way in which the Conservatives lost is clear enough. They were swamped by a big rise in the number of Liberal or Labour voters. Their own vote per opposed candidate, *c.* 4,300 was much the same as in the 1900 election, but the Liberal vote shot up by over 25 per cent from *c.* 4,100 to *c.* 5,200. This suggests, though it does not prove conclusively, that the turnover of seats was not caused by a mass conversion from Conservatism to Liberalism but because a large number of people who had abstained in 1900 were stirred to vote for the Liberals or – if one prefers it – against the Conservatives five and a half years later. The result was all the more devastating in terms of seats owing to the bargain between Liberals and Labour.

We can at least make some plausible guesses at the causes of the landslide. It is clear, if only from the collapse of Conservative support in Lancashire and in the poorer districts of London, that a great number of working class voters declared against the Conservatives, and that their effect was particularly potent because of the Lib–Lab pact. It is reasonable to surmise some of the causes that were operating: the trade unions' grievance over the decisions in the Taff Vale case and the case of *Quinn* v. *Leathem*; 'Chinese slavery' with all that it implied; 'the big loaf and the little loaf' – the fear that tariff reform would lead to dearer food; party discord on the fiscal question; general exhaustion after ten years in office, which was perhaps reflected in a lower quality in public debate compared with the Liberal leaders – especially after the departure of Chamberlain.

It is a moot point how far these or other issues cost the Conservatives the loss of middle class support too. The 'Nonconformist Conscience' which characterised a section of both the middle and the working class was certainly affronted by 'Chinese slavery' for reasons besides emigration and the commodity view of labour. It is also true that the Nonconformists were incensed by Balfour's Education Act. The theory has been advanced that from 1886 they had been drifting away from the Liberal party, and that the Act abruptly reversed this trend. Yet the researches of Pelling and others do not suggest that in 1906 the Nonconformist areas of Britain swung more markedly to the Liberal side than anywhere else – indeed the contrary is true; nor for that matter does there seem any clear evidence that there had ever been a major move away from the Liberals in 1886. The electoral consequences of the Education Act were perhaps exaggerated by tariff reformers in search of a scapegoat. The place where the Act provoked greatest wrath was Wales, and it was difficult for Wales to be much more Liberal than it already was.

Nevertheless, setting aside nonconformity which was anyway on the decline, we can still discern a considerable middle class swing away from the Tories. It was nearly 15 per cent in the richer London constituencies, and these figures could be matched elsewhere. To what extent was the swing the signal of an intellectual revolt by what are sometimes called the opinion-forming class against current orthodoxies? Of course the middle class is not coterminous with the intellectuals. Far from it. But it includes them, and one or two figures may suggest that something of the sort was happening.

For instance, the universities which in both Scotland and England normally returned Conservatives or Liberal Unionists unopposed showed at least signs of a move in the other direction. True, even in 1906 no contest took place in Oxford University; and in Cambridge the battle was between different sorts of Conservative. But a Liberal nearly won London – only losing by 26 votes; and in both Glasgow and Edinburgh there were contests for the first time since 1880, though the Liberals did not win, or indeed do as well as their forbears a quarter of a century earlier.

A rebellion by the intellectuals usually accompanies and probably in some measure causes a great political shift, a major loss of central ground, such as evidently occurred at this time. One can compare the anti-Conservatism of the intelligentsia in the 1930s and early 1940s, the swing the other way in the late 1940s and early 1950s, and the reversal in its turn of that trend in the early 1960s. If a party is to have a broad base of political power it needs the support of at least a section of the intellectuals. It is clear that from the fall of Peel to the early 1870s their predominant sentiment was Liberal, but it was beginning to change in the late 1870s. In his analysis of the 'Atrocitarians' in 1876–7 Dr Shannon[1] shows how the intelligentsia divided, and lists the formidable figures who

[1] R. T. Shannon, *Gladstone and the Bulgarian agitation 1876* (1963), 211–20.

were sceptical or positively hostile to the agitation – Fitzjames
Stephen, Frederic Harrison, Matthew Arnold, Sir Henry Maine,
George Eliot, and Richard Congreve, the apostle of Comte.

If this loss of intellectual support for Gladstonian Liberalism
was apparent as early as that, it was even more obvious ten years
later. J. L. Hammond shows[1] the extent to which Gladstone
stood alone in the intellectual world in his attitude to the Irish
question. The tide was going in the Conservative direction from
then onwards. Of course it was not a smoothly flowing surface.
There were many eddies and cross-currents. But throughout the
1890s the 'national idea', the concept of empire linked with
social reform, the decline of nonconformity, and much else, combined to give the Conservatives a preponderance, though not of
course a monopoly, in the world of thought and literature. Even
the Webbs believed around the turn of the century that they had
more chance of getting their ideas accepted by gradual permeation
of the Conservative establishment than by converting a Liberal
party still haunted by the ghost of Gladstone.

Yet all this changed quite suddenly. No doubt many things
combined to do it. One of them was the temporary disappearance
of the Irish question. This was bound to be a good thing for the
Liberals. Home Rule was always unpopular in England. True, it
had not been an issue in 1900 either, but the Conservatives then had
all the assets of the 'patriotic cry' in wartime. These had vanished
long before 1906, and in so far as they were remembered had
become positive liabilities. Fear of Home Rule might have been a
card to play now. Indeed, Balfour played it by resigning rather than
dissolving, in the hope that Campbell-Bannerman would find that
Home Rule created such divisions in the Liberal party that he
could not form a government. Nothing of the sort occurred. The
Liberals, released from Gladstone, were sick of the subject, and in
any case John Redmond, Parnell's successor as leader of the Irish
party, undertook not to press it in the next parliament.

But above all what wrecked the intellectual support of the
Conservatives was disillusionment with the 'imperial idea'. This
stemmed from the Jameson Raid and the South African War. Both
outraged the conscience of the intelligentsia, and in the not very

[1] In that great historical work, *Gladstone and the Irish nation* (1938).

long run affected a much wider range of public opinion. The Jameson Raid in particular looked fishy from the start. It was widely suspected to be a conspiracy – and rightly, though it was to be many years before the full facts emerged. What is more it was a conspiracy that did not come off. Perhaps the British politico-administrative system is naturally unreceptive to conspiratorial methods. Sixty years later 'Suez' emphasised the point, and had something of the same immediate effect on the moral sensibilities of the intellectuals and the same delayed effect on the political fortunes of the party then in power. We can perhaps compare the election of 1900 with that of 1959: the patriotic idea prevailed over the 'Nonconformist conscience'. But the adverse delayed effects upon the Conservative party were seen in 1906 even as they were to be seen sixty years later in the elections of 1964 and 1966.

4

The Conservative party machine had worked without any serious criticism under Salisbury, but this halcyon period came to an end soon after 1902. There was a new Chief Whip, Acland Hood, who seems to have lacked the drive of his predecessors, and in 1903 Middleton retired. It is a moot point whether organisational trouble is a symptom or a cause of party decline – perhaps a bit of both. At all events it is often an accompaniment. From 1876 to 1885, when the Conservatives lost two successive elections, the machine was working stiffly and erratically. In the next seventeen years the party won four out of five elections, and all seemed smooth and harmonious. But the ensuing decade which saw the loss of three elections running was marked by acute dissension, much recrimination and a major reorganisation.

The trouble basically stemmed from Joseph Chamberlain's tariff reform crusade. He determined to capture the National Union and his bid to do so was much more formidable than Lord Randolph's twenty years earlier. Chamberlain had a clear cut policy which everyone could understand; Churchill had not. Moreover, Chamberlain from long experience of the Liberal Caucus, was a past master at the art of mass organisation – a real professional; whereas Churchill for all his genius on the platform was a mere amateur at the game. Chamberlain's path was perhaps eased by the decision of Middleton's successor, Perceval Hughes, not to take on the honorary secretaryship of the National Union. By the autumn of 1905, the tariff reformers had captured that body entirely, but they did not control the Central Office which remained a bastion of Balfourism.

The débâcle of 1906 led to a move towards intra-party democracy which alarmed Balfour. Chamberlain in February insisted on a meeting of peers, MPs and candidates to decide the party line on tariffs. Balfour reluctantly gave way. '*If you desire it* a Party Meeting must be held,' he wrote. But he revealingly continued:

> There is no case in history, as far as I am aware, in which a Party Meeting has been summoned except to give emphasis and authority to a decision at which the Party have informally already arrived; still less is there an example of a vote being taken at such a meeting.

Rather than risk such a perilous democratic precedent he decided to move towards Chamberlain's position. Hence the correspondence known as 'the Valentine Letters,' which, though it marked a major concession to Chamberlain, at least obviated the need for a vote.

Chamberlain genuinely disclaimed any ambition for the leadership; he was seventy, and he was well aware that the same obstacles stood in his way which had barred his path to 10 Downing Street in 1902. Nevertheless no one can be sure what would have happened but for the stroke which reduced him to a semiparalysed and incoherent wreck of his former self. It is hard to believe that there was not in this personal tragedy an element of reprieve for Balfour, even although both tariff reform and the demand for more democracy in the party continued to go ahead. The National Union successfully staked a claim to control propaganda and speakers, and to give its constituency branches complete autonomy in the choice of candidates. Balfour preferred to concentrate on opposition to Liberal legislation but against his will was forced into a more and more acquiescent attitude to tariff reform which its supporters boosted as a 'positive' policy. Tactically Balfour was entirely right. Modern party history strongly suggests that electorates vote against the government not for the opposition, and that the fewer the hostages it gives to fortune the better. But this did not inhibit the ardent tariff reformers in the least.

The consequences of the insane decision to reject the budget of 1909 in the Lords added new discords to the party. Balfour cannot be acquitted of blame here. There is nothing to suggest that he doubted its wisdom or tried to restrain the backwoodsmen. At first the budget had a healing effect, for both the tariff reformers who might in some ways be regarded as the left wing of the party – one should not forget the connection of fiscal policy and social reform – and the old guard who disliked what they called 'confiscatory' legislation were united in their indignation with Lloyd George. But the repercussions of their rejection of the budget had a more divisive effect than ever, and the struggle between the Hedgers and the Ditchers over the Parliament Act was to unseat Balfour himself and produce a major convulsion in the party.

Why did such a balanced man as Balfour see nothing objectionable in this use of the House of Lords? Deep in the subconscious mind of the party was a sense of prescriptive right to rule, inculcated by twenty years of domination after 1886. This was an error that neither Disraeli nor Derby would have committed. The most revealing remark of all was made by Balfour just after his personal defeat in Manchester in January 1906. It is the duty of everyone, he said, to ensure that 'the great Unionist party should still control, whether in power or whether in opposition, the destinies of this great Empire'. If this proposition is taken literally it is a denial of parliamentary democracy. Indeed many Conservatives behaved as if the verdict of 1906 was some freak aberration on the part of the electorate and that it was their duty, through the House of Lords, to preserve the public from the consequences of its own folly till it came to its senses.

It is worth noting *en passant* that the whole parliamentary process was beginning to be questioned to a degree unparalleled for two centuries. This was especially so on the Right. For the public did not 'come to its senses' in 1910. Indeed the elections left a classic situation of the sort which discredits the system. The two great parties were virtually equal, but the Irish Nationalists, holding the balance of power, were in a position to bargain with the government. In return for swallowing their own distaste for the budget and thus keeping in office Asquith who had succeeded Campbell-Bannerman in 1908, the followers of Redmond, so the Tories argued, insisted on a constitutional revolution for which there was no mandate. With the powers of the House of Lords clipped, they could blackmail the government into passing a Home Rule Bill which would have been decisively rejected by the popular vote on a referendum, the more certainly since it involved the coercion of the Protestant loyalists of Ulster. Now indeed was the moment for the Conservatives to play the Orange card, and, under their new leader Bonar Law, himself an Ulsterman, they played it for all it was worth, straining the constitution to the uttermost limits.

There are many signs in the years before the First World War that parliamentary democracy was in trouble. Basically the reasons were the same as in the 1930s and 1960s. The nation was confronted with problems and uncertainties that seemed incapable of resolution: in the 1960s the balance of payments and the decline of empire; thirty years earlier unemployment and a resurgent Germany; fifty years earlier Ireland, defence, the suffragettes, militant trade unionism. There was a hankering for Caesarism, which goes far to explain the extraordinary adulation in some quarters of Milner as a 'strong man' who could somehow put things right.

There was also a hankering for coalition, another symptom of breakdown. In March 1910 Lloyd George was flirting with the idea of a 'Government of Business Men' under his leadership – the then equivalent, presumably, of Lord Robens's soon forgotten 'Great Britain Ltd.' The idea of coalition was further stimulated by the inter-party truce following the death of King Edward and the abortive efforts to reach agreement over constitutional reform. Asquith sceptically allowed Lloyd George to discuss with Balfour a coalition to carry compromise proposals on Home Rule, the Lords, tariffs, and conscription. It is significant that Churchill, Austen Chamberlain, F. E. Smith and Balfour himself, all destined to be last ditch supporters of the 1918-22 coalition, took this improbable proposal quite seriously. But Balfour in the end vetoed it, observing with his hand on his head, 'I cannot become another Robert Peel in my party.'

These were also the years of Belloc and the Chestertons with their ceaseless hammering of 'the system' and their disagreeable streak of anti-semitism – partly a French importation, partly a reaction to the great break-through of the rich Jewish financiers into society and politics under the earlier patronage of Edward VII. The Marconi scandal in 1913 gave it a notable impetus, and seemed a demonstration of corruption in high places. This was a gross exaggeration. Nevertheless, the indiscretions of which Lloyd George and Rufus Isaacs were guilty would undoubtedly have resulted in their political extinction today.[1] Asquith's decision to make Isaacs Lord Chief Justice only six months later still remains scarcely credible. It inspired one of the greatest hate poems ever written – Kipling's *Gehazi*, and those who wish to catch the envenomed flavour of the period cannot do better than read it.

The Conservative party did not, however, become an authoritarian party of the Right on the continental model. Its parliamentary tradition was too strong. Yet it did undergo something of an upheaval. On the organisational side Balfour felt obliged, after losing two elections, to set up a committee under Akers-Douglas to investigate the trouble. The result was the resignation of the Chief Whip, Acland Hood, and the creation of a new office, that of Chairman of the Party Organisation. The whip's job of organising the party both in and out of parliament was too much. In future he would confine himself to the House, and the Principal Agent would be responsible to the leader through the chairman who would be appointed by the leader and would be a member of parliament. The first chairman, Sir Arthur Steel-Maitland, presented to Bonar Law when he became leader in 1911 an alarming picture

[1] The rumour was that Sir Herbert Samuel, Postmaster-General, Lloyd George, Chancellor of the Exchequer, and Sir Rufus Isaacs, Attorney-General, had corruptly used information available to them as ministers to speculate in the shares of the Marconi Company whose tender to build a chain of wireless stations over the empire had been provisionally accepted by Samuel. Samuel was wholly innocent. Lloyd George and Isaacs were cleared of corruption but the Conservative minority on the Select Committee which investigated the affair stigmatised their conduct as 'a grave impropriety'.

of the incompetence and financial chaos which prevailed at the Central Office – overlapping of functions, absence of records, irregular accounts. 'I was prepared for a lack of system but not for what I found,' he wrote. The only consolation was that by dint of mortgaging a year's peerages in advance Acland Hood had built up a 'nest egg of over £300,000'.[1]

Clearly reform was needed, and it was achieved. The National Union and the Central Office were put into much closer harmony. Even more important, the Liberal Unionist organisation was amalgamated with the Conservatives. The National Union was now known by the remarkably clumsy title of the National Unionist Association of Conservative and Liberal-Unionist Organisations. But despite this drawback the new system was more efficient than the old.

Meanwhile, a more important change occurred. Balfour resigned in November 1911, ostensibly on grounds of health, really because his leadership, long the subject of fierce criticism, was being openly challenged by the formation of the Halsbury Club which was clearly intended to perpetuate the split between the die-hards and the moderates. In fact if not in form he was pushed out. His resignation left vacant only the leadership of the Commons, for, in accordance with usage, that of the whole party now went into commission between the leaders of the two Houses, as it had in 1881 after Disraeli's death. There was no exact precedent for the situation. The last time that the Conservative MPs had independently elected a leader had been in 1846, and there had been no opposition to Lord George Bentinck. All subsequent leaders from then till 1911 in the House of Commons began as virtual nominees of a peer who was the recognised leader of the whole party. Thus Granby was chosen in 1848, Disraeli in 1849, Northcote in 1876, Hicks Beach in 1885, Lord Randolph Churchill in 1886, W. H. Smith in 1887, and Balfour himself in 1891.

The new Chief Whip, Lord Balcarres, had to manage the election without the guidance of any written procedure. In the event of more than two candidates standing, it was not clear whether the winner would be the man who got a plurality or whether there would be a second ballot with all but the top two

[1] Robert Blake, *The unknown Prime Minister: the life of Andrew Bonar Law* (1955), 100.

eliminated. It would not have mattered had there been an obvious winner; but, far from this being so, there was evidently going to be a close and bitter struggle between Austen Chamberlain and Walter Long. Austen Chamberlain, son of Joseph, and Balfour's last Chancellor of the Exchequer, stood for the 'progressive' wing of the party. Walter Long, a country squire of ancient lineage though of sadly diminished estate, Chief Secretary for Ireland in 1905, represented the right wing and seemed to symbolise the old 'Country Party'. The two men were personally on very bad terms at this time. Matters were further complicated by Bonar Law allowing his name to go forward, though no one expected him to get anywhere near to the votes of the others. It was an awkward situation for the time servers. One at least, Sir Samuel Hoare, later Lord Templewood, solved the problem by pledging support in advance to both Long and Chamberlain. But with the best will in the world one cannot always get these things right. He did not think it worth while to write to Bonar Law. In the end the two principal contestants withdrew rather than face a battle which would have shattered party unity even further, and the dark horse, Bonar Law, whose campaign had been skilfully managed by his friend, Max Aitken, was elected *nem con.*

Of course he was not such a dark horse as all that or he would not have been a runner at all. He already had a name as a keen tariff reformer and a hard-hitting debater. His social orgins, born in New Brunswick son of a Presbyterian minister of Ulster origin, educated at Glasgow High School, in business as a merchant in the Glasgow iron market, made him at first sight an incongruous leader of the Tory party, perhaps not more incongruous than Disraeli, though for different reasons. He was moreover quite indifferent to society, he had a Scottish accent, and his favourite diet was chicken followed by milk pudding, which he washed down with ginger ale. This melancholy teetotal widower must have seemed a strange figure at a ducal dinner or at one of Lady Londonderry's grand receptions, but he met the needs of a demoralised party better than Balfour. It was a matter of style not policy – bluntness, vigour and invective, instead of dialectic, urbanity and subtlety. Bonar Law also had the advantage of batting on a better wicket. Irish Home Rule was disliked and the coercion of

14a (*left*) Winston S. Churchill, Prime Minister 1940–5, 1951–5, at his country house, Chartwell (*Paul Popper Ltd*)

15a (*right*) Harold Macmillan, Prime Minister 1957–63 (*Central Press Ltd*)

15b (*above*) Sir Alec Douglas-Home, Prime Minister 1963–4 (*Popperfoto Ltd*)

15c (*right*) Edward Heath, Prime Minister 1970–4 (*Central Press Ltd*)

16a Margaret Thatcher,
Prime Minister 1979–90
(*Conservative Central Office*)

16b John Major, Prime
Minister 1990–97 (*Camera
Press Ltd*)

14a (*left*) Winston S. Churchill, Prime Minister 1940–5, 1951–5, at his country house, Chartwell (*Paul Popper Ltd*)

15a (*right*) Harold Macmillan, Prime Minister 1957–63 (*Central Press Ltd*)

15b (*above*) Sir Alec Douglas-Home, Prime Minister 1963–4 (*Popperfoto Ltd*)

15c (*right*) Edward Heath, Prime Minister 1970–4 (*Central Press Ltd*)

16a Margaret Thatcher,
Prime Minister 1979–90
(*Conservative Central Office*)

16b John Major, Prime
Minister 1990–97 (*Camera
Press Ltd*)

13a (*above*) Neville Chamberlain and Stanley Baldwin leaving 10 Downing Street after a meeting with Ramsay MacDonald on August 13, 1931 (*Press Association Ltd*)

13b (*left*) Sir Robert Topping, Director-General of the Conservative party 1928–45 (*Radio Times Hulton Picture Library*)

14b Anthony Eden in November 1954 (*Vivienne Studios, London*)

14c Lord Woolton, Chairman of the Conservative party 1946–55 (*Conservative Central Office*)

5a (*left*) The 3rd Marquess of Salisbury, Prime Minister 1885–6, 1886–92, 1895–1902 (*Paul Popper Ltd*)

5b (*above*) Lord Salisbury. *Spy* cartoon, *c.* 1895

5c (*left*) Richard W. Middleton, Principal Agent of the Conservative party 1885–1903 (*Conservative Research Department*)

6 Lord Randolph Churchill in 1887 (*Paul Popper Ltd*)

7a (*above*) Sir John E. Gorst (*Radio Times Hulton Picture Library*)

7b (*left*) Sir John E. Gorst. Cartoon by F. Carruthers Gould (*National Portrait Gallery*)

8a (*above*) A. J. Balfour, Prime Minister 1902–5 (*Mansell Collection*)

8b (*left*) Balfour at the Dispatch Box (*Mansell Collection*)

Ulster was indefensible on its merits. The party for the first time since 1900 could identify itself with the 'national cause', and its greatest liability, tariffs, dropped into the background. Nor did Bonar Law's atavistic extremism over Ulster do him any harm. In the prevailing atmosphere of violence and ill feeling it was probably respected rather than otherwise, and if the Conservatives could have engineered an election in 1913 or 1914 on the straight question of Ulster they would probably have won it.

Yet, whatever the errors of the Liberals, the fact remains that the Conservatives were launched on a very perilous course. They could not force an election. If the First World War had not broken out in 1914, something like a unilateral declaration of independence would have been made in Ulster – and made, moreover (unlike the case of Rhodesia) with the full backing of the leader of the Conservative party and the vast majority of his followers. It is hard to imagine a greater strain upon the tacit usages and conventions which alone make possible the smooth working of the British Constitution; an election fought, not on the merits of Home Rule but on the constitutionality of the Conservatives' behaviour might well have gone against them.

5

The war was in some respects a boon politically to Asquith. The government now had the asset of the 'national' cause. 'Patriotic opposition' hamstrung the Conservatives. If the war had been over quickly, if most of the fighting had been done by continental armies, if Britain's role had been mainly naval, the Liberals would have gained ground – and one should remember that many people expected the war to be just like this. But when it became obvious that the war was not only going to be long but also to be 'total' – i.e. involve the mobilisation of all the resources of the nation – the Liberals were fatally handicapped.

There is no need to say much about war politics, despite their fascinating dramas and intrigues, because for the purposes of this account of the changing fortunes of a political party, what happened can be stated fairly simply. On almost every issue that came up Conservative tradition and ideology was better suited than

Liberal to meet the needs of the hour. Conscription, 'defence of the realm', Ireland, indeed all the necessities of a prolonged war, tended to create doubts and divisions in the Liberals. After all they were the party of liberty, and liberty is the first casualty of war. They were the party of moral conscience – and that is another casualty of war. They were the party of legalism, parliamentary forms, constitutional propriety – and these also are casualties of war. Then there was sheer pacifism and its watered down version – belief in the evil of war and of any British government that waged it. True, the pro-Boers had no analogy. There were no Liberal pro-Germans. But the scruples, doubts, misgivings were there. It was the Conservatives who before the war had been anti-German, who had pressed for conscription, for greater armaments, for a tougher foreign policy, for the French and later the Russian alliance.

Asquith was far from being an extreme representative of Liberal tendencies. But he was a quintessential Liberal deeply imbued with the party traditions, leader of the party since 1908 – a position he could have had ten years earlier – and in a sense guardian of its conscience. His whole way of thought was one that found war in its new, unprecedented and terrifying form profoundly distasteful. He thus came to symbolise to the impatient men of action everything that led to sloth and procrastination. It was inevitable that he should be elbowed out. The 1915 coalition was the first step; the Conservatives were now in office again but Asquith's chilly and jealous treatment of his former opponents boded no good for the government lasting long. The convulsion of December 1916 and the emergence of Lloyd George cracked the Liberal party in half. It was another step forward politically for the Conservatives, who dominated the new coalition; but if Lloyd George had not been prepared to act, the Liberals would have ceased altogether to be a party of wartime government. There was no room now for the 'doves'. The 'hawks' were in the ascendant.

With Lloyd George the Caesarism, craved before the war by some, really came into being. The business men and tycoons, the Geddeses, Harmsworths, Beaverbrooks, Weirs poured in. It was 'Great Britain Ltd' with a managing director of formidable power. Lloyd George was the nearest thing to a popular dictator since Cromwell and at times he treated parliament almost as contemptuously. It was wholly appropriate that Milner, the Caesar *manqué* of the Right, should have been a member of the new small war Cabinet to which in theory all power was now given. The leading Conservatives, however suspicious, were prepared to serve under a Prime Minister who, in spite of his defects, was an indubitable fighter and who cared nothing for the traditional Liberal shibboleths if they interfered with the remorseless prosecution of the war.

The continuation of the wartime coalition into peace has often been criticised by historians – usually of Asquithian Liberal persuasion. But at the time it seems to have been expected, and by most people taken for granted, that the man who won the war should try to win the peace. There is no sign among Bonar Law's papers of prolonged discussions or doubts among the top Tories about the advisability of carrying on under Lloyd George's leadership. If the Conservatives had reason to do so from a party point of view, it is also true that they had good reason to expect that they would win an election on their own. The Liberals were already deeply divided. The Labour party had decided to strike out as an independent force and cut loose from their alliance with the Liberals maintained during the last three elections. The anti-Conservative vote in the country was bound to be weakened by these divisions. Even if the coalition had broken up, it is likely that Conservatives would have won on their own, as they did in 1922 when the 'Left' was divided in this way.

Of course, with Lloyd George at their head, they were even more certain to win in a landslide, and this was what happened at the celebrated 'coupon' election[1] of 1918. But the motive behind the continuance of the coalition genuinely seems to have been a desire for national solidarity in the post-war years rather than party calculation. The alliance with Lloyd George came near to crystallising into permanency. In 1920 there was a serious movement towards 'fusion', as it was called, between the national (i.e. coalition) Liberals and the Conservatives. It came to a head

---

[1] So called because Asquith thus described the joint letter of Lloyd George and Bonar Law endorsing coalition candidates. It was an ironical reference to the coupons in war-time ration books.

in March. Bonar Law was not enthusiastic but he would not have blocked it. Lloyd George would have been the beneficiary. It would have given him a real base, a party machine and party funds. At the moment he had neither, for the Asquithians retained control over what remained of the old Liberal organisation. But he ran into opposition from some of the Coalition Liberal members of the Cabinet, and he did not push the matter very hard.

It was a fateful decision or lack of decision. The chance did not recur. The 95 Conservative back-benchers who had in March 1920 petitioned Lloyd George and Bonar Law would probably not have done so even one year later, certainly not two. Disenchantment with the Prime Minister began to set in almost at once. In the grass roots of the Conservative party the coalition was unpopular from the start, and was particularly disliked by the agents. Many Conservatives had never trusted Lloyd George very far, and his highly untraditional conduct of the premiership enhanced their doubts. No one had ever in peace time behaved in a more 'presidential' manner. The Cabinet was habitually by-passed. At the beginning of 1919 Lloyd George told Austen Chamberlain that, because of their need to be present at the Paris Peace Conference, he and Bonar Law were thinking of doing without the Cabinet altogether. This may have been a joke; a sense of humour was not Austen's strong point. Nevertheless, Lloyd George behaved more like a one man band than anyone else in the period, and when things began to go wrong he was naturally the target for attack to an even greater extent than a Prime Minister normally is.

Most governments drift into trouble after two or three years, though they can often recover. But the adjustment of Britain to the stresses of the post-war situation was bound to be particularly difficult and to make the government particularly unpopular – and this odium was bound to stick on Lloyd George whose personal role was so conspicuous. Normally a Prime Minister can rely on the loyalty of his party to counteract these trends. The party has every reason to support its leader, to gloss over his errors, defend his failings. Party members cannot turn against him while he is in office without admitting a major error in having ever chosen him. This is why it can be hard to remove a Prime Minister even though he has become a palpable electoral liability.

But the situation is quite different where the Prime Minister, though heading a coalition, is not the leader of the majority party in it. Then, success becomes the only criterion, and when once success disappears, the majority party has every reason to look elsewhere – to its own leader, or if he will not gratify them, to the election of a new one and the break up of an arrangement which is no longer an asset. By the beginning of 1922 more and more Conservatives were coming to think in just this way about Lloyd George.

Note

Regional strength of the parties

The general elections of 1910 are of some interest in assessing the geographical strength of the parties. Broadly speaking Liberals and Conservatives scored roughly the same totals in England, Wales, Scotland and Northern Ireland if these four countries are lumped together. Asquith was enabled to carry on because he could rely on the votes of some 40 Labour MPs and over 80 Irish Nationalists from the south. But it is worth pursuing this analysis rather further. We can concentrate on the election of January 1910, for the figures of the December election are almost identical. If we exclude Ireland, north as well as south, the Conservatives won 254 seats, the Liberals 274, Labour 40. The Conservative strength lay in London (33 out of 59), the rest of the south of England (107 out of 155), and the Midlands, defined for this purpose as Hereford, Worcester, Warwick, Northants, Lincs, Notts, Leicester, Stafford, Shropshire, Derby (49 out of 88). These areas along with nine university seats account for 198 out of 254, i.e., four-fifths of their total.

The Liberal strength was rather less concentrated than the Conservative, but there is a marked regional bias all the same. Of their 274 non-Irish seats they had 86 out of 154 in the north of England, 27 out of 34 in Wales, and 59 out of 70 in Scotland. These areas therefore account for 172 out of 274 – just over three-fifths; and if we remember that 29 out of the 40 Labour seats were also in these areas and that there was as in 1906 a Lib–Lab anti-Conservative pact which at any rate in England minimised the numbers of three-cornered contests, the weakness of the Conservative party in northern England and the 'Celtic fringe' becomes clear enough.

It is interesting to notice how this pattern has become crystallised in the twentieth century. Whenever the Conservatives and their opponents, whether Liberal or Labour, are fairly near to equality it reappears. In 1929 the Conservatives won 111 out of 164 seats in southern England (excluding London) and only 51 out of 171 in northern England. In 1950, the corresponding figures were 144 out of 199 and 61 out of 169; in 1964, 157 out of 206, and 53 out of 167; in February 1974, 172 out of 219, and 47 out of 164. The elections of 1906 and 1945 are the only ones during this century where the Conservatives were out-voted in southern England. The elections of 1900, 1924, 1935 were the only ones where they were not out-voted in northern England.[2] Wales too has followed the pattern of 1910. In a close election the Conservatives have always been heavily beaten there. In 1950 they only won 4 out of 36 seats; in 1964 only 6; and in February 1974 only 8.

The areas where change has occurred are Scotland where the Conservatives never again did so badly as in December 1910 for, although they rarely got a majority they managed much better than in Wales; London where after a goodish run in the inter-war years their fortunes have slumped since 1945 – only 12 out of 43 in 1950, 10 out of 42 in 1964, and only 6 out of 35 in February 1974; and the Midlands where, after flourishing in the inter-war years, their numbers have fallen, 1959, 1979 and 1983 being the only years when they had a majority – 49 out of 96, 57 out of 98, and an astonishing 88 out of 120.

---

[1] There have been twenty-three general elections in the twentieth century.

[2] I have excluded those of 1918 and 1931 which must be regarded as highly abnormal for obvious reasons.

CHAPTER VII

The age of Baldwin
1922–40

I

In his study, *The downfall of the Liberal party* (1966), Dr Trevor
Wilson denies that the cause of the break-up of the coalition is
to be found in any of the usual episodes cited: the alleged sale of
honours by Lloyd George; the Irish Treaty of 1921; the failures of
the international conferences at Cannes and Genoa; or the
Chanak incident of September 1922 when the cabinet was
stigmatised, though quite unjustly, as 'war-mongering'. It is, he
says, rather to be sought further back in a basic lack of sincerity
in the alliance of the Conservatives with Lloyd George. In 1922
the trouble was 'not that by then the Prime Minister had become
a liability; he had simply ceased to fulfil any essential purpose'.
Perhaps Dr Wilson is right about Chanak. It was a last straw,
rather than a heavy piece of baggage. The crucial moment when
the guardians of the Conservative party's conscience – or at
any rate of its independence which is perhaps not always the
same thing – declared themselves was in January 1922, nine
months earlier. This was Sir George Younger's public denunciation of the idea of an early general election to be fought on a
coalition basis. His action was prompted by a report from Sir
Malcolm Fraser, the Principal Agent, to Austen Chamberlain
who had been leader for nearly a year, owing to Bonar Law's resignation in March 1921 on grounds of health. fraser reckoned
that the coalition would lose 100 seats and the Conservative
party would be split from top to bottom, if an immediate election
was held on a coalition basis. A month later Younger made

THE DOG THAT BROKE HIS LEAD.

MR. LLOYD GEORGE. "CALL OFF THAT DOG OF YOURS, AUSTEN."

MR. CHAMBERLAIN. "I'M NOT QUITE SURE THAT HE'D DESCRIBE HIMSELF AS MY DOG."

MR. LLOYD GEORGE. "WELL, ANYHOW, IF YOU DON'T CALL HIM OFF I'M GOING HOME."

March 8, 1922. Reproduced by permission of Punch

another statement in reply to a speech of Chamberlain's and urged 'a bill of divorcement' to end the coalition.

The coalition was henceforth doomed. Such public dissension between the party leader and the party chairman is unexampled before or since. Moreover, there was no suggestion of Younger's resignation. It was clear that the party leader did not feel himself in a position to force the issue then. What remains extraordinary is that after this Chamberlain should have readily agreed to a coalition dissolution in the autumn without consulting the party managers in advance. He must have realised the probability that the National Union, due to meet on November 15, would declare against the continuance of the alliance with Lloyd George. Nevertheless, he acquiesced in the Cabinet's decision on September 16 to hold an election as soon as possible, and only then told the party managers. They were horrified. Younger, Fraser, and Sir Leslie Wilson, the Chief Whip, protested strongly, the latter informing Chamberlain that 184 constituency parties had already proclaimed their intention of running independent non-coalitionist candidates, though he conceded that some of them were sitting on the fence.

It was only the threat of public repudiation by Younger and Wilson that obliged Chamberlain to 'consult the party'. But it was, of course, a moot point exactly what this meant. Chamberlain was determined not to put the matter to the National Union -- for which there would indeed have been no precedent. But then there was no precedent for consulting the party at all on such a matter. The body chosen in the end consisted of all Conservative MPs, to which were added those members of the upper House who were in the government, but not the back-bench peers who accepted the Tory whip. This proviso caused much umbrage for it included a number of 'placemen' and kept out a body which would certainly have been for the most part anti-coalition. However, the peers were not allowed to vote, and so the exclusion of the back-benchers made little difference. In any case the verdict was conclusive – rejection of coalition by 185 to 88.[1] The

[1] Robert Rhodes James, *Memoirs of a Conservative: J. C. L. Davidson's memoirs and papers 1910–37* (1969), 129. There was one abstention. Mr James, who prints the details of how everyone voted, is the first historian to produce the correct figures. For some reason they were announced at the time as 187–87.

most eloquent speech against Lloyd George was made by Stanley
Baldwin, President of the Board of Trade, who thus appeared for
the first time on the stage of history. The most important speech,
however, was that of Bonar Law whose attitude had been hitherto
unknown. His declaration against the coalition must have swung
many votes. Chamberlain at once resigned the leadership and
Lloyd George the premiership – his last gesture being a capital
imitation to his courtiers of his own reception as head of a delegation from Wales begging a favour at 10 Downing Street from
Bonar Law. He never held office again. —

To say that Lloyd George 'had simply ceased to fulfil any
essential purpose', as far as the Conservatives were concerned
is to beg a number of questions. It may be true; but why, what
purpose, and who were the doubters? If Chanak was merely the
last straw, this does not mean that the Irish Treaty – clearly a
bitter mouthful for the Conservative back benchers to swallow –
or the Honours scandal – a source of gossip and innuendo long
before it broke – counted for nothing in the increasing disenchantment with the Prime Minister. Surely, they counted for a great
deal. Nor can one disregard Lloyd George's private life. He has
been described as 'the first Prime Minister since Walpole to leave
office flagrantly richer than he entered it, the first since the Duke
of Grafton to live openly with his mistress'.[1] These facts were well
known at the time, though they did not appear in print till quite
recently.

One can easily see the causes of the Conservative rebellion. It
was a matter of morality with Baldwin who in his speech at the
Carlton Club displayed a passion that threw a new light on his
character. With Bonar Law it was a matter of party unity. He
knew his Lloyd George. In his sad, upright, world weary, gentle,
slightly cynical way he had had an admirably deflatory effect on
his ebullient, gay, inventive, amoral senior colleague. His departure in 1921 was like the ejection of ballast from a balloon. His
successor never carried the same weight, and it is arguable that
Lloyd George would not have headed for disaster quite as he did
if Bonar Law had remained in office. Bonar Law's role at the Carlton Club was crucial. As an ex-leader of the party, out of office

[1] A. J. P. Taylor, *English history 1914-45*, (1965), 74.

solely for health reasons which seemed to be no longer applicable, he was in a unique position to replace Lloyd George. Perhaps the party would not have been wholly at a loss even if he had failed to speak up. Curzon or Derby might have formed a government, but neither of them had his authority. His speech settled the fate of the coalition.

The real problem is not why the 185 members voted against the coalition on October 19, 1922, at the Carlton Club, but why the minority of 88 voted for it. Historians have not looked closely enough at this side of the question. What, in other words, was the motive force behind the Conservative coalitionists? The answer has to be sought in the rise of Labour. In dealing with the history of any political party one has constantly to bear in mind the political forces on the other side. A party's fortunes for good or ill depend as much on the example of its opponents as upon its own exertions. The great post-war question mark was the Labour party. Balfour had seen its significance as long ago as 1906. But the importance of Labour had been hitherto masked by its role as an appendage or satellite of the Liberals, and, by the readiness of a section of its leadership to join the war-time coalition. In 1918 the Labour party took a step which had very considerable long term consequences. It not only adopted a specifically socialist constitution, but it decided to break the pact with the Liberals and strike out on its own. What was more, Labour did remarkably well in the coupon election. The party fielded 388 candidates – the previous maximum had been 81 – and secured 2·4 million votes, 22 per cent of those cast. It is true that only 63 Labour MPs were returned – not a startlingly larger figure than the 42 of December 1910. But they had won on their own against all comers. What was more, the party was clearly gaining ground between 1918 and 1922. They won no less than 14 by-elections – most of them against coalition Liberals. In 1922 they were to secure over 4·2 million votes and over 140 seats.

The leading members of the traditional parties viewed this progress long before 1922 with misgiving, made the greater because of the extremist language of the Labour left, and because of the widespread working class unrest exemplified by the strikes. How was the Conservative party to cope with this danger?

Broadly speaking, there were two solutions discussed. They correspond to two views of the past role of the Conservative party. Was it to be the Peelite solution – a cautious anti-'movement' alliance of property and order, making moderate concessions to the forces of change? Or was it to be what many people believed – and still believe – to be the Disraelian solution – a direct appeal to the working class over the heads of the bourgeoisie, a new form of Tory radicalism? The practical form that this would take, as in Joseph Chamberlain's day, was tariff reform with a new emphasis on protection for industry, and hence, it was hoped, reduction of unemployment.

Tariff reform was simply not 'on', as far as the coalition was concerned. The coalition Liberals were bound to oppose it. Bonar Law fully recognised this and he had made no attempt to bring it in. But as unemployment rose and economic conditions became worse, pressure grew within the Conservative party for a more radical solution. Baldwin adhered to this view. He had entered parliament as a tariff reformer. Another leading exponent was L. S. Amery, though he was not yet in the Cabinet, being Parliamentary Under-Secretary to Milner at the Colonial Office till the latter retired in 1921, then Under-Secretary to the Admiralty. Milner was himself an ardent supporter of tariff reform, and indeed resigned partly from lack of sympathy in the Cabinet.

To those of Milner's and Amery's persuasion, Peelism as practised by Lloyd George, Churchill, Birkenhead, Balfour and Austen Chamberlain was the recipe for disaster. 'Anti-Socialism and the defence of the constitution,' writes Amery, were from the very first the coalition policy.

But nothing could have been more short-sighted politically than a purely negative policy. Such a policy could make no appeal to the great mass of industrial workers who would be bound sooner or later to swamp the middle class once the issue was interpreted as one between classes.

Where Amery was less than fair was in omitting the other side of the coalitionist policy. It was not for nothing that Birkenhead had been the moving spirit in the Tory Social Reform Committee before the war. In fact the policy of the coalitionists was not purely negative. On the contrary, their plans on housing and unemployment insurance went a long way, in contemporary terms, towards alleviating the hardships of the poorer classes – or would have done, had they been properly implemented. The coalitionists had a policy which combined all the most characteristic features of successful Conservatism in the past, an appeal to the forces of law and order, an alliance of the small 'c' conservative classes, defence of property, Treasury economy, cautious piecemeal social reform, a 'patriotic' foreign and imperial policy judiciously tempered by liberal internationalism and respect for the League. These indeed, with variations, were to be the general themes of the policy that Baldwin in fact pursued after 1924 and again in another coalition government after 1931. And in electoral terms it was to be highly successful under him.

Why then did the coalition of 1918–22 founder as it did? The answer is not that the Milner–Amery view converted the party, although it certainly was held by some of the rebels, including Baldwin at that time. What really caused the revolt was personal distrust of Lloyd George. By 1922 this had become acute, as even his allies recognised. For example, in October 1922 Balfour wrote to his sister, 'There is no doubt of course that Ll.G is violently disliked by great bodies of his fellow-countrymen.' One might have thought that this was a good reason, if only on practical electoral grounds, for dropping him. To be violently disliked by great bodies of one's fellow citizens when an election is imminent seems *prima facie* a drawback. But Balfour drew no such conclusion. The coalition still seemed to him an essential means of coping with post-war reconstruction and dealing with the Labour party, if only because, like many of his colleagues, he could not believe that the Conservatives on their own were capable of winning an election.

There could be much argument about the justification of the anti-Lloyd George view held by so many Conservatives. What matters more in this context is its existence. Undoubtedly a large majority of back-benchers felt profoundly antipathetic to him. If he had changed places with Austen Chamberlain, as he offered to do, the situation would have been different. But Austen was too loyal, too gentlemanly – in a word, too unlike his hard, ruthless, almost fanatical father – to accept. He once told Beaverbrook that tariff reform – his father's panacea – had been all his life a millstone round his neck. The coalition gave him a chance to rid himself of the burden for a time: he welcomed this relief and, one of the most honourable figures in British twentieth-century politics, he refused to show the slightest disloyalty to the man who made it possible.

The coalition was overthrown by an alliance of overlapping groups: die-hards who detested the Irish Treaty; middle-of-the-road back benchers who believed that Lloyd George would be a liability at the next election; tariff reform enthusiasts who saw the prospect of a new Tory-Radical break-through. They were heavily backed by the party managers who rightly calculated on a straight Conservative victory. It was very marginal in terms of votes, only 38 per cent of the total, but in seats it was decisive – 354, a majority of 77 over all other parties combined.

The attitude of Bonar Law is of interest. Like Balfour, like Salisbury, he was actuated above all else by his determination that the party should not be broken up. His late and genuinely reluctant intervention at the Carlton Club was for this reason only. No one had been more obedient to the concept of intra-party democracy. His own elevation in 1911 had been essentially the product of an election, and not of a nomination. He returned to politics as a result of a vote against his successor. He even refused to accept the premiership till he had been formally elected as leader of the party – an unprecedented course of action and one which no subsequent Conservative Prime Minister has felt himself obliged to follow; neither Baldwin, Neville Chamberlain, Churchill, Eden, Macmillan, nor Douglas-Home.

Bonar Law was faced with a difficult situation in spite of his majority. Most of the able and experienced Conservative politi-cians followed Austen Chamberlain. 'What is going to happen?' the lobby correspondent of the *Yorkshire Post* asked J. C. C. David-son, Bonar Law's intimate friend, just before the Carlton Club meeting. 'A slice off the top,' replied Davidson. This was indeed what happened. Bonar Law had to form what Churchill called a Cabinet of 'the second eleven'. A. J. P. Taylor may be a little harsh in saying that 'there had been nothing like it since Derby's "Who? Who?" ministry of 1852', but it was not a very distinguished

THE IDEAL HOUSEHOLDER.

SCENE—*A Blasted Common, Mitcham.*

MR. BONAR LAW. "NOW, THAT'S MY NOTION OF A GOOD CITIZEN: CARRIES HIS HOME WITH HIM, PROGRESSES WITHOUT UNDUE PRECIPITANCY AND NEVER BITES YOU IN THE BACK."

At a by-election at Mitcham Sir Arthur Boscawen, Minister of Health, who had lost his seat in the General Election, was defeated because of the intervention of a Conservative coalitionist

March 14, 1923. Reproduced by permission of Punch

body compared with its predecessor, and Bonar Law had to rely heavily on the right wing of his party. The Cabinet contained seven peers, including a duke and two marquesses, and there was an almost Disraeliesque touch in the representation of the great houses of Cecil, Stanley and Cavendish, and the less great but even more venerable house of Curzon. The coalition Conservatives – 'Peelites without a Peel', as they have been described – muttered crossly in the wilderness. But they accounted for most of the talent in the party, and Bonar Law regarded it as one of his main objectives to secure their return. He was tired and unwell, and he envisaged handing over to Austen Chamberlain in a year or two when feelings on both sides had had time to cool down.

But illness, diagnosed in May 1923 as cancer of the throat, compelled Bonar Law's immediate resignation after only seven months in office. This at once transformed the political situation. It was too soon for Austen Chamberlain and his colleagues to be acceptable to the rank and file of the party. The choice of a successor was therefore confined to the second eleven. A great deal has been written about the manœuvres which followed.[1] Today there would be a party election, but this procedure was only introduced in 1965 by Sir Alec Douglas-Home. In those days the accepted method of settling the succession lay in 'soundings' of opinion by the king's private secretary, Lord Stamfordham. The matter was made more difficult because Bonar Law asked, in view of his illness, to be excused from making any recommendation himself to the king. His closest intimates were Lord Beaverbrook and J. C. C. (later Viscount) Davidson.[2] Each favoured a different candidate, Beaverbrook preferring Curzon for reasons which are not wholly clear but which certainly did not include personal admiration of the marquess, Davidson preferring Baldwin with whom he was on terms of close friendship.

Colonel Waterhouse, Bonar Law's private secretary, when conveying Bonar Law's resignation to the king on Sunday, May 20, gave a memorandum to Stamfordham which he said, according to Stamfordham's own note in the Royal Archives, 'practically

[1] See Robert Blake, *The unknown Prime Minister*, 516–28; and R. R. James, *Memoirs of a Conservative*, 149–65.
[2] See p. 221, n. 1, for Davidson's career.

expressed the views of Mr Bonar Law'. The memorandum which is unsigned was prepared by Davidson and was a strongly worded plea for Baldwin.[1] There is no internal evidence in the document to suggest that it expressed Bonar Law's views. According to Lord Davidson it was written in fulfilment of a promise to give Stamfordham 'the point of view of the average back bencher in the House of Commons',[2] and Waterhouse who never saw what was in the sealed envelope which he handed to Stamfordham had no authority to say that it represented Bonar Law's opinions.[3] If this is so – and there is no reason to doubt Lord Davidson's word – then it is perhaps a pity that he did not sign the memorandum, for in that case Lord Stamfordham could not have been misled – if he was misled.

The question arises whether in fact the memorandum did correspond with Bonar Law's views, even though no one had any authority to say that it did. Lord Davidson is inclined to think that Bonar Law was in favour of Baldwin. He agrees that the memorandum was an expression of his own views not Bonar Law's but says that 'it was produced after several most intimate talks with Bonar Law'.[4] There is little doubt that Bonar Law, a sick man under heavy sedation, was torn on the one hand by doubts about a peer as Prime Minister – especially a peer of such peculiarly undemocratic demeanour – and on the other by a feeling that someone of Curzon's eminence and long service simply could not be passed over. Moreover, Beaverbrook seems to have been backing Curzon, partly no doubt from dislike for Baldwin but partly because he believed that Curzon could reunite the party whereas Baldwin could not – and the reunification of the party was something which he knew to be very dear to Bonar Law's heart.[5] Bonar Law may well have said different things to different people, but Davidson's memorandum was, surely, a much clearer and more decisive recommendation than anything that Bonar Law was prepared to make. To that extent Waterhouse, whatever his motives, did misrepresent the facts when he asserted that it 'practically expressed the views of Mr Bonar Law'.[6]

---

[1] It was printed for the first time in Blake, *The unknown Prime Minister*, 520–1.
[2] James, op. cit., 151.   [3] ibid., 156.   [4] ibid., 163.
[5] ibid., 158–61.   [6] See ibid., 522 n.

It is, however, another matter to suggest that the final decision was in any way affected. Lord Stamfordham, according to Lord Derby who had it from the king himself, advised the king to send for Curzon.[1] So the memorandum evidently did not convert Stamfordham. The king, as is well known, decided for Baldwin, and everything suggests that he was influenced above all else by the fact that Curzon was a peer. His strong inclination to keep the premiership in the Commons was heavily reinforced by the advice of Balfour whom he consulted as an ex-Tory Prime Minister and the leading elder statesman of the party. Balfour was staying with friends in the country but he hastened to London on Whit Monday, May 21, to give his advice to Stamfordham. We know that he privately had long regarded Curzon with a mixture of dislike and contempt. He was, however, careful to say nothing personally detrimental. He merely pointed out that a Cabinet already over-weighted with peers would be open to even greater criticism if one of them actually became Prime Minister; that, since the Parliament Act of 1911, the political centre of gravity had moved more definitely than ever to the Lower House; and finally that the official Opposition, the Labour party, was not represented at all in the House of Lords.

Balfour returned that evening to the house party at Sheringham in Norfolk, where he was staying. The story is well known that one of the ladies there asked him, 'And will dear George be chosen?' To which he replied, 'No, dear George will not.'[2] The continuation of the dialogue is not so well known. To understand the point one should bear in mind the Christian name of Curzon's rich second wife, Grace Duggan. The guest who had asked the question went on, 'Oh I am so sorry. He will be terribly disappointed.' Balfour replied. 'I don't know. After all, even if he has lost the hope of glory he still possesses the means of Grace.'[3]

There remains some mystery about these transactions, and it may be that further details will emerge. But it is clear the principal reason for the choice of Baldwin was the difficulty of having a peer as Prime Minister. There is no reason to think that Curzon could

[1] Randolph Churchill, *Derby, king of Lancashire* (1959), 503, quoting Lord Derby's diary.
[2] Winston Churchill, *Great Contemporaries*, 287.   [3] Private information.

not have formed a government, but there is every reason to think that the king's choice coincided with the choice which would have been made by the party if there had existed an appropriate electoral machinery for making it. According to Baldwin's biographers, Stamfordham was told on the Tuesday morning by Sir Stanley Jackson, the chairman of the party, that all the constituency agents were telegraphing their support for Baldwin, and Jackson himself, though personally respecting Curzon, believed that on a free vote he would not be supported by more than fifty Conservative MPs.[1]

There can be little doubt that the king made the right decision. Even if we set aside the constitutional point, Curzon's character and public image made him a questionable candidate for the highest post in the land. A man who when Viceroy of India was so reluctant to delegate that he used to write out in his own hand and personally place the cards of the guests at his immense dinner parties lacked the ideal temperament for a Prime Minister. The blow was bitter, and in a moment of despair he protested to Stamfordham that Baldwin was a person of 'the utmost insignificance'. But magnanimity prevailed. He agreed to remain at the Foreign Office and he made a generous speech proposing Baldwin for the leadership of the party.

2

The choice of Baldwin was much the most controversial and nicely balanced of the appointments made to the premiership of the Tory side during this period. Salisbury in 1885 is the nearest parallel, but not very near. For closer comparisons one must look more recently; Harold Macmillan in 1957, Sir Alec Douglas-Home in 1963. The king's decision was right, though not inevitable. If it had gone otherwise political history would not have been the same. Baldwin would have missed his chance entirely. On the assumption that Curzon would have died when he did in 1925 and that Conservative reunion had occurred long before that, his successor would presumably have been Austen Chamberlain who in his turn would have been succeeded by his brother Neville,

[1] Keith Middlemas and John Barnes, *Baldwin: a biography* (1969), 167.

probably a good deal earlier than 1937. Curzon would not have held an election on tariffs within seven months of taking office. The short-lived Labour administration of 1924 would not have come into being, nor would there have been a second election that autumn.

But there is no end to the 'ifs' of history. What sort of a character was the man who 'emerged' as a result of the events described above? Baldwin remains to this day the subject of widely divergent judgments. He has been condemned for failure to solve Britain's economic problems and also to rearm against the German threat during the inter-war years. He has been depicted as a dreamy indolent figure, bored with foreign affairs and ignorant of economics. On the other hand his recent biographers have endeavoured to draw a very different and much kinder portrait as a new style of leader. They even go so far as to compare him with Disraeli.

One can dismiss many of the charges against him without swinging to quite such an opposite extreme as that. Nothing can disguise the fact that Baldwin's elevation was an extraordinary stroke of luck. Seven years earlier he had been an unknown nonentity on the back benches. He seriously contemplated retiring altogether from politics. He owed his first step to Bonar Law who made him Financial Secretary to the Treasury in 1917. It was not till 1921 that he entered the Cabinet – as President of the Board of Trade. The famous 'slice off the top' at the Carlton Club gave him a further chance, though he was not Bonar Law's first choice for the Exchequer, and only received the appointment after Reginald McKenna had refused it.[1] But for Bonar Law's premature resignation he would never have leap-frogged his way into 10 Downing Street, over such figures as Austen Chamberlain, Birkenhead and Sir Robert Horne.

It is true that Disraeli owed his rise to a similar slice off the top when so many official men followed Peel over the repeal of the corn laws; it is true that in his case also the accidents of health, the death of Lord George Bentinck soon afterwards, made him the

---

[1] At any rate this is the usual version, but Middlemas and Barnes, op. cit., 124, say that it was Baldwin who received the first offer and that he suggested an approach to McKenna.

only plausible candidate for the leadership of the Protectionist party in the House of Commons. But there were two important differences. First, Disraeli still had to work his passage to the premiership. For the next twenty years he fought under the leadership of Derby, and he proved himself in single combat against all the ablest debaters of the day. Secondly, Disraeli was an extremely clever man.

Baldwin may not have been, in Neville Chamberlain's words 'so simple as he makes out', but he was not clever. He regarded it as a compliment when Birkenhead claimed that Bonar Law's Cabinet was one of second class intellects. He prided himself on being a practical man of business, and he detested the intelligentsia – 'a very ugly word for a very ugly thing'. It was the paradox of the period that the public mood welcomed humdrum routine commonsense at precisely the moment when the problems of the day demanded something more than commonsense. Intellectual brilliance was at a discount when it should have been at a premium. Brains were too readily associated with personal corruption and rackety private lives. What Lloyd George has to answer for is not his own dubious morals but the fact that they discredited him and indirectly his companions, some of the ablest men in public life, at just the time when the baffling questions of the inter-war years needed originality, energy, improvisation and adventure if they were to be answered.

Baldwin represented with singular accuracy the mood of a nation wearied by the sufferings of war and its aftermath. He was peace-loving at a time when Britain hated the memory and dreaded the prospect of war. He was insular at a time of political isolationism, conciliatory in an age of compromise. He was easy-going at a time when his fellow-countrymen wanted nothing so much as to be left alone. If he misconstrued the European situation so did most others. If he evaded realities, the nation was glad to follow. To the public he seemed to embody the English spirit and his speeches to sound the authentic note of that English character which they so much admired and so seldom resembled. Pipe-smoking, phlegmatic, honest, kind, commonsensical, fond of pigs, the classics and the country, he represented to Englishmen an idealised and enlarged version of themselves. While the political climate remained calm they venerated, almost worshipped him. His tragedy was that the weather changed and in the end his worshippers, like some primitive people, sought to beat the tribal god whom they once adored.

In reality he was by no means what he seemed to be. For one thing he was only half-English, and, although it is rash to make too much of racial inheritance, the Celtic streak which Baldwin inherited from his mother, Louisa Macdonald, cannot be ignored. She was Welsh on her mother's side and Highland Scots on her father's. Her family was very talented and her sisters made notable marriages. One became the wife of Burne-Jones, another of Edward Poynter. A third married J. L. Kipling, and their son, Rudyard, the strange uneasy genius who acted as both herald and Cassandra to the age of Britain's imperial grandeur, was thus Baldwin's first cousin. It may not be unduly fanciful to discern in Baldwin's sensitivity, impulsiveness, intuition, and occasional bouts of melancholy and inertia, something of this Celtic inheritance. Certainly he was far from being the unimaginative, stolid, Anglo-Saxon figure depicted by the popular press.[1]

Baldwin had many merits. There was the quixotic generosity of his anonymous gift in 1919 of £120,000, one-fifth of his fortune, to the Treasury in the vain hope that it would inspire other men of means to repay the debt of sacrifice owed to the generation that perished in the war. He was a decent and honourable man. He was modest. He had a high sense of duty. He had no delusions about the extraordinary series of accidents which had brought him to the top. 'I need your prayers rather than your congratulations,' he said to the journalists who thronged Downing Street when he returned from the palace. The very chanciness of his rise led him to see the hand of God and to believe that he was in some sense 'the chosen instrument to heal the wounds left by war on English society'.[2]

According to his lights he tried to do this. He led the party from a position of moderate centre, seeking to conciliate his opponents, to blur the harsh edges of class conflict, and to display as far as he

[1] This paragraph and the preceding one are adapted by the author from the passage in his essay, 'Baldwin and the right', first published in *The Baldwin age*, ed. John Raymond (1960).

[2] Middlemas and Barnes, op. cit., 168.

could the more humane aspect of Conservatism. Up to a point he succeeded. If Winston Churchill or either of the Chamberlains had been at the head of the party they might have accomplished more in the way of legislation, but they would not have conveyed the same impression of friendliness, sympathy and consideration. Yet in the end Baldwin failed because the wounds on English society were not the result of malice, cruelty or spite, and could not be cured by kindness. They were the result of the collapse of the pre-war economic system, and they could be cured only by thought and the intellectual effort involved in reconsidering the basic presuppositions behind the conventional wisdom of city and Treasury. Lloyd George might have done it, but no one trusted him. Oswald Mosley too, if he had been content to work within the framework of the Labour party; but he was a young man in a hurry. Baldwin was simply not the person to deal with this kind of problem.

Nor was he the man to deal with the great question which dominated the latter half of his political career – the resurgence of Germany. His biographers show that he did a good deal more about rearmament than is usually believed. But he was not prepared to risk a real challenge on the matter. Perhaps he never forgot that Chanak, the one occasion in the inter-war years when Britain stood up – and stood up successfully – to an aggressive nationalist military dictatorship, had as its immediate sequel the fall of the Lloyd George government. On a simplistic view it could be argued that tough foreign policy had resulted in the cry of war-mongering, and in electoral disaster. It was an unfortunate political lesson, and Baldwin was not the only person who learned it all too well.

3

The second unfortunate political lesson for Baldwin was the events of 1923. That autumn, faced by mounting unemployment, he made his only obeisance to the spirit of Tory radicalism and decided that something positive must be done. He had moved a good way from the tariff reform policy of Joseph Chamberlain, but he believed that protection of British industry was a possible solution to the problem of 'the intractable million', as Professor Pigou described the hard core of 10 per cent of the working population which remained out of work through the inter-war years. He said so in a speech at Plymouth on October 25. This was a dangerous line to take, for Bonar Law, perhaps ill-advisedly, had given a pledge during the 1922 election that 'this Parliament will not make any fundamental change in the fiscal system of this country'. Baldwin had consulted some, though not all members of the Cabinet, but his speech came as a surprise to the rank and file.

Although he had warned the chairman of the party to be ready for an early election, Baldwin's speech did not in itself commit him to an instant dissolution, and it could be read as the opening of a campaign to educate the country. Common prudence would have suggested such a programme. Nevertheless, for reasons still not wholly clear Baldwin on November 12 asked the king to dissolve parliament, fixing the election day for December 6. Even such ardent tariff reformers as L. S. Amery were apprehensive about an election sprung so suddenly and with such little preparation so soon after the previous one. Baldwin endeavoured to placate public opinion by disclaiming any intention of imposing what Lord Northcliffe at the time of Joseph Chamberlain's campaign had called 'stomach taxes', i.e. taxes on imported food. But the public evidently did not believe him, and both the Labour and Liberal parties campaigned largely on the fear of dearer food. It was the big loaf and the little loaf all over again.

The election was not a landslide like 1906 but it was a severe slap in the face for Baldwin. The Conservatives remained the biggest single party with 258 seats – a loss of 87 compared with the previous year. Their proportion of the total poll was almost the same but, as they had over sixty more opposed candidates than in 1922, this represented a sharp decline in support. The Liberals were at least in appearance reunited by the challenge to free trade. Asquith and Lloyd George concealed their mutual detestation under a temporary concordat. It was destined to be the last occasion when the party could be regarded as a serious runner for victory at a general election. They put up 453 candidates, and won 151 seats. Labour was the beneficiary of the oddities of the the British electoral system. Although their share of the poll, and their average vote per opposed candidate was only 1 per cent more than in 1922, they gained almost fifty seats, rising to 191.

Baldwin was widely condemned by his party for what seemed the totally unnecessary abandonment of a position of strength. If there had been any sort of consensus for an alternative leader he would almost certainly have been ousted. But no such agreement existed. He rode out the storm successfully. His motives for this premature dissolution remain something of a puzzle. It has been suggested at one extreme that he made his speech by accident without appreciating the significance of Bonar Law's pledge, at the other that it was a far-sighted calculation, that he expected to lose the election of 1923 but also to reunite the party and come back stronger than ever at the next election – *reculer pour mieux sauter*. Neither of these theories is very plausible. Twelve years later he gave Thomas Jones[1] his own version of what moved him. He was, he said, convinced that the problem of unemployment could only be solved by a tariff. He also believed that it was the one issue which could reunite the party 'including the Lloyd George malcontents'. He went on:

> The Goat [Lloyd George] was in America. He was on the water when I made the speech and the Liberals did not know what to say. I had information that he was going protectionist and I had to get in quick. No truth that I was pushed by Amery and the cabal. I was loosely in the saddle and got them into line in the Cabinet. Dished the Goat, as otherwise he would have got the Party with Austen and F.E. and there would have been an end to the Tory Party as we know it. I shall not forget the surprise and delight of Amery. It was a long calculated and not a sudden dissolution. Bonar had no programme, and the only thing was to bring the tariff issue forward.[2]

Baldwin's official biographers are justifiably rather sceptical about such a clear-cut *ex post facto* description of what happened. While not denying the part played by these considerations in Baldwin's mind they suggest that the course of events was influenced as much

[1] Assistant, later Deputy Secretary of the Cabinet, 1916–30, and an intimate friend of Baldwin. His diaries are a valuable source of information on the politics of the inter-war years.

[2] From Jones's papers, quoted, Middlemas and Barnes, op. cit., 212.

by 'the conjuncture of mere circumstance' as by deep laid plans.

However, there is no need to doubt that Baldwin was influenced by some of the factors mentioned in Jones's account. Both at this time and later he had an almost pathological fear of a revival of some kind of centre coalition under or including Lloyd George. He feared the prestige of Austen Chamberlain as an ex-leader of the party, and the cleverness of Birkenhead for whom he felt something of the same moral disapprobation that he had for Lloyd George. It is highly probable that Baldwin's intimates dwelt much on the threat constituted by the ex-coalitionists.

As late as 1925 J. C. C. Davidson,[1] one of Baldwin's closest friends, was obsessed with the fear that Churchill, then Chancellor of the Exchequer, intended to use a dispute in the Cabinet over naval construction as a ploy to oust Baldwin. 'I had warned him that this was an attempt to get rid of him and that the Old Gang [i.e. the ex-coalitionists] nursed a hatred for him that had never been entirely broken.'[2] Davidson was by no means alone in harbouring these suspicions. Yet as R. R. James points out,[3] it is quite possible that no ulterior motive lay behind the row; it may well have been one of those straight clashes between the Treasury and a great spending department, which perpetually recur in modern British history. But, if Baldwin's closest friends felt like this in 1925 when the breach was supposed to be healed and when Baldwin had secured the services of those ex-coalitionists whom he wanted, how much more apprehension would there have been in 1923 when the ex-coalitionists were out of office and palpably unfriendly? It may be that Baldwin exaggerated the danger. There is no means now of assessing its reality. But one can well believe that, real or not, the threat played a part in his decision.

It is also true that he was acutely worried about the unemployment problem which by 1923 was at last beginning to appear in its true light as the product, not of cyclical depression, but of some deeper malaise in the structure of British industry. Baldwin certainly believed that tariffs might provide the answer, and this was

[1] The first Viscount Davidson, b. 1889. In 1925 he was Parliamentary Secretary to the Admiralty, and later, 1927–30, Chairman of the Conservative Party. R. R. James, *Memoirs of a Conservative*, gives a good account of his career based on his papers and reminiscences.

[2] James, op. cit., 213.   [3] ibid., 211.

his primary motive in raising the matter at all. But there was no obvious need to hold an immediate general election; he could have done much by merely extending the existing McKenna duties on 'luxury' imports;[1] this would not have been a breach of Bonar Law's pledge. Even if he envisaged a greater degree of protection than that, there was still no reason to dissolve so suddenly without giving time for a preparatory campaign of persuasion and propaganda.

There is no contemporary evidence to show that Baldwin anticipated a *volte face* over free trade on the part of Lloyd George, or that such a suspicion had any foundation. But it is in keeping with character that, just as Baldwin suspected Lloyd George of deliberately engineering a war over Chanak in order to cash in on the patriotic cry, so too he might have regarded the Liberal leader as capable of repudiating his allegiance to free trade if there seemed a chance of winning Chamberlain and Birkenhead over to a newly formed centre party. Baldwin always believed that cleverness and unscrupulousness went together. Suspicion of Lloyd George is the most plausible explanation of an otherwise incomprehensible decision.

Whatever his motives may have been, Baldwin seems to have drawn an important conclusion from the election result – the moral that political success will not come to a party calling itself Conservative if it embarks on a policy of avowed innovation. Electorally this may be true. It is hard to think of an example of Conservative victory on a programme of publicly proclaimed reforms; although there are plenty of examples of empirical reforms carried out when the party has been in power, and they may well have contributed to the retention of power. But Baldwin's experience in 1923 made him not only reluctant in future to fight an election on any kind of active policy – which may well have been correct – but also reluctant to embark on any positive plans, even after he was in power – which from the point of view of the public interest was a disaster.

The curious balance of the parties in the House after the 1923 election led to a host of ingenious proposals about alliances and

---

[1] These had been imposed during the war by Reginald McKenna, Chancellor of the Exchequer, 1915–16.

personalities for the new parliament. Baldwin took the sensible view that to keep out Labour would store up trouble in the long run, that the election anyway had been a straight repudiation of the only party advocating tariffs and the two free trade parties must solve their own problems. He met parliament and was duly defeated early in 1924. In accordance with the rules of the Constitution Ramsay MacDonald was sent for by the king and accepted office. The Liberals were in a dilemma. We can see now that they made a fatal error in not securing some sort of agreed terms of cooperation with Labour.[1] It might not have worked but it ought to have been attempted. Failing that, they should have turned out MacDonald at the earliest plausible occasion. As it was they supported Labour from an entirely independent position, with no written treaty, not even an informal understanding. Those Liberals who hoped for tacit, unspoken cooperation were soon disillusioned. There was none.

Meanwhile, the fortunes of the Conservative party revived. The tariff issue had brought back the ex-coalitionists. Although a series of personal tiffs and misunderstandings had prevented them actually joining Baldwin before the election, it was clear that they would be members of any future Tory Cabinet. Baldwin's dreaded centre party had been dead as soon as Lloyd George declared his adherence to free trade. The blunders of Labour and the confusion in the Liberal party helped Baldwin to recover. Perhaps paradoxically, he was helped by a protest which seemed to be a severe criticism of him. This was a resolution unanimously passed by the Lancashire Division of the National Union under Lord Derby's chairmanship. It was moved by Sir Archibald Salvidge, the great Tory 'boss' in that important county where the party had suffered particularly heavy losses in the recent election. The gist of it was a charge that the Central Office had made no attempt to ascertain opinion before rushing into an over-hasty general election. There had been nothing like this, as Baldwin's biographers point out, since the days of Lord Randolph Churchill; but, together with the strong opinions of some of his ex-Cabinet colleagues, it enabled Baldwin to climb down without loss of face.

[1] Trevor Wilson, *Downfall of the Labour party*, 264-5, unduly minimises the possibilities open to Asquith at this time.

He could present himself as an honest politician who believed in tariffs, held an election rather than break his predecessor's pledge, and, having lost it could honourably abandon his policy until public opinion was ready to reconsider the matter.

Baldwin may have had to give up his convictions on one particular issue but he was far from being as passive as the cartoonists made out. He attended at once to the party organisation. As is always the case when the Conservative party has been in office for a long while, the organisation needed an overhaul. The Conservatives had not been in opposition for nearly ten years. During that time ministers had the benefit of the civil service and the usual official sources of help and information. All this was now denied to them. The 'shadow Cabinet' in the form that we know it today dates from 1924. In a sense it had of course existed long before that. As far back as Peel's day meetings were held of ex-Cabinet ministers to consider the line to take in opposition. The expression 'shadow' seems to have come into regular use after 1906,[1] but it was not till 1924 that the Consultative Committee, to give it its official name, was provided with a policy secretariat, and organised on a regular official basis. The shadow Cabinet had separate committees to handle the various subjects, and these could include outside experts. The whole structure was independent of the Central Office, being directly responsible to Baldwin, and at Baldwin's request Austen Chamberlain was associated with him at the top.

The party was thus well placed to exploit the weaknesses of the government and plan for the next election. In June a manifesto was published, *Aims and principles*, largely drafted by Neville Chamberlain, but much helped by the resources of the new organisation. At the same time Baldwin came to the end of a series of major public speeches in which he outlined his concept of the 'new Conservatism', dwelling *inter alia* on the importance of reforming the constituency parties and persuading selection committees to be less chary of choosing candidates who could not afford heavy subscriptions to party funds.

Baldwin's organisational and oratorical efforts have not been remembered as the corresponding efforts of 1945–51 are remem-

[1] Geoffrey Block, *A source book of Conservatism* (1964), 90.

bered. This is largely because the period of opposition was so short and the election, when it came, was apparently fought on issues which had little to do with the new Conservatism. It would, however, be wrong to underestimate what was achieved in 1924 in terms of restructuring antiquated and creaking party institutions.

4

The crisis came over the Campbell case in the summer – an allegation that the government had from political motives forced the withdrawal of a prosecution for incitement to mutiny. The Liberals refused to support MacDonald who on his defeat in the House asked for a dissolution. The events of 1924 resulted in a revival of the anti-socialist alliance which had been one of the main justifications of the Lloyd George coalition of 1918-22 in its latter years. But the new alliance was one in which the Liberal ex-ministers, apart from Churchill, played no part; nor did the Liberal party. What mattered was the Liberal vote frightened by the antics of Labour into a massive shift towards the Conservative side. This confirmed the rightness of the instinct of the Conservative party managers in 1922 that those elements of the Liberal party which believed in property, law and order could in the end be brought over to the Conservative side without the need for any formal treaty. The publication of the Zinoviev letter,[1] for which the Conservative Central Office, unaware that it was a forgery, paid handsomely, contributed something to the party's victory; but there were many other causes – among them MacDonald's evasiveness and the wild utterances of some of his supporters.

If the election was a setback for Labour, for the Liberals it was a calamity. Their popular vote fell from 4·3 million to 2·9 million. This was partly because they put only 340 candidates in the field – a virtual admission that they had no chance of forming the next government. Their vote per candidate opposed fell from 37·8 per cent of the total to 30·9 per cent, and their number of members

[1] This purported to be a letter from Zinoviev, President of the Comintern, to the British Communist party. It was full of advice on various methods of fomenting revolution, and, if genuine, seemed to be a condemnation of the Labour government's policy of better relations with Russia.

returned fell from 159 to 40. They were never again to be serious contenders for power. The collapse of the Liberal party was a triumph for Baldwin's middle of the road policy – or rather not so much his policy as his image. A great many right wing Liberals who disliked Lloyd George and saw the control of their party slipping away to him from Asquith's hands could vote with a clear conscience for Baldwin now that the tariff issue was dead. It had not been so easy to vote for Bonar Law, associated as he had been with the bitter feuds about Ulster and Irish Home Rule not very long before.

The Labour party's popular vote actually rose by a little over a million, but this reflected the increased number of candidates – 512 instead of 453. Their average share of the vote for opposed candidates fell from 41 per cent to 38 per cent, and they lost forty seats, 151 compared with 191 in 1923.

The Conservatives swept home to a conclusive victory. Their popular vote was up by nearly 2·5 million, from just over 5·5 million to 8 million in round numbers. They too had a larger number of opposed candidates in the field, but even so their average percentage rose from 42·6 to 51·9 (in 1922 it had been 48·6). In terms of seats they had an overwhelming majority over the other two parties combined, 419 out of a total of 615.

Baldwin had no difficulty in securing the services of those ex-coalitionists whom he wanted. The only one he did not want was Horne, a haunter of night clubs, once described by Baldwin as 'that rare thing – a Scots cad'. He offered him the Ministry of Labour which he was certain to decline. But Austen Chamberlain, Birkenhead and Worthington Evans rejoined as colleagues of the promoted under-secretaries whom they had sought to browbeat in 1922 and served under the man whom they had regarded as the outstanding mediocrity of the coalition Cabinet. Curzon, Baldwin's former rival, was quietly relegated from the Foreign Office to the Lord Presidency. When he died seven months later, the final *imprimatur* of respectability was put on to the Cabinet by the succession of Balfour who had been one of the strongest opponents of the revolt in 1922. As he himself was wont to observe, 'I never forgive but I always forget.'

But perhaps the most notable adherent was an erstwhile

Conservative turned Liberal, one of the pillars of the coalition. Winston Churchill had already decided that there was no future in the Liberal party. At a by-election in 1924 he stood for West-minister under the tongue-twisting name of 'anti-Socialist Constitutionalist'. He ran second by only a handful of votes to the official Conservative who was a tariff reformer. 'n the general election he stood under the same colours for Epping and was not opposed by the Conservatives. Amidst much surprise, Baldwin offered him the Chancellorship of the Exchequer. No one was more surprised than Churchill himself who, so the story goes, when he accepted with alacrity Baldwin's offer to be 'Chancellor' thought that it was the Duchy of Lancaster that was intended – not the Exchequer. Churchill was not even a Conservative at the time – he joined the party a year later – and he never wavered in his support of free trade. As events turned out it was an unhappy choice, but no appointment could have more clearly symbolised Baldwin's determination to avoid the neo-Tory radicalism of the tariff reformers, and his own conversion to the policy of the anti-socialist alliance against which the Carlton Club revolt had been partly aimed.

It had also been aimed at Lloyd George, and he was the one notable figure excluded from power by the new alliance. This was not so much because of his policies as his character. Baldwin, moved by moral rather than political considerations, believed him to be 'a real corrupter', and nothing would have induced him, save the direst emergency, to sit again with Lloyd George in the Cabinet room. Here he was heavily reinforced by Neville Chamberlain who now emerges for the first time as an important figure in the Conservative party. Neville Chamberlain considered with some justice that he had never been fairly treated by Lloyd George when he took on the job of Minister of National Service in the war. Lloyd George, who was a great believer in the connection of character and physiognomy, took an instant dislike to the shape of Neville Chamberlain's head – it was far too long, he said – and he never ceased to regret having appointed him without seeing him first. He proceeded to harass him by alternate complaint and neglect, and Chamberlain resigned in a resentful huff. By such curious accidents is the course of history sometimes turned.

For Neville Chamberlain, who had first entered the Cabinet in 1923 because Bonar Law regarded him as a possible bridge to his brother Austen, proved to be one of the ablest and most energetic administrators that the Conservative party produced in the inter-war years. He was Minister of Health from 1924 to 1929 – a post which then comprised not only health but also the functions now discharged by the Ministry of Housing and Local Government. He was responsible for a whole series of very important piecemeal reforms in this very important area of government. He was the equivalent of Sir Richard Cross at the Home Office under Disraeli. Administrative capacity is not always the *sine qua non* of rising to the top. Disraeli, Salisbury, Bonar Law and Baldwin got where they did without displaying those qualities very obviously. But there are occasions when they can matter. Even as Balfour made his reputation as a tough administrator when he was Chief Secretary for Ireland from 1886 to 1891, so Neville Chamberlain established himself as the second man in the party by his tenure of the Ministry of Health. He consolidated it, no doubt, as Chancellor of the Exchequer from 1931 to 1937, but by then he was already unchallengeable. With him as well as Baldwin irrevocably hostile, there was little chance of Lloyd George being included in any possible reshuffle and realignment of the anti-Socialist alliance.

This was in many ways a tragedy. In his *Politicians and the slump*, Mr Robert Skidelsky well shows that the real issue in 1929–31 was not capitalism against socialism, but interventionist capitalism against *laissez-faire* capitalism.[1] The point applies not only to those years, it applies to the whole period in which unemployment was the dominant issue in politics – unsolved and ultimately despaired of as insoluble. The notion that an interventionist cure was only advocated by Keynes who was a solitary voice crying in the wilderness, is untrue. There was a formidable body of economists, indeed most of them, on the same side and profoundly sceptical of the 'conventional wisdom' of the Treasury and the city; and there was a substantial element of the business world thinking on similar lines.

But in politics the only man who really took up the cause in a

[1] Robert Skidelsky, *Politicians and the slump*, (1967), p. xii.

big way was Lloyd George. It was he who brought the question on to the political stage with his pamphlet, *We can conquer unemployment*, which appeared early in 1929. This was a real challenge to the front benches of both parties. It held far more promise of a cure than either the rigid deflationism of Montagu Norman, the Governor of the Bank of England, or the woolly socialist idealism of Ramsay MacDonald. But it had a fatal handicap. It emanated from the most mistrusted man in politics and it appealed neither to Labour, who regarded 'the system' as anyway hopeless and only to be endured pending the arrival of the socialist millennium, nor to the Conservatives who reckoned, not without reason as it turned out, that they could float on the current of anti-socialism – no doubt with an occasional backward eddy, but fairly safely all the same.

The Conservatives, moreover, never abandoned the tradition of Disraeli, Salisbury and Balfour of doing something about social reform. The mere fact of being in office made this natural, almost automatic. This was particularly Neville Chamberlain's contribution, and, supported by this practical record of achievement on the part of his colleague, the Prime Minister's Disraelian belief in 'one nation' and his almost poetic declarations of patriotism, opposition to class conflict, belief in paternalistic welfare, did not seem mere humbug. There were real achievements to back it. His handling of the General Strike not only seemed but was another instance of conciliation, goodwill, and a genuine effort to unify the nation. The Trades Disputes Act of 1927, however, cut disagreeably across this picture though it seems to have had little effect at the next election. It was a minor contribution to the defeat of 1929, but not more. The anti-Conservative trend was clear before the Act had been passed. By-elections went against the Conservatives from early 1926 onwards. The Act of 1927 may have enhanced this tendency, but other matters, such as derating of agriculture and industry, were probably more important. Derating of these, whatever its justification on general economic grounds, was bound to increase the domestic rates of the ordinary householder, and therefore lose votes.

Nevertheless it is something of a puzzle to answer quite why the party's fortunes slumped so much. It appears to have been to some extent due to organisational defects. J. C. C. Davidson, who took over the party chairmanship from Jackson at the end of 1926, was, it is true, successful both in raising funds and streamlining the Central Office. Money was certainly needed. The Conservatives had done very badly in their relations with the coalition. Sir George Younger alleged much 'poaching' on the part of Frederick (Freddie) Guest, the coalition Liberal whip. It was said that between 1918 and 1922 many gifts meant for the Conservatives somehow found their way into Lloyd George's mysterious 'Fund'. Matters were not made better by the fact that Lord Farquhar, the treasurer of the party, was rapidly failing in mind. By the end of 1922 in the words of Lord Edmund Talbot, the former Chief Whip, to Bonar Law, 'He is so "gaga" that one does not know what to make of him.' He was paying sums intended for the Conservative party into his own account and generally behaving with total irresponsibility. Bonar Law dismissed him in January 1923, but by then the harm was done.[1]

On the organisational side too Davidson found that all was far from well. The Principal Agent appointed in March 1923 in succession to Sir Malcolm Fraser had been Admiral Sir Reginald Hall, former Director of Naval Intelligence and a Conservative M.P. since 1919. His biographer describes his acceptance as 'one of the few big mistakes he made in his life'.[2] The party machine was not in good condition, and Hall had no past experience that fitted him for the task of putting it in order. He was blamed for the loss of the 1923 election, in which he lost his own seat, and early in the next year resigned after a breakdown in health.

His successor, Sir Herbert Blain, was a business efficiency expert pulled in by Jackson to overhaul the party organisation. Davidson gives a rather sensational account of what happened when he became chairman. His story is that at their first interview Blain made it clear that his objective was to oust Baldwin whom he regarded as 'a semi-socialist'. Davidson goes on: 'I had a tremendous row with Blain on the first and only time that I saw him and talked to him, and I dismissed him. He never came back to the

---

[1] See Blake, *The unknown Prime Minister*, op. cit., 496–8; and Lord Beaverbrook, *The decline and fall of Lloyd George* (1963), for further details of this curious episode.
[2] Admiral Sir William James, *The eyes of the navy* (1955), 183.

office.'[1] No date is given and the story is *prima facie* improbable. There may have been a row but the two men certainly met on other occasions, notably December 14 when the National Union Executive passed, under Davidson as chairman for the first time, a highly complimentary resolution of regret at Blain's resignation. Blain was unpopular with some sections of the party, but his job was mostly completed by the time Jackson resigned on October 5 to become Governor of Bengal. He probably took the occasion to send in his own resignation too, though it was not formally accepted till six weeks later, and he did not actually hand over till the end of the year. The story that he was dismissed abruptly after a single interview seems to be a myth. Reminiscences long after the event are not always reliable,[2] though one can assume that it is at least true that Davidson and Blain did not get on well together.

Davidson, however, seems to have had great difficulty in finding a satisfactory successor as Principal Agent. Sir Leigh MacLachlan whom he appointed, not without misgiving, lasted little over a year. He proved to be obstructive and particularly bad at organising the women's vote – a very important matter since universal suffrage at the age of twenty-one had been enacted in 1928. Davidson wrote that 'he is most unpopular with MPs and is regarded with disfavour by some and with ridicule by others of the Executive of the National Union and by the local leaders of the party in the country'.[3] We depend on Davidson's authority, but such unpopularity certainly seems a defect and it makes one wonder about Davidson's own judgment in choosing him at all in the first place.

His successor, Robert Topping, chosen in February 1928, was the first person to be appointed from an area agency to the post. He became Director-General in 1931, the position of Principal Agent having been abolished, and remained in that office till September 1945. Topping too did not prove entirely satisfactory. Davidson doubted whether he quite 'carried the guns',[4] and his behaviour towards Baldwin during the leadership crisis of 1930–1 seems to have been equivocal to say the least. He was

[1] R. R. James, op. cit., 265-6.
[2] I am indebted to Mr J. A. Ramsden of Nuffield College for drawing my attention to the discrepancies in Davidson's account.
[3] R. R. James, op. cit., 275.   [4] ibid., 266.

described as 'an excitable Irishman'. However, if length of
tenure is anything to go by, he cannot have been too bad. He held
the office longer than anyone before or since – with one exception,
'Captain' Middleton, who beat him by a year. The job of principal
party organiser is in many ways a thankless one. After so many
changes the Conservative leadership must have been thankful to
find someone who would stay.

Davidson instituted various reforms, some of which, according
to him, have been incorrectly attributed to his successor, Neville
Chamberlain. He rationalised the rules and procedure of the
National Union; he separated the chairmanship of the party
from that of the Executive Committee of the National Union;
and he created the Conservative Research Department.[1] He also
recruited two highly capable henchmen in Patrick Gower, a very
able civil servant and Joseph Ball, an officer of MI5. Ball is an
enigmatic figure who appears from time to time in some of the more
mysterious transactions of the period. His agents managed to
penetrate the Labour party headquarters and secure advance
copies of its propaganda.[2] One would like to know more about his
activities. He was director of the Research Department from 1930
to 1939.

These reforms took time to have any effect, and they were
largely confined to the centre. The constituency parties remained
much as they were, in spite of the efforts of Davidson and the
advice of Baldwin. The election was fought on the uninspiring
slogan of 'Safety First' for which Davidson had at least some responsibility. In retrospect he recognised that it was a mistake.
Baldwin, however, had also been a bad tactician. It was clearly an
error to bring in unpopular legislation, however desirable on
public grounds, just before an election. All parties have learned
this now, largely because of what happened in 1929. As for the
great new element in electoral politics, 'the flapper vote' as current
slang termed the extension of the franchise to girls at twenty-one,
it is impossible to say what was its effect; but there is no reason to
suppose that it was especially anti-Conservative.

[1] Lord Eustace Percy was its first chairman, Chamberlain its second. Its creation is
often attributed to the latter, but incorrectly.
[2] R. R. James, op. cit., 272.

The defeat was by no means decisive. The new franchise makes statistical comparison with previous elections difficult. It is enough to say that Lloyd George's great campaign mounted regardless of cost with 513 candidates, though it brought him 27 per cent of the poll, gave him only 59 seats. Labour on a bare minority of the poll (39·3 per cent to the Conservatives 39·4) obtained 288 seats to the Conservatives' 260. Baldwin at once resigned.

As in 1924 there was a good deal of intra-party recrimination but there was more time for it to build up. As with some medieval monarch the attack began against 'evil counsellors'. Davidson was blamed for the loss of the election, and Baldwin could not preserve him. He was succeeded as chairman in 1930 by Neville Chamberlain, a unique appointment, for Chamberlain was very obviously Baldwin's most probable successor. In matters of policy two principal lines of attack were pursued against Baldwin. The first concerned tariffs, the second India. Both were essentially problems of empire. The tariff reformers came out in force using the familiar argument that if only there had been more emphasis on tariffs and less on 'Safety First', the party would have won the election. One can compare those Labour supporters who were sure that if only there had been more emphasis on nationalisation they would have won the 1951 election. A vigorous campaign was launched by the press lords – Rothermere and Beaverbrook – in favour of Empire Free Trade. This slogan was adopted by Beaverbrook for a very simple, almost naïve reason. The British electorate, he argued in private, seemed to be irrevocably wedded to free trade. No party which opposed free trade or supported tariffs had ever fared anything but disastrously at the polls. But if you called tariff reform by a name which somehow incorporated the words 'free trade', then it might make all the difference.[1]

The press lords waged their war persistently, but in the end ineptly. When Rothermere actually put in writing a demand to see the composition of the next Conservative Cabinet as a condition of support by his newspapers, he over-stepped the limit. Baldwin hit back at him in a speech at Caxton Hall in June 1930, 'A more preposterous and insolent demand was never made

[1] Private information.

on the leader of any political party.' The campaign continued
however, and in March 1931 a by-election at St George's,
Westminster, seemed to put Baldwin in grave jeopardy. It was an
overwhelmingly Tory seat, and for a while no Baldwinite could
be found to contest it against the Empire Free Trade candidate,
Sir Ernest Petter. Eventually Duff Cooper[1] agreed to stand. At one
of his meetings Baldwin rounded on the press lords in words
borrowed from his cousin Rudyard Kipling, words which still
echo across the years: 'What the proprietorship of these papers is
aiming at is power, and power without responsibility – the
prerogative of the harlot throughout the ages.' Duff Cooper won.
Baldwin stayed.

Baldwin was fortunate that the second line of attack on him
did not coincide with the first. Winston Churchill bitterly opposed
his attitude to India. This was a new issue and, in the light of our
modern experience of the problems of a declining empire, a very
important one. Baldwin, influenced by the success of the Irish
settlement, strongly supported Lord Halifax's liberal view as
viceroy towards the demand for dominion status for India.
Naturally the Labour government was on the same side. But the
subject brought out all the most rigid, paternalistic, authoritarian
views of the man who had served in India as a cavalry subaltern
and fought in the frontier wars at a time when Indian self-
government seemed an absurd dream. Churchill, however, had
little sympathy with Empire Free Trade. The two rebellions were
mounted separately and Baldwin in the end repelled them both,
although he considered that he owed little to Neville Chamberlain
whose role as chairman of the party seems to have been ambiguous
and not wholly loyal. Baldwin's position was at one time so shaky
that the editor of *The Times* actually set up in proof a leader
entitled 'Mr Baldwin withdraws'.

It is hard to underestimate the harm which Churchill's attitude did – not over India, for he was totally defeated – but in
terms of the personal doubts which he gratuitously raised about
his own character. It was a disaster that his diehard stand on India
which he carried to great lengths in his opposition to Sir Samuel

---

[1] Secretary for War 1935–6, First Lord of the Admiralty 1936–8. Resigned over
Munich. Created Viscount Norwich.

Hoare's India Bill in 1934 should have, as it were, contaminated his stand on defence and foreign policy. The tragedy was not only that by resigning early in 1931 from the shadow Cabinet he excluded himself from office. The tragedy, rather, was that his criticism of British foreign and defence policy carried less weight in the Conservative-Liberal consensus world of the 1930s because it could be presented by its enemies as coming from an old-fashioned reactionary. A glance at the files of the *New Statesman*, or even at Low's cartoons in the *Evening Standard*, shows how Churchill was regarded by the 'good left'. He was regarded with equal misgiving by the moderate right. One should, however, beware of over-estimating Churchill's own consistency in matters of defence, nor should one forget his earlier responsibility for the low state of British arms in his capacity as Chancellor of the Exchequer in the 1920s. His colleagues certainly did not.

5

The failure of the Labour government to produce an intelligible policy on unemployment together with the gathering economic storm swept the Conservatives back. They were out of office for too short a time to re-think their attitudes. Neville Chamberlain was active in organisational matters but he had neither time nor inclination to re-examine Tory economic policy. He was too much occupied by a plethora of complaints against Baldwin and with his own personal position if Baldwin went.

The coalition which followed the break-up of the Labour Cabinet represented the anti-Socialist consensus at the height of its success. Socialism was now wholly discredited. The policy at which Lloyd George, Churchill, and their Conservative colleagues had aimed in 1918-22 was triumphant, but not as far as Lloyd George and Churchill were concerned. They were out, and the anti-socialist coalition was headed by the former Socialist, Ramsay MacDonald, in a duumvirate with Baldwin. Almost all the Liberals were behind it. The general election swept Labour almost out of existence. Their popular vote was not too badly eroded, all things considered; it fell from 8·4 million in 1929 to 6·6 million, but they won only 52 seats. The Conservatives rose from 8·6 million to nearly 12 million with 473 seats. The combined coalition forces mustered 14·5 million – 67 per cent of the poll – and 554 seats. It was an absurd and unhealthy situation, well calculated to muffle important issues and obscure the realities of the times.

For four years MacDonald presided over the government of the country, towards the end with rapidly diminishing mental power. The temperamental similarity of MacDonald and Baldwin has often been pointed out, for Baldwin was at heart as much of a romantic Celtic visionary as MacDonald. The resemblance has even made people fancy a plot between the two men planned long before the crisis of 1931. This is of course nonsense. But the coalition undoubtedly suited them both. MacDonald had for years been remote and inaccessible to his Labour colleagues, preferring a very different company. As Beatrice Webb sadly noted in 1930, observing that his itinerary included visits to the king, Lord Londonderry and the Duke of Sutherland:

> Alas, alas! Balmoral is inevitable but why the castles of the wealthiest, most aristocratic, most reactionary and by no means the most intellectual of the Conservative party?... He *ought* not to be more at home in the castles of the great than in the homes of his followers. It argues a perverted taste and a vanishing faith.

It would be wrong to infer from this that MacDonald meant to ditch his party all along. But it is true that when events fell out as they did and patriotic duty seemed to point to his heading a 'national' government, he felt something of a sense of release. As for Baldwin, he was quite content to be the right hand man, the ultimate controller of the government's destiny and yet not to be Prime Minister. The coalition excluded just the man he wanted to exclude – Lloyd George; and he may well have been glad that Churchill too had put himself out of court.

In terms of economic policy, it was the worst possible combination. MacDonald regarded in his vague way all tinkering with capitalism as meaningless, just as Lansbury and the utopian socialists did. Therefore one might as well accept 'the conventional wisdom' of the Establishment. Baldwin had never seriously thought about the problems. Nor had Neville Chamberlain. He was indeed a social reformer, but essentially in terms of palliatives of the existing system, not in terms of interventionist capitalism. It is true that statistically the worst of the unemployment problem gradually disappeared from 1932 onwards. But statistics masked very bad conditions in some areas. These were the years of the hunger marches and the tragedy of Jarrow, the years of the means test and the cuts. In so far as things improved, the cause was just those impersonal and uncontrollable forces which the Establishment had always argued to be the only thing that mattered. The rearmament boom had a good effect, just as the world depression had had a bad effect. There was little attempt to do anything positive about the situation.

Politics, given this broad consensus of inability to solve unemployment, turned on matters which ministers thought they could do something about. From 1932 onwards one of these was India. Baldwin faced this first challenge to the whole imperial position with courageous liberalism. It raised many of the problems familiar to us in the last fifteen or twenty years. The India Act was to be swept into oblivion by the tide of events, but in terms of its own time it was a generous and far-sighted measure.

The other issue on which the government might have done something even within its own terms of reference was foreign policy which was inseparably entangled with the problem of defence policy. The question was already important before MacDonald and Baldwin exchanged offices preparatory to the election of 1935. The threat of Hitler was perhaps then less obvious than the danger to international law and order presented by Mussolini, but both were serious questions and demanded an answer which they never got. It is true that the election of 1935 was fought largely on collective security and that the promise of rearmament was not the swindle later alleged. It is also true that Baldwin did not, as Churchill alleged in the most celebrated item in any index of any book, 'admit putting party before country'. He neither admitted it, nor did it. But there was ample cause for Baldwin to press for much greater armaments than he actually advocated, and the fiasco of the Hoare–Laval pact was a heavy blow to his credibility as a supporter of the League and collective action.

The election of 1935 was another triumph, though diminished, for the anti-Socialist alliance. The Labour party still suffered from the stigma of incapacity to govern – like the Conservatives in the mid-nineteenth century. The success of the Conservatives in the 1930s, as in the 1920s, was largely due to the feebleness and divisions of the opposition – even as these had been the key to the success of Palmerston and Salisbury and Campbell-Bannerman. Division is always a barrier, if unity is not always a passport, to political success. But in the second half of the 1930s, divisions became far more acute in the Conservative party than they had been since 1922. The battle over appeasement was even more important than dissension over India.

The differences were sharpened and clarified by Baldwin's retirement in a glow of glory after the settlement of the abdication question. No Prime Minister has ever chosen a better moment to bow himself out. He could not have foreseen the storm of obloquy which was to descend on him a few years later. Neville Chamberlain, his long pre-ordained successor, was a wholly different character. He had been mayor of the palace in Baldwin's last years. His influence on armament policy had been decisive. He had a clear cut view of how to deal with the dictators – clear cut and wrong. It is an irony of history that Anthony Eden, successor at the Foreign Office to the ill-fated Hoare, should actually have welcomed Chamberlain's succession on the ground that the new Prime Minister would take a more active interest in foreign affairs than his predecessor. Chamberlain certainly did, but not in the direction that Eden hoped.

Chamberlain's desire to seek a settlement with Mussolini and Hitler, his conviction that war was a terrible evil, his horror of a repetition of 1914, were attitudes which deserve commendation, not censure. But he was too reasonable, too moderate, too parochial perhaps, to see that he was not dealing with people who were even remotely like himself. Hitler really was a Genghis Khan, 'a demon figure sprung from the abyss', as Churchill called him. Mussolini was an erratic adventurer. It may be that by the summer of 1937 things had gone beyond recall. But Chamberlain's attitude, even if it made in the end no more difference to the international crisis than Baldwin's policy of drift, had its effect on

THE WORCESTERSHIRE LAD

Farmer Bull. "WELL DONE, STANLEY : A LONG DAY AND A RARE STRAIGHT FURROW."

May 26, 1937. Reproduced by permission of Punch

the divisions within the Conservative party. These became harder, harsher, and longer lasting than they would have been under Baldwin. They left a lasting mark on the party, not wholly obliterated even as late as 1957.

The split in the Conservative party on this issue was vital. Labour opposed Chamberlainism but its opposition was rendered morally and intellectually ineffective because of the party's failure to give rational consideration to the armament problem. The only clear cut consistent opposition came from Churchill, and it was based not on idealistic international grounds but on the old fashioned Disraelian view of 'the permanent and abiding interests of England'. Churchill, however, had scarcely any supporters. Between 1935 and 1938 he was a lone voice occasionally aided by Brendan Bracken, Duncan Sandys and Robert Boothby but by scarcely anyone else. Nor was he anything like so consistent an enemy of the treaty-breaking powers as his supporters later maintained. He did not oppose Japan over Manchuria or Mussolini over Abyssinia. But he was right about Hitler, and this mattered more than anything else.

The first occasion on which an organised group of MPs manifested dissent was after Eden's resignation in February 1938. About twenty Conservatives abstained from supporting the government against the opposition's motion of censure. Twenty-five to thirty did the same thing over Munich eight months later.

Meanwhile, during the summer a number of Conservative MPs began to meet informally under the chairmanship of Eden. They became known as 'the Eden Group' – or derisively in the whips' office as 'the Glamour Boys'.[1] The group was, and continued to be, distinct from the smaller one which centred around Churchill. This was still the case even after the Munich crisis. Harold Nicolson, who was not a Conservative but a National Labour MP and first joined them in the autumn of 1938, notes in his diary on November 9:

I went to a hush hush meeting with Anthony Eden. Present Eden, Amery, Cranborne, Sidney Herbert, Cartland, Harold Macmillan, Spears, Derrick Gunston, Emrys Evans, Anthony

[1] The Earl of Avon, *The Eden memoirs: the reckoning* (1964), 31.

Crossley, Herbert Duggan. All good Tories and sensible men. This group is distinct from the Churchill group. It also includes Duff Cooper . . . It was a relief to me to be with people who share my views so completely, and yet who do not give the impression (as Winston does) of being more bitter than determined, and more out for a fight than for reform.[1]

There was evidently still much reluctance to be too closely associated with Churchill, and still a certain feeling, not unreasonable in the circumstances, that more could be done by reasonably polite pressure than overt opposition to Chamberlain. On November 24 Nicolson wrote, 'We still do not really constitute a group and Anthony still hesitates to come out against the Government.'[2] This state of affairs continued right up to the war, and there was never a fusion between the Eden and Churchill groups, although there was cooperation on certain matters, and the two leaders kept in touch with each other.

It is unlikely that the activities of either group had any serious influence on government policy – with one possible exception. Rumour was widespread that the Conservative managers were pressing Chamberlain to hold a snap election on the morrow of Munich in order to exploit the undoubted popularity of his policy. Sir Sidney Herbert, the wealthy and much respected member for the Abbey division of Westminster, on October 4, in spite of failing health, made a memorable speech. 'There may be some tiny Tammany Hall ring who want such a solution,' he said, 'but my solution would be quite different.' And he made an eloquent plea for a genuine national coalition government. Nothing came of the plea, but the reference to Tammany Hall went home.[3] Chamberlain had already been strongly urged by Halifax not to take this course. Whether for that reason or because of Herbert's speech there was no dissolution.[4] In the event this decision was fully justified. The Conservative party would have suffered immense retrospective moral damage, if they had cashed

---

[1] Nigel Nicolson (ed.), *Harold Nicolson: diaries and letters 1930-9* (1966), 377-8.
[2] ibid., 381.
[3] Harold Macmillan, *Winds of change* (1966), 571.
[4] Disraeli had similarly abstained in 1878 but there is nothing to show whether Chamberlain was influenced by the precedent.

in on Munich. But the temptation, especially if Chamberlain really believed in 'peace in our time', must have been considerable. He should be given some credit for resisting it.

The importance of the anti-appeasers does not lie so much in their influence as their existence. No doubt many of them vacillated, hesitated and behaved inconsistently. But they did at least perceive the danger. Had they been in power they might have averted it. There is a modern tendency to say that the 1939 war was inevitable. But the inevitable in history is too often merely something which people have not tried hard enough to avoid. Perhaps, given Hitler's ambitions, war with Germany at some time was inevitable; but it need not have been at that particular time and in those particular circumstances. The existence of a group of dissident Conservatives with some important names among them was a crucial matter for the repute of the Conservative party when war came and Chamberlain's policy collapsed in ruins. Churchill had said all along that this would happen and he was proved right. A number of Conservative MPs had in differing ways and much later in the day said more or less the same thing. The party held an overwhelming majority in the House. A general election in time of war was regarded as impossible – or very undesirable. If Churchill and the anti-appeasers had not existed, it is by no means easy to see how in 1940 the government could have been carried on with any credit at all.

It would be nice if one could draw some sort of economic or sociological dividing line between the appeasers and the anti-appeasers. Attempts have been made to do so. It is said that the appeasers were really pre-war Liberals in disguise, alternatively that they represented the tired second or third generation of the industrial bourgeoisie. The anti-appeasers in contrast were the representatives of an older landed aristocratic tradition which did not bother about self-determination or newfangled notions of that sort, but took a straightforward view of the balance of power and British survival. It is certainly true that Sir John Simon and Walter Runciman, arch-appeasers, were former Asquithian Liberals, that Hoare with his Quaker background was more like a Liberal than a Tory, that Neville Chamberlain was an erstwhile Liberal Unionist, and that both Baldwin and Neville Chamberlain represented a second generation of heavy industry. It is also true that Churchill, Eden, Cranborne came from great landed families.

But so did Lord Halifax. So too did Lord Londonderry. And there were plenty of non-aristocratic figures on the anti-appeasement side. Austen Chamberlain, had he lived, would certainly have opposed Munich. And as for pre-war liberalism, who could have been more tarred with that brush than Churchill himself? The truth is that the difference was one of temperament, outlook, and judgment. It could and did divide families, sever friendships, and break up dinner parties as well as political parties. There was no obvious common bond linking the anti-appeasers. Some were die-hards on India, others were liberals. Some were interventionists in economic affairs, others were for *laissez-faire*. Some were social reformers, others did not care.

There was not much the anti-appeasers could do. The government's policy of drifting under Baldwin and briskly rowing in the wrong direction under Chamberlain was not in the least affected by Churchill's diatribes. It was only the inexorable march of events which obliged Chamberlain to change course, half-heartedly, in March 1939, and to go to war in September. Even then his speech summoning the nation to arms sounded a cracked and wavering note. He seemed more concerned at the collapse of his personal policy and all that he had stood for than at the critical situation of the nation that he led. He was ill-equipped to lead a nation in war, far worse than Asquith. That he should have been forced out at the first major disaster to Allied arms is scarcely surprising.

A political party has two main problems: how to obtain power, and what to do with it once obtained. In the inter-war years the Conservatives solved the first problem more successfully than the second. They won five out of seven general elections and were in office either on their own or as dominant partners in a coalition for eighteen out of twenty-one years. This success, like most political successes, was compounded of good luck, the defects of their opponents, and their own merits. The revival of the party was greatly helped by the First World War whose effects were in almost every respect favourable to the Conservatives and adverse to the Liberals. After the war they were helped by the divisions among their opponents: the severance of the Lib–Lab alliance and the feuds within the Liberal party itself, for the breach between Asquith and Lloyd George was never really repaired. In two of their five electoral victories (1922 and 1924) the Conservatives got in on a split vote. In two more (1918 and 1935) they won less than half the popular vote though it is true to say that in both cases they would have scored a higher total, if they had not concluded with a section of the Liberal party an electoral pact which operated very favourably in the more important matter of winning seats for a coalition. Only in 1931 did the Conservatives actually win more than half the votes cast. The last time they had done so was in 1900.[1]

The phenomenon of a split vote is significant also as a symptom of something else. If the Liberal and Labour parties had regarded Conservative rule as the ultimate in evils, they would have cooperated. The very existence of division on the Left suggests that the Right is regarded as at least tolerable. The truth was that the Conservative party under Baldwin had managed to recover a large area of that middle ground in politics which is the key to electoral success and which they had lost in 1906, after being in possession for nearly twenty years before that. By the mid-1920s they no longer had the harsh appearance that they had displayed in the immediate pre-war years. From 1906 to 1914 they had seemed too often to be the party of rich men reluctant to pay taxes, of Englishmen determined to retain control over the 'Celtic fringe', of Ulstermen ready to rend the fabric of the constitution and subvert the loyalty of the army in order to uphold the Protestant ascendancy. The Conservatives seemed to lack compassion.

Under Baldwin the picture was different. Their social composition did not, it is true, greatly change. The movement of the business men, bankers, industrialists into the party, which had begun well before the turn of the century, continued – a reflection of a general process of absorption and amalgamation which had been affecting the governing class for the last thirty years. The

[1] No party since the Second World War has won over half the popular vote. The Conservatives came nearest to doing so, with 49·7 per cent in 1955.

Conservatives were still the rich man's party. But there was a new
awareness of social problems, a new consciousness of poverty and
unemployment. The party no doubt contained its quota of 'hard
faced business men who looked as if they had done well out of the
war', but it was significant that their leader should have been the
man who coined the phrase. Obliged to choose between a Liberal
party torn by strife, a Labour party incapable of governing, and a
Conservative party which appeared reliable and reasonably
humane, the electorate not surprisingly voted for the latter. Under
Baldwin the Conservatives did not seem to lack compassion.

But what did the party do with the power it secured? In the
inter-war years there were three great problems. These were the
condition of the people, the future of the empire, the rise of
Germany.

On the first the Conservatives failed to deal with unemployment although there *were* alternative policies which might have
solved it or softened it – policies not the monopoly of cranks or
even of voices crying in the wilderness. On the other hand, Neville
Chamberlain by his social reforms, and Baldwin by his genuine
kindliness, generosity and goodwill did something to soften the
stark confrontation of the classes and the masses, something too in
the case of Baldwin (not Chamberlain whom they hated for his
blunt contemptuousness) to bring the Labour party towards
constitutionalism and ease it into the parliamentary system.

On the second problem – the empire – the party's policy
was much more successful. Ireland was a lesson never forgotten.
The Statute of Westminster and the India Act were both in their
contemporary setting notable advances. Baldwin deserves much
of the credit for this, but he could not have done it if the party's
outlook had remained crystallised in the climate of 1914.

On the third problem – resurgent Germany – the Conservative leadership has a record that is hard to defend. It is true that
rearmament went a good deal further from 1935 onwards than has
always been appreciated. It is true that in certain crucial areas –
particularly radar and fighter planes – the country was much better
equipped than Germany; and those are big items on the credit
side of the balance sheet. But, whatever the reason, the Conservative leaders never perceived till too late the nature of the threat

posed by Hitler. If they had, it is hard to imagine that they would not have pursued a more realistic foreign policy. On the most important asset in their normal political armoury, national security, they had failed.

When all is said and done, it is difficult not to feel that Churchill's famous words could be applied in an even wider context to the whole history of the Baldwin–Chamberlain administrations:

They are decided only to be undecided, resolved to be irresolute, adamant for drift, solid for fluidity, all powerful for impotence.

Their successors were to pay a heavy price for these failings a few years later.

CHAPTER VIII

The ascendancy of Churchill
1940–55

I

The fall of Chamberlain in 1940 is the last example of a Prime Minister who had inherited or won an electoral victory being ousted by parliament. He was also ousted by his own party. Indeed the two things go together, for only a party revolt can bring such a consummation. One has to go back to Gladstone in 1886 to find a comparable loss of support on a matter of major importance (neither MacDonald in 1924 nor Rosebery in 1895 is quite parallel: MacDonald's was a minority government depending upon Liberal support; Rosebery's defeat was the result of a snap vote which he could have disregarded or rescinded).

Chamberlain was not, like Gladstone, actually defeated. But a fall in his majority from 200 to 80 was, especially in war time, the equivalent of defeat. Nor had he, like Gladstone, the reserve weapon of dissolution, generally deemed unusable in war. He had no real option but to resign though he tried to avoid it. He also tried to keep out Churchill from the succession. There is no doubt that to the leaders of the Labour and Liberal parties, Attlee and Sinclair, Halifax would have been just as acceptable – strange though this may seem in retrospect – while to most Conservatives he would have been more so. But Halifax knew that he was not the man, just as Derby had known in 1855, and Bonar Law in 1916. In spite of all the barriers the 'will of the people' somehow gets its way in hours of crisis. Churchill was the man the nation wanted even as Lloyd George and Palmerston had been in their day.

Churchill's appointment was far from popular in the Conservative party. The cheers which greeted him when he first entered the House as Prime Minister came from the Liberal and Labour benches. The Conservatives reserved theirs for Chamberlain who, significantly, retained the leadership of the party. It was like Asquith and Lloyd George after 1916, though with this difference: Chamberlain agreed to serve under his successor; Asquith did not. If Chamberlain had lived, the situation could have been a delicate one. But he fell ill and resigned in October, dying a few weeks later. There was no lack of high minded persons to advise Churchill that he would be better placed to unify the nation if he was not tied to the leadership of a party. Churchill had more sense. He had seen the fate of Lloyd George. To the end of his political career he regarded the Conservative party machine and many of the party faithful with suspicion and dislike. For that very reason he was determined to be on top of it and them. He at once indicated that he would accept the leadership, and by now his prestige made his unanimous election a certainty.

Churchill was markedly unvindictive towards the appeasers. It was partly his natural generosity, partly too perhaps a gesture of prudence in view of his chilly reception from the party when he first became Prime Minister. He would even have made Chamberlain leader of the House, if Attlee had not objected. But Mr A. J. P. Taylor goes too far when he claims that Sir Samuel Hoare was the only 'man of Munich' to be removed.[1] Of the Chamberlain Cabinet as it was in October 1938 fourteen men of Munich were still serving in May 1940; seven of them were removed, and seven of them were retained by Churchill in offices of Cabinet rank. Mr Taylor is right, however, when he says that the Conservative anti-appeasers received few rewards, though one can add to his solitary example of Duff Cooper given the Ministry of Information, those of Lord Lloyd (Colonies), L. S. Amery (India), and Lord Cranborne (Paymaster-General).

The government was a coalition of men of all parties (bar the Communists) and of no party. Churchill was careful to blend the various colours in the House of Commons in the best way to minimise offence. But he had no hesitation in bringing in purely

[1] *English history 1914-45*, 478.

personal appointees devoid of any party backing – and highly unpopular – such as Lord Beaverbrook and Lord Cherwell. Britain was governed as much by an elected monarch and his court as by a traditional Prime Minister and his Cabinet. Yet Churchill despite his eccentricity, his midnight conclaves, his tyranny and bluster, paid the most careful attention to the correct procedure of the constitution, the sovereignty of parliament, the authority of the Cabinet, the powers of the Crown. He was not a classless iconoclast like Lloyd George. He was as cautious as Augustus in preserving the traditional outward forms. No doubt he was perfectly sincere in doing so. The fact remains that behind this façade he ruled England for five years with a degree of authority such as no Prime Minister has ever possessed before or since.

Of Churchill it could be said that the circumstances of war made assets not only of his virtues but of all those defects which had hitherto impeded his political career. His old fashioned *simpliste* views on India, the empire, and Britain's role in the world had been liabilities in the 1930s. So too had been his obvious fascination by war and the problems of war. Now in a desperate struggle for national survival they became positive virtues, along with his courage, tenacity, and a command over language unsurpassed by any previous Prime Minister, equalled by very few. Moreover, he was temperamentally designed to be a far better chief than colleague. The single-mindedness verging on fanaticism with which he had supported the interests of whatever department – Board of Trade, Admiralty, Treasury – he happened to head was a defect in a departmental minister, the more irritating because it was not accompanied by any corresponding inclination to leave other departments alone. On the contrary he had bombarded successive Prime Ministers with his opinions on the widest range of topics. But now that he was Prime Minister himself this immense energy and unity of purpose were real advantages in the object to which he and the whole nation devoted themselves – the winning of the war.

But were they correspondingly advantageous in the subsidiary object of winning the next general election for the Conservative party? It would be an over-simplification to say no, just because in fact the election was lost. Everything depends on the assessment of why it was lost. Was it a landslide resulting from long and slow subterranean subsidences – like the 1966 tragedy of Aberfan? Or was it an avalanche set off by the sudden report of a gun, as can sometimes happen in the snow-laden slopes of the Alps?

2

The Conservatives did not neglect the problems of the peace. Various committees investigated them and their reports were to form the basis of an election programme in 1945, in many ways as forward-looking as that of Labour. Nor is there any truth that the leadership encouraged local constituency organisations to shut up shop for the duration of the war. Nevertheless, by 1945 the Conservative machine was in general more rusty than that of Labour, and, however 'progressive' their programme, what most candidates really relied on was the name of Churchill, basing themselves on a false analogy with Lloyd George in 1918.

Churchill wished to keep the coalition in being till the end of the war with Japan, expected in May 1945 to be anything up to eighteen months ahead. He proposed to solve the problem of his pledge that an immediate general election should be held after the defeat of Germany by submitting a proposal for delay to a national referendum. Attlee and the Labour members of the Cabinet were against postponement till Japan had been defeated but preferred to hold an election on party lines in the autumn rather than at once. Churchill rightly considered that the coalition would never work properly with a partisan election at a known date hanging over it. He insisted that if there was to be an election it should be held as soon as possible. Accordingly he formally resigned on behalf of the coalition. The king at once reappointed him. He formed a 'caretaker' Conservative government and recommended a prompt dissolution of parliament.

There is a general agreement that the Conservative election campaign in 1945 struck the wrong note from the start, and for this Churchill must bear the blame. Even if the trouble was that he leaned too much on Lord Beaverbrook's advice – a charge which has been denied – the fact remains that Churchill's was the ultimate responsibility. He certainly started in a tone of extreme aggressiveness with his first broadcast. A touch of Eatanswill had rarely been wholly absent from his electioneering style.

There can be no doubt that Socialism is inseparably inter-woven with totalitarianism and the abject worship of the State. . . . Socialism is in its essence an attack not only on British enterprise, but upon the right of an ordinary man or woman to breathe freely without having a harsh clumsy tyrannical hand clapped across their mouth and nostrils. A free Parliament – look at that – a free Parliament is odious to the Socialist doctrinaire.

There followed his notorious warning that a socialist system could only be established with the aid of a political police or 'Gestapo'. To most people these threats and this language about people who till a few weeks ago had been his Cabinet colleagues seemed ludicrous. Attlee effectively caught the serious reflective mood of the nation in his reply. He ironically thanked Churchill for want-ing

the electors to understand how great was the difference between Winston Churchill the great leader in war of a united nation and Mr Churchill the party leader of the Conservatives. . . . I thank him for having disillusioned them so thoroughly. The voice we heard last night was that of Mr Churchill, but the mind was that of Lord Beaverbrook.

The exchanges between the rival leaders continued in this idiom. They were later largely concerned with an interminable dispute about the role of Professor Harold Laski who – unluckily for Labour – happened to be chairman of the National Executive that year and made a pronouncement on Attlee's decision to accept Churchill's invitation to go to Potsdam with him. Attlee, he said, would be only an observer; there was no necessity for continuity in foreign policy; Labour's attitude could only be settled by debate 'either in the Party Executive or at meetings of the Parlia-mentary Labour Party'. This did raise a genuine constitutional issue and the Conservatives could legitimately ask questions about the possible dictatorship of the party Caucus – a criticism of

TWO CHURCHILLS

July 31, 1945. Cartoon by David Low reproduced by arrangement with the trustees and the Evening Standard

Labour dating back to the days of the Campbell case and the Russian Treaty in 1924, and only finally killed by Attlee's own conduct of affairs after he won the election.

Attlee was too good a tactician to accept this criticism during the election campaign or to reprove Laski in any way then. He reserved that till after he had won, ending a letter to Laski with one of his most famous laconic observations: 'a period of silence from you would be welcome'. The Conservatives, in spite of having a real point, incurred the charge of 'stunting' when they used such expressions as 'Gauleiter Laski'.

But, however inept the Tory campaign, it is unlikely to have accounted for their defeat. The wartime by-elections showed a strong trend towards radical candidates fighting official Conservatives, even though Labour obedient to the party truce gave them no sort of official countenance. By-elections can be misleading but the trend from 1942 right up to April 1945 is too consistent to be ignored. Moreover, the Gallup Poll from 1943 onwards showed a big Labour lead. This suggests a deeper dissatisfaction with Conservatism than could be explained by the most incompetent electioneering. Moreover, great turnovers like that of 1945 do not occur for trivial or personal causes.

Attlee has been well compared with a sound batsman keeping up his wicket against a demon bowler rapidly losing pace and length. But it is clear that the demon bowler was still a highly popular figure. If the British premiership had been an elective office like the American presidency and the voter could have split his ticket, Churchill, like Eisenhower in 1956, might have been elected, but he would have faced a legislature dominated by the other party. The Conservatives fared badly in 1945 but who can say how much worse they might have done without Churchill? In 1945 they won 213 seats. In 1906 with no such asset as a national hero at their head they won 56 fewer.

On the face of things Churchill's defeat contrasts strangely with the triumph of Lloyd George in 1918. Yet there may be more similarity than difference. It is arguable that every war of any importance has resulted in disaster at the next election after its end for the party in power when it began. The Crimean War was started under a Peelite–Whig coalition with a Peelite Prime

Minister. The Peelites were virtually extinguished in the election of 1857. The South African War was followed by the greatest Conservative disaster of all time. The First World War did, it is true, begin with the Liberal party in power, and the 1918 election gave a gigantic majority to a nominally Liberal Prime Minister. But Lloyd George was in effect the non-party head of a coalition overwhelmingly dominated by the Conservatives – the party of opposition in 1914. The Coupon election killed the Asquithian Liberal party – that is to say it killed the real Liberal party. The 1945 election did not kill the Conservatives but it gave them a very heavy blow. Churchill, by an ironical turn of events, was tied to a party which, rightly or wrongly, was by 1945 discredited – and discredited partly because of the retrospective cogency of his own brilliant pre-war onslaughts upon its official leadership. How, one wonders, would Lloyd George have fared in 1918, for all his great record as a war leader, if he had sought to reunite the Liberals in a straight fight against the Conservatives? The question needs only to asked in order to be answered. He would almost certainly have lost.

Every war into which Britain has entered during the last century and a half has found her disorganised, unprepared and surprised. It is in no way odd that the electorate should subsequently have wreaked their vengeance on the party in power when war broke out. Nor is this a cynical reflection upon the electorates which at the time supported those parties. It is the business of people in power to give a lead and get their answers right. If they fail, they have no cause for complaint at subsequent defeat. True, it is sometimes bad luck on the individuals who have come to personify a party which had been represented by quite different figures a few years earlier. But, after all, this is what party politics is about.

Churchill lost because his party was discredited, not because he listened too much – if indeed he did at all – to Lord Beaverbrook's advice on electioneering. And his party was not discredited because its programme was reactionary, or even static, for it was neither. It did not lack content, but it lacked credibility. The trouble was that people did not believe that the Conservatives meant what they said, whereas they thought on the whole that Labour did. Nor did Churchill lose simply because the party machine was rusty. No doubt it was rusty. No doubt the sort of people who constituted the local organisations of the party – agents, workers, etc. – were more likely to be away from home than the trade unionists who played the same key part in the Labour party's constituency organisations. But it would be absurd to suppose that these deficiencies could account for such a huge swing in votes.

Churchill lost because the Conservatives were associated with most of the ills of the inter-war years: unemployment, depression, failure to prevent war, unreadiness for it when it came. It is not relevant to these criticisms that they may have been ill-founded and that no plausible alternative policy was ever put forward by anyone who had a chance of forming an alternative government. It was the Conservatives who were in, and they were bound to take the rap for what went wrong.

That mysterious, indefinable, but nevertheless real element in political change – 'the climate of opinion' – was against them too. Just as the Utilitarians prepared the way for the long Liberal ascendancy after 1832, just as intellectual imperialists like Seeley were precursors of the Conservative break-through under Lord Salisbury, so too did Professors Laski and Cole aided by Victor Gollancz and the Left Book Club in the 1930s open the first breaches in the dyke through which Labour was to pour ten years later. In the 1930s it was intellectually disreputable to be a Tory – anyway if you were a young man. One should not exaggerate the political significance of the intellectuals, but, when they incline with near unanimity in a particular party direction, that party is likely, if after a time lag, to find itself politically as well as intellectually in the ascendant. This was what was happening to Labour from the 1930s onwards.

There was too another change in the climate not so much of opinion as of sentiment – a reaction against heroism, grandeur, and effort. For five years Britain had been mobilised for war more fully than any country in the world except perhaps Russia – certainly far more than Germany or America. And the moment had come when the nation was beginning to feel that it had had enough. True, the war with Japan was not yet over. It is a very moot point how far the nation's morale would have held up if the struggle had been at all prolonged. But even already the great Churchillian language of 1940 and 1941 was beginning to sound slightly hollow. Attlee might be a humdrum figure, but he accorded more with the spirit of the hour than his mighty predecessor. Nothing better symbolises the contrast between their styles and between the moods to which their styles appealed than the account which some years later each of them has left of his reaction on becoming Prime Minister.

Here is Churchill on his summons to the highest office in 1940:

> I cannot conceal from the reader of this truthful account that as I went to bed at about 3 a.m. I was conscious of a profound sense of relief. At last I had authority to give directions over the whole scene. I felt as if I were walking with destiny and that all my past life had been but a preparation for this hour and for this trial. . . .[1]

And here is Attlee on his rise to the top in 1945:

> . . . by the middle of the afternoon it was clear that we had won a great victory.
>
> Lord Portal who was Chairman of the Great Western Railway gave the family tea at Paddington, and presently I was told by the Prime Minister that he was resigning. A summons to the Palace followed. My wife drove me there and waited outside for me. The King gave me his commission to form a Government. He always used to say that I looked very surprised as indeed I was at the extent of our success. We went to a Victory Rally at Westminster Hall where I announced that I had been charged with the task of forming a Government, looked in at a Fabian Society gathering and then returned to Stanmore after an exciting day.[2]

3

The Conservatives now faced a period of opposition comparable only with the years after 1906. But they behaved much more

---

[1] W. S. Churchill, *The gathering storm* (1948), 526-7.
[2] C. R. Attlee, *As it happened* (1954), 148.

sensibly. It is often said that history teaches no lessons or else the wrong ones. Yet it is not always the case, and after 1945 the party leaders did manage to avoid the major errors of Balfour and his shadow Cabinet. They were helped by two great contrasts between the situation then and that of forty years earlier. They were not divided on a major issue of policy like tariffs, and they had in Churchill a leader who was a figure of world fame and prestige. Balfour was in a very different position. His authority had been tottering for two years before his defeat, and he had the greatest difficulty in reasserting it in opposition.

Yet, in spite of their more favourable position after 1945, it took two elections to bring the Conservatives back to power – and even so they won by the narrowest of margins and on a minority of the popular vote. Most of the ground was regained at the first election – held in February 1950. The Conservatives rose from 213 in 1945 to 298, and Labour fell from 393 to 315. Labour's bacon was saved by the Celtic fringe. In England the Conservatives had a majority of one. The psephologists have calculated that the total result reflects a 3·3 per cent swing to the Conservatives since 1945. The turnout of 84 per cent was the highest since the first election of 1910.

What were the reasons for the Conservative gains? One must as so often in this survey look both at what people were voting for and what they were voting against. The Conservative party undoubtedly made a major effort to re-think its political programme, reorganise its internal constitution, and recover its parliamentary morale. It was over thirty years since the party had had occasion to give any prolonged thought to its role in opposition. From 1915 to 1945, the Conservatives whether on their own or as partner of a coalition – usually the dominant partner – had been in office nearly all the while. Two brief intervals – ten months in 1924 and twenty-six months in 1929–31 – were not enough to alter the fact that the party had been essentially the party of government for longer than almost any of its members could recall. In the art of conducting His Majesty's opposition the Conservative front bench was either wholly out of practice or wholly inexperienced.

A party in office inevitably gives little thought to ideology or principles. Indeed, why should it as long as things are going well?

Problems come up one after another and are solved – or not solved – by empirical criteria. Advice from Whitehall, reports of royal commissions, external pressures, the trade cycle, the need to meet sudden crises blowing up from nowhere, or to placate a public uproar – these are what actuate governments. No doubt their reactions are influenced by some sort of vague ideological colours, but the need to make those colours into a coherent pattern does not arise. Anyway it is often impossible, given the contradictions, reversals and inconsistencies which events may force upon even the most honourable and efficient of ministries.

But in opposition the situation is quite different. A party has to avoid on the one hand the charge of peevish factiousness and on the other that of pallid imitation of the government. It is necessary to steer a tricky line between policy statements so clear that they give hostages to fortune or so vague that they offer no alternative at all. Churchill at first was strongly against giving hostages to fortune. At Edinburgh in 1946 despite much pressure for a 'programme' he defined the Conservative policy as 'Liberty with security; stability combined with progress; the maintenance of religion, the Crown, and Parliamentary Government'[1] – points from which scarcely anyone in any party would have dissented. Nor was he much more specific when Eden and Oliver Stanley later that year pressed him to give a clearer lead at the Blackpool conference. His 'eight points', observed the *Scotsman*, 'would describe Conservative economic policy at any time in the past 30 or 40 years, if not further back than that.'[2]

Churchill was more interested in the world scene. His experience as Chancellor of the Exchequer in Baldwin's second government had not been happy. He had never been very good on 'bread and butter politics'. Economic affairs engaged his interest only sporadically, though if he was interested he could act decisively – witness the veto that, on Lord Cherwell's advice, he imposed in 1952 on the proposal of the Treasury to establish a floating pound. He seems to have taken a good deal of persuasion to give his *imprimatur* to the most important policy document issued by the party in these years – R. A. Butler's Industrial Charter.

[1] Quoted, J. D. Hoffman, *The Conservative party in opposition 1945–51* (1964), 140.
[2] ibid., 143.

The significance of this document is not that the Conservatives acted on it at all obviously when they got back into power, for in fact it was largely concerned with problems that were to be irrelevant in the 1950s such as unemployment, deflation, etc; resembling in this respect of course the preponderance of Labour thought at the time. Still less was it important because it converted the ordinary voter. Its effect was essentially on the opinion-forming classes. It was a successful attempt to counter the Labour argument that the Conservatives were the party of industrial *laissez-faire* and 'devil take the hindmost'. It did indeed emphasise the importance of removing 'unnecessary' controls, and it was this part of it on which the Conservatives may claim to have acted when they got back – although a host of other reasons would have made any government inclined by then to cut away the under-growth of restrictions surviving from the war, and any opposition inclined to press more keenly than any government for such a popu-lar move. But its importance at the time of issue was comparable politically to the Crystal Palace and Manchester speeches of Disraeli in 1872. Given the modern world of collective committee work, it naturally lacked the rhetoric and colour of Disraeli. Yet in its cool, humdrum and slightly flat language it did present a recognisable alternative to the reigning orthodoxy.

The reorganisation of the party was probably no less important than re-thinking of policy. As after every defeat – 1868, 1880, 1906, 1910 – there was a constitutional reshuffle, change of committee nomenclatures and relationships, and a general move for better representation of party sentiment. If one asks why this always happens, the answer is that defeat gives a lot of people much annoyance and much time on their hands. No party in power bothers very much about this sort of thing.[1] Yet we should not dismiss it as merely a matter of mutual recrimination and pro-spective window-dressing. Every now and then the moment of defeat does produce a real change.

The post-war reforms which took place in the party organisa-tion are usually attributed to that greatest of all Conservative party managers, Lord Woolton. The magnitude of his achieve-

[1] J. C. C. Davidson's efforts from 1926 to 1930 are perhaps an exception, but much of what he did took place after the defeat of summer 1929.

ment is beyond dispute, but it is fair to say that some significant developments took place under his predecessor, Ralph Assheton (Lord Clitheroe) who was chairman at the time of the election and remained in office for another year till July 1946. These included the revival of the Research Department, founded by Davidson in 1929, the formation of the Conservative Political Centre, the growth of the Young Conservative organisation, and a major expansion of the work of the Advisory Committee on Local Government.

Lord Woolton was a late convert to Conservatism. Although a member of Churchill's Cabinet he remained independent, and only joined the Conservatives on the morrow of their crushing defeat – a gesture which greatly touched Churchill. He had begun life as a Fabian and a social reformer. He subsequently went into the retail business and became chairman of Lewis's stores. In the war, thanks to his administrative genius and talent for public relations, he was appointed Minister of Food. He had a soothing if somewhat plummy mode of speech which inspired confidence. Housewives munching a dreadful wartime comestible named after him as 'Woolton pie' came to regard him with certain wry affection. Long before the end of the war he was a national figure; the first chairman of the party, apart from Neville Chamberlain, who could be thus described.

When he first took over he was horrified at the apparent lack of system that prevailed, but he quickly realised that the organisation of a party is not the same as that of a business. Excessive streamlining by causing offence to a multitude of faithful workers might defeat its own purpose. He decided instead to concentrate on membership, money and propaganda. He was determined to make the party spend and not hoard. He adopted a seemingly paradoxical technique. He deliberately resolved to over-spend on publicity, propaganda, etc., and thus force the local party organisations to raise the necessary funds. At the same time he decided to cut off one of their traditional sources, the heavy personal subscriptions through which in some safe constituencies the member virtually bought his seat.

The latter step was formally recommended in 1948 by a committee under Sir David Maxwell Fyfe and was adopted at the party conference. It had a double purpose: first, to demo-cratise the selection process, in order that no financial barrier need inhibit the choice of candidates who were now forbidden to subscribe more than £25 p.a. to the local fund (or £50 if already a member); secondly, to force constituency parties to collect money from local supporters and thus in that very process to secure wider contacts which would be the basis for a far more efficient electoral organisation. Of these two purposes the second proved much more important. The type of candidate could not greatly change in the immediate future, for most of them had already been adopted under the old rules, and so the personnel involved in the elections of 1950 and 1951 was scarcely affected by the Maxwell Fyfe recommendations. Nor in fact has there been any great change in the type of person seeking Conservative nomination since then, still less in the type actually nominated. The most that can be said is that one cause of egalitarian criticism has been cut out, and the party's 'image' to that degree improved.

The effect on the local parties themselves, however, was much more important. There can be no doubt that the need to collect a very large number of very small subscriptions, instead of relying on a very small number of very large subscriptions – perhaps only one – gave the constituency organisations a notable impetus to-wards recruitment of members. Lord Woolton's appeal for central funds – an extra £1 million – was a great success and his appeal for an extra million members equally satisfactory. The figures went up from 1,200,000 in 1947 (itself an increase of 226,000 on the previous year) to 2,250,000 by the end of June 1948. Thus, by gross over-expenditure and cutting off a major source of income, Lord Woolton had achieved a great step towards the restoration of the party's prosperity. No doubt there is a moral to be drawn from this, but not, alas, one that applies to private life.

Lord Woolton faced the problem too of the party's name. As had occurred already after defeat, there was an agitation in some quarters to change it. There has always been a section of the party which regards the title 'Conservative' as a vote-loser. Lord Woolton favoured 'the Union Party' as a substitute – not a very inspired idea, in view of its similarity to the old but now irrelevant name of 'Unionist'. Luckily he decided that he could only lead this particular card from strength, not from weakness after defeat. However, the next best thing to changing the name of one's own party favourably is to change that of one's opponents unfavourably. He declared that henceforth in speech and writing Conservatives should never use the word 'Labour' with its suggestions of honest British toil, but always substitute 'Socialist' with its alien, doctrinaire, continental overtones. This practice was dropped in 1959 when some voters were found who believed 'Labour' and 'Socialist' to be different parties.

The Conservative revival was helped by an intellectual movement in their favour. *Etatisme* which had been all the rage in the 1930s lost its charm in the highly regimented England of the war and post-war years. A very influential book at this time was Professor F. A. Hayek's *Road to serfdom*, published in 1944. It was essentially anti-socialist in its implications. The universities saw a notable revival of Conservative sympathies among the undergraduates and to some extent among the dons too. The Conservative Research Department headed by R. A. Butler contained as members at times during the period Iain Macleod, Reginald Maudling, and Enoch Powell – people of whom many things have been said, but not that they are or were stupid. The Labour party had lost its near monopoly of intellect and ideas.

The least easy aspect of the Tory revival to assess is the effectiveness of the parliamentarians. This is because of the general difficulty of deciding just what a parliamentary opposition can be expected to achieve in modern conditions. It certainly cannot block legislation. The Conservatives probably extracted the maximum concession that could be squeezed out of Labour by a judicious use of the Parliament Act to postpone the vesting date for steel nationalisation till after the next election. Otherwise the most that an opposition can do is to present itself as a plausible alternative, trip up the government whenever it safely can without incurring the charge of factiousness, and build up as odious a picture as possible of the majority party against the day of the next election.

On the whole the Conservatives managed all these tasks quite well. If Churchill was often absent, and did not always fire at the right target, he was invariably 'news' whatever he said or did –

and he possessed a devastating turn of phrase. Anthony Eden was sweetly reasonable. Harold Macmillan, Oliver Stanley and Oliver Lyttelton were acidly unreasonable, and did much to create a popular image of Labour ministers as either sour, puritanical, doctrinaire pedagogues or else as frenzied rabble rousers actuated by malice and class hatred. Sir Stafford Cripps, who was not only a vegetarian and a teetotaler but looked like it too, seemed to epitomise the first category, and Aneurin Bevan the second.

And this brings us to what is surely a much more important factor in the electoral change than any positive action by the Conservatives. The elections of 1950 and 1951 were as much votes of no confidence or lack of confidence in Labour as of confidence in the Conservatives.

Labour had won in 1945 because it had appeared as something more than a working class party. It had carried a substantial section of the middle class, and this was a major element in its victory. But a great deal happened during the next five years to alienate that section of the community. Emmanuel Shinwell[1] and Aneurin Bevan did their bit. The working class was all that mattered, said Shinwell in a public speech; for the rest he did not care 'two hoots or a Tinker's cuss'. Bevan, in an even more famous speech emphasised the theme of two nations. He declared his hatred of the Tories. 'So far as I am concerned,' he said, 'they are lower than vermin.' He got the maximum of publicity. As he had recently described the British press as 'the most prostituted in the world', it was not surprising. The Conservatives evinced great fury. Elderly colonels in Midland spas and south coast watering places formed 'vermin clubs'. When Attlee addressed an eve of poll meeting at Leicester in 1950 he was greeted to his surprise with cries in upper class accents of, 'What about the vermin!'

Professor Laski, himself an expert if ever there was one in the art of dropping electoral bricks, maintained that the 'vermin' speech cost two million votes at the next election. This seems unlikely, but the episode certainly did Labour no good. What is more it was symbolic of a real change of allegiance. If there is one conclusion that does emerge from the electoral statistics of 1950 it is the markedly bigger pro-Tory swing in the suburban areas

[1] Raised to a life baron in the 1970 dissolution honours list.

of the large towns, especially London, compared with the rest of the country. It is clear that long before 1950 there had grown up in that class a real detestation of the Labour government. One must remember that the middle and upper classes, the professional men, lawyers, civil servants, doctors, were going through a particularly thin time just then. They were very heavily taxed. Their incomes did not rise with the cost of living to anything like the degree that wages did. Later this lag was made up but not in the 1940s.

Moreover, these years can be seen in retrospect as a sort of twilight period between the era of cheap servants and the era of cheap washing machines. The effect of the disappearance of servants constituted a revolution in the middle class way of life far more drastic than anything that followed the First World War; and the effects were more acutely felt at this time than later when prosperity returned, labour-saving devices became the norm and people had recognised the need to adjust themselves to a change which, they now saw, would never be reversed. However illogically, this state of affairs greatly conduced to middle class disenchantment with Labour.

If one wishes to catch the flavour of that aspect of opinion one cannot do better than glance at some of the novels of Angela Thirkell. It is true that they deal with the country rather than the town, and with a class that could not be described as disenchanted with Labour for it had never been enchanted. Rather it was a disenchantment with post-war England as symbolised by controls, petty bureaucracy, red tape, racketeers, government extravagance, politicians' complacency – 'the Gentleman in Whitehall really does know best'. Her novels such as *Peace breaks out* (1946), in itself a significant title, *Private enterprise* (1946), *Love among the ruins* (1948), are in some ways excruciating and they set one's teeth on edge for many reasons, but they were best sellers in their day, and they have their value as social documents reflecting something – though no doubt in extreme form – of the sour bitterness with which the Labour government was regarded by an influential section of the community.

It was a black period as all who have lived through it can attest. Restrictions were more severe than in the worst days of the war.

The contrast with the seemingly rapid return – anyway from the tourist's point of view – to 'normalcy' in France and Italy was startling. The Ministry of Food encouraged the consumption of whale steaks, or as an alternative a disagreeable form of tinned fish from South Africa known as 'snoek'. There were shortages naturally of almost everything that could even remotely be described as a luxury. The *Daily Mirror* tried to cheer up its readers with a headline, 'Wine from weeds'.

The government, obsessed with the dollar gap and a determination, ultimately unsuccessful, to preserve the value of the pound, seemed at times oblivious of the fact that the consumer is also the voter. Probably the worst mistake in this field was to underestimate the immense post-war demand for new houses. The priority given to construction of factories was understandable but electorally unwise. Moreover the housing shortage hit Labour's natural supporters in the working class with particular severity. The Conservatives were quick to see this, and made it a major issue in the election of 1951.

The election of 1950 took place in February. It was a disappointment to all three parties. Labour received a palpable rebuff. Its majority in 1945 over the Conservatives had been 166, over all parties combined 136. In 1950 these figures were respectively 17 and 6. The government could carry on, but only just; it was a depressing prospect. Although the Conservatives had staged a good recovery and palpably given the lie to those who said in the aftermath of 1945 that the party was extinct, they were disappointed that the neck and neck finish had not gone in their favour. The saddest, however, were the Liberals. Fielding no less than 475 candidates – a triumph of hope over experience if ever there was one – and shunning any sort of local agreement with the Conservatives they won only 9 seats and 9·1 per cent of the poll. No less than 319 of their candidates forfeited their deposits.

The election was fought almost exclusively on domestic issues. Foreign defence and imperial affairs played little part. Even Conservatives had to concede that Labour was 'sound' over the cold war and the atom bomb. The real opposition to Ernest Bevin came from the Labour left. As for the empire, Indian independence together with that of Ceylon and Burma were *faits accomplis*, recognised as irreversible. The emergence of Israel, though highly controversial, cut across party lines. The main problems of the Middle East and Africa lay in the future.

In his book, *The general election of 1880*, Mr Trevor Lloyd, disclaiming originality, advances the theory that elections are usually conducted on two levels. The bulk of the electorate is cautious, uninterested, slow to move. It tends to vote defensively and in support of its material standards and its economic interests – or what it deems those to be. But the party enthusiasts, the minority who are prepared to work in order to get out the vote, to knock on doors, put election addresses in envelopes, and attend to the postal vote require something more – an ideal to admire or an ideology to hate. They can be stirred by non-material considerations at home and by questions of policy abroad which have little direct effect on the prosperity of the ordinary voter. The great turnovers of seats occur when at both these levels one party has the advantage over the other.

This does not purport to be an exhaustive theory of elections, but it does contribute something. In 1880 the Liberals gained from 'hard times' – the economic depression – and also from the moral enthusiasm inspired by Midlothian. In 1906 they gained from the fear of higher prices and the anxieties of the trade unionists, reinforced by the enthusiasm of party workers enraged by the Education Act of 1902 and scandalised by 'Chinese slavery'. In 1931 it was the Conservatives who had on their side the defensive sentiment aroused by the Labour Cabinet's 'running away' from the crisis and breaking up in disorder.

If we apply these criteria to the post-Second World War elections we can see why Labour won in 1945. The mass of the electorate was voting in defence of full employment and against a reversion to the economic depression of the 1930s. To this sentiment was added the impetus of socialist utopianism inspired by the anti-capitalist writings of a whole intellectual generation. On neither level could the Conservatives bring anything like such strength to bear. In 1950 the defensive argument was still a very strong Labour asset. Indeed full employment was one of the party's main themes, and by far the smallest pro-Conservative swing occurred in the areas of high pre-war unemployment. But even on the defensive level the advantage did not lie wholly with Labour. Cripps's devaluation of the pound in 1949 operated in the opposite sense for obvious reasons. And on the positive level, that of party enthusiasm, the Conservatives undoubtedly had the edge over Labour. The various conflicting forces virtually cancelled each other out in 1950.

Twenty months later with a swing of 1 per cent the Conservatives just managed to get in with a majority of 17 over all other parties but a minority of the total poll. No one can say why. Perhaps the fears of unemployment had become that much less. Perhaps the increased emphasis on Tory freedom, after another year and a half of restriction, made just the difference. 'Set the people free' was an effective slogan. Combined with the *Industrial Charter* it gave the Conservatives a distinctive colour that was neither reactionary on the one hand nor a smudged copy of Labour's on the other. True, Labour had itself by now gone in for 'a bonfire of controls'. But it is seldom a good sign when a government starts adopting opposition policies, e.g. the abrupt conversion of the Conservatives in 1963-4 to planning and 'modernisation'.

Another factor may have been the 'patriotic card' which Churchill played for all it was worth. Herbert Morrison, Bevin's successor at the Foreign Office, seemed less robust. There was trouble over the Sudan and he incurred much criticism. Then came the blow to British prestige when Dr Mossadegh, a fanatical Iranian nationalist who had temporarily ousted the Shah, took over the Anglo-Iranian Oil Company and seized its great refinery at Abadan. Morrison was criticised by nearly all Tories as feeble. The Korean War landed the Labour government with even greater trouble. A large increase in defence expenditure appeared necessary. The Conservatives did not criticise this, although when they entered office they greatly reduced it because of the practicalities involved. Aneurin Bevan, their *bête noire*, had spotted this difficulty, and when Hugh Gaitskell, the Chancellor of the Exchequer, insisted upon charges in the health service to compensate for the rise in the cost of defence Bevan, along with Harold Wilson, resigned from the Cabinet. Churchill inveighed against what he called three great disasters – 'Sud*a*n, Abad*a*n, Bev*a*n!' The *Daily Mirror* countered with an attack on Churchill as a war monger using the famous slogan, 'Whose finger on the trigger?' The ensuing libel action was settled out of court in Churchill's favour several weeks after the election. The Korean War had other consequences: a rise in commodity prices, a worsening of the terms of trade and a renewed crisis in the balance of payments.

A major issue in the election was the shortage of houses. Labour had underestimated the demand for accommodation, and there were many other important calls on the construction industry. The Conservatives were nearer to the public sentiment in this respect, just as they were thirty years later over the sale of council houses to sitting tenants. At the Party Conference in October 1950, a Conservative MP, Harmar Nichols (later Lord Harmar-Nichols), demanded from the floor a pledge in the next manifesto to build 300,000 houses a year. It was carried overwhelmingly. Such a motion does not bind the leadership, but Churchill, with one or two reservations – he had in mind the potential cost of the Korean War – decided to accept it. The pledge was an asset in the election a year later.

Probably the most important element of all in the result was something for which the Conservatives could take no direct credit. The number of Liberal candidates fell from 475 in 1950 to 109 in 1951. It has been reckoned that, in the absence of a candidate of their own, Liberals divided at that time in the proportion of three to two in favour of the Conservatives.[1] The latter were no doubt lucky that so few Liberal candidates came forward. On the other hand they could take some satisfaction that their policies were marginally more attractive to the middle ground than those of Labour. Together with a few people who moved over from Labour to Conservative, these ex-Liberals, in David Butler's words, 'were enough to change the Government and sway the course of history'.

The election of 1951 was followed by thirteen years of Conservative government. Few people would have expected such a span. Fewer still, even if they had, would have predicted the crises and vicissitudes which successive Conservative administrations had to survive in order to achieve it. Churchill's Cabinet laid the foundation stone of this success. The electoral promises made

[1] See D. E. Butler, *The British general election of* 1951 (1952), 270-2.

in 1951 were largely fulfilled. A government possessing even a small majority has the initiative, and initiative can be the key to survival – compare Harold Wilson in 1964 and again ten years later in 1974. Labour barely won but in each case retained office after a second election for over five years. In 1951 the Conservatives were given the opportunity to show that they were not only the party of freedom and free enterprise but that these virtues could be combined with full employment, rising prosperity and the preservation of the welfare state. It was scepticism about their ability to do this which probably accounted more than anything else for their defeat in 1950 and the narrowness of their win in 1951. It was a scepticism which could only be dissolved by victory. We are back with the old problem: a party cannot convince those who doubt its capacity to govern, except by governing; but how is it ever to govern unless it has already convinced the doubters?

There was a further point for the pessimists who had studied history. No government in the twentieth century had ever increased its majority at the next election. Seventeen left very little leeway. The answer is not to take historical precedents too seriously. They are always being broken by something or other. Harold Macmillan wrote in his diary:

> The truth is that the Socialists have fought the election (very astutely) not on Socialism but on fear. Fear of unemployment; fear of reduced wages; fear of reduced social benefits; fear of war. These four fears have been brilliantly, if unscrupulously, exploited. If, before the next election, none of these fears has proved reasonable, we may be able to force the Opposition to fight on Socialism. Then we can win.[1]

Although Churchill was nearly seventy-seven and past his peak, there was no question of anyone else being Prime Minister; but there was a general belief that he could not, and would not, stay for long. He had proved his ability to win and to avenge the defeat of 1945. Meanwhile Eden, the heir apparent, was inevitably given the Foreign Office. The two most significant appointments, neither of them at all inevitable, were Butler to the Exchequer and Macmillan to Housing. Foreign policy has seldom mattered much

[1] Harold Macmillan, *Tides of fortune* (1969), 361.

in terms of votes. Taxation and accommodation were much more important. Butler was not the obvious appointment. Many people 'tipped' Oliver Lyttleton (later Lord Chandos), an aristocratic industrialist of much ability. But he had entered the House relatively late in life, and lacked experience of its incalculable vagaries, its strange taboos and its mysterious usages. The government faced a major economic crisis. Unpalatable measures would be necessary. The handling of the House would be difficult. Butler was a master of the art. Lyttleton was not. Churchill put him into the less contentious Colonial Office.

Butler was a highly successful Chancellor. He had to take drastic initial steps – a cut of imports by £600 million and a rise in bank rate from 2 to 4 per cent. This was a notable attack on one of Labour's sacred cows, cheap money. Confidence in sterling was restored. Thereafter he was much helped by a favourable change in the terms of trade, thanks to the end of the Korean War, which resulted in a fall in commodity prices and Britain's import bill. The period of Churchill's premiership was the first since the war in which there was not a biennial balance of payments crisis. Whatever long-term opportunities were missed in terms of restructuring British industry or taking the lead in Europe – and these are imponderable speculations – the Tory freedom on which the party had campaigned appeared to work. Restrictions were relaxed, rationing eliminated, living standards rose, taxes fell, employment remained as full as ever and the welfare state was not dismantled. Moreover, despite all the difficulties, Macmillan managed to build 300,000 houses in the government's first year. Critics said that he only did it at the cost of other important construction work, factories, hospitals, etc. But the fulfilment of the pledge was certainly a score for the party. The second Churchill government was perhaps the most successful that Britain has had since the war.

One opportunity for freedom was, to Butler's regret, not taken. This was the chance to free the pound and make it convertible to non-residents at a floating rate of exchange. Early in 1952 the idea was mooted by Butler with the support of the Treasury and the Governor of the Bank of England. But the only other member of the Cabinet in favour was Lyttleton. Churchill hesitated. His instinct was for 'freedom', in this as in every other sense, but Eden was strongly opposed, and so were nearly all senior members of the Cabinet. Lord Cherwell, to whom Churchill always listened, argued that it was a dangerous gamble. Butler considers that if the pound had been freed in 1952, 'Conservatives would have been saved some of the indignities of "stop-go" economics and the Socialists the traumatic experience of a second devaluation.'[1] Ironically the episode produced the word 'Butskellism'. This has now become shorthand for an alleged front bench consensus claimed by a later generation of right-wing Tories to have been a betrayal of the party's principles. The phrase was in fact coined by the *Economist* and referred to the support which Gaitskell, who deeply disapproved of floating the pound, gave to Butler's, privately reluctant, announcement that the plan had been dropped. On most matters Butler and Gaitskell were by no means in agreement. Gaitskell was a sincere socialist, a believer in *étatisme*. Butler was an economic libertarian. If they both used the language of Keynesianism, 'We spoke it with different accents and with a differing emphasis,' as Butler puts it in his autobiography.[2]

Churchill could still make wonderful speeches and command the attention of the nation and the world. The war was not so far distance that he yet seemed, as he would a few years later, antiquated and irrelevant. But he took little interest in home affairs. He still thought of Britain as a great power. How could he do otherwise after his colossal career? His eyes were set on a grand summit meeting to bring an end to the Cold War. The election of Eisenhower as President in 1952 fortified his resolve. Eisenhower was politely sceptical. Nothing came of Churchill's vision. At the end of June 1953 he had a severe stroke. The secret was kept with much success; the public was told that on medical advice he would be resting from his duties for a few weeks. As Eden was also ill, with gall bladder trouble, Butler acted as head of the government and Lord Salisbury took charge of the Foreign Office.

Churchill made a remarkable recovery and successfully addressed the Party Conference at Margate in October 1953. But behind the facade of loyal support there was much misgiving.

[1] Lord Butler, *The art of the possible* (1971), 158-60.
[2] ibid., 160.

Mentally he was never the same again, and Cabinets degenerated into monologues. There was a lack of grip and decision. He should have resigned as soon as Eden was back in the autumn. He could not bring himself to do so. He continued for another year and a half. Harold Macmillan, who was in a position to give disinterested advice, for he had no prospect at this stage of becoming Prime Minister himself, was the man who pressed Churchill most strongly to fix an early date for retirement. Churchill celebrated his eightieth birthday in November 1954 amidst tributes from all over the world and much jollification. In February 1955 he decided to resign in April.

And so the greatest statesman to have led the party bowed out. He had been leader for nearly fifteen years, but the relationship was often uneasy, especially after the war. He was a man of genius, energy, vision, a master of the spoken and written word. He had saved England in 1940. But was he really a Conservative, and if so in what sense? Perhaps the answer is that he was an anachronism. It was as if time had been warped in some strange way, and an eighteenth-century Whig was leading a twentieth-century Tory party.

CHAPTER IX

The Macmillan years
1955–65

1

Macmillan was not leader of the party for the whole of the ten years covered in this chapter but he was the dominant figure in the Cabinet under Eden and he virtually nominated his successor, Lord Home. To call the period the Macmillan Years is therefore not a misnomer, but it is fair to say that in 1955 the prospect of him becoming Prime Minister at all must have seemed remote. Eden was younger, and Butler, who had acted as head of the government in 1953 when both Churchill and Eden were out of action, was younger still. No one disputed Eden's succession though there is some evidence that Churchill was not entirely easy about it.[1] The relations between the two men were not as harmonious as it suited both of them to claim in their memoirs. Eden was justifiably impatient to succeed, and Churchill was well aware of the fact. Eden decided to have a general election as soon as possible. Parliament was three and a half years old. A fresh Prime Minister had every right to a fresh mandate, and the opinion polls were encouraging. He made few changes in the Cabinet, fewer perhaps than he should have. Macmillan went to the Foreign Office and Lord Home to the Colonial Office replacing Lord Swinton whom Eden disliked but compensated with an earldom. Butler remained at the Treasury.

The election was held on 25 May 1955. The Conservatives

[1] T. F. Lindsay and Michael Harrington, *The Conservative Party 1918–1979* (2nd edn, 1979), 184, n.4, reporting a conversation with Sir Desmond Morton, Churchill's wartime personal assistant who dated the latter's misgivings back to 1942. Lord Cherwell told me much the same thing in 1956 during the Suez crisis.

were expected to win it and, helped by a budget which took sixpence off income tax, they did. The Labour party was in a state of conflict and disarray. It was hard to attack the government's record in foreign policy; it had obviously done its best about the Cold War and Eden could claim to have ended hostilities in Indo-China, although not for long as events turned out. In home affairs also there was little cause for serious criticism and much to boast about. Not that Eden boasted. He made an excellent impression of sincerity and modesty on television and, contrary to received wisdom, spoke solo, face to unseen face, with much success. His theme, the need for 'a property owning democracy', went down well. The Conservatives won 49.7 per cent of the vote against Labour's 46.4 and increased their majority in the House from 17 to 59.

Seldom has the euphoria of success been so quickly followed by the disillusionment of failure. Eden lacked the prime ministerial temperament and his health was by no means good. He was not the only holder of his office to be taut, tense and nervous. Macmillan was too, but he did not show it. Eden did, and he was a bad delegator; after so many years as Churchill's heir apparent he seemed to have inherited something of his predecessor's habit of badgering his colleagues day and night. Perhaps he was over-conscious of succeeding to a world-famous statesman. He was ill at ease in domestic matters and unlucky. Almost at once the economic situation worsened, partly because of strikes by the dockers and the railwaymen. Another balance of payments crisis impended. Butler had to bring in an austerity autumn budget and incurred the charge of electoral bribery in the previous one. He too was tired and far from well. At the end of the year Eden made Macmillan, who certainly did not welcome the move, Chancellor of the Exchequer and gave the Foreign Office to Selwyn Lloyd. Butler became Lord Privy Seal and Leader of the House. The press received this reshuffle badly. The *Daily Telegraph*, normally the most faithful of Conservative papers, was highly critical of the Prime Minister. The *People*, a Sunday paper, prophesied that he would soon resign. Eden took the unprecedented step in January 1956 of issuing a denial. A journalist asked Butler, who was about to board a plane for the Riviera: 'Mr Butler, would you say that this is the best Prime Minister we have?' Butler writes: 'My hurried assent to this well-meant but meaningless proposition was flashed round the world: indeed it was fathered upon me. I do not think it did Anthony any good. It did not do me any good either.'[1]

Although Eden's first year in office had been far from happy, he had not passed the point of no return. The visit of Bulganin and Khruschev in the spring, despite the *contretemps* of an unauthorised piece of underwater espionage on the part of MI6, enhanced his prestige as a peacemaker. The origin of the débâcle which culminated in his resignation in January 1957 was the nationalisation of the Suez Canal Company by the Egyptian dictator, Colonel Nasser, on 26 July 1956. But one must go back before that date to see its full significance. In 1954 Eden as Foreign Secretary had persuaded a reluctant Churchill to agree to withdraw British troops from the Canal Zone. There was bitter dissension within the party, and a number of right-wing Conservative MPs, who came to be known as the 'Suez Group' and included Enoch Powell, Julian Amery, Ralph Assheton (Lord Clitheroe), Fitzroy Maclean and Captain Charles Waterhouse, argued – correctly as it turned out – that the withdrawal meant the end of Britain's powerbase in the Middle East. Whether the base was sustainable anyway or even whether it greatly mattered were more arguable questions. Atavistic memories of the route to India, that jewel in the Imperial Crown, and of Disraeli's purchase of the Canal Company shares blurred post-war realities.

Eden was highly sensitive on the question. He had come to regard himself, and to be regarded by many others, as the personification, after Churchill, of resistance to 'appeasement'. It would be a major blow to his prestige if his public confidence in the *bona fides* of Nasser turned out to be as misplaced as Chamberlain's in that of Hitler. A barrage of pan-Arab and anti-Western propaganda blazed away from Cairo. Was it fireworks or gunfire? On 1 March 1957 the King of Jordan dismissed General Glubb, Jordan's Chief of Staff, creator of the

[1] Lord Butler, *The art of the possible* (1971), 183.

Arab Legion and symbol of British prestige. Eden believed that Nasser's influence was the cause. He now saw the politics of the Middle East in terms of a personal duel. The nationalisation of the Suez Canal Company brought matters to a head. He was determined, in conjunction with France, to restore the situation by diplomacy if possible, force if necessary. Diplomacy failed. The USSR vetoed the relevant resolution in the Security Council. Although it was clear that Eisenhower would strongly disapprove, Anglo-French intervention began on 31 October after war had broken out between Israel and Egypt. Port Said was quickly captured and the troops were twenty-three miles along the Canal when on 6 November a ceasefire was ordered.

A great deal has been written about the Suez crisis. The details cannot be analysed here. It is enough to say that the expedition was a military success but a political disaster. Eden underestimated American opposition, although the published evidence makes it clear that Washington was strongly averse to the use of force. The intervention was based on an obviously bogus pretext, the need to 'separate the combatants' in an Israeli-Egyptian war and safeguard the Canal. Eden and Selwyn Lloyd knew in advance that the Israelis would only move towards the Canal if they had a guarantee that the RAF would 'take out' the Egyptian airforce, which was duly done. The real objects were to 'internationalise' the Canal and 'topple Nasser'. It might have been better if these had been openly avowed. The facts about 'collusion' were soon known, though never so far revealed by any member of the Cabinet, with the exception of Selwyn Lloyd who made a partial admission in his memoirs twenty years later.[1] But the French were not reticent and Eisenhower must have known the facts from secret sources very early. The trouble was that when once the combatants had separated there was no plausible reason for going on. Even so Eden might have tried to brazen it out but for a run on the pound which the American authorities were not prepared to stop while the Anglo-French forces were in the Canal Zone. At this juncture Macmillan, one of the strongest supporters of intervention, went abruptly into reverse incurring with some

[1] Selwyn Lloyd, *Suez 1956* (1976).

justice the frequent criticism of 'first in, first out'.

Eden, who had felt the strain intensely – the House of Commons was in a continuous uproar – was now taken ill and decided, astonishingly, to recuperate in the West Indies. Butler acted as head of government from 23 November to 14 December. The Conservative party was in a turmoil. The Suez Group, who had carried a motion for tough action at the October party conference and had acclaimed the Anglo-French intervention, were now once again alienated by the withdrawal. To them was added another set of dissidents from the opposite end of the Tory spectrum. They considered that the expedition should never have been launched in the first place. Two of them, Edward Boyle and Anthony Nutting, resigned from the government. Eden seems to have intended to carry on, though whether he could have done so in practice must be very doubtful. The matter was not put to the test. On medical advice he resigned on 8 January 1957.

The Conservatives had not yet devised a system of electing their leader while the party was in office. The situation remained the same as when Bonar Law resigned in 1923.[1] Ever since that controversial occasion the Crown had been able to appoint an obvious successor; Chamberlain in 1937, Churchill in 1940, Eden himself in 1955; and it was customary for the new Prime Minister to be at once ratified as leader by acclamation at a ritual mass meeting of Tory MPs, peers, candidates and members of the Executive Committee of the National Union.[2] The succession lay between Butler and Macmillan. Most press commentators assumed that Butler would be chosen. Fleet Street can be out touch with Westminster, especially Tory Westminster. It is fair to say that Butler's position as temporary head of the government for the second time understandably fostered the delusion. In fact, as Nigel Fisher, himself a Conservative MP at the time, writes in his life of Macmillan, 'Although Parliament was in recess at the time of Eden's resignation, anyone in close touch with Conservative opinion in the House of Commons should have known that Macmillan was

[1] See above, pp. 211–14.
[2] This was not done at once in the case of Churchill in 1940 – see above, p. 248 – but the circumstances were abnormal.

the Party's probable choice as his successor." Butler had a reputation for equivocation, ambivalance and delphic utterance. His
doubts about Suez were well known largely because he
expressed them so often in society. Yet he had not resigned.
Macmillan may have been 'first in, first out' but at least he was
definite, right or wrong, in both cases. What the mood of a badly
bruised party needed was decisiveness, vigorous language and
a clear lead. Butler would have been unacceptable to the Suez
Group and to the Tory right. Macmillan raised no
corresponding antipathy among the Tory left.

The initiative was taken by Lords Salisbury and Kilmuir[2]
who jointly saw each member of the Cabinet separately and
asked them to give their choice. The verdict was strongly in
favour of Macmillan. The two peers also sounded the Chief
Whip, Edward Heath, the Chairman of the Party Organisation,
Oliver Poole, and the Chairman of the 1922 Committee, John
Morrison, who assessed back bench opinion with surprising
confidence from the Isle of Islay. The general verdict was for
Macmillan. The Queen consulted Churchill, who also advised
in favour of Macmillan, and Eden, whose advice is not known.[3]
On 10 January Macmillan kissed hands as Prime Minister.

2

The Conservatives made the right choice – or had it made for
them. Macmillan was the man for the hour – one of the worst
crises in the history of the party. He appreciated the dangers.
He told the Queen that he might not last six weeks. She
reminded him of this six years later when he was still Prime
Minister. The party was in a state of acute dissension. High
words were spoken even within the august portals of White's
Club and the Carlton. The word 'traitor' was heard more than
once. The right and left wings were, for opposite reasons,
equally disturbed and angry, though it was the left that fared
worse with their constituents. There was widespread belief that

---

[1] *Harold Macmillan* (1982), 175.
[2] Lord Privy Seal and Lord Chancellor respectively.
[3] It is very unlikely that he recommended Butler.

the next election would produce a landslide defeat; after that the Conservatives might well be out for twenty years as a result of the 'humiliation' of Suez.

Macmillan, however, possessed some assets. The next election could be postponed till early 1960. He had a safe majority in the House. The 'rebels' had no intention of carrying rebellion into the division lobbies. Nor was the effect of Suez on public opinion as damaging as it seemed to be in the hothouse atmosphere of Westminster and Fleet Street. The 'nation', as far as any judgment can be made about that intangible entity, felt bewildered rather than humiliated. It is not true, as sometimes said, that public opinion was strongly pro-Suez, but it was not against. BIPO polls on 11 November and 2 December 1956 recorded slightly over 50 per cent in favour of Eden's policy. The 'moral issue' cut little ice. Gaitskell, Attlee's successor as leader of the Opposition, did himself harm by pressing it, and even more harm when at the height of the crisis he appealed on television to the Conservative dissenters to overthrow the government – an overture certain to rally the Tory ranks. A guess may perhaps be made that most Conservative supporters and quite a number of Labour too – many with unflattering memories of wartime Egypt – felt that Eden's heart was in the right place, even if his head had miscalculated the odds. Sentiment was far more anti-American than anti-Eden. On the whole people wanted to forget Suez. The débâcle played little part in the next election.

On a longer view, however, it may have done more harm to the Conservative cause than seemed in the aftermath of their 1959 victory. At least one shrewd observer, Iain Macleod, believed that it was the biggest factor in losing the 'intellectual vote', which for whatever reason the Conservatives certainly did lose in the early 1960s.[1] They had never commanded more than a part of it, but there had been substantial support for the party in the previous decade among the economists, commentators, journalists and academics – the 'opinion formers' in general. Their votes are not many but their influence is important. A party which alienates them does so at its peril. Suez had this effect. The Conservatives did not recover the lost ground till the late 1970s.

[1] Conversation with the author in 1968.

Such long-term considerations could not play much part in Macmillan's policy. He had more immediate problems: first to restore the unity and confidence of the party; secondly, to repair the breach with America. The second was not too difficult. Although Macmillan had, like most of the Cabinet, condoned the disingenuous behaviour of Eden, he was not involved directly. Eden could hardly have hoped to restore good relations. Macmillan was helped by friendship with Eisenhower dating from their wartime period in the Mediterranean. The President too was anxious to make up the quarrel. There was a cordial meeting in Bermuda at the end of March.

The restoration of party confidence was more difficult. He began with the Cabinet. Butler was bound to be disappointed. Macmillan was ready to offer him almost any post he wanted, together with the leadership of the House, apart from the Foreign Office. To remove Selwyn Lloyd would look like an admission of guilt over Suez. The Prime Minister, though determined to say as little as possible about it, was equally determined not to apologise. Butler accepted the Home Office. He writes in his memoirs: 'Dining a few nights later at the Beafsteak I was reminded by a young spark that Home Secretaries scarcely ever become Prime Ministers.'[1] He could have replied – perhaps did reply – that Chancellors of the Exchequer frequently do. Macmillan gave the Treasury to Peter Thorneycroft and the Ministry of Defence to Duncan Sandys, Churchill's son-in-law. Macmillan dominated his Cabinet from the start. He knew what he wanted but he was a believer in delegation and he did not bother his colleagues with detailed supervision. They were expected to get on with the job. He was not prepared to give way to threats of resignation. When in March Lord Salisbury offered his, on a question of policy in Cyprus, it was promptly accepted; there never had been much love lost between the Cecils and the Cavendishes.[2] A year later the entire Treasury team of Peter Thorneycroft, Enoch Powell and Nigel Birch proffered their resignations because the

[1] Butler, op. cit., 96.
[2] Macmillan was married to Lady Dorothy Cavendish, daughter of the Duke of Devonshire.

Cabinet would not agree to their proposed cuts in expenditure. Macmillan perhaps had too much fear of unemployment and too little of inflation, although it is fanciful to argue that this episode was some kind of turning point in the battle for fiscal probity. He promptly accepted their resignations, appointed Derick Heathcoat Amory in Thorneycroft's place, and, as he departed on a tour of the Commonwealth, contrasted 'the wider vision' with 'these little local difficulties'.

By now he had come to dominate the House. A Prime Minister always has the advantage over a Leader of the Opposition, and Macmillan exploited it to the full. Although he tells us that he was very nervous at first, he did not show it and he soon outpointed Gaitskell. In a manner difficult to analyse, ascendancy in the House quickly radiates outwards. He was, moreover, determined to pursue an expansionist economic policy, not simply for electoral advantage but for its own sake. His celebrated remark on 20 July 1957, 'Let's be frank about it; most of our people have never had it so good,' may have been part of a warning against excessive wage claims, but it was also a statement of facts which he welcomed. Much disapproval was evinced by the killjoys. One can only echo the words of Lindsay and Harrington: 'The barely concealed hostility to mass affluence which was felt and expressed by large sectors of the British political and cultural establishment in the later 1950s provides the student of national psychology with a fascinating theme for investigation.'[1]

The next general election was in the forefront of Macmillan's mind from the beginning. The prospect was daunting. The Conservatives were consistently behind Labour in the opinion polls throughout 1957 and the first half of 1958 by figures ranging from 5 to 13 points. Moreover, there was no instance in the twentieth century of a party winning three successive general elections since the Liberals in December 1910 – and this had been a very marginal victory. Macmillan decided that the party organisation needed to be revigorated. Oliver Poole loyally agreed to stand down from the post of chairman and act

[1] op. cit., 203. A similar phenomenon was the bitter opposition to the introduction of Independent Television a few years earlier.

as deputy to his successor. The new chairman appointed on 17 September 1957 was Lord Hailsham who moved from the Ministry of Education to the post of Lord President. No better choice could have been made. Poole was an organisation man. Hailsham was a showman. Of course there was and is much more to him than that, including a first-class brain, but showmanship was needed at this stage and he provided it in good measure, ringing a large bell at the end of a messianic speech at his first party conference in October.

The party put its publicity in the hands of a well-known public relations firm, Colman, Prentice and Varley; between January 1957 and September 1959 almost half a million pounds was spent on advertising. The theme of the election was planned to be prosperity and peace. The slogan was to be 'Life's better with the Conservatives. Don't let Labour ruin it'. To begin with, the emphasis was on positive Conservative achievement. The Labour party was not attacked but ignored. Little publicity was at first given to the Prime Minister himself who had the 'image' of being somewhat remote and aloof. But after his Commonwealth tour of 1958 which was a great success his personal prestige rose. His visit to Russia in February 1959, the first by any Western leader since the Second World War, gave him another boost. He wore a white fur hat a foot high, which had been found in a toy cupboard at Birch Grove, his country house. What with 'little local difficulties' and Edwardian attire, he was becoming a 'character'. Preparations were made for a summit meeting in 1960. In August President Eisenhower paid a five-day visit to England and the two appeared together on a television discussion programme. Macmillan now seemed something of a world statesman and he overcame the impression of aloofness by a series of short speaking tours in marginal constituencies.

The key question was the timing of the election. On 10 April Macmillan met Butler, Hailsham, Poole, Amory and others to discuss whether or not it should be in the summer, which in practice meant June. The opinion polls showed the parties exactly equal at this stage. Hailsham and his advisers, after a careful survey, considered that an immediate dissolution would

VITAL STATISTICS

August 27, 1958. Reproduced by permission of Punch.

give a majority of 13. Macmillan decided that he would wait at least till the autumn. A few days later Amory introduced a highly popular budget which took ninepence off income tax. The opinion polls gave the Conservatives a lead throughout the summer. On 7 September Macmillan asked for a dissolution, and the election was fixed for 8 October. The situation looked promising. The year 1959 was one of the few years in which low unemployment, stable prices and a favourable balance of payments coincided. The Conservatives were tipped as favourites, and their position was strengthened by a *gaffe* on Gaitskell's part when he claimed that the expensive programme of social expenditure promised in the Labour manifesto could be met without raising income tax. The Conservatives won 365 seats with 49.4 per cent of the vote. The Labour figures were 258 and 43.8. It was widely regarded as a triumph for the Prime Minister, already depicted as 'Supermac' by the cartoonist Vicki.

3

The Conservative party rode high for the next twenty-one months. They were ahead on the opinion polls, often by large margins, until August 1961. Thereafter they were behind Labour for the rest of Macmillan's time and indeed well beyond it. Macmillan made some changes in the government, the most important being Iain Macleod as Colonial Secretary in place of Lennox Boyd who had been anxious to retire earlier and did not contest his seat in the general election. Edward Heath replaced Macleod as Minister of Labour and Reginald Maudling became President of the Board of Trade. Hailsham ceased to be Chairman of the Party and was appointed Minister of Science – a new invention. Butler took on the Chairmanship, adding yet a third to the two onerous posts he already held as Home Secretary and Leader of the House. Nine months later when Heathcoat Amory insisted on retiring from politics Macmillan moved Selwyn Lloyd to the Treasury and replaced him by Lord Home, firmly disregarding Opposition protests at a peer becoming Foreign Secretary.

Home was to be highly effective, but Selwyn Lloyd less so.

The year 1960 saw Macmillan riding high. True it was marred by the collapse in May of the long-awaited summit meeting because of the shooting down of an American spy plane over Russia, but this was no fault of Macmillan. On the positive side, he conducted a highly successful tour of Africa early in 1960, during which he made his celebrated recognition of the growth of African nationalism in a speech to both Houses of the South African Parliament in Cape Town on Monday, 3 February: 'The wind of change is blowing through this continent and, whether we like it or not, this growth of national consciousness is a political fact.' This and other phrases aroused resentment in right-wing Conservative circles. The Monday Club was formed to commemorate 'Black Monday', the day of the speech. But middle-of-the-road Conservatives welcomed it, and it spiked some of the guns of the Labour and Liberal anti-colonialists. The speech was a clear declaration of the policy of African decolonisation, an important, though highly controversial, feature of his premiership.

A second decision, which was connected with decolonisation, was to seek membership of the EEC. Thanks largely to Eden's opposition, Britain had failed to accede to the Treaty of Rome in 1957. The argument had been that it was incompatible with the Commonwealth, the sterling area and Britain's ties with the USA. Macmillan's attitude towards the Commonwealth was ambivalent. Certainly he could speak at times with romantic enthusiasm about the concept, but it may be significant that on one occasion he asked Lennox Boyd for a profit and loss account of each colony – how much Britain spent on it and what she got back in return. By 1961 he had become convinced that Britain's future lay in Europe rather than the Commonwealth. There had been nothing about this in the 1959 election manifesto, and Macmillan, having no mandate, had to tread delicately. After careful sounding in Washington and among the Commonwealth governments, he announced on 31 July the Cabinet's decision to apply for membership of the EEC. Though not at once there was soon strong opposition from Labour and from the more imperially minded elements of the

Conservative party. The negotiations were entrusted to Edward Heath, undoubtedly one of the ablest of the younger ministers; but the process clearly would not be at all easy either at home or abroad.

During Macmillan's premiership many things happened which were important but had little effect on the history of the Conservative party. For that reason such events as Duncan Sandys's revolution in defence policy which increased Britain's dependence on nuclear weapons and led to the abandonment of conscription in 1960, or the controversy about Skybolt and Polaris, or the Immigration Act, or the Cuban crisis or the Test Ban Treaty will not feature in this narrative. What affected the party's fortunes far more than any of these was the government's failure in the very field where its success had led to victory in 1959 – economic management. The four desiderata – full employment, stable prices, a favourable balance of payments and rising productivity – have never been achieved since 1945 other than for fleeting periods which soon came to an end. The years 1958–60 were one of these but the experience was not to be repeated in Macmillan's time or that of his successor.

Heathcoat Amory produced a neutral budget in 1960 but the signs that his expansionary budget of the previous year had 'overheated' the economy soon began to multiply. His successor, Selwyn Lloyd, took the Treasury and Bank of England view that there must be restraint. In 1961 he produced a mildly deflationary budget and in July raised the bank rate from 5 to 7 per cent. He also introduced what was called the 'pay pause', an attempt to moderate wage increases till March 1962. The only sphere in which the government had any direct authority was the public sector. It could merely preach elsewhere, and in practice it was pretty ineffective even with public employees – a conspicuous example being the electricity workers to whom the Electricity Board and the Minister of Power feebly surrendered in November without even consulting the Prime Minister or the Chancellor. The pay pause was a failure widely resented as arbitrary and unjust. In fact all efforts at a statutory or exhortatory incomes policy – NEDC, NIC and a long series of well meaning attempts – have foundered so far. It is a depressing reflection on British labour relations that the only thing that has ever yet induced wage restraint is fear of unemployment. To encourage this was totally contrary to Macmillan's outlook. He was determined to find a way round what he regarded as the deflationary obstinacy of the Treasury.

Selwyn Lloyd had done nothing other than loyally carry out the policy endorsed by the Cabinet but he was bad at public relations and he had none of the politician's gift of dressing up unpopular policies in a popular – or at least a not too unpopular – guise. By the end of 1961 the Prime Minister was beginning to regard him as an unimaginative liability though he gave no hint of his feelings to the Chancellor himself. Macmillan's discontent was enhanced by the recovery of the Labour party which since August had been ahead in the opinion polls. In the aftermath of Labour's third successive defeat many commentators had written off its prospect of ever recovering. Their opinion seemed to be confirmed by nearly two years of internecine struggle over nuclear disarmament and nationalisation. On the former Gaitskell reversed in 1961 his defeat in the previous year. On the latter he compromised, and he now led a reasonably united party which was clearly going to be a formidable challenge. Macmillan, who disliked him and in private referred to him as a 'sanctimonious Wykehamist', became less and less effective at answering him as the months went by, indeed less effective generally in the House than he had been at first. This, as Nigel Fisher observes, was 'mainly through lack of practice. He seldom spoke, and even a good speech on South Africa was more acceptable to the Labour Party than to his own Back Benchers.'[1] Macmillan was not the first or last Prime Minister to neglect the management of the House for the lure of orbiting the globe as a world statesman. The trouble was that Britain had ceased to be a world power and even if she had not, the world is not where one wins general elections. A series of disastrous by-elections culminated with the loss of the Conservative stronghold of Orpington to a Liberal in March 1982.

[1] Nigel Fisher, *Harold Macmillan*, 268.

Macmillan's nerve was evidently shaken. He resolved, with the assent of one or two of his leading colleagues, to get rid of Selwyn Lloyd; this was not an unreasonable step if taken in isolation and suitably prepared. But the Prime Minister decided to combine it with a complete reconstruction of the government. This involved the dismissal of one-third of the Cabinet and was effected on 13 July with the minimum of warning or even ordinary courtesy. Whatever the causes of such uncharacteristic conduct – and bad advice from a dud Chief Whip is said to be one of them – it created bitter resentment and was highly damaging to the party's morale. Selwyn Lloyd refused a peerage and insisted on a public exchange of letters. His own was frosty. Eden, most unusually for him, publicly stated that Lloyd had been 'harshly treated'. Special criticism was evoked by the dismissal of the Lord Chancellor, Lord Kilmuir, a loyal and long-serving minister for over ten years. He was replaced by the Attorney General whose virtues included neither legal distinction nor common courtesy.[1] Another much criticised dismissal was that of Charles Hill, the former 'Radio Doctor', a good speaker and a popular Minister of Housing. When Macmillan took his seat at Question Time on 17 July he was received in dead silence. The Press of course had a field day on the theme of the 'Night of the Long Knives' or the 'July Massacre' as it was alternatively described, and 'Supermac' gave way to 'Mac the Knife'.

Lloyd was replaced by Reginald Maudling whose expansionist views on the economy were far closer to the Prime Minister's. His stewardship of the nation's finances was to be more helpful to the party than Lloyd's would have been; his autumn budget of 1962 and spring budget of 1963 produced a pre-election boom which nearly carried Macmillan's successor to victory. Whether it operated in the long-term interests of the country is more questionable. Lloyd was the second case of a Chancellor being jettisoned by Macmillan for trying to restrain public expenditure. Today the risk of inflation seems a greater danger to the economy than a marginal increase in

---

[1] Sir Reginald Manningham-Butler, who took the title of Lord Dilhorne and was nicknamed 'Bullying Manner'.

unemployment. But hindsight is perilous; one needs to have lived through the 1960s to appreciate the role of unemployment in public demonology. The raging inflation of the 1970s lay ahead and Maudling's budgets were not more than a marginally contributory factor.

The fortunes of the party deteriorated during the rest of 1962. Decolonisation in Africa was pursued with energy by Macleod, but it alienated the right – Lord Salisbury described him in the House of Lords as 'too clever by half' – and it was never the subject of much enthusiasm among the majority of Conservative MPs, let alone the constituency parties. Macmillan himself came to be bored by the endless constitutional proposals about the Central African Federation and its Territories, which, as he says in his memoirs, were as ephemeral and complicated as those of the Abbé Sièyes. He moved Macleod to the Leadership of the House in October 1961. The unremitting London propaganda machine of Sir Roy Welensky had a certain effect on Conservative sentiment, and Macmillan whose premiership began with the support of the right had ceased to command it before the end.

Early in 1963 he received the worst setback of all. De Gaulle vetoed the entry into the EEC upon which the Prime Minister had set his heart. The veto, though predictable, does not seem to have been predicted – anyway by Macmillan who had been hoping to fight the next election on the theme of Europe and its opportunities which he hoped would act as a catalyst to the 'modernisation' of Britain – a slogan much in vogue at the time. The Conservatives now had no theme, and they were to be plagued by a series of misfortunes for the rest of the year. The details do not concern us. There was the revelation that Kim Philby, now in Russia, was the 'third man'. There was the Vassall case where it was rumoured that a homosexual spy had an improper relationship with Tam Galbraith, a junior minister. Galbraith offered his resignation which was accepted too readily by the Prime Minister. A judicial tribunal found that the story was a total *canard* and imprisoned for contempt of court two journalists who refused to reveal their sources. As in the case of the July dismissals, Macmillan's great assets of 'unflappability' and loyalty to colleagues seemed to have vanished. The year of scandal culminated in the Profumo episode. The Minister of War had to admit having lied to the House when he denied that he had been involved in an affair with one, Christine Keeler, who was also the mistress of the Russian naval attaché. London buzzed with rumours of the most lurid nature about the private lives of prominent people. In his memoirs Macmillan evoked the parallel of Titus Oates. He took the drastic step of appointing a one-man tribunal, Lord Denning, to conduct in secrecy an inquiry with no holds barred. The Denning Report dispersed the rumours, but Macmillan, who had been censured for being too suspicious over Galbraith, was now attacked for being too gullible over Profumo whom he had not even personally interviewed. He gave the impression of being old and tired and out of touch. Nigel Birch in the debate on 17 June made a devastating attack, and 27 Conservatives abstained in the ensuing division. It is said that there would have been more if the Whips had not hinted that the Prime Minister would retire after a decent interval.

Macmillan did indeed consider doing so though not at once, for that would have done the government even more harm. The opinion polls, however, after giving Labour an immense lead, began to be slightly less discouraging. After some consultations which produced no clear result except that the Cabinet would abide by his decision, he resolved on 7 October to stay on and announce at the imminent party conference that he would fight the next election. He could justify this questionable conclusion on the ground that there was no indisputable successor. Butler, Hailsham, Maudling and Macleod were, for different reasons, unlikely to command universal party assent. Home at this stage did not seem to be a runner at all. Nevertheless the same fortuitous event which made Hailsham a possibility also applied to Home. A recent Act of Parliament allowed hereditary peers to renounce their peerages within one year of succession and thus become eligible to sit in the Commons. The Act also gave a 'one off' chance for all existing hereditary peers to renounce, provided they did so within a year of the date when the Act came into effect. The government had intended to postpone this till after the end of the existing parliament in order to avoid inconvenient by-elections, but Macmillan accepted a last-minute amendment by the Lords, which made the Act effective from the date of the Royal Assent, 31 July 1963. In this accidental manner a peerage, albeit for a short period, ceased to be a bar to the premiership.

No sooner had Macmillan made his decision than he was taken ill with an inflamed prostate gland. He had to have an immediate operation and he decided to resign. It is by no means clear why. A prostate operation is not normally a very serious matter and there seems no obvious reason to have prevented him from acting as Churchill did in 1953 and appointing a deputy for a month or two. To throw open the whole question of the succession in the midst of a party conference was a recipe for trouble. Not that Macmillan intended to throw the matter completely open. He was not so ill that he felt obliged, like Bonar Law in 1923, to decline to advise the Crown on the succession. On the contrary, the key to what followed is his negative decision that he would not, if he could possibly avoid it, recommend Butler. His first choice was Hailsham who amidst much panache announced at Blackpool his intention to renounce his peerage. Had the conference been a nominating convention on the American model, he would probably have won on the first ballot, but it was not, and his popularity was far lower among MPs and ministers than constituency representatives. His candidature, despite much ballyhoo, soon ran into the sand. It now looked as if Butler must be the choice. Macleod had alienated the right, and Maudling had bored the conference with a lacklustre speech. Macmillan was not disconcerted. He sounded Home who let it be known, after initial hesitation, that he would be available. The Cabinet, MPs, peers and elements of the party organisation were consulted by Lord Dilhorne, the whips and Oliver Poole respectively.

Much has been written about what followed, and it is by no means certain that the Lord Chancellor was correct in reporting as he did an overwhelming Cabinet consensus for Home.[1] Nor

[1] Iain Macleod, *Spectator*, 17 January 1964 – a most important source. The article is reprinted in George Hutchinson, *The last Edwardian at No. 10* (1980), 123–41.

is it clear that Martin Redmayne, Chief Whip in the Commons, gave an accurate numerical estimate of the support for Home. By his own admission it was weighted in favour of 'people on whose opinion one would more strongly rely than on others'.[1] As Nigel Fisher points out: 'It is at least questionable whether he should have made so personal a judgment about his colleagues in the Party.'[2] Even so he gave Home only a marginal lead. It is perhaps significant that Macleod who was, after all, joint chairman of the Party with Oliver Poole was not consulted whereas Poole was, though his verdict was for Hailsham. Macleod was a strong supporter of Butler.

The pro-Butler ministers learning on 17 October that Home was to be the man were filled with consernation. They consulted Hailsham, and Butler endeavoured early on 18 October to telephone Macmillan for authority for a Cabinet meeting under Dilhorne to discuss the matter. There was no reply.[3] The Prime Minister, warned by the Chief Whip, submitted his formal resignation to the Queen at 9.30 a.m. She came to see him in hospital at 11 a.m. and he read a memorandum summarising his findings and advising her to send for Home. At 12.15 p.m. she invited Home to form a government. On Macmillan's advice she did not actually appoint him as Prime Minister till he had had a chance to see his colleagues. At first Butler, Hailsham, Macleod, Maudling, Enoch Powell and Edward Boyle declined to join. Home offered the Foreign Office to Butler who said he would think about it. At this juncture Hailsham, who had been warned by Selwyn Lloyd that refusal would look like sour grapes, changed his mind. Butler then changed his. In the end only Macleod and Powell refused and Home was able to go ahead. If the group had been united they could certainly have blocked him, but in such circumstances Butler's position as the only alternative would have been difficult, though not necessarily hopeless.

One cannot, however, help speculating on what would have happened if Macmillan had used his influence for and not against Butler. Despite all the disadvantages of the 'grouse

[1] Interview printed in the *Listener* and quoted by Nigel Fisher, op. cit., 345.
[2] ibid.
[3] Nigel Fisher, *Harol MacMillan* (1982), 346–7

moor image', the loss of two outstandingly able colleagues and the general ill-feeling created by the process of succession, Home only lost the 1964 election by four seats. One can but speculate on what would have happened if Butler had been the successor. There were certainly elements in the party which distrusted him, but it is unlikely that any major figures in the Cabinet would have refused to serve and he had much more of a 'middle ground' appeal than Home. Four is not many, and it is hard to believe that Butler would not have won. He would have been better than Home at dealing with Harold Wilson who had succeeded to the Labour leadership after Gaitskell's tragic death at the beginning of the year and soon proved himself to be a masterly leader of the Opposition.

The Labour party was approaching a point where its road forked. It could take the path of 'socialism' or the path towards what now would be called 'social democracy' or it could stop where it was 'adamant for drift, resolved to be irresolute'. A fourth successive defeat might have forced a decision. If so Labour would either have condemned itself to being a perpetual left-wing minority or converted itself into a progressive non-ideological alternative to Conservatism. In the event Wilson in office was able to manoeuvre rather than decide; and Labour's dilemma remained for another twenty years till Kinnock and Blair modernised the party.

4

Home was the first peer to be Prime Minister, however briefly, since Lord Salisbury in 1902. He at once disclaimed his peerage, and, as Sir Alec Douglas-Home – he was a Knight of the Thistle – was elected on 8 November as Member for Kinross and West Perthshire, said to be the third safest Conservative seat in Britain. The sitting tenant, George Younger, was generous to vacate it. Sir Alec entered office under many disabilities: he was not a public figure; he had left the House of Commons where he had never been a notable performer as long ago as 1951; he was not telegenic; he was an Old Etonian fourteenth earl when the 'spirit of the times' was anti-aristocratic and anti-traditional; he seemed hardly the man to 'modernise' Britain; he knew little of economics which, he said, he could only understand by using matchsticks. Moreover, the circumstances of his appointment were unhelpful. When the dust had died down many Conservatives must have felt it odd, even bizarre, that apparently no one out of 363 Conservative MPs was regarded as fit to be Prime Minister. Sir Alec was not devoid of assets. He was generally respected for his probity and honesty. He was one of the least devious politicians. He was also one of the nicest and least conceited or pompous men to become Prime Minister. Most Conservatives respected his views on foreign policy, his firm stance on Russia and his uncompromising attitude towards nuclear disarmament. He led the party from right of centre, the first Prime Minister to do so since Salisbury. This was not necessarily a handicap in the second half of the twentieth century, witness the success of Mrs Thatcher. But in the early 1960s it was. The revolution in Conservative ideology which helped her and which she largely created did not occur for at least another decade.

Macmillan soon recovered and has been in excellent health ever since. He remained in the House of Commons till the next election but spoke on only three occasions. He refused to accept an earldom, though he changed his mind just before his ninetieth birthday in February 1984. He solaced his long retirement with many interests, above all his Chancellorship of Oxford University. There are many puzzles about his career and personality, but they will not be solved, if they ever are, till after the end of his long life.

From the moment that Sir Alec became Prime Minister until two and a half years later when Harold Wilson in March 1966 won his second victory at the polls, this time with a conclusive majority, British politics were dominated by electioneering. Sir Alec's first problem was to decide on the date. It could not be later than October 1964, but Maudling, who was advised that the balance of payments despite a surge in imports would remain more or less even for the next few months, favoured May or June. He produced a neutral budget in the spring but the balance did not remain even. There was a deficit of £73 million in the second quarter and £192 million in the third quarter of 1964. These deficits would not have figured in a May/June election, but there were other snags. The Resale Price Maintenance Bill introduced by Heath in January proved to be highly divisive. It was much resented by the small shopkeepers who were for the most part Conservative supporters. To bring in a highly controversial measure at the fag end of a Parliament is usually bad tactics, witness Neville Chamberlain's rating proposals carried just before the 1929 election.[1] The opinion polls gave the Conservatives little hope of success in an early general election. On 9 April the Prime Minister announced that he would not ask for a dissolution before the autumn.

Oliver Poole, now Vice-Chairman of the Party Organisation (he had already been Chairman, Joint-Chairman and Deputy-Chairman), was effectively in charge of the election campaign, under Lord Blakenham who had taken the place of Iain Macleod. The problem was the theme. Macmillan's plan had been to make it Europe and modernisation. Europe was out, and modernisation did not exactly sound the trumpet in the ears of the party faithful. In any case first Gaitskell and then Wilson had for years been plugging it, and arguing that British industry and institutions were obsolete. If people wanted a change they were more likely to vote Labour than Conservative. There were, it is true, important reports from Commissions set up by Macmillan's Cabinet, on higher and secondary education, on railways and on traffic in towns, and technological research, but there was no obvious reason why the Conservatives would implement them more effectively than Labour, and an element in the party viewed them with scepticism as enlarging yet further the public sector and public expenditure.

Nor was the mood of the early 1960s favourable to the Conservative party. It was a period of satire, cynicism and disillusionment. In 1961 *Beyond the Fringe* was staged, *Private Eye* began publication, and *That Was the Week that Was* appeared on television – all three with notable success. Michael Shanks's book, *The Stagnant Society*, sold 60,000 copies. The publishers,

[1] See p. 229 above.

Penguin, then launched a series entitled *What's Wrong with* . . . These and many other anti-establishment manifestations were in one sense non-political but the attitude they embodied could not be helpful to a party which had now been in office for nearly thirteen years. It was hard to fight against a pervasive sentiment that it was time for a change.

Sir Alec Douglas-Home did his best. He never mastered Wilson in the House, but he prudently appeared there as seldom as a Prime Minister can and concentrated his efforts on speaking tours to make himself better known in the country. He had considerable success. The opinion polls unexpectedly showed a steady reduction in the Labour lead during the summer, and one of them even put the Conservatives fractionally ahead in August. On 15 September he announced that polling day would be on 15 October. In the end the theme chosen for the campaign was much the same as it had been in 1959; Conservative-created prosperity and the threat posed to it by Labour's plans for nationalisation and expansion of social services adumbrated in their manifesto, *The new Britain*, which appeared on 11 September, a week before the Conservatives' *Prosperity with a purpose*. For a moment it looked as if, despite the July massacre, despite Profumo, despite Blackpool, the party would pull off a fourth victory. On 30 September the National Opinion Poll gave them a lead of 2.9 per cent. But the adverse balance of payment figures of the second quarter were published that day, and Labour speakers harped on the forthcoming economic crisis – a largely self-fulfilling prophecy which they must have regretted after their narrow win. The Prime Minister came in for some rough treatment from hecklers who virtually shouted him down on 8 October at the Bull Ring in Birmingham.[1] The scene on television caused contempt rather than sympathy. It was an error of the party managers not to have arranged in advance for a final 'ticket only' meeting where he might have had a chance to remove this impression of ineffectiveness.

The end result was far closer than anyone would have predicted a year earlier. Labour with 44.1 per cent of the vote

[1] There is no reason to believe that Labour instigated this.

won 317 seats, the Conservatives with 43.8 per cent won 304, and the Liberals with 11.2 per cent won 9. Wilson thus had a majority of 13 over the Conservatives, but only 4 overall.

Few Conservatives expected to win the 1964 election, nor was there much optimism about the next one which was bound to be held fairly soon. Wilson would have the initiative and, unless the Labour leaders made a notable hash of things in their early months, they were likely to build on their slender majority. The immediate problem that the party faced was the future of the leadership. In the twentieth century this has been a frequent sequel to electoral defeat, e.g., Balfour in 1911, Baldwin in 1923 and 1929, and Heath in 1974. Churchill in 1945 was an exception and so was Heath in 1966. It has not necessarily resulted in the leader's resignation or deposition but the possibility is almost always canvassed in private if not in public. In fact most people thought that Sir Alec Douglas-Home had done very well to have come so near to success. It was his ability to lead the Opposition which aroused misgivings. His defects as a parliamentarian were now far more damaging than in office. He was too much of a specialist and he lacked the speed of repartee or the ability to coin phrases which enable a politician to cut a figure in the House.

The circumstances of his appointment were still a matter of high controversy. By inviting Macleod and Powell to join the Shadow Cabinet he did something to heal the breach, and both accepted. There was, however, general agreement that some recognised process of election should be devised for the future. A young Conservative MP on the left of the party, Humphrey Berkeley, suggested that the parliamentary party should be the sovereign body. Home agreed, and the new system was adopted in February 1965. There would no longer be any question of the 'customary process of consultation' or choice by an alleged 'magic circle'. The voting was confined to Conservative MPs and this would apply whether the party was in office or in opposition. The special role that the Cabinet had played both in 1957 when it, in effect, elected the new Prime Minister and in 1963 when its views were regarded as of crucial importance, disappeared. Nor would the House of Lords or the party organisation have any say in the matter. Although the opinion of the Lords would be communicated to the members of the parliamentary party they were free to ignore it, as in fact they did in 1975. On the first ballot the winner needed an overall majority of 15 per cent of those voting. If no one achieved this there would be a second ballot in which a bare majority would suffice.[1]

The next six months saw no improvement in Sir Alec's standing. A powerful group of MPs was now working for his removal. Edward Heath was not one of them and there is no reason to believe – certainly Sir Alec did not believe – that he took any part at all in these activities. Home's personal rating in the polls not only lagged well behind Wilson's – surprisingly even on the criterion of sincerity – but behind that of the Conservative party. The one thing that might have kept him in the battle, the possibility of a snap general election, disappeared in June when Wilson announced that he did not mean to ask for a dissolution that year. Sir Alec's position was not hopeless. Baldwin fought back from a worse situation in 1931, but he was fighting against what he considered the forces of evil in the persons of Lords Rothermere and Beaverbrook. There was no comparable menace in 1965. On 22 July Home announced his resignation at a meeting of the 1922 Committee.

The party now proceeded to hold its first genuine leadership election. There were three candidates – Heath, Maudling and Powell. The latter had no chance; he was putting down a marker for a future which has never come. Of the two serious candidates Maudling was better known to the public, but the Labour claim that his budgets were responsible for the balance of payments crisis stuck to some extent, even among his colleagues, and he had the reputation of being casual and slightly lazy. Heath had won golden opinions as Chief Whip by keeping the party together during Suez. More recently he had made a great impression with his attack on Callaghan's Finance Bill. At the ballot held on 27 July he won 150 votes to Maudling's 133 and Powell's 15. This did not meet the 15 per cent requirement, but Maudling at once withdrew, and Heath was declared winner.

[1] These rules were redrawn early in 1975. See below, p. 317.

CHAPTER X

Heath and Thatcher
1965–79

1

There was nothing of the 'magic circle' about the new leader. Edward Heath had had a longer upward path to climb than any of his predecessors since Disraeli, with the possible exception of Bonar Law. Not that he was in the least like Disraeli. If he resembled any previous leader it was Peel. But Peel belonged, despite his social awkwardness, to the élite which produced prime ministers, and from his youth was regarded as a likely candidate. Heath had a working-class background and a maintained grammar school education at Chatham House, Ramsgate. He gained a place at Balliol College, Oxford, and, later, an organ scholarship. At Oxford he was President of the Union and the University Conservative Association. He was not a conformist. He supported the all-party anti-Munich candidate, A. D. Lindsay, Master of Balliol, against the official Conservative candidate, Quintin Hogg, at the famous Oxford City by-election in the autumn of 1938. After a distinguished war career ending as a colonel in the Royal Artillery he passed the Civil Service examination at the top of the list. But he did not take up the offer. In 1950 he entered parliament as member for Bexley, winning by only 138 votes.

Edward Heath is not an easy person to categorise politically. At the time of his election he would probably have been regarded as likely to lead from the left of centre in contrast to Sir Alec Douglas-Home who led marginally from the right. But a closer scrutiny does not quite confirm this picture. It is true that Heath was very much a protegé of Macmillan, and most people would put Macmillan on the left of the party insofar as the label has any meaning. Yet the programme which Heath put forward in many ways marked a shift to the right. He had become chairman of the Advisory Committee on Policy in October 1964 while Home was still leader. A large number of study groups were set up and, after a great deal of high-pressure work, since an election was expected at any moment, a comprehensive document was ready in July 1965 at precisely the time of change of leadership. Called *Putting Britain right ahead*, it was to be published for the party conference in October.

The manifesto embodied a clear departure from the paternalistic progressivism of 1959–63. It did so both in what it said and in what it did not say. Positively the manifesto reemphasised 'setting the people free'. The main themes were: lower direct taxation; less governmental interference; reduction in public expenditure; selectivity in the social services and a shift of the burden from the Treasury to the employers; legislation to restrain the power of the unions; and entry into the EEC. Negatively its message was no less important; it said little or nothing about an incomes policy or a national economic plan. The document reflected Heath's belief which was shared by a great many Conservative MPs of his generation and younger – in particular the 1959 entry – that no country can flourish if it does not encourage personal initiative, individuality and self-help. 'It was in freedom not reliance on the State that Britain achieved greatness,' he said on one occasion. He was not an all-out *laissez-faire* advocate, like Enoch Powell, but he certainly thought that the frontiers of the State, as they were currently drawn, should be pushed back. The question of just how far back has vexed the Conservative party from that day to this.

He also believed, as Harold Wilson did, that Britain needed to be jerked out of the lethargy which seemed to have blighted the country's industrial performance and to be putting it ever further behind in the European league table. But, whereas Wilson saw the answer in terms of collectivism – more efficient and purposeful guidance and direction by the State – Heath saw it in terms of freedom for individuals to pursue their own economic advancement. This would produce an expanding economy with benefits for everyone and an even higher safety net for the poor, the deprived and the unfortunate. It was a clear ideological cleavage. Long before 1970 Butskellism, if it had ever existed, was dead, and party politics had become polarised to a degree unknown since 1945.

There is little in all of this with which Margaret Thatcher would have quarrelled ten years later. Her own programme after 1975 was no doubt presented in a different style with more emphasis on general Conservative 'philosophy' – a concept which did not appeal to Heath who preferred to spell out specific policies on specific issues. But the content and theme were very similar. Both leaders were ideologists in a sense that none of their four post-war predecessors were. The key to the leadership crisis of 1975 does not lie in Heath's programme before 1970, but in his performance afterwards.

The Conservative defeat of 1964 was followed by some important changes in the personnel and structure of the party organisation, most of which were made by Home before Heath had become leader. Martin Redmayne, who had incurred a good deal of criticism, was replaced as Chief Whip by Willie Whitelaw who proved to be much better at the job. Lord Blakenham was replaced as chairman by Edward du Cann early in 1965, and Butler at the end of 1964 was persuaded to retire from the post of Chairman of the Conservative Research Department which he had held since 1945. The position was a quasi-independent one which provided its incumbent with a potential power base. It could be a challenge to the chairman of the party or even to the leader himself. Poole had considered centralisation in the 1950s but abandoned the idea because of possible offence to a major Conservative figure. Butler, however, had had enough of politics, and, on Harold Wilson's recommendation, became Master of Trinity College, Cambridge (a Crown appointment), and a member, as a life peer, of the House of Lords where he sat on the cross benches. The post was not filled for the time being, and Sir Michael (later Lord) Fraser, the Director of the Research Department, was appointed Deputy Chairman of the Party with a new Director,

Brendan Sewill, under him. Michael Fraser, who will, when the full story is written, go down to history as a figure comparable only to Gorst under Disraeli or the famous Captain Middleton under 'Salisbury, now became the lynch pin of the party organisation. He was its top administrator servicing the Shadow Cabinet rather as the real Cabinet is served by its Secretary, and he was also given a special responsibility for the Research Department. It was also his job to coordinate the activities of the Central Office and the parliamentary party. A long overdue cohesion was thus achieved.

There was only one snag in the new arrangements. Du Cann had been appointed by Home, and, for whatever reason, did not enjoy harmonious relations with Home's successor. It is hard to see why. A young man – the youngest to hold the post – he had already made his own way in the world of the City and politics. He seemed the sort of person to appeal to the new leader. He worked assiduously, effectively and at considerable financial sacrifice for the party. It was perhaps natural that Heath would want 'his own man' in such a key position, but there must have been more to the discord than that or even the fact that du Cann had voted for Maudling. In 1967 du Cann resigned. He was to be a leading supporter of Margaret Thatcher eight years later. He was replaced by Anthony Barber who also proved to be an able chairman.

Heath's election as leader made a good impression at first on the public. In August 1965 he was actually ahead of Wilson in the opinion polls, though never again. Thereafter his rating fell. He was not very good in the House. His gift was clear exposition of detail – no asset in opposition. He had a respectable front bench. Home accepted with characteristic magnanimity the job of Shadow Foreign Secretary, Macleod that of Shadow Chancellor of the Exchequer, and Powell Shadow Minister of Defence. But the team was up against difficulties from the start. After the initial economic crisis Labour seemed to have turned the corner; its small majority precluded the thorough-going socialist policies which would have been a liability; and then, inopportunely for the Conservatives, the Rhodesian Declaration of Independence and the question of sanctions came up in November – an issue on which the party was split three ways between the right wing who sympathised with the settlers, the left who wanted a tough line to be taken with 'rebels', and the centre who, though disapproving of Ian Smith, did not want to be too severe over sanctions. Heath found it impossible to keep a united front, and Wilson gained prestige by his non-partisan handling of the situation. In general he made rings round Heath as easily as he had round Home.

On 28 February 1966 he announced that there would be an election on 31 March. There was little doubt about the outcome. Labour began the campaign, which was rather dull on both sides, with a six-point lead in the opinion polls. In the end there was a national swing of 3.5 per cent to Labour. The figures were: Labour 363 with 47.9 per cent of the vote; Conservatives 253 with 41.9 per cent; Liberals 12 with 8.5 per cent. It was and remains the Conservatives' worst performance since 1945, but no one was inclined to blame Heath who conceded defeat with dignity after fighting as good a campaign as could be expected. For there was no real answer to two questions: if the panaceas in *Putting Britain right ahead* were the correct answers to Britain's malaise, why did the Conservatives do so little about them when in office, and, if after thirteen years the Conservatives left the country in a parlous state, why deny Labour a chance to carry out their programme when they had been in office for little over thirteen months? There were some Conservatives who wondered, after Heath's poor performance in the House and his slump in popularity, whether it had been wise, after all, to press for Home's resignation, but there could be no question of reviving the leadership controversy at this stage. Clearly those who thought that they had elected a second Wilson to cope in debate with the first Wilson were wrong, but they could now only let events take their course.

Events did; for nearly three years they were almost wholly disastrous for Labour. It was clear very soon after the election that Britain, as one economic crisis succeeded another, had not turned the corner. The Conservatives shot up in the opinion polls by huge figures and won by-election after by-election. In 1967 Wilson's insistence on preserving the value of sterling, a position incidentally shared by Heath, was defeated by reality (why do countries regard their currencies as a symbol of *machismo*?). Sterling was devalued, and Wilson made an imprudent comment about 'the pound in your pocket' not being devalued.

Meanwhile the new professionalism of the party organisation resulted, under Michael Fraser, in a far more scientific investigation of voting attitudes than had been hitherto undertaken by any party. The conclusion was that the accepted stereotype of two monolithic blocs competing for a small middle-of-the-road floating vote was no longer correct. There was now much more volatility among the electorate than hitherto appreciated. It seemed possible to identify a 'target voter', in the jargon of the time – a group of up to 14 per cent of the total who were 'weak' Conservatives, 'weak' Labour, or 'weak' Liberals, or had no party preference at all. The target vote was analysed as being fairly young, slightly inclined to Labour, largely belonging to the skilled working class, primarily concerned with problems of housing, coloured immigration, and the economy (prices and costs) rather than the condition of old-age pensioners. Only one in six was bothered about international affairs. The researchers discounted the very big pro-Conservative swings in by-elections and opinion polls but assessed that the party by April 1970 had a 10 per cent lead on voting intention which could in practice for various reasons be reduced to 4 per cent at an election – a remarkably accurate prediction of what happened two months later. The survey did not alter the policies laid down in 1964–5 but it had an important effect on presentation and electioneering technique. Some seventy Labour marginal seats were selected for special attention, and in the event sixty-four of them were gained. The analysis also had a valuable side-effect. Just as it discounted startling pro-Conservative swings in the opinion polls, so too it encouraged Heath and the party managers not to be shaken by the sudden swing the other way, which occurred in the early months of 1970. Michael Fraser continued to predict a Conservative win by between 30 and 40 seats, and Heath remained, except for one brief moment, confident of victory.

Meanwhile a curious flurry in the course of the party's history has to be mentioned. This was the dismissal of Enoch Powell from the Shadow Cabinet – an episode which seemed much more portentous then than in retrospect. The Conservative attitude to coloured immigration was ambivalent. Macmillan's Act of 1962 had worried the 'liberals' and by its inept timing actually made the problem worse. In 1968 James Callaghan, the Home Secretary, brought in a highly restrictive Bill to deal with the possibility of mass Asian immigration by British passport holders threatened with racialist legislation in Kenya and Uganda – two countries whose illiberal practices contradicted their liberal professions at the time of independence. The Bill undoubtedly went back on previous promises, but Heath felt obliged to support it in view of the strong feelings in the rank and file of the party. Macleod, his biographer Nigel Fisher, and thirteen other Conservatives voted against it. Macleod evidently had tacit permission to do so.

The Bill was closely followed by another, the Race Relations Bill. The Shadow Cabinet decided not to oppose it but to move a 'reasoned amendment' expressing support for its objectives but fear that an attempt to outlaw racial discrimination would do more harm than good. At this juncture on 20 April Powell made a speech at Birmingham which became famous or notorious according to taste. The Bill, he said, was like 'putting a match to gunpowder'. He used lurid language:

We must be mad, literally mad, as a nation to be permitting the annual inflow of some 50,000 dependants who are for the most part the material of the future growth of the immigrant population. It is like watching a nation busily engaged in heaping up its own funeral pyre ... As I look ahead I am filled with foreboding. Like the Roman I seem to see 'the River Tiber foaming with much blood'. That tragic and intractable phenomenon which we watch with horror on the other side of the Atlantic, but which there is interwoven with the history and existence of the States itself, is coming upon us here by our own volition and our own neglect.

These words, along with other allegations of even more sweeping nature produced a tremendous furore. The speech was varyingly regarded as an irrevocable blow to racial harmony or a catalyst for freedom to discuss openly a subject hitherto swept under the carpet. The 'classes', to use the categorisation of the 3rd Marquis of Salisbury, were shocked, but the 'masses' were delighted. Five thousand dockers went on strike to demonstrate support for Powell who received no less than 110,000 letters, the vast majority strongly in his favour. Heath was outraged. Denouncing the speech as 'racialist in tone', he promptly and curtly, though 'with great regret', dismissed Powell from the Shadow Cabinet. One may wonder how great the regret really was. Powell had become something of an embarrassment. There was his espousal of extreme *laissez-faire* economics; there was his contempt for incomes policies and planning; there was his scepticism about the value of the Commonwealth (itself a factor in the Birmingham speech). Finally there was his strong hostility to an east of Suez defence policy – a matter on which he thought he had Heath's backing till the latter without consulting him expressed the contrary view. Powell too may not have minded the parting of the ways. He had become increasingly disenchanted with his leader.

Nevertheless Heath, if in one sense relieved, remained under pressure. Although most members of the parliamentary party did not support Powell, a great many people in the constituency organisations did. Like Rhodesia it was a divisive issue. Powell had not departed from official Conservative policy, whatever his 'tone' may have been. Yet Heath allowed another member of the Shadow Cabinet, Edward Boyle, to vote in favour of the Labour Bill – which was certainly contrary to policy. There was talk at the time of an alliance between Powell and the newly resurgent Monday Club. Powell, who was and is a marvellous orator with a command of language seldom rivalled in modern public life, seemed a possible contender for the leadership, but nothing came of it. He was too idiosyncratic. He never joined the Monday Club and many of his ideas clashed with theirs. Nevertheless the effect of the rumpus was to edge Heath and the party appreciably further to the right. It was significant that one of the most prominent figures on the 'liberal' side of the party, Edward Boyle, withdrew from politics early in 1970 to become Vice-Chancellor of Leeds University. Education, of which he was Shadow Minister, had become a controversial issue within the party and he was not prepared to accept the right's blanket support of grammar schools and condemnation of comprehensives.

At about this time the opinion polls suddenly began to show a slump in the hitherto long Conservative lead. When this turned into an actual Labour lead in May, Wilson decided to hold an election on 18 June. He believed that the well publicised Shadow Cabinet at Selsdon Park had damaged the Conservative image and that this was the moment to strike. Wilson was probably wrong about 'Selsdon Man'. The emphasis on tax cuts, selectivity in social services and above all on law and order did the Conservatives good rather than harm. But of course there were other elements in his calculation. The pollsters had correctly predicted the winners, though not their exact majorities, in almost every post-war general election. So it was not unreasonable to expect a repetition. However, for reasons that have never been satisfactorily explained, on this occasion the polls were wrong, with one last-minute exception, ORC (Opinion Research Centre) which gave the Conservatives a 1 per cent lead on 17 June, the day before the election; the others put Labour ahead by figures varying from 2 to 8½ points. In the event Heath won with a 4.8 per cent swing from Labour, and an overall majority in the House of 30. Michael Fraser's prediction was confirmed and Heath's consistent confidence and courage were vindicated. The result was a profound shock to Wilson and his colleagues, and a surprise not only to most political commentators, but a great many Conservatives too. They had been whistling to keep their spirits up but few were at heart at all confident of victory. Heath, one of the exceptions, thus had a strong position on the morrow of the election.

The pollsters tried to argue that there had been a last-minute swing, possibly caused by the late publication of unexpectedly high unemployment figures and the announcement on 15 June of a trade deficit of £31 million. This theory has been discounted by most of those who later analysed the figures. It seems more likely that the Conservatives had been gaining their 'target vote' ever since 1966.[1] The Labour party was generally regarded as having conducted an inept campaign, and Wilson seemed tired. He showed the strain of six years as Prime Minister and his contemptuous attitude to Heath, shared by most of the Labour party, led him to underestimate his opponent. Heath lacked warmth but he showed himself vigorous and resourceful in attack, and the Conservative campaign was far better organised than Labour's. How much difference the leaders and their campaigners made, it is hard to say. But one not very attractive factor may have helped the Conservatives. Whereas Labour regarded Heath with condescending superiority, he and his followers regarded Wilson with positive hatred. One would have to go back to the days of Lloyd George or even Gladstone to find a similar Tory *bête noire*. Increasing dislike of Wilson together with rising prices and a seemingly endless series of financial and economic crises may well explain the conversion of the target voter and the vigour of the Conservative constituency organisations in exploiting it.

One subject which caused much discussion at the time was the effect of Enoch Powell. He issued a personal manifesto in the form of his election address on 30 May. He identified three great threats to Britain; socialism, the Common Market and immigration. All good Tories could agree on the first. Since entry into the Common Market was the official policy of all three parties at that time, the second played little part in the campaign. Immigration was a different matter. No one can be sure of his impact. He must have alienated immigrants, but it could be argued that immigrants would vote Labour anyway. He certainly embarrassed the Tory leadership at an awkward moment. On the other hand in the Midlands, where immigration was largely concentrated, some of the constituencies in which Powell spoke, including his own Wolverhampton North West, registered a far higher than average pro-Conservative

[1] See Robert Rhodes James, *Ambitions and realities* (1972), 272–5, analysing the figure in Banbury.

movement. Yet overall the Midland region displayed only marginally more support for the Conservatives than the country as a whole, and in some Midland constituencies where the immigration issue might have been expected to be significant the swing to the Conservatives was much lower than average. In one or two there was even a swing to Labour. On the face of it Powell's manifesto and rhetoric would seem to have had a neutral effect, but the fact remains that immigration was one of the issues which most worried the target voter. Powellism may have had an effect which cannot be statistically demonstrated. We will never know. What we do know is that Powell and his supporters believed that his campaign was a major element in the Conservatives' success.

2

To put into historical perspective a premiership which ended as recently as 1974 and was one of the most controversial in Conservative party history since that of Peel cannot be easy. Government and party papers are not available. There have been scarcely any diaries or memoirs published about the period; Conservatives tend to be more discreet than their opposite numbers; most of the key figures are alive at the time of writing (1984) and many of them are still active in politics. It is generally agreed that Heath's tenure of office was not a success. For that reason, like Balfour and Eden, he will probably never occupy a very high place in the Conservative pantheon, but the apportionment of responsibility between him, his colleagues, the Opposition, external events and sheer bad luck will long be disputed.

As has already been said, the statements of policy which the party put forward at the election were not very different from those of Margaret Thatcher nine years later. Heath wanted, so he said at the October Conference of 1970, 'to embark on a change so radical, a revolution so quiet and so total that it will go far beyond the programme of a Parliament . . . We were returned to office to change the course and the history of this nation, nothing less.' In 1983 Margaret Thatcher, commenting on the 1979 election, said: 'We offered a complete change of direction – from one in which the state became totally dominant in people's lives . . . to a life where the state did do certain things but without displacing personal responsibility.' Both leaders were saying that collectivism had gone too far. Both were repudiating the consensus of the fifties and sixties.

There was, however, an important difference in their situations. Heath did not have what Margaret Thatcher had – the backing of an intellectual revolution. This only occurred after the failures of 1974 when the views of a group of Conservative thinkers from the universities became increasingly articulate.[1] It is worth quoting Robert Rhodes James who was writing immediately after the 1970 general election and with no benefit of hindsight:

> Another disturbing trend has been towards what must be described as the revival of 'anti-intellectualism' in the Conservative Party. The Party, no less than the country, requires men and women of first-class brains, not necessarily as candidates or MPs but involved in its activities. It is a striking feature of British politics in the 1960s that, with few exceptions, the Conservative Party failed to attract many people of this calibre; even more alarming, from the Conservative point of view, is the fact that many have been positively alienated.

He goes on to contrast the situation in the late 1940s and early 1950s – 'a distinct movement to the party in the universities and the remarkable popular success of the Young Conservatives'. He adds: 'Conservative suspicions of "intellectuals" and "the intelligentsia" places it in danger of forfeiting not only much goodwill but also much ability.'[2] Anyone who lived in the university world from the late 1940s to the end of the 1970s will endorse this argument and appreciate what the author of course could not foresee – the drastic change which was to occur only a few years later. Neither Heath nor Margaret Thatcher is an

[1] See below, pp. 321–3.
[2] op cit., 290–1.

'intellectual', and they would not describe themselves as such, but Margaret Thatcher had the advantage of an intellectual tide which was and still is flowing in her favour. Heath lacked this asset. If I may quote myself:

> The outlook of commentators, economists, intellectuals, journalists – the opinion formers in general – was anti-Conservative. The accepted philosophy was still *dirigiste*. Planning, high public expenditure, high taxation, a rising role for the state remained the accepted shibboleths, however doubtful some people may have become about their practical manifestations during the chaotic last years of Harold Wilson's first administration. There was no serious challenge in intellectual circles to this orthodoxy. The Conservatives did not win the election because they had won 'the battle for the mind', rather because of a general discontent about high prices and sheer governmental incompetence.[1]

Heath formed his government on predictable lines. Sir Alec Douglas-Home returned to the Foreign Office. Iain Macleod became Chancellor of the Exchequer and Reginald Maudling Home Secretary. Defence went to Lord Carrington, Health to Sir Keith Joseph, Education to Margaret Thatcher. Quintin Hogg was made Lord Chancellor and became Lord Hailsham for the second time.[2] Willie Whitelaw, who had been a highly successful Chief Whip, was appointed Leader of the House of Commons.

The government and party sustained a heavy blow at the very beginning. On 20 July Iain Macleod suddenly died from a heart attack after an operation for appendicitis. The party lost its greatest orator and its most charismatic personality. He had invested the humdrum processes of politics with a colour, warmth and wit which no one in the front bench could rival. There were those who maintained that the government never

---

[1] Lord Blake and John Patten (eds.), *The Conservative opportunity* (1976), 2.
[2] He had succeeded to his father's peerage as Viscount Hailsham in 1950, disclaimed it in 1963, and now became a life peer (baron) as Lord Hailsham of St Marylebone. The Earl of Home went through a similar metamorphosis becoming a life peer in 1974 as Lord Home of the Hirsel.

recovered from this blow. He could be replaced as Chancellor of the Exchequer, for he was never much at ease in matters of finance and economics. What could not be replaced was his feel for public opinion, his tactical skill and his shrewd political advice. If he had lived, the government might not have made the blunders which brought it down in 1974.

The new Chancellor of the Exchequer was Anthony Barber who had previously been given the task of negotiating Britain's entry into the EEC. His place was now taken by Geoffrey Rippon who was to play a crucial part in what Heath later regarded as the most important achievement of his government – the reversal of the rebuff delivered to Macmillan by de Gaulle in 1963. Despite the tragedy of Macleod's death, the morale of the party remained high. It had come in on a programme of libertarianism, lower direct taxation, reduction of trade union power, support for law and order, selectivity in social services and minimal state intervention in industry. It was pledged to abolish the Labour-created Land Commission, Industrial Reorganisation Corporation and Prices and Incomes Board. This can be seen in retrospect as a highly 'Thatcherite' platform, and Heath at once set about implementing it. More interested than most Prime Ministers in administrative reform, he was also keen to change Whitehall procedure and reorganise the judiciary, local government and the national health system.

He got off to a good start. The Queen's Speech in July announced many of these measures, and the principal Labour 'quangos' either had been or were about to be wound up by the end of the year. In October Barber's 'mini-Budget' cut income tax by sixpence and corporation tax by 2½ per cent. The reductions were balanced either by cuts in some of the social services or by increased charges. There was to be no question of a wages policy, or of intervention to help industrial companies that got into trouble. John Davies, Minister for Trade and Industry, said in a speech at the October party conference, 'I will not bolster or bail out companies where I can see no end to the process of propping them up', and in November during a debate in the House on public expenditure he declared: 'We believe that the essential need of the country is to gear its policies to the great majority of the people who are not lame ducks.'

He had scarcely spoken these words when the Aviation Minister announced that the government would lend £42 million to Rolls-Royce which was in financial trouble. Early in 1971 the firm went bankrupt, and the government brought in an emergency Bill to nationalise its aero-engine division. These actions from an administration pledged to leave lame ducks alone and reduce public ownership caused consternation among the party faithful. It was all very well for the Prime Minister to say on 7 February: 'Governments must rid themselves of the illusion that you can find the way to prosperity by pouring out the taxpayer's money on perpetual subsidies for uneconomic ventures.' What else were they doing? And the *volte face* was emphasised by the government reversing its decision to cut subsidies to the Upper Clyde Shipbuilders whose militant workers had occupied the yards.

If this was a U turn, at least the government did not go back on its promise to reform the law about the trade unions. The Industrial Relations Bill introduced early in 1971 contained a number of provisions which curbed the unions' powers. Agreements between employers and workers were to be legally enforceable. The closed shop was to be banned. A special Industrial Court was set up to try cases arising under the Act, its President being Sir John Donaldson, later Master of the Rolls. Among other powers, it could order a sixty-day 'cooling-off period', if it thought a dispute dangerous to the national interest, and insist on a secret ballot before a strike was called. These and other provisions infuriated the unions. In fact they were very similar to measures which the Labour government would have liked to carry in 1969 but called off under union pressure. This did not of course stop the Labour leadership from opposing the new Bill with all the strength at its command. Seldom has the confrontational aspect of British politics appeared in a worse light. The Bill became law on 6 August after 450 hours of parliamentary time.[1]

The government soon ran into trouble over enforcing the Act,

[1] Lindsay and Harrington, op. cit., 267.

but, even before that, they received a major setback from the coalminers' union. This had nothing to do with the new legislation. It was a straight strike for higher wages, and the miners who in those days had considerable public support – their work was hard and their wages had fallen relatively to others – won easily by picketing the power stations. An inquiry by Lord Wilberforce on 18 February conceded most of the miners' case. It was a heavy blow to the policy of controlling inflation. There followed a series of legal disputes arising from the Industrial Relations Act. These which were sometimes farcical involved a battle with the dockers and the railwaymen. There were two cases in June and July where dockers were jailed or threatened with jail for contempt of the Industrial Court. The government was by now anxious to secure union cooperation. The last thing it wanted was union martyrdom. Whether by luck, or something more, a mysterious figure called the Official Solicitor suddenly emerged and appealed successfully against both of Sir John Donaldson's decisions; he thus got ministers off the hook – temporarily.

By early 1972 unemployment had passed the million mark and there was still no sign of the rise in industrial investment which the government optimistically expected to follow the tax concessions in Barber's budgets although they had not been very generous. To the outside observer – and one must emphasise the lack of inside knowledge – it looked as if Heath and his colleagues lost their nerve at about this time even as Macmillan had in 1962. They seem to have decided that 'Selsdon' would no longer do, and that their 1970 manifesto was impracticable. Margaret Thatcher's refusal to do the same thing in 1981 was the biggest contrast between her and her administration. Heath now embarked on a policy of humouring instead of cold-shouldering the unions in order to secure an agreement to limit price and wage increases. It was hoped that this would reflate the economy without debasing the currency, and thus secure fuller employment and higher economic growth. Barber's budget on 21 March 1972 cut taxes and increased public expenditure – perhaps the last Keynesian 'fling' by the Treasury. It was followed by the establishment of an Industrial Development Executive with the power to pump public money into industry. Compulsory wage controls were introduced in November. Early in January 1973 Phase Two of this counter-inflationary policy was announced, to be followed by Phase Three in November. A Pay Board and a Prices Commission were to be set up.

This announcement merely confirmed what was already obvious – the total reversal of the policies propounded before the 1970 election. There is of course an argument for accepting reality. As someone said at the time, if you are driving along a mountainous road and suddenly encounter a landslide, the case for a U turn, if there is room to execute it, cannot be denied. But the analogy was hardly fair. There was no specific intervening event which unpredictably caused this *volte face* to be necessary. True, the Egyptian-Israeli War of October 1973 made things much worse, but, well before then, the government had already gone back on nearly everything it had stood for in the field of economic management. It seemed to have returned to just the sort of 'corporatism' which Conservatives had been first repudiating for themselves, then condemning in Labour during the 1960s.

Nor were there notable successes in other areas to offset this general sense of let-down. Britain's decision to enter the EEC was carried in Parliament in 1971 and accepted by the Community in 1973. This was certainly an important event but it rang no vibrant bell in the public ear. The reforms of local government, the judiciary and the health service were equally uninspiring to the party's grass roots; the abolition of the old order in local government made far more enemies than friends and proved immensely expensive, as many people predicted. By the autumn of 1973 the government seemed to be animated by technocratic *ad hoc* expediency rather than by ideas, or principles.

Then came a double blow in October; first the Yom Kippur War which produced a gigantic rise in oil prices, the main cause of the ensuing worldwide economic recession; and then the second miners' strike which, it is claimed, 'brought down the government'. That claim can be disputed; the Prime Minister was in a very difficult situation, but he might have played his cards differently. The Coal Board foolishly offered a rise of pay which was so high that it left no margin for bargaining. The miners (NUM) stuck out for more at a moment of acute fuel shortage. This was blackmail, but blackmail that could perhaps have been defeated by different tactics. There was admittedly a major industrial and domestic crisis – power cuts in home and factories – and Labour supported, as it had all along, every union move, though some of its members wondered about how they would react, if in office, to a similar confrontation.

But public opinion was by no means all on the Labour side. If Heath had called the election earlier, as some of his colleagues advised, he might have won on a programme of 'Who governs Britain?' Having missed that option, he could have supported a case for special concessions to the miners in view of the oil crisis and a plausible if specious offer by the TUC. He could have postponed the election till as late as June 1975.

On 7 February, however, he announced to a shivering and darkened public that an election would be held three weeks later. He made that very day a promise which many believe to have been fatal – a special investigation into wage relativities by the Pay Board. This was bound to help the NUM. Why in that case have an election at all? The public, insofar as one can judge, was bewildered and confused. The coal strike was not the only issue. High prices, a huge rise in land values, an alarming trade gap, were no less important. Enoch Powell refused to stand, denounced the election as a fraud and said he would vote Labour since they were prepared, after another quick reversal of policy, to hold a referendum on entry into the EEC. The Conservatives had a further setback when the Director-General of the CBI denounced the Industrial Relations Act. The election resulted in Labour obtaining 310 seats on a slightly lower popular vote than the Conservatives who got 296. The Liberals won 14, the Scottish and Welsh Nationalists 7 and 2 respectively. The Ulster Unionists, who had broken with the Conservatives because of the abolition of Stormont, won 11 seats.

There was no majority for any party, and this ambiguous

situation made it legitimate for the Prime Minister to stay in
office and see if he could obtain some kind of coalition. His
overtures to the Liberals failed on the question of proportional
representation; even if they had succeeded, 310 seats were not
a majority. Heath resigned on 4 March, and Wilson formed his
second administration. Clearly it would not be long before he
went to the polls. On 18 October there was a second general
election. Wilson was expected to win but his victory was far
from overwhelming: 319 to the Conservatives' 277. There were
13 Liberals, 11 Scottish and 3 Welsh Nationalists. There were
12 Ulster Members, mostly Unionists – among them,
unexpectedly, Enoch Powell. Wilson's overall majority was
only 3.

3

Edward Heath had lost three out of four elections within nine
years. Gone were the days when Lord Derby could be defeated
five times in succession and remain unchallenged as leader.
There was bound to be a question mark over Heath's future. On
14 October, four days after the election, the executive of the
1922 Committee whose chairman was Edward du Cann, agreed
that if Heath did not as they hoped resign, there must be a
fresh election for the leadership. It was unfortunate that du
Cann had to convey this message to Heath, for their relations
had been cool ever since du Cann's resignation as Party
Chairman in 1967. Moreover there were rumours that du
Cann intended to run for the party leadership himself. Heath
refused to discuss the matter till the 1922 Committee had
held their elections for the executive, which were due on 3
November.

These were a trial of strength and the members of the existing executive were re-elected to a man, defeating the pro-Heath
slate. Their victory was a set-back for Heath. It could no longer
be argued that he was the victim of an unrepresentative faction.
Under the current rules the leader, once chosen, did not have to
submit himself for re-election at any particular time or indeed
ever. Although Heath had no intention of 'going quietly' like

Balfour and Sir Alec Douglas-Home, he recognised that he must face an election, or else his position would be impossible. On 14 November, declaring that he was the 'Servant of the Party', he agreed to an election after the rules had been revised, as general opinion seemed to require. For the second time Sir Alec Douglas-Home (now Lord Home of the Hirsel) presided over a committee to deal with the matter. The new rules were promulgated early in January 1975 and promptly accepted.

There were important changes from the 1965 procedure. In future the leader would be elected annually. As before, the electorate would be the parliamentary party which would receive, though in no way be bound by, the opinions of the peers and the party in the country. But instead of the winner needing an overall majority of 15 per cent of those actually voting in the first ballot, he would need the same percentage of those entitled to vote – a stiffer hurdle. If this figure was not achieved on the first ballot, there would be a second ballot a week later. The winner would only need a simple majority over the combined votes of his opponents, but, unlike the previous procedure, the second ballot would be open to entry by candidates who had not stood in the first. Constitutions are seldom constructed on abstract principles. One can guess that this was a device to enable a pro-Heath candidate who would not wish to challenge Heath on the first ballot to make a bid in the second if Heath was defeated. If the second ballot was inconclusive there was to be a third which would be a run-off between the first three candidates under the method of the Single Transferable Vote. This must produce an absolute majority for the winner. It was agreed to hold the first ballot on 4 February 1975 and the second if necessary on 11 February.

The great question now was who would stand against Heath. If he had resigned, his obvious successor would have been Whitelaw who would almost certainly have won on the first ballot. But, displaying the loyalty which has always been one of his most engaging features, he was not prepared to fight against someone with whom he had worked so closely and for so long. Of the anti-Heath party the two names most widely spoken of were Edward du Cann and Sir Keith Joseph. The former decided for personal reasons not to be a runner. Sir Keith Joseph was the figure who most clearly posed an ideological as well as a personal challenge. In a number of speeches between the two elections he argued that the Conservative party had lost its way in the last four years, had deviated from the programmes put forward in 1966 and 1970, and had forgotten the case for monetary control, the free market economy, and the cuts in public expenditure, substituting the false gods of governmental intervention and prices and incomes control – a policy scarcely distinguishable from the policies of Wilson and Callaghan. 'It was only in April 1974', he said, 'that I was converted to Conservatism. I had thought that I was a Conservative but now I see that I was not one at all'[1] – a remarkable statement from a man who had adhered to the Conservative party for most of his life, had held high office for several years, first entering the Cabinet in 1962, and had never shown any signs of dissent during the Heath administration.

Sir Keith Joseph was a man of some wealth, son of a Lord Mayor of London and the second Baronet. He was educated at Harrow and Magdalen, and became a Fellow of All Souls. He had a distinguished and courageous war record. He was a highly sensitive intellectual concerned deeply – perhaps too deeply – with Conservative ideology. His effect on the new course which the party was about to steer is difficult to assess, but there is no reason to doubt the claim – made by others, not by him – that his arguments greatly influenced Margaret Thatcher. In the end he decided not to stand. He had made a speech in October in which he seemed to be suggesting that special provisions for contraception ought to be made for girls of the lower socio-economic groups in order to prevent the cycle of poverty and deprivation being perpetuated. It was not the only occasion when he had made observations that caused embarrassment.

Sir Keith's withdrawal in October 1974 resulted in the candidature of Margaret Thatcher whom he fully supported and who had associated herself with him since April in criticising the party's conduct of affairs. Most people were surprised when she let her name go forward. She was not well

[1] K. S. Joseph (with J. Sumption), *Reversing the trend* (1974), 4.

known to the public and, although it was clear that she was on the right, she was not a thinker like Keith Joseph. She had never indicated any serious doubts about Conservative policy while she was in the Cabinet, but it is fair to say that the posts which each of them held were peripheral to the issues of economics, finance and industrial relations which had dominated the political scene. However, she soon showed herself well versed in these matters, and made a considerable impact in the House by hard-hitting attacks on the government's Finance Bill during the winter of 1974–5. Her campaign was skilfully managed by Airey Neave. There were three candidates on the first ballot: Edward Heath, Margaret Thatcher and Hugh Fraser who stood as a romantic figure of the old Tory right. To the amazement of the public and the press, Heath was defeated. The figures were Thatcher 130, Heath 119, Fraser 16; there were 12 abstentions. Heath at once resigned. Margaret Thatcher had not reached the figure required to win on the first ballot – 159 out of 277 – and a second had to be held. Whitelaw and three other newcomers entered the contest. The target figure was now 139. Mrs Thatcher was victorious, though not by much. She won 146 votes to Whitelaw's 79, 19 each to James Prior and Geoffrey Howe, and 16 to John Peyton. There were 2 abstentions. Mrs Thatcher had an overall majority of 16. On 11 February for the first time in British history a woman became leader of one of the great political parties.

4

Mrs Thatcher's victory was largely confined to the indisputable arithmetic of the parliamentary party vote. She was very much the beneficiary of the amended version of the system first introduced in 1965. She would not have won if the Lords had had any say in the matter, or if the Shadow Cabinet had decided the result, or if it had depended on the verdict of the constituency organisations. Opinion polls suggest that, although most voters thought Heath should go, there was overwhelming support for Whitelaw as his successor. She won because she was not Heath and because she was the only person to challenge him on the first ballot among an electorate far less favourably disposed to him than the other elements in the Conservative party. It is, however, by no means clear, though nothing can be proved, that this disfavour stemmed from a preference for her ideas to his. It may have done so to some extent, but desire for change, resentment at the aloofness[1] of the former leader and a feeling that he had become an electoral liability were probably the strongest motives.

Although the new leader in no way intended to backpedal, as far as her ideology was concerned, she kept most of Heath's former colleagues in the Shadow Cabinet. Heath himself refused an offer to join it, saying that he preferred to be free to speak from the back benches on 'the great issues of the day'. He no doubt had in mind among others the question of remaining in the EEC, on which Wilson had promised to hold a referendum. His refusal was probably a relief to all concerned and certainly was to his successor. It would have been more generous if he had followed the examples of Balfour in 1911 and Home in 1965. But the circumstances were not quite the same. Both of them had resigned to allow an election in which they did not intend to compete. Heath had fought an election as leader and lost it. Perhaps it would have been better if he too had resigned. But to serve under the person who had just deposed him was very difficult. It was not so much his refusal to join as his palpable and public resentment at the conduct of his successor, which damaged his reputation. As time went on he looked more and more like a 'bad loser'.

Margaret Thatcher kept the Shadow Cabinet much as it was. Peter Walker was excluded and Geoffrey Rippon, knowing that he would be, resigned in advance. But Reginald Maudling served for a time and James Prior, Lord Carrington and Ian Gilmour remained. So did the most important of all, Willie Whitelaw, the runner-up in the second ballot. They fully balanced any incipient swing to the right. Lord Hailsham, who cannot easily be categorised, also remained a member. The right comprised Keith Joseph, Angus

[1] Mrs Thatcher was far better on the personal side. She remembered people's names, even their wives, and would talk informally in the division lobbies and elsewhere in a way which gratified her supporters and made them feel that they mattered.

Maude, Airey Neave and Geoffrey Howe; there were many others who were more or less neutral. Mrs Thatcher was careful not to alienate Heath's supporters. He was shown in advance the new party document, *The right approach*, and commended it at the 1976 party conference. The front bench did not oppose the rescue of British Leyland or the government's £6 pay limit. The new leader adopted a cautious attitude towards the unions and accepted James Prior's approach – or at any rate did not dissent from it. She was equally cautious over the EEC referendum. Although known to be unenthusiastic about Europe, she did not put any brake on the Conservative pro-marketeers in the referendum campaign which gave an overwhelming victory to those who wanted Britain to remain in the EEC.

Yet, although Margaret Thatcher was careful not to commit herself too far on specific policies, and although there was plenty of fine print in the party statements to reassure those who worried about such concepts as 'one nation', she did undoubtedly project a very different public image from her predecessor's. The tone and style marked a shift from con-sensualist centrism to something that has been described as the Radical Right; and this shift corresponded to a distinct change in the general climate of opinion on social and economic matters against 'big government', high spending, Keynesian economics and the more extravagant aspects of the welfare state. An important feature was repudiation of the 'middle ground'. The first prominent Conservative to do this was Bonar Law's son, Lord Coleraine, in a chapter entitled 'The myth of the middle ground' in his book *For Conservatives only* (1970), but the climate then was not propitious. The argument was sharpened by Sir Keith Joseph. He distinguished between 'common' ground and 'middle' ground. The former might cover proposals which a large number of voters from every party favoured, e.g. sale of council houses to tenants. The latter was merely the half-way house between Socialism and Conservatism. Whenever the Labour party was in office it gave a turn of the ratchet to socialism. Every time the Conservatives got back the middle ground had moved further to the left. In theory the Conservatives could have turned the ratchet their way. In practice loss of nerve, lack of confidence, absence of a clear ideology and fear of the electorate had made them merely react to the initiative of Labour rather than take it for themselves. This territorial analogy may well not stand up to philosophical examination, but it became a part of the political discourse of the time, and certainly influenced Margaret Thatcher. She was determined to turn the ratchet her way – and she has.

There was much intellectual ferment on the anti-socialist side. The Institute of Economic Affairs had for years been hammering at the alleged abuses of the welfare state. One of its leading figures, Ralph Harris, author of many books and pamphlets such as *Down with the poor* (1971), *Freedom of choice* (1976), *Not from benevolence* (1977) and *The coming confrontation* (1978), was to be made a life peer in Mrs Thatcher's first honours list. The view that public expenditure must be controlled and inflation eliminated or at least reduced by a curb on the monetary supply was supported vigorously by two high-powered non-Conservative journalists, Samuel Brittan in the *Financial Times* and Peter Jay in *The Times*. In the general field of economics as far as Conservative practitioners were concerned Adam Smith was 'in' and Keynes was 'out'. There was a widespread feeling that the state was playing too big a role. The economist John Redwood pointed out that in 1963 when public expenditure was 43 per cent of gross domestic product no one would have dreamed that it would rise to 60 per cent by 1975. 'If recent policies are extrapolated, the public sector will consume the whole of the gross national product before the end of this century.'[1] An important book on this subject appeared in 1976 – *Britain's economic problem: too few producers*. It was written by two Oxford economists – Robert Bacon and Walter Eltis – who argued that the rising amount of resources devoted to unmarketed goods and services as compared with those that were bought and sold was increasing inflation and unemployment while reducing investment and growth. The book was serialised in the *Sunday Times* and had much influence on Conservative policy-makers, although the

[1] Lord Blake and John Patten (eds.), op. cit., 76.

argument was far from being fully accepted by all or indeed most economists.

The most intractable problem for the Conservative party was what to do about the unions. There can be no doubt of the Conservatives' bitter hostility to the force that had, as they saw it, brought them down in 1974. That union power 'has increased, is increasing and ought to be diminished' was universally agreed. Even such a moderate Conservative as Sir Ian Gilmour made a devastating comparison of the inordinate power of the trade union movement with that of the medieval Church:[1]

> For some trade unions the picket line has become as sacred as any image or holy place. To join a picket line is as meritorious as going on a pilgrimage while in British life today the only mortal sin is to cross one. The ultimate sanction of trade unions like that of the Church is excommunication.[2]

But having made this interesting analysis Sir Ian seems to have been as much at a loss as anyone else about how to curb the powers and privileges which like almost every Conservative, and a great many non-Conservatives, he deplored. The party did not wish to burn its fingers. In the end there was commitment to postal strike ballots, limitation of picket rights and the reversal of some of the highly pro-union legislation passed by Labour after the October 1974 election, but no more than that.

Much of the Conservative approach from 1975 to 1979 was influenced by the belief that Labour had since the loss of the 1970 election moved strongly to the left. In opposition the language of some of the shadow ministers did sound like that, and the plans for nationalisation, change in labour law, and devolution foreshadowed during the short parliament of 1974 could be regarded as radical and were certainly provocative to most Conservatives. Moreover despite Labour's small majority the legislation was enacted, though, in the case of devolution,

[1] *Inside right* (1977), 237–8.
[2] ibid., 238.

the referendums in Scotland and Wales did not produce the result which Labour wanted. The threatened wealth tax and withdrawal of charitable status from the independent schools were not carried, but no Conservative believed that this failure stemmed from any change of heart. Nor did they regard the moves towards monetarism and the cuts in public expenditure which took place in 1976–7 as anything other than the price insisted upon by the International Monetary Fund as a condition for a huge loan to prevent the collapse of sterling.

The Conservatives believed that the government was carrying highly left-wing proposals on an exiguous parliamentary majority backed by only 39 per cent of those who voted in a low turnout. In order to retain office it had given in to the unions, and it was about to give in to the Scottish and Welsh nationalists. Scotland in particular was crucial to Labour. Without Scotland they would have lost the elections of 1964 and February 1974; and they might well in each case have lost the ensuing election too, for the timing would have been in their opponents' hands. At the back of many Conservative minds was the fear that if James Callaghan, who had succeeded Wilson in April 1976, could somehow carry on, despite perpetual economic crises, he would benefit from the coming surge of North Sea oil and win the next election which could be held as late as October 1979.

These considerations made constitutional matters unusually prominent during the 1974–9 parliament. The spectacle of radical measures being carried on the basis of a minority popular vote produced two reactions. Margaret Thatcher's was to concentrate on winning the next election with a clear majority in the House. She could then reverse Labour's policies and set out on her new course. If she won, as Wilson had, on a minority of the popular vote, that was one of the rules of the game. No party since 1935 had won over half. Although 39 per cent was exceptionally low, she was not prepared to make it a reason for changing the rules.

The other reaction was to do just this. In his book *The dilemma of democracy* (1978), Lord Hailsham, following his celebrated Dimbleby Lecture, raised the whole question of the sovereignty

of Parliament. Was Britain becoming what he called an 'elective
dictatorship'? Ought the case for a 'written constitution' to be
reconsidered? Should there be a Bill of Rights and, if so, should
it be entrenched so that a simple majority of the House of
Commons could not destroy it? Another possibility, though
Lord Hailsham was not in favour, was to change the voting
system. The unofficial Hansard Society Committee, chaired by
the author, produced a much publicised report in June 1976
commending proportional representation on the lines of an
amended version of the system in the Federal Republic of West
Germany.[1] Such a change would at least prevent Labour
securing full power on a vote which could be even lower than
the October 1974 figure. In 1977 the National Campaign for
Electoral Reform was launched with much Conservative as well
as non-party support. There was already a body called CAER
(Conservative Action for Electoral Reform). In 1978 the
Confederation of British Industries which was in general pro-
Conservative endorsed the concept, and on 1 March that year
as many as a third of the Conservative MPs voted for
proportional representation in the proposed Welsh Assembly.

Mrs Thatcher viewed this trend with disfavour accentuated
by the Lib/Lab pact of March 1977. Just at a moment when it
seemed possible after repeated Labour by-election losses to
defeat the Government on a vote of confidence, James
Callaghan did a deal with the new Liberal leader, David Steel.[2]
Neither could afford an election. Labour stood very low in the
opinion polls, and the Liberals were reeling from the effects of
their ex-leader Jeremy Thorpe's alleged involvement with a
male model, Norman Scott, which received wide publicity and
caused his resignation.[3] The deal which was far more favourable
to Callaghan than Steel confirmed the Conservative leader's
instinct; PR would make such bargains a normal feature of
politics, and if the Liberals held the balance they would support

[1] *Report of the Hansard Society Commission on Electoral Reform* (1976).
[2] The leadership of all three parties had changed in seventeen months between 11
February 1975 and 7 July 1976.
[3] The matter came to a head in August 1978 when Thorpe and three other men were
charged *inter alia* with conspiracy to murder Scott. They were acquitted ten months
later on all charges but the facts that emerged in evidence irretrievably ruined Thorpe's
political career.

Labour, not the Conservatives. The Lib/Lab pact saved the Labour government for the moment, but Callaghan could not deliver what the Liberals really wanted – the pledge of a referendum on PR. On 25 May 1978 it was announced that the pact would end in August.

The change in the Conservative leadership had been followed by changes in the personnel of the party organisation. Whitelaw, chairman since June 1974, resigned. He was replaced in February 1975 by Lord Thorneycroft who remained in office till 1981 and was extremely effective, one of the most successful holders of the post since Lord Woolton. Michael Fraser was due to retire and departed in October. In April 1974 Heath had appointed his confidant and speech-writer Michael Wolff to the newly created post of Director-General, which was clearly intended to be the key position. Inevitably he was regarded as a committed Heathite. He could hardly have expected to survive for long, and, apart from other considerations, he did not achieve happy relations with Sir Richard Webster, Director of Organisation since 1966. Nevertheless his dismissal by Thorneycroft within a week of the latter's appointment caused a good deal of criticism. Webster himself, after disagreements with the chairman, left in 1976 and was replaced by Anthony Garner, the area agent for the North West, who has remained there ever since.

Thorneycroft was anything but a part-time chairman. He was much in demand as a constituency speaker and his advice on strategy and tactics carried great weight with the leader. His resignation in 1958 from the Chancellorship of the Exchequer on what would later be called 'monetarist' grounds gave him impeccable credentials. From 1977 he was helped by an important figure in the organisation, Baroness Young, who became deputy chairman till the election and was later to be Leader of the House of Lords. Thorneycroft made major changes in the financial affairs of the party, separating expenditure from fund-raising. He appointed Alistair McAlpine as joint Treasurer with Lord Ashdown (known in jest as 'Lord Cashdown') who had been appointed by Heath in April 1974. The drain on party funds caused by the two elections of 1974 had been considerable. In the year ending March 1975 there was a deficit of £1.2 million. But the situation was soon restored. There was a small surplus in 1976, and by 1979 it was clear that the party would not lose the election through lack of funds.

5

A party in opposition has to play a waiting game. The government may not be able to control the course of events, but it normally can at least choose what it thinks the best time for a general election. The Conservatives watched the polls which in early 1975 gave Labour a 10-point lead and yet in late 1976 gave an 18-point lead to their own party. They had to watch with the frustrating knowledge that there need be no election before the autumn of 1979. They remained ahead till late in 1978 when Labour took a narrow and, as it turned out, short-lived lead. The government was in dead trouble during 1976–7 with a major sterling crisis. Survival depended upon loans from the US and Western European banks, and from the International Monetary Fund. The conditions of the loans included a reduction in the public sector borrowing requirement (PSBR), cuts in the rise of public expenditure and in the printing of money. Possibly influenced by his son-in-law, Peter Jay, the Prime Minister at the Labour conference in September 1976 proclaimed the new doctrine with much emphasis. He overruled the alternative 'Fortress Britain' proposals of a group in the Cabinet headed by Tony Benn. Although it suited neither side to say so later, the 'monetarist' policy of Mrs Thatcher from 1979 onwards had ample precedent in that of Mr Callaghan after 1976.

Between the election of February 1974 and that of May 1979 the general index of retail prices more than doubled. Inflation on this scale was too injurious to be tolerated by any government, but Labour faced a major problem of relations with the unions. After the defeat of the Conservatives in 1974 Labour's great asset seemed to be their claim to work with the unions; and the public, influenced by a combination of dislike and fear for those increasingly unpopular organisations, regarded a Labour government as a safer alternative to confrontation. But how could IMF conditions be put across to the unions? In the end they could not, and the failure of the Cabinet's incomes policy, along with many other manifestations of industrial unrest, two of which involved calling in the army, undermined the credibility of the government. The 'winter of discontent' in 1978–9 was to be the last straw.

The pact with the Liberals had saved Labour in March 1977. If Mrs Thatcher had carried her no-confidence vote then, she would certainly have won the ensuing election. The pact ran out in July 1978. But by then the economic position had improved, North Sea oil was beginning to flow and prospects looked brighter. Most people expected an autumn election. Mr Callaghan, an avuncular, small 'c' conservative figure, had much going for him. He seemed more composed and calmer than Mrs Thatcher, more relaxed, less intense, less shrill. There has been much controversy over what would have happened if he had dissolved in October, but it seems that private polls conducted by Labour suggested a less favourable outlook than was generally believed by the public.[1] On 7 September he announced that there would be no election that year. He took most of the Cabinet by surprise and he had a bad reception from the broadcasters and journalists who felt that they had been led up the garden path. Many Labour officials and supporters were equally annoyed. The Conservatives were on balance pleased. Although the polls were marginally in their favour in September, they believed that the situation would be even better in 1979, and they were soon gratified by a major dispute at the Labour party conference which appeared to repudiate the government's main economic policies.

The Prime Minister probably reckoned, however, that the economic improvement which by October indicated a 6 per cent rise in the standard of living – the best for twenty years – would need time to impinge on public opinion. He may also have believed that the unions would accept his 5 per cent limit on

[1] David Butler and Dennis Kavanagh, *The British general election of 1979* (1980), 44–6.

incomes if only for fear of a Thatcher administration, and he must have been pleased by the palpable dissension in the Conservative party conference, at which wide publicity was given to the difference between Mr Heath's support for a statutory incomes policy and Mrs Thatcher's obvious scepticism. Although she agreed not to rule it out in the event of an emergency, the gap between her and her predecessor, delicately papered over in 1976, was now more obvious than ever; a disastrous by-election at Berwick together with further opinion poll reports implied that there was more public support for the Heath than the Thatcher approach. Then in November there was yet another intra-party row about the perenially divisive issue of Rhodesia. Sir John Biggs-Davison and Winston Churchill, the great man's grandson, were sacked from the front bench for voting along with 116 other Conservative MPs against the renewal of sanctions. At this stage the result of the next election looked wide open. Gallup gave the Conservatives a 5-point lead, NOP 1-point and MORI a 1-point lead to Labour.

Three months later the situation had been transformed. The polls gave an 18- to 19-point lead to the Conservatives. The reason was an outbreak of industrial trouble which, had it been foreseen by Mr Callaghan, would almost certainly have caused him to dissolve earlier. There was a spate of damaging strikes settled by breaking the wage guide-lines first in the Ford Motor Company and later – and even more damagingly – in the public sector. The BBC technicians got a 15 per cent rise. 'We sold our pay policy to have *The Sound of Music* on Christmas Day,' as one disenchanted Labour supporter put it.[1] Militant picketing, violence and walk-outs occurred soon afterwards among tanker, lorry and ambulance drivers, and also local government workers. Rubbish piled up in the streets, corpses queued for the crematorium, patients waited upon the whims of hospital workers. No respectable Conservative wanted these things to happen, but, accompanied by the worst winter for many years, they greatly damaged Labour's credibility as the party which could manage the unions. Mrs Thatcher's views on trade union reform gained ground and her principal spokesman on

[1] Quoted Butler and Kavanagh, op. cit., 120.

industrial relations, Jim Prior, conceded the need for at least some legislation.

Damaging though all this was, the Prime Minister still had plenty of leeway if he could avoid parliamentary defeat. He did not need to dissolve till October 1979 and much could happen before then. What wrecked his plans was Scottish devolution – a question which had been rumbling on since the late 1960s but especially loudly after the election of eleven Scottish Nationalist MPs in the October 1974 election. A devolution Bill for Scotland and Wales had foundered in February 1977 when to the wrath of the Scottish Nationalists the government failed to muster a majority for a guillotine motion. In November the Cabinet had another go. This time separate bills were introduced for each country so that they did not have to sink or swim together. Early in 1978 the House of Commons forced on a reluctant government important amendments to both bills. A devolved assembly could only come into being if a referendum was carried in favour of it, not merely by a simple majority of those who actually voted but also by over 40 per cent of those eligible to vote. If the Secretary of State considered that less than 40 per cent of the electorate had voted for the Act, he had to lay an order for repeal before parliament; otherwise he had to lay a commencement order.

The bills became law in the summer of 1978, and the referendums were fixed for 1 March 1979 to take advantage of the new register. Wales need not concern us. There was never any likelihood of a pro-devolution vote there, and in the event it was rejected by a majority of nearly four to one. As Kenneth Morgan puts it, 'Welsh devolution was promptly wiped off the political agenda.'[1] The Conservative attitude towards Scotland had been ambivalent in the past. Logically one could have expected the party to favour any move that might lead to ultimate separation, given the dependence of their opponents on the Scottish vote; but the same argument could have been used of Irish Home Rule, and it cut no more ice in 1979 than it had ninety years earlier. The Conservatives are there to conserve, and they are the party of Unionism and British nationalism. It

[1] Kenneth O. Morgan, *Rebirth of a nation, Wales 1880–1980* (1981), 405.

is true that in 1968 Mr Heath and Sir Alec Douglas-Home, in the long-forgotten Declaration of Perth, had put forward the idea of a tentative and cautious step towards devolution, though nothing was done about it by the 1970–4 government. It is also true that Mrs Thatcher, soon after her election as leader, made a speech in Glasgow where she supported a Scottish Assembly as 'a top priority to ensure that more decisions affecting Scotland are taken in Scotland by Scotsmen'.[1] But the Scots who supported the Conservative Party were divided, and it was not long before Unionism prevailed. In any case there were strong arguments which Conservatives could use against this particular Bill without necessarily committing themselves to opposing all forms of devolution. Mrs Thatcher, helped by a powerful speech from Lord Home, displayed much skill in uniting Conservative pro-devolutionists and anti-devolutionists. The referendum produced a bare majority of votes (52 per cent), but only 33 per cent of the electorate, in favour of devolution. The government dithered about what to do next. The Scottish Nationalists decided to press for an election as soon as possible. On 28 March Mrs Thatcher, aware of their support, moved a vote of no confidence. It was one of the most dramatic debates of the century. The motion was carried after an evening of excitement and intrigue by a single vote – the first occasion since 1924 when a government lost such a motion – and was therefore forced to dissolve at a time it did not choose. It is, however, at least doubtful whether the Prime Minister could have carried on much longer even if he had won.

Mr Callaghan announced that parliament would be dissolved on 7 April and the election held on 3 May. This meant that there would be the unusually long campaigning period of five weeks. The reason was partly because the five days around Easter including two bank holidays do not count against the statutory minimum of twenty days between dissolution and polling day; but the Prime Minister could have dissolved earlier and held the election on 26 April. He chose 3 May because he believed that Labour's best hope lay in a long campaign, during which the Conservative leader might lose her voice, or commit

[1] Quoted Butler and Kavanagh, op. cit., 109.

some indiscretion. Labour was very much on the defensive. The Conservatives entered the campaign with a longer lead at that stage than any party since 1945. On the other hand their lead had been even longer in February and time might be on Labour's side.

One terrible event shook everyone at the outset. On 30 March Airey Neave, shadow spokesman on Northern Ireland, one of Mrs Thatcher's closest aides and architect of her campaign for the leadership four years earlier, was killed by a time bomb planted in his car at Westminster by IRA terrorists. Fearing that it might be the prelude to a series of assassination attempts, the police insisted on the most elaborate security precautions at public meetings and elsewhere. These affected all parties and had no discernible effect on the outcome. As time went on, politicians, though not the police, became more relaxed, and there was in fact no repetition of the atrocity. The campaign, despite allegations of left and right extremism, was marked by relatively good humour and a welcome absence of rotten eggs, tomatoes and other missiles.

The Conservatives under Lord Thorneycroft's chairmanship had a smooth and highly efficient party machine. They employed an able and aggressive advertising agency, Saatchi and Saatchi, and they had in Mr Gordon Reece a highly capable Director of Publicity. Their campaign had both a negative and a positive side. Negatively, the party leader and her acolytes emphasised the hardships of the winter strikes, the failure of Labour's claim to work with the unions and the need for legislation to prevent the worst abuses of picketing. Positively, the leadership reverted largely to the manifesto of 1970.[1] In February 1974 the manifesto had been mainly concerned with a statutory incomes policy. In October 1974 the theme had been a government of national unity. Now the emphasis as in 1970 was on law and order, lower taxation, lower public expenditure, except on defence and police, less state intervention, reduction of bureaucracy, and getting government 'off our backs'. The manifesto entitled *Time for a change* had a foreword by the leader claiming that the election was perhaps 'the last chance' to

[1] See above, p. 300.

restore the proper balance between the state and the individual. As in 1970, the party managers concentrated on the target of the 'soft', i.e. convertible, voter and on a group of some 80 marginal constituencies. The 'soft' voter watched ITV rather than BBC, read the *Mirror* or the *Sun* and belonged to the skilled working class described in social surveys as C2. It was, perhaps surprisingly, not true that the highest taxpayers were the only category to favour lower taxation. Those whose incomes were rising from whatever base felt even more strongly about the matter. It was clear too that a large section would be happy to opt out of parts of the Welfare State. The principal points in the Conservative party manifesto (which attracted twice as much attention as Labour's) were, according to the polls, endorsed by a majory of Labour as well as Conservative supporters.

Mrs Thatcher struck a populist note which was unmistakeable. The proposal to sell council houses to tenants at half price, whatever its economic or ethical merits, was a signal that the Conservatives could rival Labour in planning to carry 'irreversible' legislation. There is no doubt that for the time being the terms of debate had been changed. The Prime Minister himself dwelt on the importance of less bureaucracy, lower income tax, a charter for council house tenants and greater freedom of choice. There was a general swing to the right, but Labour was not likely to benefit from a deathbed conversion. The libertarian and Adam Smithian doctrines of the Institute of Economic Affairs, after years of what has been called 'near exile in a kind of intellectual Siberia',[1] had great influence on Sir Keith Joseph and Mrs Thatcher. It was an appropriate recognition of the IEA's contribution when Mrs Thatcher created one of its co-directors, Ralph Harris, a life peer in her first honours list. There were at this time some interesting conversions to the Conservative side: Lord Vaizey, Hugh (now Lord) Thomas, Max (now Lord) Beloff, and Paul Johnson, ex-editor of the *New Statesman*.

An uneventful low-key campaign was only punctuated by one minor surprise, Mrs Thatcher's refusal to engage in a television debate with the Prime Minister. She would have liked to accept

[1] Hugh Stephenson, *Mrs Thatcher's first year* (1980), 27.

the challenge, but her advisers were against, not because they thought she would be worsted but because they wanted the campaign to turn on Labour's general record, not on a single, much publicised encounter which might go wrong. The Conservative lead fell as expected during the campaign: it began at an average of 11 per cent, declining to 5 per cent. There was a nervous hiccough on 1 May when the *Daily Mail*'s NOP gave Labour a 0.7 per cent lead. No other polls confirmed it, and two days later the Conservatives won a conclusive though not ovewhelming victory, gaining 51 seats with a swing of 5.1 per cent – the biggest since 1945. They won 43.9 per cent of the popular vote to Labour's 36.9, and 339 seats to Labour's 269. The Liberals won 11 seats on 13.8 per cent of the popular vote. The Scottish Nationalists collapsed from 11 seats to 2. The Conservative share of the vote was not much above its post-war average of 43.5 per cent, but the party was home and dry as far as the House was concerned. On 4 May at 2.30 p.m. Mr Callaghan resigned. An hour later Mrs Thatcher was appointed – the first woman prime minister in British history.

CHAPTER XI

The Thatcher government
1979–83

This chapter must begin with a warning. It is very difficult to put into historical perspective an account of events so recent, and the task is made even harder since it is an incomplete story. One has only to imagine a history of the first three years of Harold Macmillan's administration published in, say, 1962, in order to appreciate that its judgments might look very strange today. On balance, however, I believe the risk is worth taking. Even if one lacks perspective one can at least chart the main outline of events, and this in itself may be of some use to the reader.

Mrs Thatcher won the election with a majority of 43 over all other parties combined. The Conservatives had enjoyed a bigger swing in their favour than either of the principal parties since 1945. There was no likelihood of parliamentary defeat in such circumstances. It is true that there were some features in the result which might be regarded as slightly disturbing. The concept of 'one nation' was contradicted by the ever more striking divergence between Conservative and Labour fortunes in the north and the south. In the south, Conservatives had 186 seats compared with Labour's 30. This however does not include the old LCC area where Labour had 25 to the Conservative score of 10. In the Midlands the Conservatives had won 57 seats against Labour's 41. But in the north the Labour party won 107 seats to the Conservatives' 53 – a loss of 10 compared with the last election, but all the same a conclusive majority. In Scotland and Wales the Conservatives made some gains but were nevertheless outnumbered by two to one in both countries (Scotland 22-44, Wales 11-22). These trends, which dated back for many years, were to be even more marked in the landslide election of 1983.

The new government was unlikely to worry unduly about the disparity. After all, the Conservatives increased their share of the vote everywhere, and Mrs Thatcher had as good grounds as any post-war Prime Minister to claim a 'mandate' for the policies she had put forward. The concept of the mandate is open to much argument, but, if it has any validity – and politicians seem to think it has – Margaret Thatcher possessed it, and was to possess it even more firmly after 1983. The Conservative manifesto by implication repudiated much of the party's post-war practice. Mrs Thatcher had proclaimed herself a 'conviction' not a 'consensus' politician. She intended to reverse the long-term decline of the economy by a policy of 'monetarism', reduction in expenditure and taxation, curbing of union power, no subsidisation of 'lame ducks', and 'privatisation' of publicly owned industry. She was sceptical about the blanket provisions of the 'welfare state'. She was against 'corporatism', 'collectivism' and 'Keynesianism' – anyway in the meaning which those somewhat ambivalent words had come to acquire. She regarded inflation as a far greater danger than unemployment. She was determined not to inject purchasing power into the economy in order to create jobs and thus involve herself in trying to control the consequential inflation by a prices and income policy. The TUC and the CBI were no longer to be regarded as estates of the realm to be consulted and cossetted. Even the NFU might not remain privileged for ever. The consumer was to come into his or her own.

The question was whether Mrs Thatcher would do what she promised, reverse the trends of the last thirty-five years. It was a programme that could be described as 'radical' or 'reactionary', according to taste. It was not radical in the sense that the expression 'Tory radicalism' has been used in the past. That normally meant assisting the cause of 'progress' even more efficiently than the 'progressive', on a common basis of movement towards the same goal. Mrs Thatcher aimed at something quite different. She was, in one sense of the Oxford English Dictionary's definition, 'reactionary'. The word has two meanings – 'tending to oppose change' or 'seeking to return to a former system'. They are very different – indeed contradictory. Return to a former system involves change from the existing one. Mrs Thatcher hoped to change it by bringing back some of the values of the nineteenth and twentieth centuries – competition, a stable currency, self-help, free enterprise, law and order. 'Reactionary' is a bad word to most people, whereas 'radical' sounds vaguely good. Mrs Thatcher's intention was to change the existing system, but it is a misnomer to call it 'radical'. Clearly the policy was one which some of the old guard in the Conservative party would regard with mixed feelings. Mrs Thatcher is said to have had a habit of writing the word 'wet' on submissions from ministers or civil servants who seemed to prefer consensus to her convictions. Whatever the reason, the terms 'wet' and 'dry' entered for the time being into the language of politics and of newspaper correspondents.

Although she had stated on 25 February 1979 in an interview with the *Observer*[1] that 'as Prime Minister I could not waste my time in having internal arguments', she was characteristically cautious when she came to form her Cabinet. She may have been conscious of her uniquely 'outsider' status in the history of the Conservative leadership. Disraeli, Bonar Law and Edward Heath, the only comparable figures, had gradually infiltrated into the Conservative establishment, and become a part of it before rising to the top. She alone had captured it by direct assault. This was an argument for initial prudence in exploiting her success. She had inherited most of her Shadow Cabinet from Edward Heath and she gave office to most of them. The 'paternalist' or 'one nation' strand of Conservatism was strongly represented: Lord Carrington and Sir Ian Gilmour at the Foreign Office; Lord Soames, Leader of the House of Lords; Willie Whitelaw, Home Office; Francis Pym, Defence; Mark Carlisle, Education; Peter Walker, Agriculture; Michael Heseltine, Environment. But she took care to have people of her

[1] Quoted David Butler and Dennis Kavanagh, *The British general election of 1983* (1984), 41.

own persuasion in the key economic posts: Sir Geoffrey Howe at the Treasury, with John Biffen as Chief Secretary and Nigel Lawson as Financial Secretary; Keith Joseph, Industry; John Nott, Trade, with Norman Tebbit as Under Secretary; David Howell, Energy. The exception was Jim Prior, Secretary for Employment. Lord Hailsham, who defies categorisation, became Lord Chancellor for the second time at the age of seventy-one. Norman St John Stevas, a great admirer of Disraeli and a notable wit, was given the leadership of the House, and perhaps proved to be too witty for his own good.[1] An awkward problem was what, if anything, to do about Edward Heath. To have him in the Cabinet was out of the question. In the end she offered him the Washington Embassy which he refused.

From 1979 to 1983 Margaret Thatcher dominated politics. Any Prime Minister is bound to play a conspicuous role on the scene, but the spotlight from the very beginning shone on her to the exclusion of almost all her colleagues. This was not true, to the same degree, of her four Conservative predecessors, even Harold Macmillan; nor was it true of Harold Wilson and James Callaghan. The history of the Conservative party in those years was largely, though not only, the biography of its leader. Her first twelve months were anything but successful. There had to be a new budget, for the previous one was by agreement merely a holding operation. The principles of Professors Hayek and Friedman – the two gurus who dominated the new Conservatism – were applied. Sir Geoffrey Howe reduced the standard rate of income tax from 33 to 30 per cent and the marginal rate of top salaries from 83 to 60 per cent. He reduced tax on unearned incomes from a maximum of 98 to 75 per cent. He also phased out exchange controls – a far-reaching step whose significance was not at first seen.[2] There were cuts

[1] He was credited with describing Mrs Thatcher not only as the 'Leaderene' but as the 'Immaculate Misconception'. Perhaps he never did, but the stories circulated. His action in creating backbench committees to 'shadow' every department on the lines of Congressional Committees in Washington was an important reform but did not endear him to his Cabinet colleagues. When he was dismissed in January 1981 – he was the first to go from the Cabinet – it did not come as a surprise.

[2] David Butler and Dennis Kavanagh, op. cit. (1984), 28, n. 1, mention the belief in some quarters that there never could be another Labour government. If the polls pointed to a Labour win, the consequential flight of capital would frighten enough of the public to vote in order to keep them out.

in expenditure but they could not at this stage be enough to counterbalance the cut in revenue. He decided, therefore, to raise VAT on those items which attracted it, from a mixture of 8 and 12½ to a uniform 15 per cent. This accorded with the view that tax should fall on spending rather than earnings but the effect was to increase the cost of living by nearly 4 per cent. Inflation was already rising. It was running at 15 per cent in the early months of 1979.

Matters were made worse by the Conservative promise during the election campaign to abide by the recommendations of Professor Clegg's Commission on pay comparability. This was an error bitterly and soon regretted. The Commission awarded rises of between 15 and 25 per cent to employees in the public sector in order, so they said, to bring them in line with wages outside; certain of their figures were, to put it mildly, eccentric. No doubt the government had some satisfaction when it send the Commission packing in July 1980, but the harm had already been done. On top of these inflationary pressures came the second great rise in oil prices, the result of the fall of the Shah of Iran and the accession of the Ayatollah Khomeini. It produced major inflation in Britain and major recession all over the world. By the summer of 1980 inflation was running at over 20 per cent and unemployment rose from 1.5 to 2 million between April and August.

The Conservatives quickly lost their lead in the opinion polls after the 1979 election. They did not regain it till the Falklands War. For nearly two years they seemed to be heading for electoral disaster, but the Prime Minister ignored these alarmist signals. She had always maintained that she needed ten years – two electoral victories – to turn round the 'ship of state', and change the course of history. She did not mean to be deflected despite a disastrous start.

In her first year her government had two successes, though her personal responsibility, despite her memoirs, is open to doubt. One was Zimbabwe where she reluctantly reversed her support for Bishop Muzorewa's government in the face of the arguments of Lord Carrington and Ian Gilmour[1] and agreed to

---

[1]See Ian Gilmour's review of *The Downing Street Years* in *Twentieth Century British History*, Vol. 5, No 2, 1994, 265-66.

the settlement which resulted in the victory of Robert Mugabe. If this did nothing else it at least got Britain off the hook. Zimbabwe after two decades of trouble and embarrassment to successive British governments faded into insignificance. It soon ran into economic and social trouble like many other post-independence African states, but this was no longer a British responsibility. The whites, however embittered, were expendable, and if the blacks chose to be ruled by a Marxist at the head of a corrupt and incompetent administration, that was their affair, not Britain's.

Her government's other success was Europe. She was anxious, with good cause, to cut the UK's contribution to the EEC budget. Carrington and Gilmour negotiated a substantial reduction in Brussels on 30 May but it was nothing like as large as the £1,000 million which the Prime Minister wanted and which there was no chance whatever of getting. According to Ian Gilmour she was 'incandescent' when they reported to her. But Gilmour managed to brief the press to the effect that the deal was a great triumph for Britain and only one member of the Cabinet objected. So she accepted a *fait accompli*.[1]

In this as in other ways she followed a traditional Conservative doctrine which had latterly become watered down: belief in British nationalism. She revived it in no uncertain way and not only in the EEC. Her hostility to the Kremlin and all its works was clear and emphatic. The victory of Ronald Reagan in 1980 was a boon. She found herself in accord with the President of the most powerful country in the world. Unlike his predecessor he was anything but 'wet'. She believed that Britain's interests by and large coincided with those of the USA. After years of compromise and conciliation in the world of UNO, UNESCO etc. a fresh wind seemed to be blowing. The Conservative party under her leadership reverted to an older outlook on the internatinal scene. It could be crudely summarised as 'Britain first', and it corresponded to a palpable shift of intellectual opinion which may have silently begun some time earlier. Few things are more difficult than to

[1]Ibid. and *Dancing with Dogma* (Simon and Schuster, 1992), 285-296.

chart the currents below the surface of affairs before they become obvious and turbulent. But it is clear that the ideological tide was carrying the Conservatives forward throughout the years between Mrs Thatcher's ascent to the leadership and the election of 1983. After 1979 their opponents seemed weak, divided, ineffective and devoid of ideas.

The fortunes of the Conservative party in the 1979 parliament cannot be explained without reference to those of Labour, which were disastrous. Defeat at the polls was followed by a prolonged *post mortem*. The left moved into the ascendancy. A new constitution was devised under which the election of the leader would be made by an electoral college composed as to 30 per cent each by the parliamentary party and the constituency parties, and 40 per cent by the unions. The previous system had been confined to MPs only, and the new one was a blow to the centre and right wing of the party. Before its machinery came into action, James Callaghan resigned, and a contest under the old dispensation took place on 15 October 1980. Michael Foot defeated Denis Healey by 139 votes to 129 on the final ballot. Although some saw in this a decision for unity and avoidance of a split, Michael Foot could not, perhaps did not, wish to check the slide to the left on such issues as mandatory reselection, unilateral disarmament, departure from the EEC and extension of nationalisation.

The result was an important secession early in 1981 when Roy Jenkins, Shirley Williams, Bill Rodgers and David Owen, 'the Gang of Four', on 25 January launched the Social Democratic Party with the 'Limehouse Declaration' supported by nine other Labour MPs. By the end of the year the SDP had recruited 28 MPs but only Shirley Williams had been elected under its colours – with a notable victory at Crosby where she overturned a 19,000 Conservative majority. Roy Jenkins was to win Hillhead in Glasgow on 25 March 1982. In the autumn of 1981 a loose alliance was established between the new party and the Liberals. The Social Democratic Alliance (SDA), as this came to be called, did remarkably well in the opinion polls till the Falklands War which broke out on 2 April 1982. It had been at one stage as high as 40 per cent but it fluctuated downwards to a figure of 20 per cent. At the 1983 general election it was to be 25 per cent. There was no single leader of the SDA. After Roy Jenkins had defeated David Owen for the leadership of the SDP in July 1982, the leadership of the Alliance was a joint one held by him and the Liberal leader, David Steel. In the event, by splitting the non-Conservative vote almost down the middle the SDA would prove a notable boon to the government at the general election. The Conservatives were to profit, under the vagaries of the first-past-the-post system, even as they had in 1922, but this was not self-evident in 1981–2. Conservative seats seemed more vulnerable than Labour seats, and the two SDP victories at by-elections were at the Conservatives' expense. There was some plausibility in the view that the SDA might hold the balance of power in a hung parliament and, if it did not actually form a government, bargain its support for one of the other parties in return for the introduction of proportional representation. The fact that none of these things occurred should not blind one to the fears and hopes of the time.

Mrs Thatcher did not allow herself to be influenced by any of these considerations. The recession, the inflation partly self-induced and partly the result of the oil crisis, together with the rise in unemployment, combined to force her into many modifications of her original programme, but these were basically tactical rather than strategic. The target of reducing public expenditure and the public borrowing sector requirement (i.e., in plainer language, the budget deficit) as a proportion of the gross national product was obviously going to be very difficult when the government was committed to a rise in expenditure for defence and the police, when social security payments were escalating and when the GNP was shrinking. Nor did the government succeed in achieving its objective during its first years. Mrs Thatcher's task was not made easier by the composition of her Cabinet. It was heavily weighted towards the traditionalists who surveyed her new course with misgivings. She is supposed to have said on one occasion: 'I am the Cabinet rebel!' She was, if hearsay is to be believed, abrasive, argumentative and aggressive. She could be argued with, and, if the arguer was clear-headed, tough and well-informed, he had a chance of prevailing, for she could be converted by reason and persuaded by facts as she was over Rhodesia. But no one who was not very much on top of his brief had a chance, and those who had doubts but were temperamentally disinclined for a fight soon became in her eyes 'wet'.

The new attitude of the government towards the economy was summed up in the 'Red Book' issued by the Treasury on Budget Day 1980:

> The Government has deliberately not set its targets in terms of the ultimate objectives of price stability and high output and employment because these are not within its direct control. It has instead set a target for the growth of the money supply which is more directly under its influence and has stated that it will frame its policies for taxation and public expenditure to secure a deceleration of money supply without excessive reliance on interest rates.

After quoting this passage Lord Bruce-Gardyne in an interesting book[1] goes on to point out that although monetary targets were not new, for Roy Jenkins and Denis Healey had both tried them in their day, they had hitherto been imposed on a reluctant Labour government by its creditors. More significantly, 'They had always been presented as adjuncts to the conventional yardsticks of . . . full employment and output growth; and they had been accompanied by attempts to restrain domestic inflation through centralized control of wage bargaining.[2] The new medium-term financial strategy was quite different. In Lord Bruce-Gardyne's words, 'It formally abandoned the pretence that full employment and economic growth were in the gift of the government, accepting by implication that the achievement of these desirable objectives depended on the ability of British commerce to meet the appetites of its customers at home and abroad.' This was a very

---

[1] *Mrs Thatcher's first administration* (1984), 58. Strictly the title is a misnomer. There has been only one administration continuously in existence from 1979 to the time of writing.
[2] ibid, 59.

important change, and it has influenced attitudes ever since. It meant that, if employers and employees continued to assume that their rewards would beat inflation regardless of the efficiency with which they conducted their affairs, they would price themselves out of their jobs – in the private sector through loss of markets, and in the public sector through cash control of government lending and spending. By the end of the 1979-83 parliament there had been a notable alteration in the electorate's expectations of what government could do. From her own point of view this was one of Margaret Thatcher's major achievements. It altered, for the time being, the terms of reference in the economic debate.

An indication of the shape of things to come was the steel strike early in 1980. It lasted for thirteen weeks and seemed to end in a victory for the strikers. Sir Keith Joseph, after a settlement recommended by Lord Lever and two others, agreed to make the necessary funds available. But it led to an immense loss of customers at home and overseas. Massive redundancies ensued, and the power of the steel unions was broken. The episode produced shock waves throughout the union world – for the time being even in the National Union of Mineworkers, although they were to return to the attack after the 1983 election. Unemployment was to be a major element in the decline of union power for the next three years.

In terms of economic policy the critical moment came in 1981 with the government's third budget. Defeated in the autumn Cabinet battle of 1980 over cuts in public expenditure, the Prime Minister and the Chancellor of the Exchequer were determined not to repeat the pattern of the past. If expenditure was to go up, taxation would have to rise too, and there would be no question of 'priming the pump' to give what they believed to be merely transitory relief to unemployment. This was the first time since 1945 that such a policy had been adopted except when the government was under pressure from its creditors. It caused alarm throughout the so-called 'wets', indignation in the City and in wide areas of industry. At the 1980 October conference the Prime Minister had said, 'U turn if you want to, the lady's not for turning.' Those who declined to believe her were in for a shock. She meant what she said, and she was prepared to risk the electoral consequences which on past precedent ought to have been disastrous, and, had there been an election that year, probably would have been.

The first Cabinet reshuffle occurred on 5 January 1981 with the dismissal of Norman St John Stevas and the removal of Francis Pym from Defence to the leadership of the House; he was succeeded by John Nott. John Biffen replaced Nott at the Department of Trade and Leon Brittan became Chief Secretary of the Treasury. These changes did not seem to indicate any particular ideological shift in the balance of the Cabinet, although there was much speculation about them in the media. But there was no doubt about the nature of the next re-shuffle on 14 September of the same year. The summer, after a budget which had scandalised the neo-Keynesians, had been one of the worst periods of the government's career. The budget was attacked in an unprecedented letter to *The Times* signed by 364 academic economists. They were anti-monetarist and largely Cambridge-based. Lord Harris of High Cross observed that, with a few exceptions, the list of the most prominent signatories looked like 'a charge sheet of those responsible for Britain's relative economic decline since the war'. The same summer saw a prolonged and damaging Civil Service strike and riots in some of the worst inner city areas – particularly those with large West Indian populations. Scenes of violence took place at Toxteth in Liverpool, Moss Side in Manchester and Brixton in South London. There seems to have been no particular correlation between lawlessness and unemployment which was indeed high in Toxteth but well below the national average in Brixton. However, the government's critics, both within and outside the Conservative party, used the riots to brand monetarism and the unemployment for which they claimed it to be responsible as proof of the divisive nature of the government's policy.

A curious coded language came to be used by Conservative critics including some inside the Cabinet. If a minister talked about 'one nation' and praised Disraeli, it was a safe assumption that he was attacking Mrs Thatcher and Sir Geoffrey Howe. The fact that Disraeli operated in a world totally remote from the Britain of a century later and that it is quite impossible to guess how he would have looked at these problems made no difference at all.[1] Lord Bruce-Gardyne thinks that the summer riots almost caused the government to waver and he surmises that a concerted attack by the critics might have forced a change of course, but he rightly points out that the 'wets' never had a clear alternative policy any more than the 364 economists who had confined themselves to observing that an alternative existed though they refrained from saying what it was. The opportunity passed away, and on 14 September 1981 the Prime Minister hit back. Lord Thorneycroft, who had said that he felt 'rising damp', was replaced as chairman of the party. Lord Soames, who had irritated the Prime Minister by his handling of the Civil Service pay claim, and Sir Ian Gilmour, whose critical speeches had gone beyond the limits normally observed by ministers, were asked to resign. The former consented in one of the coldest and curtest letters ever written to a Prime Minister in such circumstances. Another minister to be dismissed was Mark Carlisle who had perhaps fought too hard for the education budget. He made way for Sir Keith Joseph. Perhaps there was a hint that a minister whose civil servants – a category not liked by the Prime Minister – had pushed him into too much conflict with the Treasury might be for the chop. Nigel Lawson, a redoubtable Thatcher supporter, was elevated to the Cabinet as Minister for Energy in place of David Howell who, though dry, was not good at arguing with Mrs Thatcher. He was shunted to Transport. Nicholas Ridley and Jock (now Lord) Bruce-Gardyne became respectively Financial and Economic Secretaries to the Treasury which was now in hands as dry as could be.

The most sensational blow to the wets, however, was the clean sweep made in the Department of Employment. Jim Prior and one of his team went to Northern Ireland, another to the back benches. The Prime Minister and the Chancellor of the Exchequer considered that legislation over and above what had

[1] Disraeli in fact had views about the limited role of government which were much nearer to Mrs Thatcher's than her critics'. Oddly enough some of the hardest liners in the administration were of Jewish ancestry – Sir Keith Joseph, Nigel Lawson and Leon Brittan.

been promised in the manifesto was needed to curb trade union power. Prior made no secret of his scepticism. He had to bring in the 1980 Employment Act which implemented these limited pledges, but he did not wish to go further. Perhaps he still believed in the sort of cosy, 'corporatist' jollying-along with the TUC which had been a feature of industrial relations over the last twenty years – 'beer and sandwiches at Number 10' etc. The Prime Minister certainly did not share this belief. Along with most Conservatives she regarded the unions, whose legal position is uniquely privileged in the Western world, as a barrier to efficiency and a major factor in pricing people out of jobs and raising unemployment. The division of opinion cut across the usual dry/wet lines. Nigel Lawson and John Biffen were against legislation, not out of any hankering for 'corporatism' but because they thought it would not work. Michael Heseltine and Peter Walker, who might have been expected to be pro-Prior, believed that if monetarism was to go, as they hoped it would, legislation that curbed the trade unions would be necessary to control inflation.[1]

Jim Prior had allowed it to be believed that he would resign rather than accept any other office. At least that was the impression gained by lobby correspondents and political editors. In the end, however, after some agonising, he accepted the move, and he was replaced by the strongly Thatcherite Norman Tebbit. The story may well be more complicated than appeared in the media, but the public impression was one of bluff being called, a triumph on the part of Mrs Thatcher and reduced credibility for Mr Prior. The Prime Minister now had a clear majority of the Cabinet on her side, and her supporters occupied all the key positions which determined economic policy.

These convulsions in the Cabinet would have been far more serious for Mrs Thatcher but for the unwavering support of Willie Whitelaw. A landowner, a paternalist and a grandee, he might have been the sort of person upon whom the new Tory tone would strike a jarring note – the more so since he was the defeated candidate in the second ballot of the 1975 contest and

[1] Bruce-Gardyne, op. cit., 35-6.

would almost certainly have won if he had put his name forward in the first. The debt she owed to him throughout the 1979-83 Parliament was immense. The only time she was in any danger was when she appeared to distance herself from him at the party conference of 1981 on a question of 'law and order', but she soon repaired the breach.

Control over her cabinet was one thing. Winning the next election was another. The government had now reached nearly half way through its maximum term of office. The party conference at Blackpool in September 1981 was, as usual, reasonably well stage-managed, but it soon became clear to those who talked to ministers and ex-ministers 'off the record' that dissent had been far from quelled. There was no longer any question of abandoning monetarism. The course was irrevocably set. The question was whether it would bring victory or disaster. Most of the commentators predicted disaster. Few people, after Blackpool 1981, would have put much money on a renewed mandate for the Conservative party. In October the Prime Minister's popularity sank to the lowest level of any Prime Minister's since opinion polls were invented – 24 per cent. By Christmas the Conservative party's rating, while slightly above its leader's, was down to 27 per cent. Unemployment, which had passed 2.5 million in April 1981, rose to over 3 million in January 1982. Labour's standing was almost as low as that of the Conservatives, the Alliance being well ahead of either.

Yet for no very obvious reason the slide in Conservative fortunes was halted in the New Year, and the trend began to move upwards. This occurred at least three months before the Falklands War which broke out at the beginning of April. Oddly enough Labour's also rose at the same time while that of the SDA sharply declined. By the end of the first quarter of 1982 the parties were running neck and neck. Too much significance should not be read into these figures, but they probably indicate something that was happening in public opinion, although they do not tell us why. One can only guess at possible reasons. The sale of council houses had been a great success – one of those populist changes, like the introduction of ITV, which infuriate the *bien pensant* establishment but please everyone else. Surveys of industrial expectations ceased to be as gloomy as they had been. Unemployment, though still rising, was beginning to flatten out and people were coming to regard it as something, like the weather, for which the government was not responsible. Nor were its social consequences as serious as predicted, anyway for the time being. Indeed one result, though no one liked to say so, could be regarded as beneficial. Unemployment was the most powerful factor in discouraging strikes, abating excessive wage demands and preventing a repetition of the 'winter of discontent' regularly predicted by the pundits. It was a major element in convincing the public that the government's ceaseless propaganda about the danger of pricing themselves out of work had a basis of truth.

How the Conservatives would have fared at the next election but for the Falklands War is anyone's guess. The likelihood is that they would have won, though not so overwhelmingly. It is hard to see how Labour could have recovered from its disastrous condition, war or no war; and the SDA was too new and untried to replace the Conservatives as the alternative to Labour. However that may be, the Falklands gave a boost to Mrs Thatcher personally, and hence to her party, which is beyond dispute. There is no need to rehearse the story of the campaign. There is a plethora of books on the subject.[1] It is enough to say that the Argentinian invasion resulted in an uproar from the 1922 Committee about the role of the Foreign Office, which caused Lord Carrington to resign despite a strong plea by the Prime Minister. Francis Pym took his place but he lacked his predecessor's talent for defending the allegedly 'wet' Foreign Office in the semi-jocose terms which deflected Mrs Thatcher's wrath. It was an unhappy relationship.

As for the war, Mrs Thatcher was fully in accord with the national mood. Whatever the errors of the past, she was determined to recover the islands if this was feasible. Her service advisers told her that it was, though they must have pointed out the risks. It was fortunate that Argentina was governed by a seedy group of right-wing generals and admirals, not by an

[1] The best is Max Hastings and Simon Jenkins, *The battle for the Falklands* (1983).

THE RESOURCEFUL LOVER
LATIN TROUBADOUR *(serenading the fair Maggie):* "IF SHE WON'T
LISTEN TO MY LOVE-SONGS, I'LL TRY HER WITH A BRICK!"

April 28, 1982. Reproduced by permission of Punch.

equally seedy collection of Cuban-type commissars. The Labour party otherwise might not have supported the government. Even so, some did not. Tony Benn was one of them and did his cause no good. The Task Force which set out for these remote islands achieved a brilliant success, though there were occasions when the situation looked bad. The Cabinet was prepared to lose up to 1000 men.[1] In the event 260 were killed, and the occupying force was obliged to surrender on 14 June.

The result was rightly attributed to the Prime Minister's nerve and determination. The 'Iron Lady' of Soviet propaganda had proved herself iron indeed. She had played for the highest stakes nationally and politically, and she had won. She was, however, careful not to exploit her victory in terms of party. There was no suggestion of a snap election. She was ready to carry on through another winter, and there was an important reason for doing so. The Boundary Commission, which is obliged by statute at certain intervals to consider the redistribution of seats and the redrawing of their boundaries, was due to report early in 1983. It could not fail to redress the highly anti-Conservative bias of the existing system. To go to the polls any earlier than the summer would have been folly. It could have cost some 30 seats.

The party organisation went through a number of changes after 1979. There were serious financial problems and awkward institutional conflicts. Lord Thorneycroft was a chairman who had the Prime Minister's support until the summer of 1981. He caused a major shake-up soon after the general election by moving the Research Department from Old Queen Street to the Central Office in Smith Square. The change had an important financial aspect. The sale of the Old Queen Street property was a help towards reducing the party's deficit. Moreover a shrewd bargain with the Westminster Council over the lease of the Smith Square property improved the situation even further. The Research Department, however, resented the move, and strong protests were addressed to Mrs Thatcher. Its members already felt that their noses had been put out of joint by Sir

[1] Private information.

Keith Joseph's Centre for Policy Studies – a much more right-wing affair than the Research Department which had the reputation of being wet or at least slightly damp.

Finance was a continuing worry. In 1980-1 the party was £2.2 million in deficit, despite an income of £3.2 million, and, although the sale of the Old Queen Street property had been a help, subscriptions from major manufacturing firms had been falling off, partly because of the recession, and partly because the boards of some were by no means happy about the government's economic policy. The Confederation of British Industries (CBI) was at times highly critical. The government commanded more sympathy from the Institute of Directors which had a higher representation of service industries and small businesses. Indeed it was from the latter and from the constituencies that the Central Office obtained most of its funding, but in 1981 it had to cut its budget by 20 per cent.

In July 1981 Lord Thorneycroft, who had already in the spring made some opaque criticisms of government policy, gave a clearly critical press conference. Mrs Thatcher decided it was time for a change. After considering various names, including Michael Heseltine who was always a highly successful orator at party conferences, she chose Cecil Parkinson, an able self-made businessman holding junior office in the Department of Trade. Unlike Lord Thorneycroft he was given a seat in the Cabinet. He promptly created a new Marketing Department in the Central Office headed by Mr Chris Lawson who had been managing director of one of the Mars companies in the United States. The department was given charge of the communications aspect of the next election campaign. Chris Lawson, who had had experience of electioneering in the USA, adopted many of the techniques of the Republican party with considerable success. Publicity as before was entrusted to Saatchi and Saatchi.

Obviously the manifesto had to be on different terms from 1979. Then the slogan was 'Time for a change'. Now it was to be 'Stay on course'. The notable rise in the public's rating of the party and Prime Minister as a result of the Falklands, together with signs during the winter of 1982 that the worst of the recession might be over, meant that an election was almost certain to be held in 1983. The only serious question was the month. The Labour party started an action in the courts in July 1982 to stop the Boundary Commission from presenting its report on the ground that it had incorrectly interpreted its duty to keep the size of constituencies as equal as possible. The Court of Appeal firmly rejected the argument and refused leave to carry the matter to the Appellate Committee of the House of Lords. In February 1983 the Lords confirmed the action of the Court of Appeal and declined to hear any further argument. Mrs Thatcher was now free to choose her date. From the beginning of the year the Central Office had favoured June. By the autumn the unemployment figures would be inflated by school leavers, and the extra time might just possibly provide an opportunity for Labour to ditch Michael Foot, the most disastrous leader the party had ever chosen; Denis Healey would be a much more formidable opponent. The local elections in May indicated a comfortable Conservative lead. On 9 May the Prime Minister announced that polling day would be on Thursday, 9 June.

The Conservative manifesto, written by Ferdinand Mount, head of Mrs Thatcher's Policy Unit, and published on 18 May, contained no surprises. It comprised reduction of inflation, lower public expenditure, lower taxes, secret ballots for union leadership elections and strike decisions, more privatisation, including British Telecom and British Airways, rate-capping, and abolition of the GLC together with the Metropolitan Counties. The proposals had been submitted to stringent financial review, and, although there was no suggestion of dismantling the welfare state, there were few promises to spend more money, apart from a pledge to protect retirement pensions and other long-term benefits against inflation. Inflation was in fact running at 4 per cent in May, the lowest figure for the past fifteen years, and this was an important talking point for the Conservatives.

Whatever doubts there might have been about the result of the election were set at rest by Labour's manifesto published on 16 May. Described by Peter Shore as 'the longest suicide note in history'[1] it featured nuclear disarmament, departure from the EEC, a massive rise in public expenditure, renationalisation of privatised assets and the end of council house sales. A less popular series of items would be hard to imagine. The likelihood of winning on this programme was small. As for the Alliance's manifesto, it was sensible and rational, as one would expect, but it never got across. The Alliance votes were still votes of protest rather than endorsements of a positive policy, and there was a credibility gap. People could not seriously see it as a government-forming party.

There was no serious doubt about the result, and it is not worth describing the various 'leaks' of confidential government papers which featured in the campaign, or the charges and counter-accusations which flew to and fro. It was obvious from the start that the Conservatives would win in a canter. Mrs Thatcher dominated the scene throughout and never put a foot wrong. The poll was low – only 72.7 per cent. The Conservatives won 397 seats with 42.4 per cent of the voters in support. The figures for Labour were 209 and 27.6 per cent, and for the Alliance 23 and 25.4 per cent. The support of the SDA was spread evenly over the country whereas Labour's was concentrated in particular areas. The north-south divide between Conservatives and Labour was more marked than ever before. The election was the biggest landslide since the war, but there were odd statistical features. The Conservatives, on a lower percentage of the popular vote than in 1979, won 58 more seats, and the disproportionate seat/vote relationship between Labour and Alliance was a strong rational argument for electoral reform, though this is not a subject in which rational argument plays much part. Labour had, on any view, fared catastrophically. The skilled working class deserted it in droves, it only secured 39 per cent of trade unionists and 38 per cent of manual workers, and its electoral support, which had been diminishing with occasional upward eddies since the high point in 1951 of 48.8 per cent, was lower than ever before, down by nearly ten points from 1979.

Any judgment on the 1979–83 administration must be

[1] Quoted Butler and Kavanagh, op. cit., 62.

tentative and interim. We are dealing with the first period of a government which looks like continuing in office till 1987 or even as late as June 1988. The picture may not be at all clear even then but it will probably be clearer than it is now. Personally Margaret Thatcher emerged as a figure with the characteristics which people look for in a Prime Minister. She had courage, clarity of mind, determination and 'guts'. She was a pragmatic as well as a conviction politician. She may not have inspired great affection but she was admired as a leader and respected as someone who knew what she was trying to do and who meant what she said. She had been lucky in various ways but luck was what Napoleon looked for in his Marshals and it may be a synonym for some personal if indefinable quality which leads to success. By 1983 she towered above the other political figures on the British scene and she had a formidable reputation all over the world.

Her government had by no means achieved everything it set out to do and, although the government that does this has never existed, there were many short-falls. Public expenditure had been more difficult to control than the Conservatives expected. Privatisation had not got very far. Relations with local authorities were in a state of confusion. Taxation was actually higher, except for the well-to-do. The unions were to some extent in retreat, and certainly the Prime Minister had established that government did not require the assent of the TUC barons to govern. But the battle had by no means been wholly won even if strikes had been fewer. Unemployment at over 3 million was up by 150 per cent – a rise which on all conventional wisdom should have been electorally disastrous.

On the other hand there were successes; in foreign affairs Rhodesia, the Falklands and the EEC; in home affairs the clear signs that British industry, after great losses, was gradually becoming more streamlined, more cost conscious, more competitive, and that small businesses were now beginning to make an impact. Above all Mrs Thatcher and the current of opinion which had borne her into office had brought about a change in expectations. Along with many other Conservatives she had always said that the state had for years been trying to do too much in fields where it could not have much effect – industrial planning, intervention to save lame ducks, pump priming to reduce unemployment – and not enough in fields where it could – law and order, defence. This message seemed at last to have got across. It explains the acceptance of unemployment, even by the unemployed. The ghost of 'Keynes' had been laid, even if the ghost of 'Beveridge' was still left to stalk abroad. The Prime Minister is cautious and the welfare state is dangerous ground.

Margaret Thatcher had said long before 1979 that she needed two terms of office, if not more, to bring about the changes which she believed were needed to reverse the ratchet and arrest the long decline in Britain's flabby degenerating economy. The election of 1983 had given her that opportunity.

CHAPTER XII

The Thatcher government
1983–87

On the morrow of the biggest Conservative victory since 1935 the Conservative leader was not inclined to rest on her laurels. Rest was no part of her temperament and she was well aware that electoral defeat of Labour had not yet achieved one of her principal objectives, 'the death of socialism'. It was for the moment moribund in Westminster but far from dead in other fields of public life: local government; the unions; education; the social services; and many Whitehall departments. The frontiers of the state needed further rolling back. Taxation was still too high. Privatisation had barely begun. But there was a problem in managing the party despite, or perhaps because of, its crushing victory. By no means all Thatcherites were convinced that the old consensus tradition should be reversed and Tory paternalism put in the dustbin. 'There was a revolution to be made,' she wrote, 'but too few revolutionaries.'[1] Ironically, there was another element in the party which feared that Thatcherism was not going far enough. The 'One Nation' supporters of consensus were counter-balanced by a right-wing group whose manifesto 'No Turning Back', published in 1986 after long gestation, advocated vouchers for education, extension of private medical insurance and radical change in the whole welfare system, which they believed to be riddled with fraud, corruption, incompetence and extravagance.

Despite her huge majority, Thatcher did not entirely have her way in Westminster. The new speaker, Bernard Weatherill,

---

[1] Margaret Thatcher, *The Downing Street Years* (HarperCollins, 1993), 306.

was not her preferred candidate. The Commons voted heavily against capital punishment, which she supported, and in favour of higher salaries for ministers, which she opposed. Nor could the normally docile House of Lords be trusted always to toe the line. In June 1984 they rejected a 'paving Bill' for the abolition of the Greater London County Council, a body which under the provocative 'loony left' leadership of Ken Livingstone particularly infuriated the Conservatives. The Bill went through in the end but only after embarrassing delay.

Although the Conservatives were safe when the Whips were on, many of them knew that there were elements of luck in their recent victory which might not be repeated. There was the 'Falklands factor', which, although probably not decisive, almost certainly gave the Conservatives a larger majority than they would otherwise have had. Then there were the divisions and disarray of an opposition split between Labour, SDP and Liberals. Labour itself was an uneasy amalgam of moderates and 'hard left'. Add to these assets a Labour election campaign of heroic ineptitude under a likeable but antediluvian leader and one has a set of circumstances which could hardly have been more propitious. There was no guarantee that all or any of these would recur next time round. Margaret Thatcher knew this well enough and was by no means euphoric. But she saw the result as a golden opportunity to complete the work of the previous parliament.

Her immediate task was to reconstruct the Cabinet. She was determined to get rid of Francis Pym whom she regarded as 'wet' over the Falklands and who had sealed his fate during the election by saying that a landslide victory might be a bad thing. Who should succeed him? Her first choice was Cecil Parkinson, young, self-made, good-looking and as party chairman largely responsible for its recent victory. But on the election night he had to inform her about his affair with his secretary, Sarah Keays, whose father told the Prime Minister the next day that his daughter was expecting Parkinson's child. Thatcher was far from puritanical but this revelation obliged her to look elsewhere. She plumped, not very enthusiastically, for Geoffrey Howe, who had certainly been a successful Chancellor of the

Exchequer but was a much more committed 'European' than she realised at the time. He was also rather slow and legalistic in Cabinet discussions when she wanted speed, clarity and decisiveness. The choice was one that she was destined to regret. In his place she appointed Nigel Lawson who was undoubtedly 'one of us' but not destined to remain in the club for ever.

She moved Willie Whitelaw from the Home Office and made him Lord President of the Council and Leader of the House of Lords. Although her views on immigration and penal reform were well to the right of his, this was not a case of 'kicking upstairs'. He had not been happy as Home Secretary and was in many ways better placed in his new position to act as a virtual second-in-command to the Prime Minister, who greatly valued his support and advice. 'Willie had become quite simply indispensable to me in Cabinet.'[1] She replaced him at the Home Office with Leon Brittan, an able lawyer but a bad presenter, who had never headed a department of state before and now found himself in command of the most difficult one of all.

Margaret Thatcher in retrospect saw three immediate political problems. First, the removal of the threat of socialism made people more and more querulous about the snags and problems of running a free enterprise economy. Second – and she agrees that the party was itself to blame – the 1983 manifesto, though electorally successful, 'did not inspire the government with the sort of crusading spirit which would have got us off to a good start in the new Parliament'.[2] The third problem – in a sense part of the more general problem of the persistence of socialism in vital areas – was the still unchallenged grip of the unions on the economy and of the hard left on the unions.

The first problem – that of reconciling the doubters to a genuine free enterprise economy – could only be solved by going ahead and demonstrating success. So the government resolved to press on with its programme of privatisation. This decision more than anything else helped to solve the second problem, the impression of staleness after four years in office. Between 10 August 1984 and 20 May 1987 nine state-owned corporations

[1] *The Downing Street Years*, op. cit., 307.
[2] *The Downing Street Years*, op. cit., 305.

were sold to the public, the largest being British Telecom (£3,916m) and British Gas (£5,600m). Total receipts were just over £15 billion. Harold Macmillan compared the decision with 'selling off the family silver', forgetting perhaps that the silver was being sold to the family. What they did with it afterwards was their business. There have been repeated complaints that these and later sales were too cheap and the controversy continues to this day. There was also the question of the enormous salaries and share options which directors, the so-called 'fat cats', voted for themselves. The plea that these were necessary for international competitiveness did not carry much conviction in the case of utilities which were national monopolies.

The policy was not unpopular, however. British Telecom was far more efficient under private than public control and British Airways, from being a byword for sloth and incompetence, became one of the most competitive lines in the world. British Gas was less successful and its problems still remain. By and large, privatisation during this and the next two parliaments (1987-92 and 1992-97) was sufficiently successful for Labour, though opposing every sale at the time, to declare eventually that it had no intention of renationalising.

The Labour party, demoralised by defeat, took nearly a decade to recover. The process began tentatively with the resignation of Michael Foot and the election on 2 October 1983 of Neil Kinnock as leader and Roy Hattersley as deputy by large majorities in the newly invented party electoral college. Kinnock, only forty-one, was apparently a figure of the left but he soon distanced himself from the 'hard' core of that faction and made it clear that Labour, however discreetly, had to drop some of the commitments of their electoral manifesto – in particular the promise to reverse privatisation. But his major problem was relations with the unions and the Conservatives had him at a serious disadvantage when Arthur Scargill called what turned out to be a year-long miners' strike on 8 March 1984. This and the ensuing print union strike were turning points in the history of industrial relations and the fortunes of the Conservative party. They enabled the Prime Minister to achieve a solution to her third problem – the excessive power of the trade unions, whose privileged legal position was unique in Europe.

Scargill, emboldened by the apparent success of the miners in bringing down the Heath government and by the seeming success of the steel workers' strike in 1980 – in reality a Pyrrhic victory – persuaded the National Union of Miners (NUM) to make an all-out attempt to repeat 1974. He openly proclaimed his intention to destroy the government. Margaret Thatcher's memoirs have been criticised, sometimes justly, but on this question it is hard to fault her. She heads the relevant chapter 'Mr Scargill's Insurrection'. Observing that the 1983 election had finally defeated 'democratic socialism', in the sense of the manifesto policies proclaimed by Michael Foot and his friends, she went on:

> But there was also undemocratic socialism and it too would need to be beaten. I had never had any doubt about the true aim of the hard left: they were revolutionaries who sought to impose a Marxist system on Britain whatever the means and whatever the cost.

This was Scargill's alleged aim and no government of any complexion – let alone Conservative – could accept it.

The prospect of such a confrontation had long been a concern of the Conservative party leaders. In the previous parliament the government had made preparations. It was not ready to have a showdown in 1981 when strike action was threatened over pit closures. Coal stocks were too low to be sure of success in the event of confrontation, but Nigel Lawson, Minister of Energy from September 1981 to June 1983, was as determined as his leader to resist any further challenge. He rightly recognised that Arthur Scargill had to be defeated if the economy was to survive.

The key issue was the closure of uneconomic pits. For years Britain had been producing far too much unsaleable coal. But it was an article of Scargill's Stalinish faith that no pit which could produce coal should ever be closed. This piece of idiocy had one useful side-effect unintended by its author – a vast stockpile of coal which would prove very handy in the event of a strike, provided it was piled up along with the necessary chemicals at the power stations, not at the pits. Lawson and his successor, Peter Walker, managed to do this with the maximum of discretion.

As well as the miners, the National Coal Board was a thorn in the government's side. A byword for all the worst features of nationalised industry, it was riddled with sloth, confusion, administrative chaos and financial incompetence. Its priorities were to keep the NUM sweet and to please the managers. The customers came bottom of the list. To run it successfully new blood was essential. Lawson appointed as chairman, at an enormous and highly controversial salary, Ian MacGregor, a tough monosyllabic Scottish-American who had already turned round the loss-making British Steel Corporation.

The strike began on 8 March 1984 as a protest against the closing of uneconomic pits. After a year of bitterness, violence and hatred, it collapsed ignominiously on 3 March 1985. The government formally distanced itself from the negotiations between the NUM and the NCB but its sympathy and support for MacGregor were unconcealed and he knew that he had Margaret Thatcher's full backing. Scargill made two major errors. Aware that his support in the NUM was half-hearted, he ignored the union's own rules about balloting when he called the strike. He also called it early in the spring, before the summer months when it would have least impact.

The unions' cause soon received a second defeat on a different front. For many years the printing unions had exercised a Luddite stranglehold on newspaper production, which combined corruption, fraud and blackmail on a scale intolerable in a free enterprise society. And it was free enterprise that ended it. Rupert Murdoch, whose company News International controlled *The Times*, *Sunday Times*, *Sun* and *News of the World*, decided that with the new printing technology he could break the power of the print unions for good. Displaying a secrecy and ruthlessness worthy of a wartime operation, in December 1985 he dismissed the whole of his production staff when they refused to co-operate in using the new machinery. He moved all four titles from Fleet Street to a new plant set up at Wapping and operated by a new force of electricians producing the papers at a fraction of their previous cost. It was the death knell for Fleet Street as the hub and symbol of the newspaper industry. Amidst numerous scenes of violence and sabotage, the 'Battle of Wapping' lasted, like the miners' strike, for twelve months, ending in January 1986 in total defeat for the unions. The miners had had a certain amount of backing from public opinion, though far less than in 1974. The print unions had none and deserved none.

The government by the end of its second parliament had gone a good way towards success in one of its prime means of reviving the British economy – defeat of the unions. Trouble rumbled on in the public sector, particularly among the school teachers, and a ballot among the unions at large calling for the abandonment of the political levy, a main source of Labour's finance, totally failed. But the combination of unemployment, privatisation and reforms in the law greatly enfeebled the union 'movement'. The government was helped by economic success during the 1983–87 parliament. True, unemployment at between 3.1 and 3.3 million throughout the period was alarmingly high, though this very fact may have played a part in taming union militancy. In other respects the scene was much more favourable. Inflation ranging between 3 and 5 per cent was well below the level of the major European countries. North Sea oil, despite a collapse in world prices between December 1985 and August 1986, remained an important element in a favourable balance of payments. More significant than either of these features was a slow but steady rise in the standard of living of the vast majority of the population who were in work. Average wages in real terms rose from £140 per week to £190 between 1983 and 1987.

Although the expression was not used at the time, 'the feel good' factor was an important asset to the party throughout these years. It contributed much to electoral success in 1987.

These were not years of calm and peace, however. The problem of the IRA brooded over the scene. In December 1983 the bomb outside Harrods, which killed five people and wounded many others, showed that terrorism was unabated. This was followed by the explosion of a bomb on 12 October 1984 in the Brighton hotel where a great number of prominent Conservatives were staying for the party conference. The intention was to murder the Prime Minister and as many members of the government as possible. There had been nothing like it since the Gunpowder Plot or the Cato Street Conspiracy of 1820. The plotters' full objectives were not achieved but five people were killed including Anthony Berry MP and the wife of John Wakeham, the Chief Whip, who was himself seriously injured. Norman Tebbit, Secretary for Industry, also suffered grave injury and his wife was crippled for life.

Despite these and many other atrocious events, the Conservative government tried to seek some agreement with Dublin to improve co-operation over security and to reduce the tacit support which elements of public opinion in Eire seemed to be giving to the objectives if not the methods of the IRA. On 15 November 1985, at Hillsborough Castle, Margaret Thatcher and Garret FitzGerald, the Irish Prime Minister, signed the Anglo-Irish Agreement. Its first article affirmed that no change in the status of Northern Ireland could take place without the consent of a majority of its population and recognised that for the present no such consent existed. In return for this declaration the British government agreed that Dublin could put forward opinions and proposals to London about Northern Ireland on a wide range of matters, one of the most important being security. There was no question of any modification of parliamentary sovereignty. Dublin could only propose. London would decide.

Despite these safeguards, Unionist opinion was outraged. The link between the Conservative party and the Ulster Unionists was broken. Fifteen MPs resigned to fight by-elections as a sort of referendum, and all bar one were returned. This defection was about the only Irish issue which affected British party politics, for in general there was bi-partisan agreement outside Ulster. The loss of the Ulster Unionists did not matter much to the Conservatives while they held big majorities at Westminster, as in 1983 and 1987. It was to be a very different matter after 1992, when their margin, small even at the outset, rapidly dwindled.

By the spring of 1985 the party was beginning to run into trouble. Efforts to keep welfare expenditure under control affected local government, the health service and education. In those quarters Margaret Thatcher soon became highly unpopular – especially in secondary and higher education. She had never concealed her contempt for local government and for the Department of Education and Science. In January 1985, the University of Oxford voted against conferring an honorary degree upon its most influential graduate and the first woman Prime Minister, as a protest against cuts in the funding of universities. This vindictive act of petty spite did Oxford nothing but harm and of course made no difference whatever to the cuts.

Early in 1985 Labour began to move ahead in the opinion polls, the Conservatives lost control of a number of shire counties in the May local elections and two months later, on 4 July, they suffered what Margaret Thatcher described as 'a spectacularly bad by-election result at Brecon and Radnor'.[1] The Alliance won with a swing of nearly 16 per cent and the Conservative candidate came in third. Opinion polls, local government elections and parliamentary by-elections are very far from being reliable indicators of what might happen in a general election unlikely to occur for at least two years. Nevertheless, any party in power is bound to feel uneasy when all three seem to be going in the wrong direction.

Francis Pym tried to capitalise on these worries by launching in May an anti-Thatcher movement called 'Centre Forward'. It was the dampest of damp squibs. But it was a symptom of doubt among the party faithful.

Was there something wrong with party policy, personalities or presentation? Policy is the last thing a party is going to change so soon after it has apparently been endorsed by the electorate at the polls. The possibility that the general election result owed more to the errors and incompetence of the Conservatives' opponent than to their own virtues and skills is seldom prominent in the minds of the winners. Personalities

---

[1] *The Downing Street Years*, op. cit., 416.

and presentation, closely connected, are in a different category.

In late May the Prime Minister began to discuss with the Deputy Prime Minister (Whitelaw) and the Chief Whip (Wakeham) the possibility of a July reshuffle of the government. They were in favour, according to her account, but she thought it was too soon.[1] Better to do it after the summer holidays and at the beginning of September. She decided to leave two of the three key posts unchanged. Lawson, after a disastrous first budget bedevilled by a 'leak', seemed a successful tax-reformer at the Treasury; and she did not yet appreciate how far away from her Geoffrey Howe was moving over Europe. Perhaps she should have listened more carefully.

The third key minister, however, she was determined to change and on 1 September she told Leon Brittan that she wished him to move from the Home Office to the Department of Trade and Industry. The Home Office is exposed to more public criticism and media attention than any other government department. Its actions or inactions are subject to incessant legal and political controversy. Brittan had many strengths but presentation was not one of them. In his place she appointed Douglas Hurd from the Northern Ireland Office, an archetypal 'safe pair of hands' with a reassuring manner.

The other important change which the Prime Minister was determined to make concerned the Conservative Central Office. As Party Chairman, Gummer had not been a success. He had been regarded at the time as a curious appointment – a junior minister not even in the Cabinet and with few presentational skills. Mrs Thatcher wrote: 'I had appointed him as night-watchman: but he seemed to have gone to sleep on the job.'[2] This may have been unfair. Arguably it was the Prime Minister's fault in the first place for choosing a lightweight. In his place she appointed Norman Tebbit, who accepted the job although he was still suffering a good deal of pain from injuries sustained at Brighton. His deputy was Jeffrey Archer whose boundless energy and popular oratory compensated for his not infrequent gaffes. David Young, an able businessman whom

[1]*The Downing Street Years*, op. cit., 418.
[2]*The Downing Street Years*, op. cit., 421.

Margaret Thatcher much admired and had already brought into the government from outside the political world, became Minister for Employment. Kenneth Baker became Minister for the Environment with the problems of rates reform on his hands.

The reshuffle went down quite well and the Prime Minister reckoned that this would be the team to fight the next election. She had not allowed for what Harold Macmillan once said when asked to name the greatest problem in politics: 'Events, my dear boy, events.' The 'event' was the Westland helicopter affair which blew up from an apparently clear sky quite suddenly at the end of November 1985 and very nearly brought the government down. Westland was a small company running into financial difficulties. Its importance was that it was the only British company manufacturing helicopters. It needed an infusion of capital from outside if it was to survive. Michael Heseltine, because of defence implications, wanted to secure support from a European consortium. The company looked towards Sikorsky, an American firm; the Prime Minister and Leon Brittan agreed that this was the better option and in any case that it was a matter for the company to judge not Whitehall.

The ensuing row involved both ideology and personalities. Heseltine was a 'Europhile' and a *dirigiste*. The Prime Minister was instinctively pro-American and although she was shortly to sign the Single European Act she was inclined even at this time to be doubtful about Europe.

The European Community had been – since 1977 – a customs union. The Single Act, agreed in February 1986, removed the 'non-tariff' barriers affecting, for example, insurance and financial services, regulations discriminating against foreign products and differences in procurement policies. A Conservative government committed to free trade could readily agree to these changes. What the Prime Minister perhaps failed to take account of at the time was the cloudy Euro-rhetoric about ever-closer union beloved by leaders of the other European nations. She wrote it off as windy waffle. But it was to lead directly to Maastricht – about the last thing she wanted.

Beyond ideological differences, Thatcher regarded Heseltine with deep distrust. There was no love lost between them. There followed a bitter conflict between Heseltine and Brittan backed by the Prime Minister.

Heseltine believed that he had not been allowed to state his case to the Cabinet. There were arguments about the minutes. There were allegations and counter-allegations, numerous leaks and a charge that the Prime Minister had authorised one of these from a letter by the Attorney General, who later threatened to resign. On 9 January 1986 Heseltine, who has a short fuse, walked out of the Cabinet but the effect was slightly marred by the impression gained by some members in the general confusion that he was merely departing to the loo. Two weeks later, Leon Brittan also resigned. The Prime Minister's ambiguous – or seemingly so – role in all this made her highly vulnerable but in the ensuing debate in the Commons Neil Kinnock fluffed his lines and she survived – just.

This battle proved to be the prelude to a war of attrition that was to bring her down in November 1990. Heseltine was a formidable and implacable enemy. He had to bide his time in the run-up to the general election. Thereafter, no holds were barred.

The years since 1983 had been full of too many banana skins for the party to be confident about the next election. This explains the divisions and doubts about who should run the campaign and on what programme. Although the extent of dissension in the party's electoral preparations has been exaggerated, Margaret Thatcher's account in her autobiography indicates that all was not sweetness and light.

The question of the programme and timing of the election had been in the Prime Minister's mind since the end of the Westland affair. She was not entirely happy with the team in place to lead the party. The occasion for a reshuffle was provided by an event which in itself was far from welcome: Keith Joseph's decision in May 1986 to leave the Cabinet. He had been a staunch ally from 1975 onwards and a notable intellectual advocate of 'Thatcherism'. His decision was purely personal. Thatcher transferred Kenneth Baker from Environment

to Education and put in his place Nicholas Ridley, whose clarity
of mind she believed might bring order and purpose to a
'sprawling department',[1] as she described it. Concerned as it
was with housing and rates, its head would have a key role in the
run-up to the general election. She also brought in one of the
rising younger figures, John Moore, as Minister of Transport.

The Conservative party conference in November 1986 – possibly the last before the general election – required careful
planning. It would give the key note for an election which was
likely to be called in early summer of the following year. The
general election did not have to be then, however, and the
Prime Minister kept her options open. But her known view that
a new mandate should be sought after four years meant that –
failing some calamitous downturn in the party's fortunes – an
election in the first half of 1987 was highly probable.

In June, at the suggestion of Whitelaw and the Chief Whip,
John Wakeham, she set up the 'Strategy Group' to deal with
plans for the next election. Its members beside herself were
Whitelaw, Wakeham, Howe, Lawson, Hurd and Tebbit, i.e. the
Deputy Prime Minister, the Chief Whip, the holders of the
three great offices of state and the Party Chairman. At the
same time she established eleven party-policy groups, each
chaired by the minister who covered its area of interest. The
object was to establish a forward-looking programme to appeal
to the electorate. The slogan devised by Norman Tebbit was
'Our Next Move Forward'. At the conference, Margaret
Thatcher made, after elaborate care, a highly successful
speech. The party's faithful were delighted. 'Westland', which
few people understood anyway, had long been forgotten. Her
scathing attack on Labour's defence policy did great damage to
Neil Kinnock, from which he never recovered and which may
well have lost him the election.

By the end of the parliamentary recess in the autumn of 1986
the party's morale seemed much better than it had been in July,
which is always an ill-tempered month in politics. Opinion polls
were favourable. No obvious storms were on the horizon. The

[1]*The Downing Street Years*, op. cit., 563.

economic prospects seemed good. In January 1987 the Prime Minister, with Norman Tebbit and others, discussed in detail (at Lord McAlpine's house for the sake of secrecy) plans for the election campaign. It was fairly clear by now that the election would take place in early June. The manifesto was more or less settled. It would, on the positive side, concentrate on economic prosperity, educational improvements, rates reform, privatisation, a 25 per cent basic rate of income tax and general encouragement of self-help. Negatively, it would attack Labour and the Alliance for confusing waffle and obscurity, especially on defence. The 'poll tax' was being planned in order to solve the rates problem but although it had been agreed, despite strong opposition from Nigel Lawson, it did not appear as a major issue before the general election. It was, however, in the manifesto and after the Conservative victory in 1987 no one could deny that the government had a 'mandate', whatever that means, to replace rates with a 'community charge', as the government officially called it. In the event the poll tax was to be a disaster of the first magnitude and contributed more than any other mistake to the fall of Margaret Thatcher in 1990.

As with the previous two elections the party machine concentrated heavily on publicity. The key players in 1979 and 1983 had been the advertising firm of Saatchi and Saatchi, whose managing director (Sir) Tim Bell was a committed Thatcherite and had an excellent rapport with the Prime Minister. The others had been (Sir) Gordon Reece, director of party publicity, who had gone to work in the USA in 1981 but had returned to help in 1983, and Harry Thomas who had managed publicity for the American evangelist Billy Graham. He was adept at the organisation and presentation of rallies, mass meetings and big public occasions – dry ice, laser beams and a theme song by Andrew Lloyd Webber.[1]

The personnel had changed by 1987. Tim Bell had virtually parted company with the Saatchis, though he still had a rather vague consultancy brief where political publicity was required. Co-operation was not smooth. Reece and Thomas were avail-

[1] *The Downing Street Years*, op. cit., 580. This was at a rally in Cardiff on 26 May 1987.

able as before. At Central Office the Party Chairman, Norman Tebbit, was a more abrasive and suspicious figure than his predecessor, Cecil Parkinson, who was smooth and emollient. Tebbit's relations with Margaret Thatcher were uneasy. He suspected her quite wrongly of feeding adverse matter about him to the press and although the misunderstanding was cleared up a certain lack of confidence remained on both sides.

On 11 May 1987 Margaret Thatcher requested the Queen to dissolve parliament. The general election would take place a month later, on 11 June. Conservative campaigns traditionally get off to a slow start but Mrs Thatcher soon wondered whether it was going to get off at all. The worry was all the greater because Labour seemed to have learnt the lesson of the 1983 fiasco. Their organisation was far more modern, streamlined and up-to-date than it had been four years earlier. The Conservatives by contrast seemed confused and divided, not on policy but on how to put it across and win votes. The story is too complicated to relate here. It is enough to say that there was in the end a dual command at Central Office. Mrs Thatcher summoned David (Lord) Young to 'help' Norman Tebbit; and there were three advertising agencies giving advice. There were many other crosscurrents in these somewhat turbulent waters.

What really mattered in the campaign was the party's leader. She had the authority of having been Prime Minister for eight years and she was a brilliant performer on the political stage. No doubt she had much private advice about her image. It was highly successful in that she came across as a powerful, respected, formidable figure. Although not regarded with much affection, she looked like a winner. And she was.

Votes are cast not only *for* a party, but *against* a party or parties. The Conservatives faced a much greater threat from Kinnock than they had from Foot. Yet, although his campaign was well organised and efficient, he somehow did not come across in parliament or the media as a plausible Prime Minister. Compared with Margaret Thatcher he seemed a lightweight. He may have suffered from his place of origin. Lloyd George is the only product of Wales ever to have become Prime Minister. Scotland seems to fare much better.

The Labour party's campaign was marred by two serious gaffes. Denis Healey on a goodwill visit to the USSR declared that Moscow would be delighted if Labour won. Neil Kinnock defending nuclear disarmament said that, if there was an invasion of Britain, the answer would be guerilla warfare against the occupying forces. The Conservatives had plenty of fun with both these remarks but it is unlikely that they affected the result of the election.

It is never clear what decides elections. Historians can only guess. The campaign ran fairly smoothly for the Conservatives. There was a slight blip a week before the crucial date – on 'wobbly Thursday', 4 June – when a rogue opinion poll suggested that the party might lose. In the event they won by a comfortable margin. The threat of the Alliance party – 'the two Davids' (Steel and Owen) – never seemed very serious. They had a substantial popular vote but they were marginalised by the electoral system and, as in 1983, were not seen as a potential party of government. The result was a win for the Conservatives by a majority of 102 seats over all other parties combined. The detailed figures in a poll of 75.3 per cent were: Conservatives 376 seats with 42.3 per cent of votes cast; Labour 229 with 30.8 per cent; Alliance 22 with 22.6 per cent; Welsh and Scottish Nationalists 6 with 1.7 per cent; others (mainly Northern Ireland) 17 with 2.6 per cent. Mrs Thatcher thus became the first prime minister since Lord Liverpool (1812–1827) to win three successive general elections.

CHAPTER XIII

Thatcher and Major 1987–97

1

In the aftermath of this triumph one of Margaret Thatcher's colleagues is said to have commented that she behaved as if she was walking on water. She was soon to find that she was sliding on very thin ice. At first no great difficulties arose. She made a modest Cabinet reshuffle. John Biffen who had become, as she put it, 'semi-detached' now found himself fully detached and was replaced by John Wakeham as Leader of the Commons. David Waddington became Chief Whip. Cecil Parkinson, one of her favourites, was brought back as Secretary for Energy. John Moore became Secretary for Health. Norman Tebbit had clearly told her that he would resign after the election. In his place she appointed Peter Brooke. The holders of the key posts – Foreign Office, Treasury, Home Office, Education, Environment (Howe, Lawson, Hurd, Baker, Ridley) – remained unchanged. Whitelaw continued to lead in the Lords and act as Deputy Prime Minister. The new Lord Chancellor and former Attorney General Michael Havers only lasted a year because his health collapsed. He was succeeded by Lord Mackay, the first lawyer whose experience was wholly Scottish to hold this office. He turned out to be a vigorous law-reformer and as a result was not loved by lawyers.

For the first eighteen months after the election the Conservatives were riding high in the opinion polls and the government was able to begin fulfilling its manifesto promises. The main objectives were reform of housing, health and education, areas in which anti-Conservative forces were most deeply entrenched. Housing was dominated by Labour local authorities which had blocked the sale of council houses as far as they could and continued to oppose any reduction of their remaining powers. The teachers' unions, as Conservatives saw them, supported a 1960s' type of permissive child-orientated orthodoxy, which had left British educational standards far behind those of Europe. Here the Prime Minister wanted fundamental change and one result of this was the 'grant maintained school'. As for health, it was a matter of increasing administrative efficiency and getting better value within a system too popular electorally to be radically altered but capable of being made more economical and cost-conscious. These were piecemeal changes which would take time to have an effect.

The most important next stage was the Budget. Nigel Lawson was determined to make a mark for the Conservative party and himself with major tax reforms. There were clear and comprehensive decisions to be made. And Lawson made them. The economy was still booming; the best time for a controversial Budget is the earliest moment in a new parliament. Lawson reduced the standard rate of income tax to 25 per cent. This came as no surprise. It had been promised in the party manifesto. What did come as a surprise and produced furious opposition reaction was a reduction from 60 per cent to 40 per cent in the top rate of income tax. Many Conservatives including the Prime Minister preferred 50 per cent but Lawson was determined to make a decisive and symbolic break with the old 'soak-the-rich' syndrome which neither Macmillan nor Heath had managed to eradicate and which Geoffrey Howe had only partly modified.

The Budget was well received. Margaret Thatcher cordially congratulated the Chancellor. But relations between them were friendly only on the surface. According to Lawson, the Prime Minister resented claims in Westminster and the media in the aftermath of the general election that he, rather than she, was the author of the Conservative success. It is true that his critical analysis of Kinnock's financial promises had been an important element in the government's anti-Labour propaganda and had received much publicity, though it was certainly not the only reason why Labour lost. He believed that she now saw him as a rival for the leadership.[1] The relationship further deteriorated following Whitelaw's resignation after he had suffered a slight stroke when reading a lesson at a carol service at St Margaret's, Westminster, on 14 December 1987. Conciliatory and tactful, he had done a great deal to oil the Cabinet wheels and to anticipate conflicts, often before they reached the confrontational stage.

The situation was made no easier by the Prime Minister's long-standing antipathy to Geoffrey Howe, the other key member of the Cabinet. This was partly personal. She found him slow, long-winded and over-cautious at Cabinet meetings. But there was more to it than that. She was becoming more and more of a Eurosceptic, whereas he was an emphatic Europhile. This latent ideological divide became overt when the Prime Minister made her famous (opponents might say infamous) speech at the College of Europe in Bruges on 20 September 1988. She had already been infuriated by the words of Jacques Delors, the President of the European Commission, when he had told the European Parliament in July 1988 that within ten years 80 per cent of all the key social and economic decisions would be taken in Brussels rather than in the member states. He capped this by addressing an enthusiastic TUC conference at Brighton on 8 September: the unions should, he said, press for collective bargaining on a European level and take advantage of the Social Chapter to achieve some of Labour's objectives which had no prospect of success at Westminster. His speech greatly strengthened the Europhile tendency in Labour and correspondingly hardened the hostility of the Prime Minister who anyway detested Delors.

Impatient with what she saw as 'the creeping expansion of the Commission's authority', Thatcher wrote in her memoirs: 'I had now heard about as much about the European "ideal" as I could take.'[2]

At Bruges she decided to strike out on a line of her own which

[1] Nigel Lawson, *The View from No. 11* (Bantam, 1992), 708. He has repeatedly denied any such ambition and there is no reason to doubt his word.
[2] Margaret Thatcher, *The Downing Street Years* (HarperCollins, 1993), 743.

was by no means agreeable to her hosts, nor to the Foreign Office which had hoped that she would confine herself to emphasising Britain's contribution to Europe. She opened her speech by doing just this but then sounded a different note.

It is ironic that just when those countries such as the Soviet Union, which have tried to run everything from the centre, are learning that success depends on dispensing power and decisions away from the centre, some in the Community seem to want to move in the opposite direction. We have not successfully rolled back the frontiers of the state in Britain only to see them reimposed at a European level, with a European super-state exercising a new dominance from Brussels.

Turning points in recent political history are notoriously difficult to identify but the Bruges speech has a better claim than most. Geoffrey Howe 'was deeply dismayed by the Bruges speech. Its impact at home as much as abroad far exceeded my initial fears'.[1] At the end of the same page appear the words which give the title to his memoirs. 'I can see now that this was probably the moment at which there began to crystallise the conflict of loyalty with which I was to struggle perhaps for too long.'[2]

Nigel Lawson had similar misgivings, not so much about the speech as about the feelings – 'intensely chauvinistic and particularly hostile to the Community' – which inspired it.[3] He and Howe did not have exactly the same views on the rising problems of ERM (the Exchange Rate Mechanism of the European Monetary System) and EMU (Economic and Monetary Union), but both their views differed sharply from Margaret Thatcher's.

'Europe' had been the subject of bitter dispute during Edward Heath's premiership and during the referendum of 1975 called by Harold Wilson. The referendum seemed to have

---

[1]Geoffrey Howe, *Conflict of Loyalty* (Macmillan, 1994), 538.
[2]*Ibid.*, 744–5.
[3]*The View from No. 11*, op. cit., 907.

settled the question of British participation *en principe*, though not the details which were and are subject to almost infinite argument. For over a decade the problem had not been a major issue in national or Conservative politics. But there was no consensus and it did not cease to smoulder. The Bruges speech revived the flames of the referendum debate. They have gone on burning ever since and, at the time of writing, show no sign of going out. They were to consume the three leading Thatcherites, first Howe, then Lawson and finally Margaret Thatcher herself.

On 4 May 1989 Margaret Thatcher had been Prime Minister for ten years. She tried to play it down but the media had a field day. Then and since many people have said that this was the right time for her to retire, not recognising that for a Prime Minister in good health there never is a right time to retire.

A new crisis loomed. A summit meeting of the EU Council of Ministers was due to be held in Madrid on 26 June. The key question was whether Britain should join the ERM. This, to quote Nigel Lawson, 'in essence was a parity grid, giving a lower and upper margin of fluctuation of each member currency against every other'. In practice this meant limited fluctuation against the Deutschmark, the only stable yardstick at the time. Lawson and Howe were in favour of joining. The Prime Minister had strong misgivings. The Madrid Summit was faced with the Delors Report. This argued for entry into the ERM as a first step towards the ultimate goal of EMU, in effect a common currency and a central European bank. No British government at that time was going to agree to EMU – a subject of intense controversy to this day. But ERM was a different matter. Believing that the Prime Minister, encouraged by a private adviser Alan Walters, would try to block entry, Lawson and Howe threatened to resign. The Prime Minister gave way, but she neither forgot nor forgave. A month later, on 24 July 1989, she reshuffled the Cabinet, removed Howe from the Foreign Office and replaced him with John Major. Howe became Leader of the House and was fobbed off with the title 'Deputy Prime Minister'. It was widely believed that Thatcher would, as soon as was politically convenient, get rid of Lawson, too, but if so he anticipated her by resigning on 26 October. He felt that his economic advice was being bypassed in favour of that of her guru Walters who, to complicate matters further, resigned himself almost at the same time. John Major, after one of the briefest tenures ever of the Foreign Office, now became Chancellor of the Exchequer. Douglas Hurd was appointed in his place.

Europe was not the only divisive party issue. Nigel Lawson was involved in another quite independent dispute over the community charge or, as it became known to the irritation of the government, the poll tax. This was an attempt to meet the manifesto pledge to reform that most unpopular of all features of local government: rates. A local tax on the rental value of property made sense when it was the local authority who provided services such as gas, electricity, water, refuse disposal and sewerage; when there was a large privately rented housing sector with which comparison could be made, and, particularly, when local suffrage was based on a property qualification. By the last quarter of the twentieth century none of this applied. The original services had long since been nationalised. The local franchise was the same as for Westminster. The privately rented sector had almost vanished. Local government now supplied a variety of services – education being the most expensive – which had no connection with property but the cost of which fell on property owners. As a result, non-property owners who constituted the great majority of voters had no reason to vote for economy in expenditure since the cost fell on the minority. Successive governments tried to alleviate this situation by grants-in-aid – the Rate Support Grant (RSG) – from central funds calculated on a formula which scarcely anyone understood. However, this did not meet the complaint of elderly pensioners living on their own that they paid the same rate as a householder in identical accommodation with three sturdy sons at home earning good wages.

The essence of the poll tax was a flat residents' charge per head for every adult (with modest rebates for the very poor) to replace domestic rates. At the same time, non-domestic rates which were said to penalise small businesses, especially in Labour-dominated authorities, would be replaced by a nation-

ally fixed business rate and thus prevent 'ideological victimisa-
tion'. This caused little controversy.

The consequences of the poll tax were disastrous and
Margaret Thatcher's relations with Lawson were made no
better when he predicted them, the only member of the
Cabinet to do so. For the poll tax was not, as is often alleged, an
example of the Prime Minister bullying the Cabinet. On the
contrary, she was not at first in favour of it, although it had been
very thoroughly analysed, researched and ably presented. The
episode, far from being an example of prime ministerial government, was the result of Cabinet government and constitutional
correctness. The only snag was that it was politically unsaleable
– a huge, unexpected rise in local taxes falling far more heavily
on the poor than the rich and widely felt to be grossly unfair.
The tax was finally withdrawn in 1991 in favour of the graduated tax on the capital value of properties which prevails today.

To agree to the poll tax, even if belatedly, was probably the
worst mistake of the Prime Minister's career. It contributed to
a large degree to her fall. One of Heseltine's planks in his platform to oust Thatcher from the leadership was the repeal of the
poll tax. It did not get him in, but it got her out.[1]

The seventeen months in 1989–90 following the Madrid
Summit saw disaster after disaster piling up for the
Conservative party. Early in 1989 there began a major recession
which affected the world economy. It followed hard on what is
sometimes called 'the Lawson boom', when house prices shot up
at 30 per cent p.a. for a brief but unsustainable period. By
spring 1990 the rise had halted and prices were soon to go down.
Many buyers had badly burned their fingers. The recession, the
longest in recent times, only began to bottom out in the mid-
1990s. The poll tax, divisions over Europe and economic depression caused a heavy slump in the party's popularity and
particularly in that of the Prime Minister, who outwardly
seemed curiously impervious to what was going on. Her unpopularity was worrying many of the rank and file of the party,
especially back-benchers with marginal seats who felt threat-

ened by the backlash from the poll tax. There was also increasing unease about her apparent dependence on advice from Bernard Ingham, her press secretary, and Charles Powell, who advised her on foreign policy and much else.

The electoral system for the leadership had been changed in 1975, the year when Thatcher had defeated Heath. Since then the election had been an annual event but despite slumps in Thatcher's popularity in 1981 and 1986 no one had challenged her and she was formally elected every year *nem. con.* In 1989, however, an unexpected rival candidate was proposed in the form of an elderly Old Etonian baronet, Sir Anthony Meyer, MP for Clwyd North-West. Geoffrey Howe had considered but rejected the idea of standing, though he was pressed to do so both privately and in the Press. Meyer was the wettest of wets and also a strong Europhile. He was far too dim a figure to have any chance. The figures announced on 5 December 1989 were Thatcher 314, Meyer 33, and 27 abstentions. The significance of 60 MPs unwilling to support Thatcher was not lost on the Whips, who are said to have hinted to her that it might be time to drop Ingham and Powell. If they did, the hint was not taken.

Events in 1990 did not improve the party's fortunes. On 31 March there were riots over the poll tax. On 3 May Labour made big gains at the local elections. On 14 July Nicholas Ridley felt obliged to resign after uttering, as he thought off-the-record, some highly anti-German remarks to the editor of the *Spectator*, who happened to be Nigel Lawson's son. On 30 July one of the Prime Minister's closest allies, Ian Gow, was murdered by the IRA. On 9 September she announced to the consternation of many Conservatives that she intended to remain Prime Minister till 1995. The impression of hubris was enhanced when she made a speech after Britain had joined the ERM on 8 October 1990 which signalled her real views on Europe. She was making a statement to the House in the aftermath of the Rome EU Summit of 27–28 October. In the House, she declared that Britain would never participate in EMU. For the first time she attacked Delors publicly. He wanted, she said, 'the European Parliament to be the democratic body of the Community ... the Commission to be the executive ... and the

Council of Ministers to be the Senate'. To these alleged objectives she said her reply was 'No! No! No!' The Commission was trying to extinguish democracy and take Britain through 'the back door to a federal Europe'.

After this the gloves were off and the split between Europhiles and Eurosceptics was there for all to see. Geoffrey Howe decided that he had had enough. After a day spent consulting his wife and friends and drafting his letter of resignation, he called on the Prime Minister soon after 6.00 p.m. on 1 November, formally resigned and handed her the letter. Parliament had been prorogued so although the news of his resignation filled the media he could not make the customary speech for several days and had plenty of time to prepare. When he did speak, on 13 November, the occasion was one of high parliamentary drama. The words were devastating. The House was stunned by an oration so lethal from someone who had seemed ready to put up with almost any insult and affront from the Prime Minister and who had once been pilloried as 'Mogadon Man'.

Howe's speech heralded the end of Margaret Thatcher as Prime Minister. Under the 1975 rules a leadership election was shortly due. If Heseltine was ever going to make a bid, now was the time. True, the Gulf War was soon to begin and there was always the cry 'not to rock the boat'. This did not deter him. On 14 November he was nominated as a candidate. On 20 November the first ballot took place while the Prime Minister was meeting President Mitterrand in Paris. It gave her 204 votes to Heseltine's 152. To the world outside Westminster this looked like a win for Thatcher, but under the arcane party rules a 15 per cent majority was needed. She was two short of that. There would have to be a second ballot in which new candidates could stand and the winner would need a simple majority over all others. There is general agreement that the Prime Minister's campaign was badly managed and that with a bit more effort and efficiency from her managers (one of whom, Peter Morrison, was a notorious drunk), she could have broken the 15 per cent barrier.

The question now was whether she would stand and could

win in a second ballot. On her return from Paris she consulted each Cabinet member in turn. The verdict in all but two cases was that each would personally support her but doubted whether she would win. She might have done better to confront them collectively. She decided to resign as leader but not as Prime Minister until the party had elected a new leader, just as Harold Wilson had done in 1976.

A great amount has been written about the feverish days of manoeuvre and intrigue between 14 and 27 November when the second ballot was held. It almost rivals the literature about the fall of Asquith in 1916. Precisely who said what, where and when to whom, who was at this or that meeting, who were the two-faced double-crossers and who if any played a straight bat will long be a matter of dispute. Diaries were kept, which may one day be published. The best account at the time of writing is by Alan Watkins.[1] It has not been seriously criticised by the principal participants but the author would not claim it as the last word. Indeed, there cannot be one for many years, if ever, on such a complicated and controversial imbroglio.

Whatever the details, the underlying reason for Margaret Thatcher's fall is clear. The Conservative party believes in winning. It has always been ready to oust leaders who seem to be losers: Balfour in 1911, Austen Chamberlain in 1922, Home in 1965, Heath in 1975. Whether because of personal doubts, hints from loyalists, or, after 1975, the brutal arithmetic of a party vote, leaders have gone because the party believed that they would lose the next general election. In Thatcher's case, the resignation of two key figures, the failure to cope with the worsening recession, divisions over Europe and, above all, the poll tax to which the Prime Minister was irrevocably committed all pointed towards electoral disaster.

Who would be Thatcher's successor? Those who voted for her in the first ballot were determined on one thing: it would not be Michael Heseltine, whatever he said about dismantling the poll tax. The old adage that the man who wields the dagger never wins the crown applied: he must be kept at all costs from the

[1] Alan Watkins, *A Conservative Coup, The Fall of Margaret Thatcher* (Duckworth, 1991).

inheritance which he sought. He had never denounced Thatcher or Thatcherism but his views were well known. Now that Thatcher had gone, her supporters still adhered to the creed but sought a less abrasive exponent. John Major, a somewhat Baldwin-like figure, was her preferred successor.

The second ballot, which was preceded by another week of political intrigue, had three contestants: Heseltine, Major and – an unexpected third candidate – the Foreign Secretary, Douglas Hurd. The vote declared on 27 November was Major 185, Heseltine 131, Hurd 56. Under the rules there should have been a third ballot since Major was two votes short of the required absolute majority over the combined vote of his rivals. But they both at once withdrew and Cranley Onslow, who as Chairman of the 1922 Committee was the Returning Officer, decided not to prolong the agony. He pronounced the winner to be Major, who next day was appointed Prime Minister by the Queen.

2

John Major's social and educational background was unlike that of any previous Conservative leader. Neither Edward Heath nor Margaret Thatcher was 'born in the purple' but both went to Oxford; later he made – and she married – money. Major's father, Tom, who was sixty-four when his son, their third child, was born in 1943, had been from 1901 to 1929 an actor, singer, conjuror, dancer and trapeze artist; later he set up a garden ornament business which fell on bad times in the war and never recovered. John Major was brought up in the shabby genteel lower-middle-class world of south London in the 1950s. Something of this is encapsulated in the Pooterish autobiography of his brother, Terry, his elder by ten years.[1]

The family was firmly Tory. John became a Young Conservative at sixteen, the earliest age of admission. He never went through the left-wing phase which affected many young people including some who later became orthodox Conser-

[1]Terry Major-Ball, *Major Major, Memoirs of an Older Brother* (Duckworth, 1994).

vatives. He did not enjoy his school-days at Rutlish. He was good at cricket but made no mark intellectually. He left in 1959. He had periods of unemployment which gave him a lasting dislike of the lazy supercilious bureaucrats who dealt with his claims. He eventually got a job in 1965 as a clerk at the District Bank, now a part of the National Westminster Bank. A year later he moved to the Standard Bank and in 1966 was posted to Nigeria. There he sustained severe injuries to his left leg as the result of a motor accident. It looked as if he might lose his limb but after a long spell in hospital in London he recovered, though never completely. His cricketing days were over and he still finds it difficult to walk more than a couple of miles. But he made good progress in the head office of the bank and now began to take part in local politics. In 1968 he was elected as a councillor for the Ferndale Ward of Lambeth, helped, in that normally rock solid Labour borough, by an extraordinary swing to the Conservatives which was largely the result of Enoch Powell's 'rivers of blood' speech. At the age of twenty-five he found himself Vice-Chairman of the Housing Committee. In 1969 he became Vice-Chairman of the Brixton Conservative Association.

In 1971 the pendulum in Lambeth swung back with a vengeance and Major was out. However, he now had the opportunity to do what he had sought to do all along - have a go at national politics. He was beginning to make money and in the same year he married Norma Johnson. In the two elections of 1974 he fought the safe Labour seat of Holborn and St Pancras where there was of course no possibility of winning. Two years later his chance came. Sir David (later Lord) Renton announced in June 1976 that he would not be contesting Huntingdon, an ultra-safe Tory constituency, at the next election. Major was chosen out of 280 applicants. In 1979 he duly took his seat.

He was not at first seen as one of the 'high flyers' in the 1979 Tory intake. He was popular and liked. He was respected for competent speeches and he always knew what he was talking about. But several of his colleagues got preferment before him. He became an Assistant Whip in 1983 and was highly successful. He was a strong runner for Chief Whip in 1987 but Nigel Lawson commandeered him to become Chief Secretary to the Treasury, a Cabinet post, even if the lowest in the pecking order. He was the first of the 1979 new entry to reach Cabinet rank. Few people guessed that he would, in the course of the next three years, be Foreign Secretary, Chancellor of the Exchequer and finally Prime Minister, the youngest Conservative Prime Minister this century and the only premier never to have sat on the Opposition benches. It was an astonishing rise. The only parallel is that of Stanley Baldwin whom Major in some ways resembled temperamentally and politically.

The first problem to face the new Prime Minister was the Gulf War. Saddam Hussein had seized Kuwait at the beginning of August. By the end of 1990 a formidable Anglo-American force had been stationed on the Gulf and in Saudi Arabia. The British role was a subsidiary one and it was not an issue in party politics, though some fifty Labour MPs defied their Whip on 15 January 1991, the day before active air hostilities began in the Gulf. On 24 February the Allied land forces invaded from Saudi Arabia and brought the war to a victorious conclusion on 28 February, one hundred hours later. Whereas Margaret Thatcher was a world figure and might have played – no one knows for certain – a crucial role in persuading the Americans to intervene, John Major was unknown in America and scarcely known among the British forces. He soon established cordial relations with President Bush, however, and made an excellent impression on the British personnel stationed in Saudi Arabia.

Meanwhile Major had to prepare for a general election which could not be more than a year and a half ahead. His immediate task was to reconstruct the Cabinet. He decided at once that his two rivals for the leadership must be included. Douglas Hurd was no problem. He would be happy to remain at the Foreign Office. It was not so easy to decide where to place Michael Heseltine. He wanted the Board of Trade (and eventually got it) but the Prime Minister felt that he was the best man to deal with the problem of the poll tax, which clearly had to be withdrawn. Heseltine accordingly became Secretary for the

Environment. There were two other key positions to fill, the chancellorship of the exchequer and the party chairmanship. Major allocated the first to Norman Lamont, who had been Chief Secretary to the Treasury and had managed John Major's election campaign, the second to Chris Patten, moving Kenneth Baker to the Home Office. In the run-up to a general election the Party Chairman is the most important player in the party game apart from the Prime Minister, and Chris Patten was to be a great success.

Patten had much to do. Such preparations as had been undertaken had naturally been based on the assumption that Margaret Thatcher would lead the party at the next election. In fact Baker, distracted by a series of by-election disasters, ministerial resignations and finally by the leadership crisis, had not covered much ground. One of the newly appointed members of the Central Office told the authors of the latest volume in the Nuffield series on British general elections, 'At the beginning of 1991 we found that the bloody cupboard was bare.'[1] It was not only bare of ideas but of money; Patten had the task of filling it with both as far as he could. Money was tricky. There was an accumulated deficit of £12 million in March. The slump in the stock market in 1990 and the recession had led to a fall in business contributions. Although this was partly offset by substantial gifts from a Greek shipping magnate and a Hong Kong multimillionaire, revelation of these sources was in itself something of an embarrassment when it appeared in the Press.[2]

Patten set about his task with vigour and efficiency. He was a good speaker and wrote cogent memoranda. His past record as a 'wet' would have made him unacceptable to Margaret Thatcher in his new role. He was very much 'not one of us'. His appointment was a sign of changing times. Major's aspirations to 'a nation at ease with itself' contrasted with Margaret

---

[1]David Butler and Dennis Kavanagh, *The British General Election of 1992* (Macmillan, 1992), 29.

[2]Ibid., 28. The Greek donor was John Latsis who presented Lord McAlpine, ex-Treasurer of the Party, with a bearer's bond of half a million pounds to pass on to his successor. See Lord McAlpine, *Once a Jolly Bagman* (Weidenfeld & Nicolson, 1997).

Thatcher's remark that she did not know what 'One Nation' meant.[1] Major's views on policy were more like Thatcher's than the corporatist outlook of Patten, who was certainly not and never claimed to be the Prime Minister's 'guru', as alleged by the Right. But Major's style was very different from Thatcher's. It was 'Thatcherism with a human face', as Kenneth Clarke called it. Major was more conscious than Thatcher seemed to be that free marketeering and privatisation could never cover all aspects of social life and that the public sector had to continue to play a very important role. Hence the announcement on 22 July 1991 of the Citizen's Charter, an effort to improve the quality of public services and give the 'consumers' more opportunities for making suggestions, airing grievances and securing remedies. How much difference it really made in the long run one cannot easily say, but it was welcomed as at least a gesture in the right direction and a good talking point in the imminent election campaign.

Major was dubious about the 'conviction politics' so often trumpeted by his predecessor. It had worked in the 1980s but the country now seemed less receptive. A lower key was more appropriate. Without in any way reneging on the past, he was prepared to listen and consult. Diplomacy rather than confrontation was the order of the day. This was particularly evident over the EU. Europe has been, was and still is the most divisive issue facing the party both at home and abroad. Major continued in speech after speech to declare that Britain should be at the 'heart of Europe'. He made this point at a meeting on 11 March in Bonn where he addressed an Anglo-German audience. However, he also made it clear that being at the heart of Europe did not mean participating in a European federal superstate: 'Europe is made of nation states: their vitality and diversity are sources of strength. The important thing is to strike the right balance between closer co-operation and a proper respect for national institutions and traditions.'[2] Major never deviated from this line and, though less abrasive than Margaret

[1]Ibid., 30.
[2]Sarah Hogg and Jonathan Hill, *Too Close to Call: John Major in No. 10* (Little, Brown, 1995), 78.

Thatcher, he made no concessions to the federalisers. He would have no truck with the so-called 'Social Chapter' nor with the minimum wage, both strongly endorsed by Labour. He secured opt-out clauses on these two crucial matters as well as on another no less important: Britain's right to refuse to join EMU. The Maastricht Summit of December 1991 had been a formidable hurdle but the Prime Minister had got most of what he wanted.

If the Conservatives were to have the slightest hope of success at the general election there was one essential preliminary: get rid of the poll tax and put something acceptable in its place. Heseltine, the only member of the Cabinet not compromised by the past,[1] had this somewhat complicated and laborious task. He managed it with great skill and remarkable speed. The new graduated properly tax, christened 'the Council Tax', together with the Uniform Business Rate have taken much of the heat out of local government finance. But it was at a cost. To be acceptable the 'headline' figure had to be reduced from £400 per person to a maximum of £250. The money to make up the shortfall had to come from central funds – in fact an increase of 2.5 per cent on VAT. It used to be said that people pay income tax with sorrow but rates with rage. Perhaps an answer to this dichotomy between attitudes towards national and local taxation lies in abolishing the latter – or at least lowering it to something trivial – and reducing local government to providers of services financed by hand-outs from the Treasury. Margaret Thatcher is said to have seriously considered such a change. John Major, who cut his political teeth on local government, was not likely to go as far. The result was a compromise which has so far lasted reasonably well. But as Sarah Hogg and Jonathan Hill observe 'no government can expect applause for solving a problem that the public considered to be of its own making'.[2]

---

[1]Heseltine had resigned over the Westland Helicopter affair before the Cabinet had opted for the poll tax. He opposed the bill on its second reading in 1987.
[2]*Too Close to Call: John Major in No. 10*, op. cit., 70.

3

By the time of Maastricht in December 1991, the choice of dates for the election had been narrowed. As early as the end of January 1991 Patten had sent a list of options to the Prime Minister. A June election had been a possibility but not after the disastrous showing at the local elections on 2 May. Central Office expected to lose some 400 seats out of the 12,000 or so being contested. In the event the Conservatives lost 900; Labour and Liberal Democrats gained 500 each. A scarcely less disastrous set-back occurred two weeks later: in a by-election at Monmouth on 16 May, Labour took the seat with a 13 per cent swing from the Tories.

The same day, coincidentally, saw the first of a series of daily meetings of what came to be called the No. 12 Committee, whose brief it was to handle electoral tactics.[1] It was chaired by the Chief Whip, Richard Ryder, and it included John Wakeham, the leaders of the Lords and Commons (David Waddington and John MacGregor), Chris Patten, Shaun Woodward (recently appointed Director of Communications and a former producer of *That's Life*), Andrew Lansley (Director of the Research Department), Sarah Hogg (head of the Prime Minister's Policy Unit) and a host of other party apparatchiks. Its remit was, as Hogg and Hill put it, 'to spot promotional opportunities and banana skins'. They add: 'This involved a fair amount of chivvying of Ministers, which did not make either the Chief Whip or committee very popular with colleagues – particularly the Chancellor, the No. 12 Committee's most frequent target.'[2]

The summer of 1991 was marked by a notable dispute about Labour's 'costings'. Just how would they pay for the various expensive extra benefits which they were promising in a series of pre-campaign documents. According to Tory calculations an extra £35 billion would need to be raised. 'Labour never really managed to undermine the figures. And it may have been this early, convincing set of spending challenges that provoked Labour into the consummate error of publishing their tax-rais-

---

[1] *Too Close to Call: John Major in No. 10*, op. cit., 110 *et sq.* for an entertaining account of its membership and proceedings. No. 12 Downing Street is the abode of the Chief Whip.
[2] *Too Close to Call: John Major in No. 10*, op. cit., 111.

ing "shadow Budget".[1]

When the political world dispersed for summer holidays in Provence, Chiantishire, Spain or wherever, the date of the election was still not settled. November remained a possibility. But in September an autumn election seemed less plausible. Polls and the economy were not encouraging. The green shoots of recovery from the recession perceived by Norman Lamont were not discerned by many others. At the end of the month Major closed his options. He was now boxed in. The election had to be in spring or early summer; theoretically it could be as late as 9 July, but the last practicable day was 18 June. Prime ministers do not like running into the fifth year of a parliament, let alone its last months. Home and Callaghan had done so and both lost, though very narrowly in Home's case. Major, however, felt he had little choice. On 1 October he allowed it to be known that there would be no election before 1992. The decision meant a long campaign.

Patten had already engaged the services of Saatchi and Saatchi, the public relations firm which had operated in the last three elections, very successfully in 1979 and 1983, less so in 1987. In fact, Margaret Thatcher had terminated the relationship in 1988, after it had caused a certain amount of bad blood between her and Norman Tebbit. Both Major and Patten were anxious to avoid the crossed wires, confusions of authority and in-fighting of the 1987 election. In this they succeeded. The long campaign of 1991–92 was far better co-ordinated.

The next hurdle was the Party Conference in Blackpool from 8 to 11 October. All sorts of worries existed. Would Margaret Thatcher be there? Would she speak? If so, what would she say? It went as smoothly as such things ever do, i.e. not very. But Major made a good impression, partly by not being Thatcher and also because he spoke, if not eloquently, with sincerity, vigour and no hint of repudiating her policies. His personal image was an asset to a party far from confident about its electoral prospects. Three victories in a row – could there be a fourth? they wondered. The answer of course is that there was.

[1] Ibid., 117.

The question is why?

For six months beginning in October 1991, Labour was ahead in the opinion polls, not by much but by enough to make the wiseacres predict a small majority or a hung parliament. The Conservatives played their hand much as they had in 1987, with many of the same players including Sir Gordon Reece and the masterly speech writer Sir Ronald Miller. Both sides were more professional, more media-minded, more dependent on clever posters and smart sound-bites than ever before. Each side concentrated on what its electoral experts believed to be its strong points and did not spend too much time repudiating the other's attacks on its weaknesses. From mid-October onwards the weekly Cabinet meeting was followed, once the civil servants had departed, by a 'political cabinet'. The government was in a state of continuous election fever throughout the autumn and winter.

A key question was when should the election be called. It was highly dependent on the Budget, which on normal form would be on 17 March. Since there was no great scope for 'give-aways', ought the election to come first? But this might look like cowardice in anticipation of a disappointing Budget and there were other reasons, partly connected with the economic climate and partly with the timing of the completion of the new electoral register, which made an election in February or March undesirable. Norman Lamont pressed for the opposite extreme: June or even July. But the consensus favoured 9 April. This meant announcing the decision on 11 March and bringing the Budget forward to the 10th. The party manifesto would be promulgated on the 18th.

The show piece in the Budget was a reduction in the standard rate of income tax to 20p for the first £2,000 of anyone's income. The advantage of this was that it did not entail a large immediate cost to the Exchequer but the government could widen the 20p band a bit at a time towards its ultimate goal of a 20p standard rate. John Smith on 16 March riposted with his celebrated 'shadow Budget' which put up the top rate of tax to 50p and effectively to 59p by removing the ceiling on national insurance contributions. It has generally been regarded as a serious mistake, confirming the Tory claim that Labour was the 'soak-the-rich' party. The Conservatives were slow to make much of this error at first but it became one of their most important propaganda points as the campaign proceeded. And they needed help: at the beginning of the full campaign the party was three points below Labour in the polls. At the end of the first week Labour led by five points. What such polls really mean is anyone's guess but they certainly affect the morale of those who read them.

The election of 1992 will be remembered for four features. First in order of time is John Smith's 'shadow Budget'. The second is John Major's soapbox. The third is Neil Kinnock's Sheffield rally. The fourth is the fiasco of the opinion polls.

From the start, the Conservatives' campaign was centred on their leader to a far greater degree than Labour's on theirs. John Major's personal popularity was always ahead of his party's. The first attempt to exploit this, however, did not work out well. The idea was to have a series of meetings under the title 'Meet John Major', where the Prime Minister, seated on a bar-stool with an audience of two or three hundred in a circle around him, answered questions in a folksy style. The model was President Bush's campaign in the Republican primary elections. Bush, however, was talking to an audience of the faithful and could buy unlimited time on television. Major could not and only got an occasional half minute on the screens with no time to develop an argument.[1]

This clearly would not do. After a lacklustre visit to Wales on 27 March 'the Prime Minister worked himself into a grump', as Hogg and Hill put it:

Why wasn't he meeting any real voters? Why wasn't he being allowed to speak to them direct? He was becoming cut off. His message was not getting across. Well, he'd had enough of it. He wasn't going to sit there while the campaign collapsed around him. Why shouldn't he do what he had done all those years ago when he first started out in politics: find a street

[1] *Too Close to Call: John Major in No. 10*, op. cit., 171–2.

corner, get on a soapbox – and talk? Damn it, he was going to do it no matter what anyone said.[1]

Most members of the election management team were aghast and Major's first bout of soapboxing, staged at Luton, confirmed their worst fears, for he was shouted down; but Luton, notorious for its high proportion of toughs and yobbos, was about as hard a place as one could find for an opener. The Prime Minister stuck to his guns and in fact the soapbox went down remarkably well. Major toured the country more extensively than any previous Conservative leader. He *did* meet a great many voters and speak to them directly. It was something which he thoroughly enjoyed. Not least of the benefits of the famous soapbox was the boost it gave to his own morale.

The third episode which made the election memorable was the Labour rally in Sheffield on 1 April. This was a mass affair – some 10,000 loyal supporters - with the maximum of razzmatazz. The opinion polls were giving Labour a lead of between 4 and 7 per cent. No wonder Kinnock believed victory was in the bag. He made a triumphal entry, punching the air, shouting to his supporters like a pop-star, 'You're all ri', you're all ri'.' The shot of this gesture was repeatedly shown on television 'and was adjudged by friend and foe to be disastrous'.[2] As someone said at the time, 'The Welsh boyo suddenly took over from the national statesman.'

Kinnock further damaged his chances by toying with constitutional reform – still in 1992 a perilous political field. Scottish devolution and proportional representation were issues on which Conservatives could take a clear and comprehensible line, viz., have nothing to do with them, though this did not help them five years later. Towards the end of his campaign Major played the 'unionist' card for all it was worth. His appeal to preserve a United Kingdom in the interest of all its component parts may have been an important element in his success.

By election day the general expectation was either a small

[1] Ibid., 225.
[2] *The British General Election of 1992*, op. cit., 124.

Labour lead or a hung parliament. The early result from Basildon put doubts to rest. It was a key marginal seat in the heartlands of 'Essex Man'. Labour would have to win it if they were to win the election. The Conservatives held it by a slightly reduced majority. Watching the results from his house in Huntingdon the Prime Minister leapt to his feet, 'That's it. We've done it. We've won the election.'[1] There was, as the results flowed in, only one black lining to a silver cloud: Chris Patten lost Bath.

Why – and this is the fourth memorable feature of the election – did the opinion polls get it so wrong? The percentage figures in a turn out of 78 per cent of the electorate were: Conservatives 42.8; Labour 35.2; Liberals 18.3. The Conservatives won 336 seats to Labour's 271, Liberal Democrats' 20, Welsh and Scottish Nationalists' 7, and 17 others in Northern Ireland. Major had an overall majority of 21. None of the polls foresaw such figures or anything near them. Their combined prediction underestimated the Conservative vote by 8.5 per cent – as it happens the exact figure by which the American polls were wrong in 1948 when Truman and Dewey contested the presidency.

The answer to the question is that there is no answer. Opinion polls had been wrong before in Britain – 1951, 1970 and 1974 – but never on this scale; and in the previous three elections they had been fairly accurate. Much talk and print has been expended on efforts to explain what happened but there is no consensus. Errors in sampling, differential refusals to answer, lying, differential turnout, late swing – all have their supporters, but no convincing answer has emerged.[2]

It is rather, though not much, less difficult to say why the results, however unpredicted, were what they were. That it was a personal triumph for the Prime Minister, though effectively helped by his heavyweight colleagues, especially Michael Heseltine, is not in doubt. Margaret Thatcher with the incubus of the poll tax would certainly have lost. This did not mean that

[1]*Too Close to Call: John Major in No. 10*, op. cit., 257.
[2]*The British General Election of 1992*, op. cit.: See chapter 7 for a full analysis.

Major would win. The longest recession since 1982 and the 'time for a change' syndrome were serious obstacles. No party victorious in three successive elections had won a fourth. True, a Liberal prime minister did so in 1918 after his party had won in 1906 and twice in 1910. But Lloyd George headed a coalition that was dominated by the Conservatives. It was not a parallel case.

How much difference did the campaigns make? The media panjandrums considered that Labour fought a 'good' campaign, better than the Conservatives. What does one mean by 'good'? It could be argued that a good campaign is one that wins. On that definition the Conservatives fought a better one than Labour. But it can also be argued that campaigns make little difference anyway and that elections are lost or won before the campaigns even begin. For example, Labour made the most of various scares and sensations during the run-up to 9 April. The most absurd of all was the so-called 'War of Jennifer's ear' – a case of a little girl whose ear operation was allegedly being delayed owing to the incompetence of the NHS. The media went to town on this with their full complement of sensational idiocy. It had no effect on anything.

The Conservatives won probably through fear of what Labour would do – high taxation, economic incompetence and trade union domination. They were helped by the Smith 'shadow Budget' and by the Sheffield rally, which William Waldegrave compared to Nuremburg.

In the end, the election reflected deep doubts in what is called 'middle England' about Kinnock and his policies. Major on his soapbox was more trusted than the Welsh boyo. Major looked like a prime minister, indeed was one. Kinnock did not.

4

The election of 1992 marked the high point of John Major's career. However, although he had won, Major's parliamentary position was very different from Margaret Thatcher's and from his own when he succeeded her. A margin of twenty-one gives little to play with.

At first, however, all seemed to go smoothly. For the next few months the Conservatives retained their advantage in the opinion polls, leading by four points in August. Then, on Wednesday 16 September, disaster struck. There was an unprecedented run on the pound. After putting up interest rates to 15 per cent and spending huge sums on the foreign exchanges to save sterling, the government was forced to devalue and leave the ERM. 'Black Wednesday' (or 'White Wednesday' to those who had always opposed entry) was a heavy blow to one of the principal claims of the party at the election, that they could deliver good management of the economy. In October the polls gave a sixteen point lead to Labour – a figure that was never to fall during the next four years and was often to be much higher.

Early in 1997 the Prime Minister, questioned on *Newsnight* about Black Wednesday, admitted: 'Events made a monkey of us.' In retrospect one might think that it was a mistake in 1990 to go into the ERM at all – and certainly an error to enter at such a high sterling exchange rate with the Deutschmark. But scarcely anyone said this at the time; even Margaret Thatcher, though sceptical and unenthusiastic, did not actually oppose the policy of her Chancellor, who was of course John Major. It had a wide measure of cross-party and cross-media support. The Treasury and the Bank of England were in favour, as was that alliance of the Great and the Good known as 'the Establishment'.

There were, it is true, during the summer of 1992, occasional calls in the Press and elsewhere for devaluation. But the orthodox view was that devaluation would make the government appear soft on inflation, unless it was part of an agreed general realignment of ERM currencies, of which there seemed little prospect. In the event, Black Wednesday did nothing but good to the British economy. The devaluation of sterling made it more competitive, gave a boost to exports and laid the foundations for recovery from recession. But this did not help the Conservative party which could hardly claim credit for the consequences of something which its leaders had done all in their power to avoid.

Black Wednesday was not the only reason for Conservative

unpopularity. There was growing discontent among house-
owners, many of whom had bought at the height of the Lawson
boom and now suffered from 'negative equity' (jargon for the
fact that the value of their houses had fallen below the value of
the mortgages with which they had been bought). At the beginning of 1992 the number in this plight was reckoned at some
300,000. By the end of the year it had more than tripled.
Repossessions rose correspondingly and contributed to a
general sense of insecurity which pervaded the early 1990s.
Patterns of employment were changing. 'Jobs for life', i.e. till
retiring age, had largely gone. Far more people were employed
on short-term contracts. Wages and salaries were good for some
but would they last? The recession did at last bottom out in the
summer of 1992 and the next three years saw a rise in real
incomes and a fall in unemployment. But the party's standing
in public opinion showed no sign of improvement.

The situation was made no better by the parliamentary
struggle over the Maastricht Treaty which followed hard on the
heels of the ERM fiasco. The treaty, with Britain's opt-outs
from Monetary Union, the Social Chapter and the minimum
wage, had been successfully negotiated and signed by John
Major on 7 February 1992, before the general election. The
problem was getting the treaty ratified, as this required legislation, although from time to time during the protracted battle
which ensued it was argued that the government could invoke
Crown prerogative and so bypass parliament. Whether or not
this was constitutionally feasible there would certainly have
been an uproar if it had been attempted and a government with
such a slender majority was not likely to take the risk.

Major's problem was that a hard core of right-wing Tory
Eurosceptics was determined to scupper the European
Communities (Amendment) Bill. The measure received its
second reading on 1 May 1992 and twenty-two Conservative
rebels voted against it. The committee stage was postponed. On
4 November the government introduced what was called 'a
paving motion' to resume the debate on the Bill, though it was
far from clear why this unusual procedure was considered necessary. It was carried by only three votes after a ruthless display

of blandishment, cajolery, threats and bullying on the part of the whips. There were thirty-two Tory rebels of whom twenty-five voted against and six abstained. But for the support of the Liberal Democrats the government would have been defeated. There followed months of seemingly endless and esoteric manoeuvres in the House of Commons involving complicated points of procedure, which even members found hard to understand, and were incomprehensible to the general public. The sceptics, led by the indefatigable Bill Cash, a constitutional lawyer of great expertise, put down amendment after amendment. He and others tried to tag on to the Bill a requirement for a referendum before it became law. This was defeated on 22 April 1993 by 363 to 124. The third reading of the Bill was passed on 20 May by 292 to 112. There were forty-six Tory rebels, the largest number so far. The Bill had occupied twenty-three days in committee and there had been 600 amendments discussed.[1]

It then went to the Lords where a similar referendum amendment was defeated by 269 votes.[2]

The Bill came back to the Commons, with the question of the Social Chapter postponed to a later vote. It became law on 20 July, but the vote on the Social Chapter went against the government by 324 to 316, with twenty-four Tory rebels. Major now had to use the 'nuclear' weapon of a vote of confidence which, if he lost, would mean a suicidal general election. He won by 339 to 299. Some members of the Cabinet stigmatised by the Prime Minister as 'bastards' were anything but helpful. There can be no doubt that the Maastricht debate was more damaging to party unity than any comparable divisions since Tariff Reform in 1903.

Meanwhile, on 26 May 1993 the Chancellor of the Exchequer had been dismissed. Norman Lamont was not a very popular figure and his Budget raising taxes, however necessary, despite the party's electioneering promises to lower them, did him no

---

[1] See *Parliamentary Affairs*, January 1994, pp. 37–60, 'The Siege of Maastricht' by David Baker, Andrew Gamble and Steve Ludlam for the best account.

[2] It was moved by the author and supported by Lady Thatcher, Lord Tebbit and Lord Parkinson.

good. He might have done better to resign after Black Wednesday as James (now Lord) Callaghan had after Labour's devaluation in 1967. He greatly resented his dismissal and made this clear in his statement in the Commons on 9 June in which he strongly attacked John Major's leadership. He was succeeded by Kenneth Clarke, a portly cigar-smoking bon vivant Europhile lawyer who was to conduct the nation's finances with much success over the next four years but was to be a divisive figure in the Cabinet's Euro-debate.

During this period there had been crucial changes in the policy and leadership of the Labour party. Kinnock quickly resigned after his defeat in 1992. The cumbrous party electoral system produced a successor in John Smith, a middle-of-the-road Edinburgh lawyer who was generally respected. He died tragically of a heart attack at a relatively young age, early in 1994. His successor was Tony Blair, a right-wing tough operator, who unequivocally recognised the Thatcher revolution and pushed the party into repudiating its sacred cow, Clause 4 of its constitution which proclaimed the doctrine of public ownership. He thus achieved something which Hugh Gaitskell had unsuccessfully attempted some thirty years earlier. He made it clear that a Labour government would not reverse privatisation and would not feel itself bound to the trade unions. He also democratised the party's internal selection process. These and other changes encouraged the name of 'New Labour'. It was a threat that the Conservatives, immersed in internal struggles and mounting accusations of financial malpractices, were slow to recognise.

The continued Labour lead in the opinion polls and the continued back-biting among the Conservatives led throughout 1994 to rumblings about the leadership. Major had put this to the test over Maastricht when, after defeat on the Social Chapter, he had won a grudging vote of confidence. But the problem did not go away. People unfairly contrasted his allegedly vacillating leadership with the firm stance of Margaret Thatcher, forgetting that she had had cast-iron majorities in the Commons whereas his, which was at first only twenty-one, had now fallen to nine. She had never had to deal with an organised dissentient minority and had enjoyed the solid support of the right-wing press which was now becoming increasingly lukewarm, even downright hostile, towards Major. He was particularly vulnerable because of the clause in the party's constitution enjoining annual re-election of the leader every November. Labour had no comparable provision. In 1991 after the ousting of Margaret Thatcher the Executive of the 1922 Committee reconsidered the procedure. It retained the clause about November re-election but rendered a challenge by a 'frivolous' candidate more difficult. The challenger could now stand only if supported by the signatures of 10 per cent of the parliamentary party. Even so, the possibility of a disputed contest remained as a stimulus to intrigue and speculation about the leadership. In summer 1994 Major considered putting the matter to a vote but decided against it. There was no challenge in November. In July 1995 he resolved not to wait to see what happened next November but to resign and by his own initiative precipitate a leadership election there and then.

It was a risky strategy. The 10 per cent requirement did not apply in a contest for a vacancy and there were many other dangers, especially when, contrary to Major's expectation, Cabinet solidarity was broken by John Redwood, Secretary for Wales, who resigned and stood against him. Major's campaign was managed by Lord Cranborne, Leader of the House of Lords, son of Lord Salisbury and heir to the great Cecil family's Tory tradition. The alliance was a good example of Major's plea for a classless society – Brixton and Hatfield. There was no question of Major losing. The only question was by how much he would win. His supporters implied that he would play by the rule-book. At least one of them advised him to say 'one is enough'. Of course it would not have been, but no harm would be done by giving that impression. The minimum number of votes he needed, if there were no abstentions, was 190. In the event Major won by 218 to 89. There were twenty-two abstentions and spoiled ballot papers. There was the usual post-mortem row. The 1922 Executive Committee and its chairman, Sir Marcus Fox, charged with the task of acting as returning officers, made no bones about their support for the Prime Minister. But the

result was not in doubt. It gave relief for the moment to a belea-
guered leader and a boost to his public and political standing.
The 1922 Committee had ruled out any further challenges
before the general election now looming large on the horizon.
John Major would undoubtedly lead the party into it. Whether
for good or ill remained to be seen.

5

The relief given to Major by the leadership vote proved temporary. The long Labour lead in the opinion polls remained
unchanged during the remainder of 1995 and throughout 1996.
It was clear that the only hope for the Conservatives was to
postpone the election to the last plausible date, as they had in
1992. But there was no guarantee that delay would help them
and the Labour advantage in the polls was much greater than it
had ever been before. Moreover, the government was now
plagued by a series of scandals and blunders. There was the
dubious conduct of ministers revealed by Lord Justice Scott's
enquiry into the arms for Iraq affair. There was the matter of
'cash for questions' when two MPs were obliged to admit that
they had each accepted £1,000 to ask parliamentary questions
in the interest of certain business firms. There were other
highly questionable episodes. These prompted the setting up of
a committee chaired by Lord Nolan to enquire generally into
Members' declaration of financial interests and to suggest
reforms. The saga of sleaze seemed to have no end, though the
number of MPs involved was very small.

By the beginning of 1997 the Conservatives were showing the
characteristic signs of a party on its way out. The parallels with
1905–6 were all too obvious: Europe was taking the place of tariffs as the divisive issue, Major substituting for Balfour as the
leader vainly trying to reconcile the divisions and to manage an
unmanageable party.

Party organisation, if anecdotal evidence is anything to go by,
was chaotic. The earlier losses in local government, which left
scarcely any counties in Conservative hands had destroyed their
grass roots. Few Conservatives can have expected to win in an

election. The only straw at which the party faithful could clutch was the erroneousness of the polls in 1992. Yet the lead they had prophesied for Labour in 1992 was small in comparison to the figures appearing in the run-up to the 1997 election. Opinion polls can be wrong but not that wrong.

Another difficulty under which the Tories laboured was the loss of the press support which they had enjoyed in previous elections. 'It was the *Sun* wot won it', that egregious organ claimed in the aftermath of the 1992 results. But in 1997 for whatever reason the Murdoch press abandoned Major and plumped for Blair, who had earlier flown out to Australia to meet the great tycoon. Around 70 per cent of the press was pro-Conservative in 1992. There has been no time to work out the figures for 1997 but the percentage was obviously far lower than that. Exactly how much influence the press really has on voting patterns is arguable but it is hard to believe that it has none at all.

Parliament was prorogued on 20 March and there began one of the longest election campaigns in history. On 1 April Major announced that the election would be on 1 May. On 8 April he formally asked the Queen to dissolve parliament. The campaign was remarkably dull. Labour's campaign, masterminded by Peter Mandelson, a grandson of one of the party's greatest past 'fixers', Herbert Morrison, was highly efficient and well targeted on 'focus groups'; it exploited tactical voting with much skill. Having such a huge lead in the opinion polls, Tony Blair was safe unless he trod on a banana skin of exceptional size and slipperiness. He publicly took nothing for granted and repeatedly warned against complacency.

Faced with such a towering mountain to climb – if the polls were right – the Conservative campaign soon took on an air of desperation. The burden was carried largely by the Prime Minister, whose personal standing was always higher than his party's – which, however, was not saying very much. As a last throw, he challenged Tony Blair to engage with him in an American-style television debate. He would probably have been better at this sort of exchange than Blair, whose evangelical style of oratory might not have come across so effectively. (Had a similar confrontation been possible in the 1870s, Disraeli could well have scored off Gladstone.) But by this stage Blair had nothing to gain. He declined the challenge. 'Funk' and 'Chicken' was the Conservative cry. An absurd look-alike of Blair as a chicken was touted around and there was also a poster of the Labour leader as a tiny puppet sitting on the knee of Chancellor Kohl, signifying Blair's alleged intention to surrender Britain's nationhood to the EU.

None of these gimmicks, which many Conservatives deplored, saved the party. It is doubtful whether any campaign could have had much influence on an electorate that had already made up its collective mind. 'Black Wednesday' may have started the decline in Tory support, but it is unlikely that many voters knew or recalled what it was all about. What they did remember was betrayal of pledges about lower taxes, unemployment, bankruptcies, rocketing interest rates and 'negative equity'. The recovery of the economy since 1992 was indisputable but the conventional wisdom that prosperity is a plus for the party in power was strikingly punctured. The Conservative claim to be the best party to manage the economy did not save them.

When the electoral figures were finally counted the result was astonishing to Labour as well as Conservatives. There was a swing to Labour of 10 per cent. Labour gained 146 seats, the Conservatives lost 178, including seven Cabinet ministers. They were wiped out in Scotland and Wales. The Liberal Democrats gained 30 and lost two. Labour had an overall majority of 177. The final score was: Labour 418; Conservatives 165; Lib Dem 46; others 29; the Speaker 1.

The share of the vote was Labour 44.4 per cent, Conservatives 31.4 per cent, Liberal Democrats 17.2 per cent, others 7 per cent. The latter included Sir James Goldsmith's Referendum party, which probably syphoned off more Tory than Labour or Liberal votes but won no seats and made little difference if any to the results. The electoral turn-out was 71.3 per cent – the lowest since 1945 and 2 million less than in 1992.

On the face of it this was a catastrophic Tory defeat and it certainly was a disaster in terms of seats. But the first-past-the-post voting system enormously amplifies the gap in votes between the parties. In an article in *The Times* Garret FitzGerald, a former Prime Minister of Ireland, reckoned the result was principally caused by massive Tory abstentions and that barely one in ten actually switched to Labour.[1] Commenting on Dr FitzGerald's article, Dr Charles Pattie and Professor Ron Johnston of Sheffield University confirmed this analysis: 'Labour's landslide victory was won with no more than 3 per cent of the electorate transferring their vote from the incumbent party to its main challenger. It has always been thus: British elections are won and lost because of changes in the voting decisions of relatively few people in a few places.'[2] Whatever the truth – abstentions or conversions – the voting figures are unlikely to be much consolation to the parliamentary rump of the Tory party. If Labour made relatively few Tory converts, the fact of massive abstentions, though more recoverable, was almost as damaging. Why did Major lose? No doubt there will be much investigation in detail by the famous Nuffield College experts. An interim opinion close after the event might be as follows.

1. 'Me-too-ism', in American parlance. New Labour stole the Tory's clothes while they were bathing – and bathing in turbulent waters where they seemed more intent on drowning than rescuing each other.

2. Longevity. No party in modern times has won four elections running. The chance of winning a fifth was always unlikely – 'Time for a change' was hard to dispute.

3. Disunity. The alleged secret weapon of the Conservatives – loyalty – broke to pieces in their hands. 'Europe' was immensely damaging.

4. Sleaze. The number of MPs involved was small and their offences trivial compared with what has long gone on in France and Italy. But sleaze, though not a determining factor, was certainly damaging. Neil Hamilton, for example, was defeated in Tatton, one of the safest Conservative seats, by Martin Bell, the

[1] *The Times*, 12 May 1997.
[2] *The Times*, 15 May 1997.

famous white-suited BBC war correspondent. Labour and Liberals withdrew to give him a clear run as the 'anti-sleaze' candidate and he won with a majority of 11,000.

5. Black Wednesday and increased taxes were very hard to laugh off – and the Party never did.

Perhaps the best verdict on the result was by 'Bagehot' in *The Economist*: 'The result is not, as it might at first appear, a sign that the electorate has turned against the Tories for ever. It's not Toryism that voters cannot stand. It's the present Tory party.'1

Major, who was more respected than any of his colleagues, and whom the party faithful least blamed for the débâcle, bowed out at once. When the curtain falls, he said, it is time to leave the empty stage.

EPILOGUE

Vast changes took place in Britain during the 125 years covered by this book. Yet the person who was a Conservative of the more thoughtful sort in Peel's day, his outlook, prejudices and passions, would have been quite recognisable to his counterpart who voted for Winston Churchill in the 1950s. There was a similar belief that Britain, especially England, was usually in the right. There was a similar faith in the value of diversity, of independent institutions, of the rights of property; a similar distrust of centralising officialdom, of the efficacy of government (except in the preservation of order and national defence), of Utopian panaceas and of 'doctrinaire' intellectuals; a similar dislike of abstract ideas, high philosophical principles and sweeping generalisations. There was a similar readiness to accept cautious empirical piecemeal reform, if a Conservative government said it was needed. There was a similar reluctance to look far ahead or worry too much about the future; a similar scepticism about human nature; a similar belief in original sin, and in the limitations of political and social amelioration; a similar scepticism about the notion of 'equality.'

Just as in Peel's day the party spectrum ran from the Ultras through the middle-of-the-roaders to the Tory radicals, so too in the 1950s a similar diversity existed. Indeed at any time in the party's history one would find analogues: Young England is followed by the Fourth party, and then the 'Hughligans'; the Protection Society has its spiritual descendants in the Cranborne 'cave', the Ditchers and the Monday Club. It would be easy to multiply instances. Most Conservatives for most of the time have wished to keep things as they are and believe along with the Duke of Cambridge that the time for change is when it can no longer be resisted; but there have always been those who on the one hand think that it can always be resisted, and on the other that the Conservatives are the true party of change.

Of course there were important differences compared with the time of Peel. The empire was not a specifically Tory cause in the 1830s; it became so in Disraeli's day and still was in Churchill's. In Peel's time the party had been very much the party of the Anglican Church, fighting its battles against Dissent both Roman and Protestant. Whoever said that 'the Church of England is the Tory party at prayer' was not far from the truth for a long period in the history of both those bodies. But it would not have been relevant in the 1950s. At some period, hard to specify, the religious question had ceased to count. There was a little comment when Balfour, a Presbyterian, became leader, less when Bonar Law did, and virtually none when the party found itself led by a Unitarian, Neville Chamberlain. To this day, however, Conservatives are more likely to have an Anglican background than Labour or Liberals; and both the Catholic and the Nonconformist votes are more likely to be anti- than pro-Conservative.

Another difference was that in Peel's time and long afterwards the party was pre-eminently the party of the landed interest. In a sense it never ceased to be so, but the conflict between the landed and the business, financial and industrial classes gradually disappeared. Peel himself tried to reconcile them but he failed and the corn law crisis marked the end of his attempt. For thirty years the party rested on the landed interest – too narrow a base for electoral success. Then for a number of reasons which had no connection with any conscious policy on the part of the Conservative leadership, the business class began to move away from the Liberal into the Conservative party at the same time as it became assimilated with the landed class. By 1900 the Conservatives were the party, not just of the land, but of the rich in general; the business man, the banker, and the financier as well as the country squire and the broad-acred peer. It was part of a general social change which was certainly advantageous to the Conservatives, and though no one made a special effort to bring it about, the landed leaders of the party were not slow to exploit it when it occurred. The leadership itself ceased to be a landed monopoly, as is shown by the succession of Bonar Law, Baldwin and Neville Chamberlain.

Yet tradition dies hard. The party retained a vaguely landed outlook even in the 1950s. Conservative managers continued to pay a degree of attention to the agricultural vote scarcely warranted by its strength. And it remains true even today in spite of all the social changes affecting the countryside that the county seats, bastions of Tory strength in every nineteenth-century election except the freak one of 1885, are those where the party does best. Everyone who has watched or listened to the results coming in on an election night knows that, however big the Labour lead may be when the commentators close down, it will be reduced by the county results which, taking longer to collect, are not announced till the next day.

Geographically too the distribution of Conservative strength in the 1950s would come as no surprise to a Tory Rip Van Winkle who went to sleep in 1840. The party then was pre-eminently the party of England whereas Scotland and Ireland were Liberal. In England the Conservatives were the party of the south rather than the north where they seldom won a majority of seats even in a good year. These features were broadly true 125 years later. There had been some changes. In Peel's day Wales had given the Conservatives a majority. This had long ceased to be true by Churchill's time. Another change, this time favourable, had been the independence of Southern Ireland. Although the Conservatives campaigned fiercely for the Union their defeat gave them a bonus of 10 seats (Ulster) instead of a deficit which from 1886 amounted to over 65 seats. One might logically have expected them to draw the lesson and advocate home rule for Wales and Scotland. But Conservatives are there to conserve.

Viewed from one aspect the Conservative party could be regarded as the party of English nationalism. Having won its struggle long ago English nationalism was and is essentially defensive. The political nation, especially in England, throughout a period of the great social, economic and technological change has been profoundly conservative – with a small 'c' – as regards its institutions, usages and habits. The sheer continuity of constitutional structure is one of the most remarkable features of

British history. For example, who would have thought in the 1830s that the monarchy, the House of Lords and the Established Church, would still be features of the British scene 130 years later? One is reminded of Hilaire Belloc's Lord Calvin:

> Lord Calvin thought the Bishops should not sit
> As Peers of Parliament. And *argued* it!
> In spite of which, for years, and years, and years,
> They went on sitting with their fellow-peers.

And they are still sitting there today. One could cite many examples of this continuity, this reluctance to change. Lord Salisbury whose career as leader is the great success story of our period 'always maintained', so his daughter tells us,

> ... that the forces which make for the defence of institutions, as well as the principles bound up with them, are immensely powerful, and sufficient in themselves to win adherence to any party that is able sincerely and loyally to place itself at their service. It was a view constantly disputed by his Tory democrat followers – but he held to it and could point to the prevailing influences which have governed every Conservative victory at the polls as proof of his contention. He used to declare ... that Mr Gladstone's existence was the greatest source of strength which the Conservative party possessed. . . . He did not shrink from facing the fact that according to his views the success of his own party was dependent on the existence of the other; 'I rank myself no higher in the scheme of things than a policeman – whose utility would disappear if there were no criminals.'[1]

If it is true that the English nation is in this sense profoundly conservative, it is also true that certain features go with that sort of conservatism. One has been 'nationalism', patriotism', whatever one wishes to call it, in many ways a defensive reaction to threats and dangers from outside. The 'patriotic' card has usually been a winner when it can be played with any relevance. Moreover, this sort of conservatism has never been totally negative – the artificial

---

[1] Lady Gwendolen Cecil, *Biographical studies of the life and political character of Robert, Third Marquis of Salisbury* (privately published, Hodder & Stoughton, n.d.), p. 84.

and obdurate freezing of a particular balance of social forces, without reference to the pressures of discontent and change. To use Disraeli's frequently quoted words in a speech in Edinburgh in the autumn of 1867:

> In a progressive country change is constant; and the question is not whether you should resist change which is inevitable, but whether that change should be carried out in deference to the manners, the customs, the laws, and the traditions of a people, or whether it should be carried out in deference to abstract principles, and arbitrary and general doctrines.

Stern and unbending Toryism has never paid dividends to the Conservative party, nor in practice when in office has the party ever taken that line. However much his 'betrayal' may have been disliked at the time, Peel taught his party a lesson that has not been forgotten. He also taught it another lesson, though unintentionally – the lesson that party disunity is something which the 'national' party cannot afford.

The party's lack of success in the first part of the period lay in its inability either to move with the times or to preserve unity over the corn law crisis, and later in its failure to present itself as a plausible alternative to the Whig-Peelite alliance established by Palmerston. Neither the 'patriotic' nor the 'constitutional' card was much use against him, and while he ruled, conservatism was not on the side of the Conservative party. This, whatever Tory radicals may say, is a very dangerous situation for the party to reach – one to be avoided at almost any cost. Gladstone transformed the scene. Disraeli profited to some extent, for he was quick to seize the Palmerstonian mantle; but it never quite fitted, and Salisbury was the real beneficiary. The 'national' cry and the 'constitutional' cry were Tory assets hard to challenge, when the Liberal party had committed itself to Irish Home Rule, Little Englanderism, and opposition to armaments. A conservative nation for the next twenty years regarded the Conservative party as the natural party of government.

But the Conservatives made a grave error – or rather Joseph Chamberlain, a non-Conservative accidentally in their ranks made it – when the party became embroiled in the campaign for tariff reform after 1903. The situation was made worse because they did not speak with a united voice, but the policy would have been disastrous even if it had been unanimous. For it was the reverse of conservatism. Unlike the repeal of the corn laws it could not even be represented as one of those reforms necessary to stave off revolution. There was no danger whatever of revolution in 1903. The tariff reform policy was a major radical innovation. It has seldom paid the Conservative party to come forward as the party of change. That is not why people vote for it. The Conservatives can accept change. They can even initiate it, once they are safely in office and as long as they do not make a song and dance about it. But experience suggests that they should be very chary about announcing major changes as the theme of an election programme.[1] If the country is in the mood for radical change it will not vote Conservative.

The result of tariff reform was to provoke a Lib–Lab alliance which, no doubt aided by other events, kept the Conservatives out at the next three elections. It was the war that brought them back. The consequential divisions on the Left were fatal, and the Lib–Lab alliance broke up in 1918. During the next thirty-seven years the Conservatives were in power for twenty-eight and for most of that time, whatever their sins of commission or omission they behaved as a Conservative party. Their worst mistake was a failure to act as the 'national party' in the 1930s. Their greatest success was to convince a large section of the working class that the class struggle was irrelevant and that they were a safer bet than the Left.

At the end of all this one may perhaps ask what difference it really makes which party is in. Do not much the same things happen whoever is in office? On this there are two views. One is epitomised again by Belloc in his lines 'On a Great Election':

The accursed power which stands on privilege
(And goes with Women, and Champagne, and Bridge)
Broke – and Democracy resumed her reign
(Which goes with Bridge, and Women, and Champagne).

[1] Change in the sense of reversing their opponent's changes is another matter.

There is another view, however, and this is that all these efforts and struggles, these dramatic changes of fortune, do mean something; that the careers devoted to politics are not a complete waste of time; that it is possible sometimes at least to reach the right answer; that some people are more likely to do this than others; and that it may make a real difference which side prevails in the unending struggle for political power. If I did not adhere to this second view rather than the first, I would not have chosen this subject for the Ford Lectures.

No one knows for certain why people voted as they did or why they vote as they do. No one knows for certain – or indeed at all – what would have happened if an election had gone differently and another party had won the day. It is an act of faith to believe that these things matter. History is not an exact science and it never will be. It is a good story. The fortunes of a political party, like those of an individual, make a fascinating tale, and that, rather than general truths or lessons from the past, must be the justification of this survey.

POSTSCRIPT

The above Epilogue was written in 1970 for the first edition of a book which took the history of the Conservative party from Peel to Churchill. Historiography is a part of history and I have left it unchanged. But one must say something even briefly as a postscript to an expanded book dealing with the years since Churchill bowed out in 1955.

During those years there were six leaders: Eden, Macmillan, Home, Heath, Thatcher and Major. Eden and Home had too brief a tenure to leave much of an imprint on the party. Macmillan, Heath, Thatcher and Major did in different ways affect its fortunes. But leaders do not operate in a vacuum. Society was changing. There were new economic forces in operation. And, although many archetypal Tory beliefs still prevailed, they were adapted to changing conditions. A Conservative Rip Van Winkle of 1955 looking at the party forty years later would see many basic continuities: the same sceptical attitudes towards 'equality', the efficacy of government, the wisdom of Whitehall, long-term planning, Utopian panaceas, international idealism, the goodness of human nature. On the other side of the coin he or she would find the same belief in the continuity of institutions and traditions, in freedom of the individual, in national unity, in 'Britain first'.

The Conservatives under John Major had much in common in their social and geographical composition with those of forty years earlier. They were still the party of England and the south, of the counties and the suburbs, of the ever-expanding class which has been called Middle England. Perhaps the débâcle of the 1997 election has changed all this and will lead to a lasting realignment of parties. Perhaps not. The Conservatives survived 1906, 1945 and 1966. They may survive 1997. Or they may go the way of the Liberals after 1918 and descend into a group of quarrelling factions. But history deals with the past, and the historian's guess about the future is no better than anyone else's.

Even if the social composition of the party has changed since 1955 – fewer old Etonian landowners and Knights of the Shire, more lawyers, accountants, estate agents and company directors – this does not explain a much bigger ideological change. From 1945 to 1975 the Conservatives broadly accepted the post-war Attlee settlement: the welfare state; high tax and spend; public ownership; regulation; redistribution; collectivism; the domination of the unions; the rule of Whitehall. They did not like it but felt that they had to lump it unless they were to deteriorate into an unelectable minority. They could tinker with the details but not reverse the principles. Hence the consensus known as 'Butskellism'. This attitude was enhanced by a singularly un-Conservative leadership. Churchill was at heart an Asquithian Liberal and he was terrified of the unions. Macmillan was the same and constantly evoked the gallantry of the miners who served in the trenches, as if this had any relevance to coal strikes twenty-five years later.

By the end of the sixties collectivism was palpably collapsing under the weight of bureaucratic over-regulation and state centralisation. Heath in 1970 seemed to have seen this but he was by instinct a technocrat and an interventionist. He made a U-turn which was neither forgiven or forgotten. A series of accidents put Margaret Thatcher in his place. She was a Conservative by conviction. The picture of her as a neo-Gladstonian is a caricature. Her mentor was Keith Joseph, subject of a Pauline conversion in 1975 from consensualism to Toryism. He was never a 'liberal', nor was she.

The fifteen years that followed her victory in the 1979 election saw a general repudiation of collectivism all over the western world and a reversion to individualism, free enterprise and low personal taxation. In Europe and much of Asia, including the USSR and its satellites, socialism collapsed and the market economy became the buzz word. The same period also saw the slaughter – at least in Britain – of two post-1945 sacred cows: the trade unions and the nationalised industries. These, especially the former, were by far the greatest impediment to Britain's economic growth. In openly regarding them as enemies to be destroyed – and in succeeding – Thatcherism did a notable service to the British economy which, despite two serious recessions, was in far better shape in 1997 than it had been twenty years earlier. The figures speak for themselves. Percentage growth of output per working hour in industry from 1960 to 1979 was lower in the UK than in almost every comparable industrial country. From 1979 to 1994 it was second only to Japan. The growth of Gross Domestic Product has slowed down in America, Britain, France and Germany since 1979 but in percentage terms Britain has done better than the others – growing by 1.85 per cent p.a. compared with USA 1.41, France 1.36 and Germany 1.40. The UK may not have performed brilliantly but it would be hard to argue at all plausibly that its record was disastrous. The worst feature of the Thatcher/Major years was high unemployment but by the end this was coming rapidly down and was considerably lower than in the rest of Europe.

Many errors were made between 1979 and 1997 and some of them stemmed from doctrinaire ideology. In a brilliant, largely hostile analysis of Thatcherism entitled *Dancing with Dogma*, Lord Gilmour, no friend of Margaret Thatcher, details some of these errors. But arguably dogma was needed to jerk the country out of the slough of despond symbolised by the 'Winter of Discontent'. Whatever her defects, Margaret Thatcher achieved one of her objectives. She destroyed 'socialism'. New Labour has ceased to be a socialist party. 'We are all socialists nowadays,' Edward VII, then Prince of Wales, said in a speech at the Mansion House in 1895. It is unlikely that his successor will say that 'we are all conservatives nowadays'. But it would be true, all the same.

Governments 1830–1997

The following list of dates for governments (name of the Prime Minister only) and general elections may be of some help to the reader. Conservative governments, or coalition governments in which the Conservative influence predominated (e.g. Lloyd George's Cabinet of 1919, MacDonald's of 1931 and Churchill's of 1940) are italicised. A list of Cabinet ministers from 1830 to 1945 can be found in the appendices of the relevant volumes of the Oxford History of England, and a full list of ministries from 1900 to 1979 in David Butler, *British political facts 1900–1979* (1980). The figures for general elections are anything but certain, especially in the early period. I have relied on F. H. McCalmont, *Poll book* (1906) for elections from 1831 to 1906, thereafter upon David Butler, *British political facts*, but I have made certain emendations of my own. For the figures of the general election of 1983 see David Butler and Dennis Kavanagh, *The British general election of 1983* (1984).

The abbreviations are as follows: C for Conservative; L for Liberal; P for Peelite; IN for Irish Nationalist; LU for Liberal Unionist; Lab for Labour. It should be noted that 'Liberal' in the elections from 1832 to 1865 covers a very heterogeneous group of Whigs, Liberals, ex-Peelites, Irish, Radicals whose principal and often only common bond was antipathy to the Conservatives.

Cabinets	General elections	Supporters of Wellington	Opponents
	1830 July[1]	348	310
1830 November, Earl Grey			
	1831 June	257	401
		C	L
	1832 December	185	473
1834 July, Viscount Melbourne			
1834 December, Sir Robert Peel			
	1835 January	279	379
1835 April, Viscount Melbourne			
	1837 August	314	344
	1841 July	367	291
1841 September, Sir Robert Peel			

[1] For the elections of 1830 and 1831 it is impossible to give exact party names. The opposition included both Whigs and Ultra Tories.

Cabinets		General elections			

1846 July, Lord John Russell

		C	P		L
	1847 July	243	89		324

1852 February, Earl of Derby

	1852 July	290	45		319

1852 December, Earl of Aberdeen
1855 February, Viscount Palmerston

	1857 March	256	26		372

1858 February, Earl of Derby

	1859 May	306			348

1859 June, Viscount Palmerston

	1865 July	300			358

1865 October, Earl (formerly Lord
    John (Russell)
1866 June, Earl of Derby
1868 February, B. Disraeli

	1868 November	279			379

1868 December, W. E. Gladstone

		C		IN	L
	1874 February	352		57	243

1874 February, B. Disraeli

	1880 April	238		62	352

1880 April, W. E. Gladstone
1885 June, Marquess of Salisbury

	1885 November	250		86	334

1886 February, W. E. Gladstone

		C	LU	IN	L
	1886 July	316	78	85	191

1886 August, Marquess of Salisbury

	1892 July	268	47	81	274

1892 August, W. E. Gladstone
1894 March, Earl of Rosebery
1895 June, Marquess of Salisbury

	1895 July	341	70	82	177
	1900 February	334	68	82	186

1902 July, A. J. Balfour
1905 December, Sir Henry
    Campbell-Bannerman

		C & LU	Lab	In	L
	1906 January	156	52	83	379

1908 April, H. H. Asquith

	1910 Jan–Feb	273	40	82	275
	1910 December	272	42	84	272

1915 May, Asquith's coalition
1916 December, David Lloyd
    George's first coalition

		Coalition		Opponents	
	1918 December 14	478[1]		229[2]	

*1919 January, Lloyd George's
    second coalition*
1922 October, Bonar Law

		C	Lab	Others	L
	1922 November 15	345	142	12	116

[1] C 335, L 133, Lab 10.

[2] Includes Lab 63; Asquithian Liberals 28; Sinn Feiners from Ireland who refused to take their seats, 73; and several other groups.

Cabinets			General elections			
1923 May, Stanley Baldwin						
			C	Lab	Others	L
	1923	December 6	258	191	7	159
1924 January, Ramsay MacDonald	1924	October 29	419	151	5	40
1924 November, Stanley Baldwin						
	1929	May 30	260	288	8	59
1929 June, Ramsay MacDonald						
1931 August, MacDonald's first national coalition			Coalition	Lab	Others	
	1931	October 27	554[1]	52	11	—
1931 November, MacDonald's second national coalition						
1935 June, Stanley Baldwin	1935	November 14	429[2]	154	11	21
1937 May, Neville Chamberlain						
1939 September, Chamberlain's war Cabinet						
1940 May, W. S. Churchill's war Cabinet						
1945 May, Churchill's caretaker Cabinet			C	Lab	Others	L
	1945	July 5	213	393	22	12
1945 July, C. R. Attlee	1950	February 23	298	315	3	9
	1951	October 25	321	295	3	6
1951 October, W. S. Churchill						
1955 April, Sir Anthony Eden	1955	May 26	344	277	3	6
1957 January, Harold Macmillan	1959	October	365	258	1	6
1963 October, Sir Alec Douglas-Home	1964	October	304	317	—	9
1964 October, Harold Wilson	1966	March	253	363	2	12
	1970	June	330	287	7	6
1970 June, Edward Heath	1974	February	297	301	23	14
1974 March, Harold Wilson	1974	October	277	319	26	13
1976 April, James Callaghan	1979	May	339	269	16	11
1979 May, Margaret Thatcher	1983	June	397	209	21	23[3]

[1] C 473, Nat. Lab 13, L 68 (after 1932 divided into National Liberals 35, independent Liberals 33).

[2] C 388, Nat. Lib 33, Nat. Lab 8.

[3] This is the figure for the SDA which consisted of 17 Liberal and 6 SDP members.

Cabinets		General Elections			
		C	Lab	Others	L
1983 June, Margaret Thatcher					
	1987 June	376	229	23	22
1987 June, Margaret Thatcher					
1990 November, John Major					
	1992 April	336	271	24	20
	1997 May	165	418	30	46
1997 May, Tony Blair					

Bibliographical note

I. GENERAL

The most reliable connected history of the political parties is Ivor Bulmer-Thomas, *The growth of the British party system*, vol. I 1640–1923; vol. II, 1923–67 (2nd edn, 1967). See also Sir Ivor Jennings, *Party politics*, 3 vols (1961–3). An essential study is R. T. McKenzie, *British political parties*, 2nd edn (1963). A useful book on Conservative attitudes is R. B. McDowell, *British Conservatism 1832–1914* (1959). Geoffrey Block, *A source book of Conservatism* (1964), published by the Conservative Political Centre, contains a valuable bibliography and six short essays on various little-known aspects of party history. A sparkling if controversial survey is Lord Coleraine, *For Conservatives only* (1970). T. F. Lindsay and M. Harrington, *The Conservative Party 1918–1979* (2nd edn, 1979) is an excellent short history of the period. Longman are publishing in four volumes *A history of the Conservative party*, two of which have appeared: Robert Stewart, *The foundation of the Conservative party 1830–1867* (1978) and John Ramsden, *The age of Balfour and Baldwin 1902–1940* (1978). See also Lord Butler (ed.), *The Conservatives, a history from their origins to 1965* (1977) and S. H. Beer, *Modern British politics* (1965). The Nuffield Election Studies are invaluable for the period after 1945.

Studies of particular periods, which constitute an indispensable background for the subject, are the following:

(i) 1830–1846

Norman Gash, *Politics in the age of Peel* (1952); and the same author's Ford Lectures for 1964, *Reaction and reconstruction in English politics 1832–1852* (1965); G. Kitson Clark, *Peel and the Conservative party* (1929); the same author's Ford Lectures for 1960, *The making of Victorian England* (1962); and the first chapters of his *An expanding society, Britain 1830–1900* (1967). A work of great indirect interest is H. Perkins, *The origins of modern English society 1780–1880* (1969). Charles Whibley, *Lord John*

Manners and his friends, 2 vols (1925) is good on 'Young England'. Michael Brock, *The Great Reform Act* (1973) is the definitive work on the subject.

(ii) 1846–1865

This period has been less closely studied than the years immediately before and after. I have tried to do something about it in my *Disraeli* (1966), ch. XII, and in the following chapters up to ch. XX; I hope to deal with the matter more fully when I write the life of the 14th Earl of Derby. There is no book on the period comparable to the studies of Professor Gash for the 1830s and 1840s, or of Professor Hanham (see below) for the period 1867–85. The most valuable recent book on the political background of these years is John Vincent, *The formation of the Liberal party 1857–1868* (1966). An important book, also relevant to (i), is Robert Stewart, *The politics of protection* (1971).

(iii) 1865–1881

On the second Reform Bill, the books are: Maurice Cowling, *1867, Disraeli, Gladstone and revolution* (1967), stiff going in places and meant for the sophisticated historian rather than the plain man, but a subtle and illuminating study of events till May 1867; and F. B. Smith, *The making of the second Reform Bill* (1966), which covers the whole story. H. J. Hanham, *Elections and party management, politics in the time of Disraeli and Gladstone* (1969) is the best study of the political system between the second and third Reform Bills. Paul Smith, *Disraelian Conservatism and social reform* (1967) is the first thorough study of the subject. Trevor Lloyd, *The General Election of 1880* (1968) investigates the election on the lines of the modern Nuffield Studies. Further monographs of this kind are badly needed. E. J. Feuchtwanger, *Disraeli, democracy and the Tory party* (1968) is a valuable analysis of the Conservative party machine from 1867 to 1885.

(iv) 1881–1902

Henry Pelling, *The social geography of British elections 1885–1910* (1967) – a mass of electoral information. A. P. Thornton, *The Imperial idea and its enemies* (1959) – a thoughtful study of the subject. Harold Gorst, *The Fourth party* (1906) – useful even now. Lord Chilston, *Chief Whip* (1961), a life of Akers Douglas, gives much information about the party machine. Michael Hurst, *Joseph Chamberlain and Liberal reunion* (1967), Peter Fraser, *Joseph Chamberlain* (1966), and Richard Jay, *Joseph Chamberlain, a political study* (1983), are valuable on the Liberal

Unionists. M. Pinto-Duschinsky, *The political thought of Lord Salisbury 1854–1868* (1967), is a valuable analysis of Salisbury's earlier writings and is also highly relevant to his career as leader.

(v) 1902–1922

A. M. Gollin, *Balfour's burden* (1965) [i.e. Tariff Reform], and Dennis Judd, *Balfour and the British Empire* (1968) are worth attention. Bernard Semmel, *Imperialism and social reform* (1960) exaggerates the connection but corrects earlier bias. A. M. Gollin, *Proconsul in politics* (1964) is an interesting study of Milner. Trevor Wilson, *The downfall of the Liberal party* (1966) is an important analysis of a controversial subject. Stanley Salvidge, *Salvidge of Liverpool* (1934); and Randolph Churchill, *Lord Derby, King of Lancashire* (1959), are valuable studies of two north country Tory 'bosses' of very different stations in life. For war and post-war intrigues, see Lord Beaverbrook's *Politicians and the war*, 2 vols (1928–32); *Men and power* (1956); *The decline and fall of Lloyd George* (1963). See also Cameron Hazlehurst, *Politicians at war* (1971).

(vi) 1922–1940

John Raymond, *The Baldwin age* (1960) contains useful essays. Thomas Jones, *Whitehall diary 1916–30*, 2 vols (1969) and *Diary with letters 1931–50* (1954) are valuable sources on Baldwin. See also Robert Rhodes James, *Memoirs of a Conservative* (1969), letters and reminiscences of Lord Davidson. Maurice Cowling, *The impact of Labour 1920–24* (1971) is essential if difficult reading. David Marquand, *Ramsay MacDonald* (1977) supersedes all previous accounts of the 1931 crisis. Sir P. Goodhart, *The 1922 Committee* (1973) is the only history of this important body. *The diaries of Harold Nicolson*, 3 vols (1966–8) and *Chips, the diary of Sir Henry Channon* (1967) throw interesting light on both this period and (vii).

(vii) 1940–1955

J. D. Hoffman, *The Conservative party in opposition 1945–51* (1964) is the only study of its kind. R. T. McKenzie, *Angels in marble* (1968), and Eric Nordlinger, *The working class Tories* (1967), are valuable investigations of a neglected topic. W. L. Guttsman, *The British political élite* (1963) confirms statistically what one would guess anyway. Ronald Butt, *The power of Parliament*, 2nd edn (1969); and Ian Gilmour, *The body politic* (1969) are books on the British system of government which throw much incidental light on party politics. A valuable book on wartime politics is Paul Addison, *The road to 1945* (1975). For the Conservative recovery after 1943 see Lord Woolton, *Memoirs* (1959), Lord Kilmuir, *Political adventure* (1964) and Lord Butler, *The art of the possible* (1971), which is also relevant to (viii).

(viii) 1955–65

The memoirs of Anthony Eden, *Full Circle* (1960) and of Harold Macmillan, the last four volumes (1969–73) contain much useful information. Reginald Maudling, *Memoirs* (1978) is important both from this period and for (ix). George Hutchinson, *The Last Edwardian at Number Ten* (1980) reprints Iain Macleod's account of the battle for the succession in 1963. Andrew Gamble, *The Conservative Nation* (1974) is a valuable study covering 1945 to 1974, though his conclusion looks odd in the light of later events.

(ix) 1965–79

Robert Rhodes James, *Ambitions and realities* (1972) is the best acount of the party from 1964 to 1970. Robert Behrens, *The Conservative party from Heath to Thatcher* (1980) is useful too. For an analysis of the modern party organization see Philip Norton and Arthur Aughey, *Conservatives and conservatism* (1981), which brings R. T. McKenzie's work up to date. The Nuffield Election studies are indispensable for this period.

(x) 1979–1983

Hugh Stephenson, *Mrs Thatcher's first year* (1980), Peter Riddell, *The Thatcher Government* (1983), and Jock (now Lord) Bruce-Cardyne, *Mrs Thatcher's first administration, the prophets confounded* (1984) are books by no means fully in agreement, but are essential reading. So is David Butler and Dennis Kavanagh, *The British general election of 1983* (1984).

II. BIOGRAPHIES

This list is roughly chronological and confined to those who either led the party or were so prominent as to count in the same category.

On the Duke of Wellington as a political figure see Elizabeth Longford, *Wellington, pillar of state* (1972). On Peel is a great biography in two volumes: Norman Gash, *Mr Secretary Peel* (1961) and *Sir Robert Peel* (1972). On Bentinck, Disraeli's *Lord George Bentinck: a political biography* (1852) still holds the field – A dramatic work as much autobiography as biography. The 14th Earl of Derby lacks a biographer with access to the papers. There are studies by G.

Saintsbury, *The Earl of Derby* (1892) and W. D. Jones, *Lord Derby and Victorian conservatism* (1956).

On Disraeli, the classic but very long biography is W. F. Monypenny and G. E. Buckle, *The life of Benjamin Disraeli, Earl of Beaconsfield,* 6 vols (1910–20). There is a single- (though large) volume biography based on the papers by Robert Blake, *Disraeli* (1966). There is no satisfactory life of Sir Stafford Northcote. Andrew Lang's 2 vols (1890) are sketchy and dull. On Randolph Churchill his son Winston's 2 vols (1906), 2nd edn, 1 vol. (1951) still make very enjoyable reading, but both this and Robert Rhodes James, *Lord Randolph Churchill* (1959) have been superseded by R. F. Foster, *Lord Randolph Churchill* (1981). There is a marvellous pen portrait by Lord Rosebery, that master of the miniature, *Lord Randolph Churchill* (1906).

Lord Chilston, *W. H. Smith* (1965) is a useful life of a forgotten but important figure. Lord Salisbury constitutes a great gap in the Conservative pantheon. His daughter, Lady Gwendolen Cecil, did not live to complete her biography which ends in 1892 – *The life of Robert Marquis of Salisbury*, vols I and II (1921), vols III and IV (1931). Joseph Chamberlain's life was once in the same uncompleted category but J. L. Garvin, *Joseph Chamberlain*, 3 vols (1931–3), which only reached 1900, has been finished by Julian Amery, vol. IV (1951) and vols V and VI (1969) – an invaluable work.

On Balfour we have a rather thin life, though interesting for personal touches, by his niece Blanche Dugdale, *Arthur James Balfour*, 2 vols (1936). The biography of Kenneth Young, *Arthur James Balfour* (1963) effectively supersedes it, but the best portrait of Balfour is Max Egremont, *Balfour* (1980). On Bonar Law the official biogaphy is Robert Blake, *The unknown Prime Minister* (1955). See also A. J. P. Taylor, *Beaverbrook* (1972). Sir Charles Petrie has written the lives of Law's two rivals, *Walter Long and his times* (1936) and *The life and letters of Austen Chamberlain*, 2 vols (1939–40). John Campbell, *F. E. Smith* (1983) supersedes the filial biography by the 2nd Earl of Birkenhead. On Baldwin one can learn all one needs from H. Montgomery Hyde, *Baldwin* (1973). Sir Keith Feiling, *Life of Neville Chamberlain* (1946) is a much better book than was appreciated at the time. The biography by David Dilks of which the first volume down to 1929 has just appeared (1984) will clearly be an authoritative work.

There have been many books on Winston Churchill. The official life begun by his son Randolph and continued by Martin Gilbert extends now to 6 vols (1966–83) reaching 1941. The best one-volume life is by Henry Pelling, *Winston Churchill* (1974). On Sir Anthony Eden (the Earl of Avon). there is an interesting but unfriendly biography by David Carlton, *Anthony Eden* (1981). If the author can find an adverse interpretation he does, but the book is essential nevertheless. On Eden's successor there is an excellent biography by Nigel Fisher, *Harold Macmillan* (1982). He has also written the life of one of the most important Conservatives not to reach the top, *Ian Macleod* (1973). The other person in this category is R. A. Butler whose brief life by Patrick Cosgrave, *R. A. Butler, an English life* (1981) is well worth reading. Mr Heath and Mrs Thatcher await to be biographised satisfactorily.

III. WORKS PUBLISHED OR COMPLETED SINCE 1983

The most important of these is the six volumes published by Longman (1978–96) entitled *A History of the Conservative Party*. These are indispensable works of learning and scholarship for the history of the party from 1830 to 1975:

Robert Stewart, *The Foundation of the Conservative Party 1830–1867* (1978);

Richard Shannon, *The Age of Disraeli 1868–1881* (1978);

Richard Shannon, *The Age of Salisbury 1881–1902* (1996);

John Ramsden, *The Age of Balfour and Baldwin 1902–1940* (1978);

John Ramsden, *The Age of Churchill and Eden 1940–1957* (1995);

John Ramsden, *The Winds of Change 1957–1975* (1996);

Other valuable works are Anthony Seldon and Stuart Ball (eds), *The Conservative Century, The Conservative Party since 1900* (OUP, 1994); Sue Onslow, *Back-bench Debate Within the Conservative Party and its Influence on Foreign Policy 1948–57* (Macmillan, 1997); Lord Gilmour and Mark Garnett, *Whatever Happened to the Tories: the Conservative Party since 1945* (Fourth Estate, 1997).

There is a plethora of books on Margaret Thatcher and Thatcherism. She has written an account of her premiership *The Downing Street Years* (HarperCollins, 1993). It is her 'case' and needs to be read in the light of Lord Gilmour's review in *Twentieth Century British History*, Vol. 5, No. 2, 1994, pp. 257–77.

An earlier critique of Thatcherism is the same author's *Dancing with Dogma* (Simon and Schuster, 1992). Margaret Thatcher later wrote a history of her previous career *The Path to Power* (HarpeCollins, 1995) which is more relaxed and less self-justificatory than her first volume.

The best account of her fall is Alan Watkins, *A Conservative Coup* (Duckworth, 1991). Other useful books about Thatcherism are John

Cole, *The Thatcher Years* (BBC Books, 1987) and *As It Seemed to Me* (Weidenfeld & Nicolson, 1995); Shirley Robin Letwin, *The Anatomy of Thatcherism* (Fontana, 1992); Dennis Kavanagh and Anthony Seldon (eds), *The Thatcher Effect* (OUP, 1989); Kenneth Harris, *Thatcher* (Weidenfeld & Nicolson, 1988); Bernard Ingham, *Kill the Messenger* (Fontana, 1991); Patrick Cosgrave, *Thatcher, The First Term* (Bodley Head, 1985); David Butler & Others (ed.), *Failure in British Government, The Politics of the Poll Tax* (OUP, 1994); Hugo Young, *One of Us, A Biography of Margaret Thatcher* (Macmillan, 1989); Alistair McAlpine, *Once a Jolly Bagman, Memoirs* (Weidenfeld & Nicolson, 1997); Morrison Halcrow, *Keith Joseph, A Single Mind* (Macmillan, 1989) is a good account of Margaret Thatcher's guru.

Not surprisingly, there are far fewer books about John Major. Bruce Anderson, *John Major, The Making of the Prime Minister* (Fourth Estate, 1991); is the best book on his career till May 1991; Dennis Kavanagh and Anthony Seldon (eds), *The Major Effect* (Macmillan, 1994) is a useful contingent work; Sarah Hogg and Jonathan Hill, *Too Close to Call* (Little Brown, 1995) is a vivid and often very funny account by two 'insiders' of the 1992 general election.

The best works on the Conservative organisation and tactics in the general elections of 1987, 1992 and 1997 are the Nuffield Studies.

Many of the principal political figures in the Thatcher/Major years have written memoirs. The most important are Nigel Lawson, *The View from No. 11* (Bantam Press, 1992); Geoffrey Howe, *Conflict of Loyalty* (Macmillan, 1994); Kenneth Baker, *The Turbulent Years* (Faber, 1993); Norman Tebbit, *Upwardly Mobile* (Weidenfeld & Nicolson, 1988); Lord Carrington, *Reflect on Things Past* (HarperCollins, 1988); Nicholas Ridley, *My Style of Government* (Hutchinson, 1991); William Whitelaw, *Memoirs* (Aurum Press, 1989); Francis Pym, *The Politics of Consent* (Hamish Hamilton, 1984); a valuable book, though not a memoir is John Ranelagh, *Thatcher's People* (HarperCollins, 1991).

Books of importance about earlier Tory figures but published since 1983 are Robert Rhodes James, *Anthony Eden* (Weidenfeld & Nicolson, 1983); Alistair Horne, *Macmillan* (Macmillan, 2 vols, 1988–89); Richard Lamb, *The Macmillan Years 1957–63* (John Murray, 1995); Anthony Howard, *Rab, The Life of R. A. Butler* (Cape, 1987); John Campbell, *Edward Heath* (Cape, 1993); D. R. Thorpe, *Alec Douglas-Home* (Sinclair-Stevenson, 1996).

General index